DEAF STUDENTS AND THE QUALITATIVE SIMILARITY HYPOTHESIS

Donald F. Moores, General Editor

DEAF STUDENTS AND THE QUALITATIVE SIMILARITY HYPOTHESIS

Understanding Language and Literacy Development

Peter V. Paul,
Ye Wang, and
Cheri Williams

Gallaudet University Press
Washington, DC

Gallaudet University Press

Washington, DC 20002

http://gupress.gallaudet.edu

Library of Congress Cataloging-in-Publication Data

Paul, Peter V.

Deaf students and the qualitative similarity hypothesis : understanding language and literacy development / Peter V. Paul, Ye Wang, and Cheri Williams.

pages cm

Summary: "Book presents the educational implications for deaf and hard of hearing children and offers reason-based practices for improving their English language and literacy development"– Provided by publisher.

ISBN 978-1-56368-584-2 (hardback) – ISBN 978-1-56368-585-9 (e-book)

1. Deaf children–United States–Language. 2. Deaf children–Education–United States. 3. Hearing impaired–Education–United States. 4. English language–Study and teaching. I. Wang, Ye. II. Williams, Cheri. III. Title.

HV2469.E5P377 2013

371.91'2–dc23

2013030545

Contents

Preface

"A conclusion is the place where you got tired thinking."
(Martin H. Fischer in Peter [1977, p. 494])

The main purpose of this book is to describe the theoretical underpinnings and to synthesize the findings of research based on or related to the qualitative similarity hypothesis (QSH). Although the targeted population is children and adolescents who are d/Deaf and hard of hearing (d/Dhh), it is important to apply our understanding of the development of English in other populations of struggling readers and writers such as children with language or literacy disabilities and those for whom English is a second language. In addition, we have synthesized and applied the findings of research on the development of English in children and adolescents who are native learners. Collectively, these research findings enable us to proffer empirical- and reason-based practices for improving the English language and literacy development of d/Dhh individuals who are acquiring English as a first or as a second language. We propose general instructional guidelines and strategies, which are contextualized with respect to the language and cognitive attributes of d/Dhh students.

Chapters 1 and 2 present the theoretical foundations of the QSH, involving constructs such as discipline structure and critical or optimal time periods of development. The manner in which the QSH is related to the development of English is discussed with applications to students who are d/Dhh. These two chapters attempt to provide a few insights into the relationship between English language and literacy, clarify terms such as language or literacy delays and disabilities, and establish the tone for the remainder of the book.

There is a critical need for educators and scholars to be cognizant of the larger fields of language, literacy, and second-language learning and the manner in which research in these areas informs or leads to empirical- and reason-based practices for the education of d/Dhh students. The research findings from these larger content fields provide further support for the tenets of the QSH and pertinent information for differentiating instruction to meet the instructional needs of d/Dhh children and adolescents. In addition, this information deepens our understanding of the relationship between English language proficiency and the development of English literacy skills.

Chapter 3 addresses the development of English as a second language—that is, English Language Learners (ELLs). Improving the literacy skills of ELLs is critical, particularly considering the increasing prevalence of ELLs in U.S. school-age children, including children who are d/Dhh. In this chapter, we assert that both hearing and d/Deaf ELLs learn to read and write English (as a second language) in a way qualitatively similar to that of their typically developing monolingual English-speaking peers, but at a quantitatively different—that is, slower—rate (for a number of individuals).

Chapter 4 synthesizes research investigations on the development of English emergent and conventional literacy, and Chapter 5 focuses on children with language and literacy disabilities. In both chapters, we reiterate that English literacy development is a complex acquisition process. Through-the-air language proficiency is certainly a foundation for the literacy process; however, the development of English reading and writing requires much more than just English language proficiency, either via the spoken or signed modes—as discussed in previous chapters. Again, despite the quantitative differences for a number of d/Dhh students and students with language or literacy disabilities, there is ample empirical evidence that the development of both emergent and conventional literacy is qualitatively similar to that of peers with typically developing English literacy skills. In essence, this evidence indicates that we should use and build on the research findings from the general field of literacy education, including the field of language or literacy disabilities.

In Chapter 6, we review literacy-focused intervention studies that have been conducted with d/Dhh students. The main goal here is to document the research effectiveness of specific instructional strategies and approaches that support early English literacy or conventional literacy learning and to build on the findings from previous literature reviews. We proffer specific evidence-based practices that show promise for supporting d/Dhh students' phonemic awareness and phonics knowledge, reading fluency, vocabulary development, and text comprehension. We compare our syntheses with those reported by the National Early Literacy Panel (2008) and the National Reading Panel (2000), which focused on typically developing learners of English literacy—and which provided further support, evidence- and reason-based, for the QSH.

In Chapter 7, we assert that there is a need for more rigorously designed research projects and for stakeholders to understand the challenges of the bench to bedside approach. Because deafness is a low-incidence condition, there have been enormous challenges in conducting research and translating theory and research into educational implications. In our view, greater attention must be paid to the complexity of the constructs, English language and English literacy, neither of which is a unitary acquisition process.

We note that there are relatively few large-scale experimental or quasi-experimental research investigations on d/Dhh children and adolescents. We assert that single-subject experimental designs and qualitative case studies have provided a growing understanding of the impact of instructional interventions. Finally, we argue that combining these research paradigms might be a fruitful approach for future investigations, especially for developing individual social-cognitive profiles.

In Chapter 8, we invited two well-known scholars to evaluate the merits of the QSH with respect to their epistemological and research paradigms. In our conclusion, Chapter 9, we provide our response to the essays in Chapter 8 as well as a summary of the salient principles of the QSH with respect to theory and research on the development of English language and literacy. Ultimately, we have attempted to offer our views on improving English language and literacy development and, consequently, the educational achievement of d/Dhh children and adolescents, based on the major tenets of the QSH. Our conclusions, however, are not the product of "where we got tired thinking," but rather—we hope—reflect the limits of current theory and research.

REFERENCES

National Early Literacy Panel. (2008). *Developing early literacy: Report of the National Early Literacy Panel—A scientific synthesis of early literacy development and implications for interventions.* Washington, DC: Institute for Literacy and National Center for Family Literacy.

National Reading Panel. (2000). *Report of the National Reading Panel: Teaching children to read—An evidence-based assessment of the scientific research literature on reading and its implications for reading instruction.* Jessup, MD: National Institute for Literacy at EDPubs.

Peter, L. J. (1977). *Peter's quotations: Ideas for our time.* New York, NY: Bantam Books.

Acknowledgments

We are indebted to all researchers and scholars who have provided the findings and ideas that undergird the foundation of this book. If we have seen far and clearly, it is because we have been standing on the shoulders of these intellectuals as we synthesize and present our understandings. Of course, our interpretations are our own; thus, we have no one to blame (or to praise!) but ourselves.

We are grateful to Dr. Donald Moores for comments and support on earlier drafts of the manuscript. The contributions of the staff in the Gallaudet University Press's editorial and business office are also appreciated. Finally, but certainly not least, we want to thank our spouses and children, who helped us to maintain our sanity and who facilitated our attempts to remain focused and to develop the inner discipline needed to complete this project in a timely manner.

1

Introduction to the Qualitative Similarity Hypothesis

In this introductory chapter we provide a general overview of the construct known as the *qualitative similarity hypothesis* (QSH) (Paul, 2010, 2012; Paul & Lee, 2010; Paul & Wang, 2012) and establish the tenor for the remainder of this book. The QSH is a descriptive, testable hypothesis (or construct), with micro and macro components (subconstructs), and is based on a synthesis of empirical and reason-integrative research concerning the acquisition of through-the-air English (i.e., speaking and/or signing) and English literacy (i.e., reading and writing). Our main thesis is that the acquisition of English by any individual is developmentally similar to that of native learners and to that of typical literacy learners of English. This developmental similarity suggests that there are certain critical fundamentals that facilitate and enhance the acquisition process. These fundamentals, discussed later, apply to the learning of English as either a first or a second language.

In this book we primarily focus on critiquing the validity of the QSH and its implications for the development of English language and literacy in children and adolescents who are d/Deaf and hard of hearing (d/Dhh). The use of the phrase *d/Deaf and hard of hearing* encompasses both audiologic and cultural parameters and is meant to be inclusive of the wide range of individuals who have been identified with a hearing loss, including those who are members of the Deaf culture, DEAF-WORLD, or have a Deaf identity. Individuals who are *deaf and hard of hearing* (dhh) are those with slight to profound hearing losses based on the pure-tone average in the better of their two unaided ears (Moores, 2001; Paul & Whitelaw, 2011; Quigley & Kretschmer, 1982). Those who are identified as *Deaf* (D) typically have Deaf parents/caregivers who use American Sign Language (ASL) or some other type of sign language, which is not based on English. *Deaf* (D) individuals also can be those who use ASL or some other type of sign language themselves, regardless of the hearing status of their parents/caregivers.

It is permissible to classify some d/Deaf and hard of hearing individuals whose home or first language is not English as English language learners (ELLs). ELL is the common term used to refer to people learning English as a second language, especially in educational settings. However, children and adolescents in special-education programs whose first language is not English may be placed in programs labeled English as a second language (ESL) (e.g., Paul & Wang, 2012). Alternatively, some of these individuals may be educated in bilingual programs, particularly ASL–English bilingual programs.

To understand the challenges of developing English within the conceptual framework of the QSH, it is obligatory for us, the authors, to synthesize theory and research on children and adolescents who are typical English language and literacy users. Throughout this book, we emphasize strongly and repeatedly that the reference standard for the QSH is the typical development of English language and literacy—and individuals may be hearing, Deaf, deaf, or hard of hearing and may even have a disability (e.g., language/learning disability; dyslexia) whose effects on the acquisition of English have been minimized or even compensated for via other avenues (e.g., use of comprehension strategies). It might not be sufficient to simply compare the language and cognitive attributes of *good* or *proficient* English users with others who are *struggling* with English language and literacy although this is one standard procedure for research under the rubric of cognitivism, particularly information processing or computational/representational theory of mind (McCarthey & Raphael, 1992; Mitchell, 1982; Paul, 2001, 2009; for popular discussion, see Pinker 1994, 2007). The social/sociocultural and affective domains also contribute to the English acquisition process and are discussed in this book; however, both of these areas are underexplored with d/Dhh children and adolescents (e.g., see Williams, 2011).

Examining the challenges of other children with either language or literacy disabilities or language or literacy difficulties (e.g., those with language or learning disabilities or those who are struggling readers/writers) should also shed additional light on the developmental trajectory of d/Dhh children and adolescents (e.g., see various perspectives in McGill-Franzen & Allington, 2011). In fact, these challenges seem to underscore not only the importance of English language proficiency for cognitive and social purposes but also the strong relationship of knowing English in the through-the-air mode to the acquisition of English print literacy (Cain & Oakhill, 2007; Kamhi & Catts, 2012; McGill-Franzen & Allington, 2011; McGuinness, 2004, 2005). Finally, investigating the complex processes involved in the learning of English as a second language or in bilingual programs by typical non-d/Dhh individuals also contributes to our understanding of the validity of the construct of developmental similarity (August & Shanahan, 2006; Paul & Wang, 2012).

HISTORICAL BACKGROUND AND THEORETICAL UNDERPINNINGS

The construct of developmental similarity has a fairly long, contentious history with scholars who have undertaken the pursuit of investigating the development of English language and literacy (Paul, 1985, 2009, 2012; Paul & Wang, 2012). Ascertaining the specific historical or even theoretical influences is not possible because this is contingent on the interpretative biases of the observers. What follows is our rendition of these influences.

The construct of developmental similarity seems to have historical connections with the debates on the relations between language and cognition (Lund, 2003) and between language and literacy (particularly, script or print reading) (Bartine, 1989, 1992; Kamhi & Catts, 2012) as well as the interrelations among language, cognition, and literacy (Paul, 1985, 2009; Paul & Wang, 2012). In these debates, the critical roles of the social interactive environment (home attributes, social practices, social artifacts, school attributes, etc.) or the affective domain (e.g., motivation, interest, self-regulation, etc.) were acknowledged; however, these entities assume a more prominent position in the later periods of the research literature (Gaffney & Anderson, 2000; McIntyre, 2011; Pearson, 2004).

In general, the QSH has been grounded in cognitive–linguistic theories and variations for both English language (e.g., Chomsky, 2006; Lund, 2003) and English reading (e.g., see a review of cognitive theories in various chapters in Section 3, Part 1 of Ruddell & Unrau, 2004). It is possible to find some support for the QSH via interpretations of research findings within a sociocultural framework or a sociocognitive framework that relies heavily on the social context (Paul, 2012; Paul & Wang, 2012; Williams, 2011, 2012), particularly when these social and contextual frameworks are considered to be a paradigm elaboration of cognitivism, rather than a paradigm shift (Gaffney & Anderson, 2000).

Chomsky's view of explanatory adequacy (e.g., Chomsky, 1988, 1991, 2006) and Lenneberg's (1967) notion of a critical period for language development undergirded much of the original theoretical background for developmental and difference hypotheses. To achieve Chomsky's interpretation of explanatory adequacy, linguists need to describe the language behaviors, processes, and mechanisms used by children throughout the language development period. Explanatory adequacy is a shift from descriptive linguistics to explanatory linguistics. Chomsky's work, especially his position on syntax, has influenced the extensive line of research on the syntactic development of d/Dhh children and adolescents as exemplified by the work of Quigley and others (e.g., see reviews in Paul, 2001, 2009). This body of research contains some of the seminal empirical and reason-integrative support for the QSH.

With respect to a biological basis and critical acquisition period for language, Lenneberg (1967) provided the impetus for research thrusts on the language development of children with language/learning disabilities as well as on individuals (hearing) learning English as a second language or in bilingual environments. For example, Lenneberg (1967; see also Rymer, 1992) hypothesized that the language development of children with developmental delays (i.e., cognitive or intellectual disabilities) differed quantitatively (i.e., rate of acquisition) from that of typical children but was qualitatively (developmentally or manner of acquisition) similar with respect to mental age. This assertion seems to be applicable to many children with language/learning disabilities as well as those with cognitive/intellectual disabilities (Cain & Oakhill, 2007; Kamhi & Catts, 2012; McGill-Franzen & Allington, 2011; Vellutino, 2003; see also Chapters 6 to 8 of Paul & Wang, 2012).

The application of a few of the basic tenets of Lenneberg's work can also be seen in the research thrusts of Stanovich (1986, 1988, 1991, 1992, 2000; Stanovich, Nathan, & Zolman, 1988), who proffered a critical or optimal period for English reading development. Stanovich's construct, coined the *Matthew effects*, has been instantiated subsequently, in part, into the *developmental lag hypothesis*, which is also similar to the basic principles of the QSH, as discussed later.

Additional foundations for the QSH (and for other developmental similarity hypotheses) can be gleaned from theories of reading motivated, in part, by memory research (i.e., working memory; Baddeley, 2006; see also the various perspectives in Pickering, 2006). The research on working memory (e.g., Hanson, 1989) has led to contentious debates on the role of phonological coding in the development of English reading for some d/Dhh children and adolescents (Allen, Clark, del Giudice, Koo, Lieberman, Mayberry, & Miller, 2009; Miller & Clark, 2011; Paul, Wang, Trezek, & Luckner, 2009; Trezek, Wang, & Paul, 2011; Wang, Trezek, Luckner, & Paul, 2008) and for other children who are struggling readers (e.g., Bruning, Schraw, Norby, & Ronning, 2004; Pickering, 2006). The importance of phonology as one critical or necessary component—either via the development of English through the air or as a part of the early English literacy period—is buttressed by major syntheses in reading research (Adams, 1990; McGill-Franzen & Allington, 2011; National Early Literacy Panel, 2008; National Reading Panel, 2000; for ELLs, see August & Shanahan, 2006; C. Shanahan, 2009; see also reviews in Paul & Wang, 2012; Trezek et al., 2011; Wang et al., 2008).

CONCEPTUAL FRAMEWORK OF THE QSH

To assert that the overall acquisition and development (i.e., manner) of English is qualitatively similar evokes the integration of two broad components: disciplinary structure and a critical or optimal period. The construct of disciplinary structure is couched within arguments about the nature of cognition (and language) and its contact with the contents or structures of particular disciplines (Carruthers, Laurence, & Stich, 2005, 2006; Phillips, 1983; Phillips & Soltis, 2004, 2009). This construct has fueled intense debates in the field of critical thinking (Johnson, 1992; Kuhn, 2005; Martin, 1992; McBurney, 2002; Moore & Parker, 2009; Norris, 1992) and other arenas such as the nature and extent of disciplinary comprehension (e.g., C. Shanahan, 2009). The structure of the discipline refers to certain content aspects on varying difficulty levels, which are necessary to acquire to make progress with one's understanding of and growth in the discipline.

The critical or optimal period involves the issue of a time frame for maximizing the acquisition and beneficial effects of a bona fide through-the-air language (Lenneberg, 1967) as well as for print literacy (Stanovich, 1986, 1988). For the purposes of this book, this entails the development of English as a first or second language. The timeline of this acquisition, particularly English as a first language, affects the subsequent development of other disciplines such as literacy, mathematics, science, and so on. In addition, there is a timeline associated with the development of mature literacy skills—that is, reading and writing. Again, it is argued that mature literacy skills need to be acquired as early as possible during the beginning school years and subsequently maintained at a proficient level because this affects the development of what is often labeled academic language and knowledge found in content areas expressed in print (e.g., Birch, 2007; for second language, see Cummins, 1979, 1984, 2007; Paul & Wang, 2012). Of course, the acquisition of more complex language and literacy usage continues to occur mainly via the use of academic language and knowledge in academic and social environments.

Both of these components of the QSH—disciplinary structure and critical or optimal period—are discussed in detail in the ensuing paragraphs. These components are pervasively influenced by cognitive and biological models of language and literacy development.

Structure of the Discipline

The construct of disciplinary structure or structure of the discipline has also been known as *knowledge structure* (Donovan & Bransford, 2005; Phillips, 1983; Phillips & Soltis, 2004, 2009; C. Shanahan, 2009; see also the discussions in Paul, 2012; Paul & Wang, 2012). Research on the nature of the structure of the discipline and the acquisition or learning of the discipline is pervasively influenced by epistemological stances or methodological approaches (McBurney, 2002; Noddings, 2007; Norris, 1992; Pring, 2004; Ritzer, 2001). There are debates on ascertaining whether a discipline can be understood or examined with the use of a scientific methodology or multiple methodologies (Paul & Moore, 2012a, 2012b; Ritzer, 2001; Wang, 2012). From another perspective on the acquisition process, Phillips (1983) remarked: "The learning process has been conceptualized in terms of entities—the "structure of the discipline" that is being learned, and the "cognitive structure" that is built up inside the learner as he or she gradually masters the particular subject (p. 60).

If a discipline has a structure, this is interpreted to mean that it has an internal logical conceptual framework that impacts the learner at various difficulty levels due to the demands of acquiring and understanding the contents (Cartwright, 2009; Donovan & Bransford, 2005; C. Shanahan, 2009). Thus, there are certain concepts and skills that are or should be easier to learn prior to others because of their inherent or conceptual difficulty. For example, it is assumed that the concept of addition needs to be mastered prior to encountering the concept of multiplication—which can be conceptualized as repeated addition (Battista, 2001; Bruning et al., 2004; R. Mayer, 1992; Mayer & Hegarty, 1996). Within this purview, there is much discussion on whether the structure of a discipline is highly logical and coherently defined as in, for example, mathematics, or loosely defined but still logical as in, for example, English reading or English writing (e.g., see Spiro, 2006; Spiro, Vispoel, Schmitz, Samarapungavan, & Boerger, 1987; see also the discussions in Cartwright, 2009; Donovan & Bransford, 2005).

We agree that it is important to understand the cognitive and social worlds (or foundations) of individuals as they attempt to learn the concepts in the various academic content areas and as they are acquiring English language and literacy skills. There is ample evidence to support the sociocultural challenges posed by poverty, educational levels, and the language usage and situations in the homes (e.g., Paratore & Dougherty, 2011). In general, there is a mismatch among the artifacts, language usage, and social practices of the home and surrounding cultural worlds of these individuals and the classroom usage, artifacts, and practices relating to the social and academic language of schools. This mismatch requires culturally relevant instructional techniques to deliver, in our view, the critical fundamentals of developing language and literacy.

From another perspective, it might be more difficult to convince us that the positing of a strong general model of cognition or even of social cognition or socioculturalism would be sufficient, by itself, for understanding the acquisition of the specific aspects of a conceptual framework of a particular discipline (e.g., see Phillips, 1983; Phillips & Soltis, 2004, 2009). There is simply no strong evidence—as of yet—that a general mental/cognitive or a general social/sociocultural model is representative or reflective of understanding a conceptual model as reflective of disciplinary structures (e.g., see related discussions in Bruning et al., 2004; Vosgerau, 2006).

This does not mean that general cognitive or social models are not necessary per se; it does mean that the development of these models needs to consider specifically the components associated with the structure of the discipline that is being acquired or learned. Understanding disciplinary structure is especially critical in educational or classroom settings, involving the use of effective instructional strategies and techniques by teachers and the use of efficient cognitive skills and strategies by students. To exemplify this issue, it has been remarked (Paul, 2012) that

> it might be that discipline structures ... are contingent on an external psychological or developmental framework on *how individuals learn* considering specifically the rate and manner of acquisition and optimal periods for development. ... That is, in the process of learning mathematics or science or in learning to read or write, there are skills that are easier or more difficult because of the complicated—often unpredictable—intertwinement of factors associated with the broad domains of cognitive (e.g., the structure of individuals' minds), sociocultural (e.g., interactions, home environment, social artifacts, or institutions), and affective behaviors (e.g., motivation, interest, demeanor). (p. 180)

In essence, we assert that understanding the structure of the discipline is critical to minimize the mismatch between the cognitive capability of the individual and their learning via the instruction of the discipline. Whether a discipline has a logically coherent or loosely defined structure might determine the rigor of fundamentals that undergird a particular discipline as well as the manner in which a discipline can be investigated or even to teach the contents of the discipline (e.g., see various perspectives in Norris, 1992; Willingham, 2007). Thus, this might be one reason for the difficulty in ascertaining what it means to think like a mathematician, a scientist, or an individual who is an expert in the use of English literacy (McBurney, 2002; Schoenfeld, 2002; Willingham, 2007). [Note: We avoid the complexities associated with subcomponents of a major discipline (e.g., algebra, geometry).]

Regardless of the nature of disciplinary structure, there are certain fundamentals that underlie the acquisition and development of English language and literacy skills. For example, individuals need a working knowledge of the specialized vocabulary (i.e., technical vocabulary) associated with the discipline, especially during classroom discourses (Birch, 2007; Kamhi & Catts, 2012; Willingham, 2007). With respect to English literacy, research has shown the importance of children understanding print concepts in the early literacy period (National Early Literacy Panel, 2008; National Reading Panel, 2000) as well as overall vocabulary knowledge of words in print throughout the entire literacy process (National Reading Panel, 2000; see reviews in Paul, 2009; Paul & Wang, 2012).

The Notion of Fundamentals The notion of fundamentals with respect to the acquisition of English as a first or second language and the development of English literacy is discussed in detail in Chapters 2 (English language), 3 (English as second language), and 4 (English literacy). The discussion here is a brief overview. The basic premise is that there are certain fundamentals that apply to all individuals in the learning of English, including the development of English literacy skills.

There is ample research demonstrating that neither the English language nor English literacy is a unitary construct (Cain & Oakhill, 2007; Israel & Duffy, 2009; Kamhi & Catts, 2012; McGill-Franzen & Allington, 2011; Ruddell & Unrau, 2004). There is no one specific or all-encompassing fundamental that can account for or explain the entire process of development from the beginning to the mature period. Although there are a number of literacy models and theories, it is possible to delineate a group of fundamentals, especially for early and later acquisition as proffered, for example, by the National Early Literacy Panel (2008) and the National Reading Panel (2000). It is even possible to argue for certain fundamentals in the development of the English language as a first or second language, despite the various renditions of different frameworks and approaches (e.g., Birch, 2007; Cummins, 2007; Lund, 2003; Paul, 2009; Paul & Wang, 2012; Pence & Justice, 2008).

The proffering of a group of fundamental attributes should not be viewed as static or even as an all-or-nothing phenomenon. As is discussed throughout this book, the nature of the contributions of the fundamental attributes varies with intensity and age (e.g., early versus later development). In addition, these attributes are subjected to the influences of a number of interactions involving the combinations of language, cognitive, social, and affective (e.g., motivation, etc.) domains (Cain & Oakhill, 2007; Kamhi & Catts, 2012; McGuinness, 2004, 2005; McIntyre, 2011; Valencia, 2011). From a strong sociocultural viewpoint, these attributes are affected pervasively by the home and surrounding cultural world experiences, especially the nature of language and literacy artifacts, practices, and communicative interactions (e.g., McIntyre, 2011; Paratore & Dougherty, 2011).

Perhaps, another feasible way to understand the notion of fundamentals is to pose a few questions, which are addressed in this book. For example,

- What is necessary to acquire or to become proficient in a phonemic-based language such as English? Is this the same for learning English as a second language? How can or should this level of proficiency be maintained throughout the formative school years?
- What is necessary to acquire or become proficient in English literacy? Is this the same as learning to read and write in English as a second language? How can or should this level of proficiency be maintained throughout the formative school years?

- Is there a relationship between proficiency in the through-the-air form of English and its written counterpart? What is the nature of this relationship? Is this relationship the same for learning to read and write in English as a second language? Do the attributes of this relationship change or become altered throughout the formative school years?

The Acquisition of Fundamentals: English Language With respect to through-the-air English, it is a challenge to delineate the fundamentals that are necessary for proficiency. There are numerous debates not only on the nature of English but also on the most efficient manner to investigate its acquisition by children (see Chapter 2). A range of theories and models can be found within the purview of cognitivism, social, contextual, or socioculturalism, or environmental/behaviorism, not to mention the array of computations or combinations of these broad frameworks or even eclectic approaches based on aspects from two or more of them (Kamhi & Catts, 2012; Paul, 2009; Pence & Justice, 2008; Reed, 2012). This situation is no different for learning or acquiring English as a second language (e.g., August & Shanahan, 2006; Birch, 2007; Paul & Wang, 2012).

What does it mean to *know* English? English proficiency, at the least, means that children have a working intuitive understanding of the integrative use of major language components such as phonology, morphology, syntax, semantics, and pragmatics (Crystal, 2006; Pence & Justice, 2008). Thus, the fundamentals of English proficiency entail the use of all of the language components in receptive and expressive communicative interactions. There may be other concepts within each of the components that are critical for obtaining proficiency in a particular component, which indicates that there is an order of acquisition due to levels of difficulty. For example, in the research on the acquisition of syntax, Quigley and his collaborators demonstrated an order of difficulty across the nine structures assessed as well as within several of the structures such as verb processes and relative clauses (see reviews in Paul, 2001, 2009). The order of difficulty was found to be roughly similar for children who are d/Deaf (90 decibels or greater in the better unaided ear) and for children who were typically hearing (i.e., native learners) at younger ages. It should be emphasized that this order of difficulty was for print comprehension of syntax, given the enormous challenges of assessing such knowledge in the through-the-air domain.

Historically, a particular component of English such as phonology or syntax or semantics has received a substantial amount of scholarly attention due to its purported prominence and criticalness, and this has engendered a strong line of research in each specific area (Crystal, 2006; McGuinness, 2005; Paul, 2009; Pence & Justice, 2008). It is assumed that the full development and, consequently, subsequent benefits of knowing and using English requires proficiency in all of its components. The nature of reaching a threshold level of proficiency in a particular language component or with the integration of all components is not completely understood. This current state affects our understanding of the specific contributions of major English language components to the development of English literacy.

There seems to be little doubt that there are important connections between English language comprehension (i.e., comprehension in through-the-air English) and the development of both early and mature literacy skills (Cain & Oakhill, 2007; Kamhi & Catts, 2012; McGuinness, 2004, 2005; McGill-Franzen & Allington, 2011). In fact, English language comprehension—often labeled oral language or through-the-air comprehension—is a major component of an influential model of reading called the "simple view of reading" (Gough & Tunmer, 1986; cf. a critique in Hoffman, 2009). English language comprehension through the air might be necessary (but not sufficient) for English literacy, but also, as stated eloquently by Pinker (1994, p. 16), "writing is clearly an optional accessory; the real engine of verbal communication is the spoken language we acquired as children."

Most young children who do not have language delays/difficulties or disabilities acquire an intuitive understanding of English by the time they start formal schooling—at about age five or six. The more difficult features of phonology are usually acquired by age eight (Crystal, 2006; Pence & Justice, 2008). Children can then use their knowledge of the English language to further their learning process—that is, growth in comprehension and knowledge. Specifically, children learn to use literate language (language to represent language and concepts as in academic content areas), and they continue to grow in their understanding and use of more complex language structures, including vocabulary knowledge (e.g., see discussions in Paul, 2009; Paul & Wang, 2012; see also Chapter 2).

Several of the challenges to the implications of the QSH, particularly within a certain structure, concern the role of phonology, especially phonological and phonemic awareness, in the development of early English literacy skills in d/Deaf children, who are heavily dependent on the use of sign with presumably little or impoverished access to the sound system of English. Implicitly and, perhaps puzzling, these challenges seem to pertain mostly to the acquisition of English literacy, not necessarily to the development of through-the-air English language (e.g., see Allen et al., 2009; Miller & Clark, 2011).

In our view, phonology represents the building blocks of a language (Crystal, 2006; Pence & Justice, 2008). For individuals to learn or acquire a language—any language—they must be able to access its phonology. In turn, phonological knowledge (on an intuitive or tacit level) facilitates the acquisition of other language components (Crystal, 1997, 2006; Paul, 2009; Pence & Justice, 2008). Some scholars argue that both phonology and morphology contribute to vocabulary knowledge in either the through-the-air mode or in the print mode (e.g., Stahl & Nagy, 2006; see also the discussion in Kamil & Catts, 2012).

For a spoken language such as English, phonology includes the development of proficiency in two broad domains: segmentals (phonemes such as consonants and vowels) and suprasegmentals (prosodic features such as intonation, pauses, etc.). Phonology is highlighted here because of its necessary, but not sufficient, role (particularly phonological processes) in the development of emergent and foundational reading skills (Adams, 1990, 1994, 2002; McGuinness, 2004, 2005; National Early Literacy Panel, 2008; Whitehurst & Lonigan, 2002; for d/Dhh children, see C. Mayer, 2007;

Paul, 2009; Perfetti & Sandak, 2000; Trezek, Wang, & Paul, 2010, 2011; Wang et al., 2008; Williams, 2004, 2011).

For a number of d/Deaf and hard of hearing children, there is at least one additional issue—that is, whether it is effective to teach English (or any other spoken language) as a *first* language if it has not been learned during early childhood (e.g., Paul, 2009). As is discussed later in this book, this issue is so critical and complex that these children are attempting to learn the through-the-air and print forms of English *simultaneously*—which is truly a challenging, almost insurmountable, task (Kamhi & Catts, 2012; Paul & Wang, 2012; Reed, 2012; Trezek et al., 2011). In fact, this critical situation is either overlooked or not addressed adequately by scholars, who seem to downplay or dismiss the role of English phonology for d/Deaf children (e.g., Allen et al., 2009; Miller & Clark, 2011). It almost seems that the crux for these scholars is that the acquisition of English through the air is not necessary or that the important working knowledge of English can occur via the use of ASL and the engagement with English print. This assertion, in our view and as argued throughout this book, does not have strong theoretical or empirical support (Paul, 2009; Paul & Wang, 2012; Trezek et al., 2010, 2011; Wang et al., 2008; Williams, 2004).

The Acquisition of Fundamentals: English Literacy   Delineating the micro and macro fundamentals for through-the-air English proficiency is a difficult feat. Establishing these two tiers of fundamentals for the development of English literacy is no less complicated. We have argued that English literacy requires more than just knowing and using English through the air, albeit through-the-air competency is critical.

For starters, the fundamentals for English literacy entail competence in, at minimum, through-the-air English plus print access skills (e.g., phonological processing, phonemic awareness, decoding, print conventions, etc.), vocabulary knowledge (meanings, nuances, figurative usage, etc.), comprehension (e.g., prior knowledge, metacognition, making inferences, etc.), fluency (reading accurately and expediently with expression), and adequate social (e.g., home environment, effective teaching, etc.) and affective (e.g., motivation, interest, etc.) factors (Cain & Oakhill, 2007; Israel & Duffy, 2009; McGuinness, 2004, 2005; McGill-Franzen & Allington, 2011; National Early Literacy Panel, 2008; National Reading Panel, 2000; Ruddell & Unrau, 2004; see further discussions in Chapters 3 and 4). The micro fundamentals involve the aspects within each of the broad domains such as decoding, vocabulary, and comprehension.

During the early literacy period, particularly while learning to read and write, children need to develop metalinguistic awareness of print (pragmatics); sounds (phonemes); letters (graphemes); the relations between letters and sound (phonics), parts of words (morphology or structural analysis), and word order (syntax); and connected text structures (i.e., connected discourse) (Cain & Oakhill, 2007; Israel & Duffy, 2009; McGill-Franzen & Allington, 2011; McGuinness, 2004, 2005; National Early Literacy Panel, 2008; National Reading Panel, 2000; Ruddell & Unrau, 2004). Based on our limited understanding of the reciprocal relations between reading and writing (e.g., T. Shanahan, 1984, 2006; T. Shanahan & Lomax, 1986, 1988), there seems to be a common set of competencies that underpins the development of both reading and writing in the young literacy learner. This becomes operationalized in the facilitative effects of one domain on the other. For example, writing behaviors in kindergarten children are predictive of subsequent reading achievement, and research indicates that the ability to engage in invented spelling is a strong and consistent predictor of success in phonological training and learning to read (Kamhi & Catts, 2012; Pressley, 2006; Richgels, 2001).

As discussed throughout this book, the development of early literacy in d/Dhh children has not been researched extensively, and similar comments can be made about research on other children, including those who are struggling readers and writers (e.g., McGill-Franzen & Allington, 2011). Nevertheless, there is some research that highlights the relative contributions of print-access or decoding skills and cognitive/language-related skills in the early literacy period to the later acquisition of conventional or mature literacy (Cain & Oakhill, 2007; McGuinness, 2004, 2005; T. Shanahan, 2006; Snowling & Hulme, 2005; Storch & Whitehurst, 2002; Whitehurst & Lonigan, 1998, 2002). For example, the relationship between phonological processing (e.g., manipulating sounds, memory, etc.) and word identification (i.e., later decoding skill) is robust. However, this relationship appears to be nonlinear and exhibits a lower predictive power (i.e., effects) for English reading comprehension at the advanced reading levels—often called the reading-to-learn phase. This has led several scholars in the field of deafness to argue that phonology is necessary, but not sufficient, for reading comprehension in the mature conventional literacy phase—at least for reading in English as a first language (e.g., Paul et al., 2009; Trezek et al., 2011; Wang et al., 2008). This differential contribution of phonology represents part of our response to the challenges of the basic assumptions of the QSH (cf. Allen et al., 2009; Miller & Clark, 2011).

The contributions of language and cognitive skills are becoming more prominent in the literature on children who are not d/Dhh (Cain & Oakhill, 2007; Kamhi & Catts, 2012; Reed, 2012; T. Shanahan, 2006; Storch & Whitehurst, 2002; Whitehurst & Lonigan, 2002). Several researchers and scholars (Kamhi & Catts, 2012; McGuinness, 2005; McGill-Franzen & Allington, 2011; T. Shanahan, 2006) have argued that the effects of language and cognition on literacy are much more pervasive than have been reported previously. The social and affective domains are also becoming more acknowledged in their roles in both the early and later literacy periods (e.g., McIntyre, 2011; Paratore & Dougherty, 2011; Hall, 2003; see also, the work of Williams, 2004, 2011, 2012).

The skills associated with the use of through-the-air English language might be more pertinent for the advanced reading or reading-to-learn phase, mainly due to the increased demands of the text on both cognition and language of individuals (e.g., McGuinness, 2004, 2005; Whitehurst & Lonigan, 2002). This situation may also apply to the advanced writing period, particularly with the composing of expository texts (e.g., Hayes, 2004; T. Shanahan, 2006). For individuals to use their higher-level language and cognitive skills, they must possess automatic lower-level decoding skills, including alphabet knowledge (knowledge of letters and sounds and the relationships between them) and morphological understanding (word parts). With automatic decoding skills in tow, these individuals can focus most of their attention, energy, and resources on making sense of and understanding the information in the text.

Automatic decoding skills are facilitated by the use of working memory, which is suited for comprehending a written language system on which the alphabetic principle is based (Cain & Oakhill, 2007; Pickering, 2006; Snowling & Hulme, 2005). In particular, the processing and comprehension of English sentences and longer discourse structures requires that specific textual aspects are maintained for a period of time in working memory (for d/Dhh individuals, see reviews in Hanson, 1989; Paul, 1998, 2009; Trezek et al., 2010, 2011; Wang et al., 2008).

In essence, Paul (2012) asserts that the critical fundamentals for the development of English literacy with respect to the QSH are the following:

- Knowledge of the language of print (i.e., components of English).
- Metalinguistic awareness of language- and print-related factors (e.g., letters, sounds, letter–sound relationships [phonology, orthography], functions of print [pragmatics], words [semantics], sentences [syntax]).
- Phonologically based working memory or phonological memory (and processes).
- Comprehension capabilities (i.e., the development of textual, intertextual, and cultural prior knowledge, metacognitive, and self-regulatory skills). (p. 186)

Critical or Optimal Period

In addition to disciplinary structure, the second major component of the QSH is the construct of a critical or optimal period. Similar to other complex constructs—which are often slippery or seem to escape strong or complete descriptions (e.g., Flavell, 1985)—the notion of an acquisition period having a critical or optimal time frame has been subjected to intense debates (see reviews in Paul, 2001, 2009; Paul & Wang, 2012; Phillips, Hayward, & Norris, 2011). From one standpoint, establishing a specific time frame is difficult because of the multitude of language and literacy challenges that are often present in struggling language and literacy learners (Kamhi & Catts, 2012; Phillips et al., 2011). The time frame has been tied to the maturation process of the brain, particularly up until the time of puberty for language development—albeit, there are challenges from the emerging research on brain plasticity (e.g., see discussions in Lenneberg, 1967; Rymer, 1992; see also the reviews in Paul, 2001, 2009) and research on children with reading difficulties (but not reading disabilities) (Phillips et al., 2011).

The growth of language is deemed to be optimal in the early years and slows down considerably—and is less optimal—after puberty. This critical or optimal period also applies to the learning of a second language, which, of course, complicates the process (Paul, 2001, 2009; Paul & Wang, 2012). Language proficiency that develops earlier has the most beneficial effects on the acquisition of skills and knowledge in other content areas, not to mention on cognitive and affective domains. The growth period of language markedly affects the development of English literacy during both the emergent literacy period and the later mature acquisition period.

The person most noted for applying this time-frame construct to the acquisition of literacy, especially English reading, is Stanovich (1986, 1988; see also, 1991, 1992;

Stanovich et al., 1988). Stanovich's *Matthew effect* is based on a biblical passage in the book of Matthew that relates how *the rich get richer and the poor get poorer*. Specifically, Stanovich has documented the negative effects of the low reading skills of struggling readers. The aggregation of low expectations, poor motivation, inadequate instruction, and poor reading skills contribute to a downward spiral of failure, which seems difficult to escape (see also Chapters 6 to 8 in Paul & Wang, 2012).

Stanovich proffered the end of the early elementary grades (i.e., grade 2 or 3) as the demarcation of the optimal period, although the optimal period for literacy growth has been debated contentiously. Essentially, this was interpreted to mean that if children can make progress in learning to read relative to their typical mental ages by grades 2 or 3, then they can read widely to learn (i.e., get *richer*) and, consequently, they will grow linguistically and cognitively. If children do not learn to read on grade level by the end of this optimal period, then they experience enormous subsequent difficulties, which affect pervasively any further growth in language and cognition. That is, these children become *poorer* with respect to the acquisition of knowledge and understanding.

Although there is no exact percentage, the assumption is that the overwhelming majority of individuals who are not reading on grade level by the end of grade 2 or 3 have extreme difficulty making up the *lost ground* in the later years (cf. Phillips et al., 2011). Some possible reasons include not only ineffective teaching and inadequate social environments but also difficulty in comprehending reading materials beyond the third grade due to the demands elicited by the complexity of the language and concepts. These challenges are due to inadequate decoding and comprehension problems as well as other cognitive issues (e.g., memory, metacognition, and self-regulating mechanisms; see Arlington & McGill-Franzen, 2009; Kamhi & Catts, 2012).

Developmental Lag Hypothesis and the QSH

The Matthew effect has morphed—so to speak—into Stanovich's *developmental lag hypothesis* (DLH; Stanovich et al., 1988), which typically compares the cognitive profiles of good and nondyslexic struggling readers (i.e., via matched comparison of reading ability levels). The DLH is similar to the basic tenets of the QSH (Paul, 2012; Paul & Lee, 2010); thus, it is discussed here. Unlike the QSH, the DLH has strong and weak forms; however, these forms can also apply to the QSH.

The strong form of the DLH contends that struggling readers of English can perform on par (i.e., catch up) with their peers who are developing at a typical pace or rate of acquisition. However, the remediation or intervention period for the struggling readers needs to be relatively brief and marked by instruction that is targeted and extensive on the reading components that have caused the delay. Although the nature of the reading process and components is extremely contentious (Israel & Duffy, 2009; Ruddell & Unrau, 2004), much of the controversy surrounding the DLH relates to the contributions of phonological processes (e.g., phonological and phonemic awareness; phonological memory). The complex relations between phonological processes and the acquisition of emergent and mature reading comprehension skills, for first- and second-language reading of English, are discussed later in this book (August & Shanahan, 2006; National Early Literacy Panel, 2008; National Reading Panel, 2000).

The weak version addresses the situation in which struggling readers (and writers) fail to read on grade level, despite intensive and extensive targeted instructional approaches. It can be postulated that this means not reading on grade level by *puberty* regardless of the reasons. In essence, the rate of acquisition is too slow and laborious—albeit, children and adolescents may continue to make progress in reading.

Stanovich's DLH seems to pertain mostly to children who have what is called garden-variety (nonspecific) *reading difficulties* or who do not have dyslexia, even though the description and reality of dyslexia are also shrouded with controversies. The weak version of the DLH, along with accompanied research data, has elicited another position to account for the lack of progress or the slow progress—the *deficit hypothesis* (e.g., see discussions in Francis, Shaywitz, Stuebing, Shaywitz, & Fletcher, 1996; O'Brien, Mansfield, & Legge, 2005; O'Shaughnessy & Swanson, 1998; Reimer, 2006; Snowling, Defty, & Goulandris, 1996). The deficit hypothesis applies to the research findings of children with severe dyslexia and even to those with severe cognitive or intellectual delays—that is, to many children with *reading disabilities* (McGill-Franzen & Allington, 2011; McGuinness, 2005). The deficit hypothesis contends that the challenges of the growth of reading cannot be remedied or intervened effectively psychologically—that is, via the use of instruction even with optimal sociocultural contexts or situations. The best-case scenario is to stabilize the reading level of these children (e.g., maintained at a certain level with some growth). There are multiple reasons for this situation, and phonological processes play only one major role, most likely during the early reading period (Paul & Wang, 2012).

Reading Disability versus Reading Difficulty

Given the research on and the underpinnings of Stanovich's DLH and the QSH, it is important to continue the discussion of the emerging views on the similarities and differences between *reading disability* and *reading difficulty* (Kamhi & Catts, 2012; Phillips et al., 2011; Spear-Swerling, 2011). (Note: Similar situations involving *language delay/difficulty* and *language disability* are discussed in Chapter 2). There is no clear consensus on the descriptions of these complex constructs (Kamhi & Catts, 2012; McGill-Franzen & Arlington, 2011), yet a few scholars have argued that a distinction can and should be explicated (e.g., Phillips et al., 2011; Spear-Swerling, 2011). A case can be made that both constructs are socially constructed with respect to ideological (or power) issues associated with the concept of literacy of which reading is a subset (e.g., Gee, 1996, 2003; Paul & Wang, 2012; Street, 1984). Our aim is to shed some light on the confusion surrounding the use of these terms, including others such as *reading challenges, reading failures, at-risk readers, struggling readers,* and so on. Then, we apply the use of these terms with children who are d/Dhh.

Reading Disability   The label *reading disability* is often reserved for individuals whose reading difficulties are due to underlying biological–psychological or neuropsychological conditions (Phillips et al., 2011; Spear-Swerling, 2011). These children have extreme challenges in learning to read on grade or chronological age levels or even in learning to read at all. In this category, there might be little debate in delineating children with severe language impairment or those with intellectual or cognitive disabilities (Cain & Oakhill, 2007; McGuinness, 2004, 2005).

Children with dyslexia, especially severe dyslexia, can certainly be labeled as children with persistent reading disabilities; however, unlike other types of children, a number of children with dyslexia can become good readers—with appropriate interventions. Some scholars actually put children who cannot access the phonological code—for biological or psychological reasons—in this category of reading disability. In addition, with respect to the effects of English language proficiency for facilitating the understanding of English reading, McGuinness (2004) asserts:

> Overall, a broad range of studies from a variety of disciplines show that no child, short of being deaf, mute, or grossly mentally disabled, is prevented by a language delay or deficit from learning reading mechanics—the ability to master the code sufficiently to read (decode) and spell (encode). The longitudinal studies, on the other hand, show that serious delays in core language functions like expressive vocabulary, syntax, and semantics put a child at high risk for difficulties with more advanced reading skills, like reading comprehension. This is due to a complex interaction of factors that, so far, have not been teased apart. (p. 12)

Thus, it can be inferred, according to McGuinness, that children who are "deaf, mute, or grossly mentally disabled" have reading disabilities that actually prevent them from learning to read. However, the meaning of the word *deaf* has not been explicated by the research synthesis of McGuiness (who, we assume, is not a researcher of d/Dhh individuals). Nevertheless, we can postulate that it refers to those students with serious delays in the language of print and the ability to access print in general—that is, "reading mechanics," which includes decoding skills.

Although there might be specific conditions that warrant the label of reading disability, this term is also considered to be predominantly socially constructed (e.g., Alvermann & Mallozzi, 2011; Phillips et al., 2011). That is, the assignment of the label, reading disability, is dependent on the results on certain tests or tasks, most of which can be described as involving the ability to perform adequately on discrete skills such as retelling, answering questions, obtaining the main idea, synthesizing information, and so on. Whether these discrete skills portray an accurate or complete picture of what it means to be a good reader is debatable (Duffy & Israel et al., 2009).

Reading Difficulty

It has been argued that a number of children with persistent reading disabilities should actually be considered as children with reading difficulties (Arlington & McGill-Franzen, 2009; Phillips et al., 2011). On one hand, the term *reading difficulty* is often used generically in regards to any individual or group who is not—for lack of a better phrase—reading (or writing) on grade level or commensurate with the achievement level of typical chronologically age peers. This term is often used interchangeably with the others, most notably *struggling readers, at-risk readers,* and so on. When reading difficulty is used indiscriminately in this manner, it might mask the actual reasons for the challenges in reading achievement and lead to issues such as a self-fulfilling prophesy (low expectations of teachers, etc.), ineffective or lackluster instructional approaches, and negative attitudes, including low self-esteem or self-concept of the affected individuals.

For some researchers, reading difficulty has descriptive connotations whereas reading disability seems to be disposed toward explanatory adequacy (Cain & Oakhill, 2007; Nation, 2005; Phillips et al., 2011). The assertion is that the so-called persistent reading difficulties of children can be ameliorated by the intensive and extensive applications of appropriate language and literacy assessments and interventions. [Note: This may also be the case for a number of children with dyslexia or others in the reading disability category.] The use of specific instructional assessment and approaches varies according to the progress and needs (phonological processes, comprehension, etc.) of children, some of whom may experience *difficulty* at different grade levels and across different reading genres. Equally as important, it is necessary to address the mismatch between the requirements of school- or academic-based literacy content, language usages, and practices and what children from nonmainstream or minority environments bring to school during the beginning or early literacy period. The development of higher-order comprehension skills, relative to the use of content areas, is also a critical need for all readers, but especially those who experience reading challenges in the middle childhood grades (6 to 9) (e.g., Wharton-McDonald & Swiger, 2009).

Running the risk of oversimplification, it is feasible to assert that researchers and educators who favor the term *reading difficulty* have argued that factors that negatively impact the acquisition of reading are predominantly the result of a disconnect between mainstream academic tenets and those associated with the child's sociocultural environment (e.g., Phillips et al., 2011). The problem is outside of or external to the child— rather than within, as is the case for reading disability. Ironically, it is possible that the inappropriate *treatment* of reading (and language) difficulties may lead to severe reading (and language) disabilities or what can be labeled as environmentally induced language or cognitive impoverishment. The longer this state of affairs continues, the more difficult it is to ameliorate the deleterious effects. This is related to Stanovich's (1986) Matthew effect construct, discussed previously.

On one level, the construct of reading difficulty is different from that of reading disability. A number of children who are struggling readers/writers can be placed in both categories—assuming that there is some consensus on the salient features of each label. Perhaps, defining or describing reading difficulty, like that of struggling readers, is as challenging as trying to nail gelatin to the wall. It might be that all terms are dependent on a definition and assessment of reading comprehension, which is also an extremely complex and slippery construct (e.g., Alvermann & Mallozzi, 2011; see also the various perspectives in Israel & Duffy, 2009).

Relation to d/Deaf and Hard of Hearing Individuals   The application of the constructs of reading disability and reading difficulties to d/Dhh individuals has not been discussed intensively or even explicitly. From one perspective, it seems to fall under the umbrella of the debate between the clinical versus cultural views of deafness or the medical versus social views of disability (e.g., for deafness, see Paul, 2009; Paul & Moore, 2012a; for research on disability, see various perspectives in Thomas & Vaughn,

2004). That is, individuals who favor the clinical or medical view might be placed, rightly or wrongly, in the camp of promoting reading disability whereas those who adhere to cultural or social views might propose that the challenges are mostly, if not predominately, reading difficulties.

In our view, this either/or syndrome or dichotomy is not only unproductive but also masks the complexity of developing proficiency in both English language and English literacy. Although we appreciate the differing worldviews or epistemologies emanating from these positions (e.g., Paul & Moore, 2012a, 2012b), the fact that some, perhaps many, d/Dhh children have difficulty with phonological processes because of the input and development of phonology needs to be considered as well as the nature of the sociocultural factors that impede both English language and English literacy development. In short, the attempt to decide on whether a reading issue is a disability or a difficulty for d/Dhh children is not as beneficial as deciding the specific issues that need to be addressed for each child. These issues may indeed be both inside and outside the child. That some d/Dhh children may also have dyslexia (and other specific reading disabilities) also needs to be considered. Obviously, d/Dhh children with cognitive or intellectual disabilities present additional challenges for the development of language and literacy.

Dissensions: A Few Summative Remarks

The QSH maintains that the English language and literacy development of all children—whether placed in the category of reading (or language) disability or reading (or language) difficulty—is qualitatively (developmentally) similar albeit it might be quantitatively delayed when compared to those who are typical readers/writers (or native English language learners). It is important to address the language and literacy challenges of these children as early as possible to minimize the quantitative gaps, especially prior to puberty, although these challenges can still be addressed throughout the school years. The focus on qualitative similarities indicates the need for differentiated treatment of various language and literacy components according to the child's needs. These components are the same for everyone attempting to learn English; however, it should be emphasized that treatment or intervention needs to be differentiated with respect to intensity and time frame.

As mentioned previously in this introductory chapter, a few of the major criticisms of the QSH (e.g., Allen et al., 2009; Miller & Clark, 2011) focus mostly on the role of phonology in the development of reading, particularly in the learning to read period. As discussed later in this book and elsewhere (Paul, 2011, 2012; Paul & Wang, 2012), this predominant focus on the role of phonology is shortsighted with respect to the construct of the QSH. Other divergent views on the validity of the QSH seem to flow from misunderstandings of the overall framework as it pertains to the development of either English language or English literacy. Still other contrarian views seem to emerge from research that falls under the rubric of *multiple epistemologies* or within the purview of strong forms of social and contextual frameworks that reject a salient or even a critical position being consigned to cognitivism or to the use of the standard epistemology within a scientific framework (Hayes, 2004; Paul & Moores, 2012b).

A wave of attacks against cognitivism, particularly information processing, has come from positions such as embodied cognition (Lakoff & Johnson, 1999) or situated cognition (e.g., Brown, Collins, & Duguid, 1989; Greeno, 1998; see also Duffy et al., 2009). These views highlight the prominence of the broader context or social world and the inseparability of learning and teaching or even cognition and the affective or motor domain. Nevertheless, it is also possible to find arguments to refute these broad attacks (e.g., Anderson, Greeno, Reder, & Simon, 2000; Anderson, Reder, & Simon, 1996).

As we have mentioned repeatedly, we do agree strongly that social and contextual factors should be considered in the discussion of developing or teaching English. We argue that such considerations serve to refine the basic assumptions of the QSH rather than to undermine our convictions. A more fruitful approach to these dichotomies, which is still relevant, has been proffered by Anderson et al. (1996):

> What is needed to improve learning and teaching is to continue to deepen our research into the circumstances that determine when narrower or broader contexts are required and when attention to narrower or broader skills are optimal for effective and efficient learning. (p. 10)

It is not possible to address adequately all of the challenges that emerge from a few social and contextual models or from the multiple epistemologies because several of these perspectives reflect radically different world views that do not involve the use of the scientific method, especially one that adheres to the principles of an objective methodology (Paul & Moores, 2012a, 2012b; Moores & Paul, 2012). The same can be said for challenges from radical interpretations of situated or embodied cognition, which seem to reject objectivism or, specifically, the use of a scientific method, to understand human behavior and action. Although we acknowledge that the use of the scientific method—especially an objective methodology—may not be sufficient to comprehend all of reality, we do believe that this approach is necessary for making progress. We also acknowledge and value the variations of the scientific method such as the use of qualitative or ethnographic research as long as the findings can be verified and validated.

CONCLUSION

Our main goal in this introductory chapter was to outline the basic tenets of the QSH with respect to the development of English language and literacy. The QSH has both micro and macro components, which should encourage a wide range of further research, including research into the acquisition of English as a second language and research on non-d/Dhh children with either language/literacy disabilities or language/literacy difficulties or both.

In this book, we synthesize extant theories and research on the development of through-the-air English and English literacy for both first- and second-language learners. We also explore these constructs for students with language/learning disabilities. In every chapter, we relate the information to what we know about students who are d/Dhh. Based on our synthesis, we proffer instructional strategies for improving the English language and literacy skills of d/Dhh children and adolescents (Chapter 6).

We provide a critique of research that has been conducted on the construct of developmental similarity to suggest needed areas and approaches for further investigations (Chapter 7). Other perspectives on the QSH (and related constructs) are presented by invited authors who comment on first- and second-language development of English (Chapter 8). Finally, in our concluding chapter (Chapter 9) we present our reflections and directions for further theorizing and research as well as our response to the reactants in Chapter 8. It is hoped that the debate on constructs such as the developmental similarity stimulate further study on the manner in which to improve the English language and literacy development of students who are d/Dhh.

REFERENCES

Adams, M. (1990). *Beginning to read: Thinking and learning about print.* Cambridge, MA: MIT Press.

Adams, M. (1994). Phonics and beginning reading instruction. In F. Lehr & J. Osborn (Eds.), *Reading, language, and literacy: Instruction for the 21st century* (pp. 3–23). Hillsdale, NJ: Erlbaum.

Adams, M. (2002). Alphabetic anxiety and explicit, systematic phonics instruction: A cognitive science perspective. In S. Neuman & D. Dickinson (Eds.), *Handbook of early literacy research* (pp. 66–80). New York, NY: Guilford Press.

Allen, T., Clark, M. D., del Giudice, A., Koo, D., Lieberman, A., Mayberry, R., & Miller, P. (2009). Phonology and reading: A response to Wang, Trezek, Luckner, and Paul. *American Annals of the Deaf, 154*(4), 338–345.

Alvermann, D., & Mallozzi, C. (2011). Interpretive research. In A. McGill-Franzen & R. Allington (Eds.), *Handbook of reading disability research* (pp. 488–496). New York, NY: Routledge.

Anderson, J. R., Greeno, J. G., Reder, L. M., & Simon, H. A. (2000). Perspectives on learning, thinking, and activity. *Educational Researcher, 29*(4), 11–13.

Anderson, J. R., Reder, L. M., & Simon, H. A. (1996). Situated learning and education. *Educational Researcher, 25*(4), 5–11.

Allington, R., & McGill-Franzen, A. (2009). Comprehension difficulties among struggling readers. In S. Israel & G. Duffy (Eds.), *Handbook of research on reading comprehension* (pp. 551–568). New York, NY: Routledge.

August, D., & Shanahan, T. (Eds.). (2006). *Developing literacy in second-language learners: Report of the National Literacy Panel on language-minority children and youth.* Mahwah, NJ: Erlbaum.

Baddeley, A. (2006). Working memory: An overview. In S. Pickering (Ed.), *Working memory and education* (pp. 1–31). Boston, MA: Elsevier.

Bartine, D. (1989). *Early English reading theory: Origins of current debates.* Columbia, SC: University of South Carolina Press.

Bartine, D. (1992). *Reading, criticism, and culture: Theory and teaching in the United States and England, 1820–1950.* Columbia, SC: University of South Carolina Press.

Battista, M. (2001). Research and reform in mathematics education. In T. Loveless (Eds.), *The great curriculum debate: How should we teach reading and math?* (pp. 42–84). Washington, DC: Brookings Institution.

Birch, B. (2007). *English L2 reading: Getting to the bottom* (2nd ed.). Mahwah, NJ: Erlbaum.

Brown, J. S., Collins, A., & Duguid, P. (1989). Situated cognition and the culture of learning. *Educational Researcher, 18*(1), 32–42.

Bruning, R., Schraw, G., Norby, M., & Ronning, R. (2004). *Cognitive psychology and instruction* (4th ed.). Upper Saddle River, NJ: Pearson/Merrill/Prentice Hall.

Cain, K., & Oakhill, J. (Eds.). (2007). *Children's comprehension problems in oral and written language.* New York, NY: Guilford Press.

Carruthers, P., Laurence, S, & Stich, S. (Eds.). (2005). *The innate mind: Structure and contents.* New York, NY: Oxford University Press.

Carruthers, P., Laurence, S, & Stich, S. (Eds.). (2006). *The innate mind: Vol. 2. Culture and cognition.* New York, NY: Oxford University Press.

Cartwright, K. (2009). The role of cognitive flexibility in reading comprehension: Past, present, and future. In S. Israel & G. Duffy (Eds.), *Handbook of research on reading comprehension* (pp. 115–139). New York, NY: Routledge.

Chomsky, N. (1988). *Language and problems of knowledge: The Managua lectures.* Cambridge, MA: MIT Press.

Chomsky, N. (1991). Linguistics and adjacent fields: A personal view. In A. Kasher (Ed.), *The Chomskyan turn* (pp. 3–25). New York, NY: Blackwell.

Chomsky, N. (2006). *Language and mind* (3rd ed.). New York, NY: Cambridge University Press.

Crystal, D. (1997). *The Cambridge encyclopedia of language* (2nd ed). New York, NY: Cambridge University Press.

Crystal, D. (2006). *How language works.* London, England: Penguin.

Cummins, J. (1979). Linguistic interdependence and the educational development of bilingual children. *Review of Educational Research, 49*(2), 222–251.

Cummins, J. (1984). *Bilingualism and special education: Issues in assessment and pedagogy.* San Diego, CA: College-Hill.

Cummins, J. (2007). Pedagogies for the poor: Realigning reading instruction for low-income students with scientifically based reading research. *Educational Researcher, 36*(9), 564–572.

Donovan, M., & Bransford, J. (Eds.). (2005). *How students learn: History, mathematics, and science in the classroom.* Washington, DC: National Academies.

Duffy, G., Israel, S., Davis, S., Doyle, K., Gavigan, K., Gray, E. S., Jones, A., Kear, K., Qualls, R., Mason, P., et al. (2009). Where to from here? Themes, trends, and questions. In S. Israel & G. Duffy (Eds.), *Handbook of research on reading comprehension* (pp. 668–675). New York, NY: Routledge.

Flavell, D. (1985). *Cognitive development* (2nd ed.). Englewood Cliffs, NJ: Prentice-Hall.

Francis, D., Shaywitz, S., Stuebing, K., Shaywitz, B., & Fletcher, J. (1996). Developmental lag versus deficit models of reading disability: A longitudinal, individual growth curve analysis. *Journal of Educational Psychology, 88*(1), 3–17.

Gaffney, J., & Anderson, R. (2000). Trends in reading research in the United States: Changing intellectual currents over three decades. In M. Kamil, P. Mosenthal, P.D. Pearson, & R. Barr (Eds.), *Handbook of reading research* (Vol. 3, pp. 53–74). Mahwah, NJ: Erlbaum.

Gee, J. (1996). *Social linguistics and literacy: Ideology in discourse* (2nd ed.). New York, NY: Taylor & Francis.

Gee, J. (2003). *What video games have to teach us about learning and literacy.* New York, NY: Palgrave.

Greeno, J. G. (1998). The situativity of knowing, learning, and research. *American Psychologist, 53*(1), 5–26.

Gough, P., & Tunmer, W. (1986). Decoding, reading, and reading disability. *Remedial and Special Education, 7,* 6–10.

Hall, K. (2003). Effective literacy teaching in the early years of school: A review of the evidence. In N. Hall, J. Larson, & J. Marsh (Eds.), *Handbook of early childhood literacy* (pp. 315–326). Thousand Oaks, CA: Sage.

Hanson, V. (1989). Phonology and reading: Evidence from profoundly deaf readers. In D. Shankweiler & I. Lieberman (Eds.), *Phonology and reading disability: Solving the reading puzzle* (pp. 69–89). Ann Arbor, MI: University of Michigan Press.

Hayes, J. (2004). A new framework for understanding cognition and affect in writing. In R. Ruddell & N. Unrau (Eds.), *Theoretical models and processes of reading* (5th ed.) (pp. 1399–1430). Newark, DE: International Reading Association.

Hoffman, J. (2009). In search of the "simple view" of reading comprehension. In S. Israel & G. Duffy (Eds.), *Handbook of research on reading comprehension* (pp. 54–66). New York, NY: Routledge.

Israel, S., & Duffy, G. (Eds.). *Handbook of research on reading comprehension*. New York, NY: Routledge.

Johnson, R. (1992). The problem of defining critical thinking. In S. Norris (Ed.), *The generalizability of critical thinking: Multiple perspectives on an educational ideal* (pp. 38–53). New York, NY: Teachers College Press.

Kamhi, A., & Catts, H. (2012). *Language and reading disabilities* (3rd ed.). Boston, MA: Pearson Education.

Kuhn, D. (2005). *Education for thinking.* Cambridge, MA: Harvard University Press.

Lakoff, G., & Johnson, M. (1999). *Philosophy in the flesh: The embodied mind and its challenge to western thought.* New York, NY: Basic Books.

Lenneberg, E. (1967). *Biological foundations of language.* New York, NY: Wiley.

Lund, N. (2003). *Language and thought.* New York, NY: Routledge.

Martin, J. (1992). Critical thinking for a humane world. In S. Norris (Ed.), *The generalizability of critical thinking: Multiple perspectives on an educational ideal* (pp. 163–180). New York, NY: Teachers College Press.

Mayer, C. (2007). What really matters in the early literacy development of deaf children. *Journal of Deaf Studies and Deaf Education, 12*(4), 411–431.

Mayer, R. (1992). Mathematical problem solving: Thinking as based on domain-specific knowledge. In R. Mayer (Ed.), *Thinking, problem solving, cognition* (pp. 455–489). New York, NY: Cambridge University Press.

Mayer, R., & Hegarty, M. (1996). The process of understanding mathematics problems. In R. Sternberg & T. Ben-Zeev (Eds.), *The nature of mathematical thinking* (pp. 29–53). Mahwah, NJ: Erlbaum.

McBurney, D. (2002). *How to think like a psychologist: Critical thinking in psychology* (2nd ed.). Upper Saddle River, NJ: Prentice Hall.

McCarthey, S., & Raphael, T. (1992). Alternative research perspectives. In J. Irwin & M. Doyle (Eds.), *Reading/writing connections: Learning from research* (pp. 2–30). Newark, DE: International Reading Association.

McGill-Franzen, A., & Allington, R. (Eds.). (2011). *Handbook of reading disability research.* New York, NY: Routledge.

McGuinness, D. (2004). *Early reading instruction: What science really tells us about how to teach reading.* Cambridge, MA: MIT Press.

McGuinness, D. (2005). *Language development and learning to read: The scientific study of how language development affects reading skill.* Cambridge, MA: MIT Press.

McIntyre, E. (2011). Sociocultural perspectives on children with reading difficulties. In A. McGill-Franzen & R. Allington (Eds.), *Handbook of reading disability research* (pp. 45–56). New York, NY: Routledge.

Miller, P., & Clark, D. (2011). Phonemic awareness is not necessary to become a skilled deaf reader. *Journal of Developmental Physical Disabilities, 23,* 459–476.

Mitchell, D. (1982). *The process of reading: A cognitive analysis of fluent reading and learning to read.* New York, NY: Wiley.

Moore, B., & Parker, R. (2009). *Critical thinking* (9th ed.). Boston, MA: McGraw-Hill.

Moores, D. (2001). *Educating the deaf: Psychology, principles, and practices* (5th ed.). Boston, MA: Houghton-Mifflin.

Moores, D., & Paul, P. (2012). Retrospectus and prospectus. In P. Paul & D. Moores (Eds.), *Deaf epistemologies: Multiple perspectives on the acquisition of knowledge* (pp. 255–258). Washington, DC: Gallaudet University Press.

Nation, K. (2005). Connections between language and reading in children with poor reading comprehension. In H. Catts & A. Kamhi (Eds.), *The connections between language and reading disabilities* (pp. 41–54). Mahwah, NJ: Erlbaum.

National Early Literacy Panel. (2008). *Developing early literacy: Report of the National Early Literacy Panel—A scientific synthesis of early literacy development and implications for interventions.* Washington, DC: Institute for Literacy and National Center for Family Literacy.

National Reading Panel. (2000). *Report of the National Reading Panel: Teaching children to read— An evidence-based assessment of the scientific research literature on reading and its implications for reading instruction.* Jessup, MD: National Institute for Literacy at EDPubs.

Noddings, N. (2007). *Philosophy of education* (2nd ed.). Boulder, CO: Westview Press.

Norris, S. (Ed.). (1992). *The generalizability of critical thinking: Multiple perspectives on an educational ideal.* New York, NY: Teachers College Press.

O'Brien, B., Mansfield, J., & Legge, G. (2005). The effect of print size on reading speed in dyslexia. *Journal of Research in Reading, 28*(3), 332–349.

O'Shaughnessy, T., & Swanson, H. (1998). Do immediate memory deficits in students with learning disabilities in reading reflect a developmental lag or deficit? A selective meta-analysis of the literature. *Learning Disability Quarterly, 21*(2), 123–148.

Paratore, J., & Dougherty, S. (2011). Home differences and reading difficulty. In A. McGill-Franzen & R. Allington (Eds.), *Handbook of reading disability research* (pp. 93–109). New York, NY: Routledge.

Paul, P. (1985). Reading and other language-variant populations. In C. King & S. Quigley, *Reading and deafness* (pp. 251–289). San Diego, CA: College-Hill.

Paul, P. (1998). *Literacy and deafness: The development of reading, writing, and literate thought.* Needham Heights, MA: Allyn & Bacon.

Paul, P. (2001). *Language and deafness* (3rd ed.). San Diego, CA: Singular/Thomson Learning.

Paul, P. (2009). *Language and deafness* (4th ed.). Sudbury, MA: Jason & Bartlett.

Paul, P. (2010). Qualitative-similarity hypothesis. In R. Nata (Ed.), *Progress in education* (Vol. 20, pp. 1–31). New York, NY: Nova Science.

Paul, P. (2011). A perspective on language and literacy issues. In D. Moores (Ed.), *Partners in education: Issues and trends from the 21st International Congress on the Education of the Deaf* (pp. 51–61). Washington, DC: Gallaudet University Press.

Paul, P. (2012). Qualitative similarity hypothesis. In P. Paul & D. Moores (Eds.), *Deaf epistemologies: Multiple perspectives on the acquisition of knowledge* (pp. 179–198). Washington, DC: Gallaudet University Press.

Paul, P., & Lee, C. (2010). Qualitative-similarity hypothesis. *American Annals of the Deaf, 154*(5), 456–462.

Paul, P., & Moores, D. (Eds.). (2012a). *Deaf epistemologies: Multiple perspectives on the acquisition of knowledge.* Washington, DC: Gallaudet University Press.

Paul, P., & Moores, D. (2012b). Toward an understanding of epistemology and deafness. In P. Paul & D. Moores (Eds.), *Deaf epistemologies: Multiple perspectives on the acquisition of knowledge* (pp. 3–15). Washington, DC: Gallaudet University Press.

Paul, P., & Wang, Y. (2012). *Literate thought: Understanding comprehension and literacy.* Sudbury, MA: Jason & Bartlett Learning.

Paul, P., Wang, Y., Trezek, B., & Luckner, J. (2009). Phonology is necessary, but not sufficient: A rejoinder. *American Annals of the Deaf, 154*(4), 346–356.

Paul, P., & Whitelaw, G. (2011). *Hearing and deafness: An introduction for health and educational professionals.* Sudbury, MA: Jason & Bartlett Learning.

Pearson, P. D. (2004). The reading wars. *Educational Policy, 18*(1), 216–252.

Pence, K., & Justice, L. (2008). *Language development from theory to practice.* Upper Saddle River, NJ: Pearson/Merrill Prentice Hall.

Perfetti, C., & Sandak, R. (2000). Reading optimally builds on spoken language: Implications for deaf readers. *Journal of Deaf Studies and Deaf Education, 5,* 32–50.

Phillips, D. (1983). On describing a student's cognitive structure. *Educational Psychologist, 18*(2), 59–74.

Phillips, L., Hayward, D., & Norris, S. (2011). Persistent reading difficulties: Challenging six erroneous beliefs. In A. McGill-Franzen & R. Allington (Eds.), *Handbook of reading disability research* (pp. 110–119). New York, NY: Routledge.

Phillips, D., & Soltis, J. (2004). *Perspectives on learning* (4th ed.). New York, NY: Teachers College Press.

Phillips, D., & Soltis, J. (2009). *Perspectives on learning* (5th ed.). New York, NY: Teachers College Press.

Pickering, S. (Ed.). (2006). *Working memory and education.* Boston, MA: Elsevier.

Pinker, S. (1994). *The language instinct: How the mind creates language.* New York, NY: William Morrow.

Pinker, S. (2007). *The stuff of thought: Language as a window into human nature.* New York, NY: Viking.

Pressley, M. (2006). *Reading instruction that works: The case for balanced teaching* (3rd ed.). New York, NY: Guilford Press.

Pring, R. (2004). *Philosophy of educational research* (2nd ed.). New York, NY: Continuum.

Reed, V. (2012). *An introduction to children with language disorders* (4th ed.). Columbus, OH: Pearson.

Reimer, J. (2006). Developmental changes in the allocation of semantic feedback during visual word recognition. *Journal of Research in Reading, 29*(2), 194–212.

Richgels, D. J. (2001). Invented spelling, phonemic awareness, and reading and writing instruction. In S. Neuman & D. Dickinson (Eds.), *Handbook of early literacy instruction* (pp. 142–155). New York, NY: Guilford Press

Ritzer, G. (2001). *Explorations in social theory: From metatheorizing to rationalization.* Thousand Oaks, CA: Sage.

Ruddell, R., & Unrau, N. (Eds.). (2004). *Theoretical models and processes of reading* (5th ed.). Newark, DE: International Reading Association.

Rymer, R. (1992, April 13). Annals of science: A silent childhood–I. *New Yorker*, pp. 41–81.

Schoenfeld, A. (1992). Learning to think mathematically: Problem solving, metacognition, and sense making in mathematics. In D. A. Grouws (Ed.), *Handbook of research on mathematics teaching and learning* (pp. 334–370). New York, NY: Macmillan.

Shanahan, C. (2009). Disciplinary comprehension. In S. Israel & G. Duffy (Eds.), *Handbook of research on reading comprehension* (pp. 240–260). New York, NY: Routledge.

Shanahan, T. (1984). The reading–writing relation: An exploratory multi-variate analysis. *Journal of Educational Psychology, 76*(3), 466–477.

Shanahan, T. (2006). Relations among oral language, reading, and writing development. In C. MacArthur, S. Graham, & J. Fitzgerald (Eds.), *Handbook of writing research* (pp.171–183). New York, NY: Guilford Press.

Shanahan, T., & Lomax, R. (1986). An analysis and comparison of theoretical models of the reading–writing relationship. *Journal of Educational Psychology, 78*(2), 116–123.

Shanahan, T., & Lomax, R. (1988). A developmental comparison of three theoretical models of the reading–writing relationship. *Research in the Teaching of English, 22*(2), 196–212.

Snowling, M., Defty, N., & Goulandris, N. (1996). A longitudinal study of reading development in dyslexic children. *Journal of Educational Psychology, 88*(4), 653–669.

Snowling, M., & Hulme, C. (Eds.). (2005). *The science of reading: A handbook.* Malden, MA: Blackwell.

Spear-Swerling, L. (2011). Patterns of reading disabilities across development. In A. McGill-Franzen & R. Allington (Eds.), *Handbook of reading disability research* (pp. 149–161). New York, NY: Routledge.

Spiro, R. J. (2006). The "new Gutenberg revolution": Radical new learning, thinking, teaching, and training with technology. *Educational Technology, 46*(1), 3–4.

Spiro, R., Vispoel, W., Schmitz, J., Samarapungavan, A., & Boerger, A. (1987). Knowledge acquisition for application: Cognitive flexibility and transfer in complex content domains.

In B. Britton & S. Glynn (Eds.), *Executive control processes in reading* (pp. 177–199). Hillsdale, NJ: Erlbaum.

Stahl, S., & Nagy, W. (2006). *Teaching word meanings.* Mahwah, NJ: Erlbaum.

Stanovich, K. (1986). Matthew effects in reading: Some consequences of individual differences in the acquisition of literacy. *Reading Research Quarterly, 21,* 360–407.

Stanovich, K. (1988). *Children's reading and the development of phonological awareness.* Detroit, MI: Wayne State University Press.

Stanovich, K. (1991). Word recognition: Changing perspectives. In R. Barr, M. Kamil, P. Mosenthal, & P. D. Pearson (Eds.), *Handbook of reading research* (2nd ed., pp. 418–452). White Plains, NY: Longman.

Stanovich, K. (1992). Speculations on the causes and consequences of individual differences in early reading acquisition. In P. Gough, L. Ehri, & R. Treiman (Eds.), *Reading acquisition* (pp. 307–342). Hillsdale, NJ: Erlbaum.

Stanovich, K. (2000). *Progress in understanding reading: Scientific foundations and new frontiers.* New York, NY: Guilford Press.

Stanovich, K., Nathan, R., & Zolman, J. (1988). The developmental lag hypothesis in reading: Longitudinal and matched reading-level comparisons. *Child Development, 59,* 71–86.

Storch, S., & Whitehurst, G. (2002). Oral language and code-related precursors to reading: Evidence from a longitudinal structural model. *Developmental Psychology, 38*(6), 934–947.

Street, B. (1984). *Literacy in theory and practice.* New York, NY: Cambridge University Press.

Thomas, G., & Vaughn, M. (2004). *Inclusive education: Readings and reflections.* Maidenhead, NJ: Open University Press.

Trezek, B. J., Wang, Y., & Paul, P. (2010). *Reading and deafness: Theory, research, and practice.* Clifton Park, NY: Delmar/Cengage Learning.

Trezek, B., Wang, Y., & Paul, P. (2011). Processes and components of reading. In M. Marschark & P. Spencer (Eds.), *Handbook of deaf studies, language, and education* (2nd ed., Vol. 1, pp. 99–114). New York, NY: Oxford University Press.

Valencia, S. (2011). Reader profiles and reading disabilities. In A. McGill-Franzen & R. Allington (Eds.), *Handbook of reading disability research* (pp. 25–35). New York, NY: Routledge.

Vellutino, F. (2003). Individual differences as sources of variability in reading comprehension in elementary school children. In A. P. Sweet & C. E. Snow (Eds.), *Rethinking reading comprehension* (pp. 51–81). New York, NY: Guilford Press.

Vosgerau, G. (2006). The perceptual nature of mental models. In C. Held, M. Knauff, & G. Vosgerau, G. (Eds.), *Mental models and the mind: Current developments in cognitive psychology, neuroscience, and philosophy of mind* (pp. 255–275). New York, NY: Elsevier.

Wang, Y. (2012). Educators without borders: A metaparadigm for literacy instruction in bilingual–bicultural education. In P. Paul & D. Moores (Eds.), *Deaf epistemologies: Multiple perspectives on the acquisition of knowledge* (pp. 199–217). Washington, DC: Gallaudet University Press.

Wang, Y., Trezek, B., Luckner, J., & Paul, P. (2008). The role of phonology and phonological-related skills in reading instruction for students who are deaf or hard of hearing. *American Annals of the Deaf, 153*(4), 396–407.

Wharton-McDonald, R., & Swiger, S. (2009). Developing higher order comprehension in the middle grades. In S. Israel & G. Duffy (Eds.), *Handbook of research on reading comprehension* (pp. 510–530). New York, NY: Routledge.

Whitehurst, G., & Lonigan, C. (1998). Child development and emergent literacy. *Child Development, 68,* 848–872.

Whitehurst, G., & Lonigan, C. (2002). Emergent literacy: Development from preschoolers to readers. In S. Neuman & D. Dickinson (Eds.), *Handbook of early literacy research* (pp. 11–29). New York, NY: Guilford Press.

Williams, C. (2004). Emergent literacy of deaf children. *Journal of Deaf Studies and Deaf Education, 9*(4), 352–365.

Williams, C. (2011). Adapted interactive writing instruction with kindergarten children who are deaf or hard of hearing. *American Annals of the Deaf, 156*(1), 23–34.

Williams, C. (2012). Promoting vocabulary learning in young children who are d/Deaf and hard of hearing: Translating research into practice. *American Annals of the Deaf, 156*(5), 501–508.

Willingham, D. (2007, Summer). Critical thinking: Why is it so hard to teach? *American Educator,* 8–19.

2

English Language Development

Historically, the development of language in children and adolescents who are d/Deaf and hard of hearing (d/Dhh) has been one of the most, if not *the* most, contentious educational issue (Moores, 2001, 2010; Paul, 2009; Quigley & Kretschmer, 1982). More than 30 years ago, King (1981) asserted that the question of language acquisition is actually a bipartite question: (1) How do deaf children learn language? and (2) How well do deaf children learn language? Setting aside, for now, the ambiguous meanings of *deaf* and *language*, it seems that King's two-part question has morphed into a controversial version: *What is or should be the first language of deaf children?*, with much of the ensuing debate in the United States involving predominantly American Sign Language (ASL) and English (Paul, 2009, 2010).

As discussed in Chapter 1, the basic tenets of the qualitative similarity hypothesis (QSH) are applicable to the primary (through-the-air) and secondary (reading/writing) development of English as a first or second language. The focus of this chapter is on the primary development of English as a first language. Our version of King's question can be stated as follows: How do and how well do d/Dhh children learn English as a first language?

To address this question, we synthesize, initially, the dialogues on the features of salient language acquisition models and present general milestones of typical English language development. This is no easy feat considering the variety of dissensions on the methodologies for collecting and analyzing language data, let alone what constitute *data* and whether the notion of explanatory adequacy for language acquisition is viable or applicable (e.g., see N. Chomsky, 2006; Lund, 2003). We contend that attempts to explicate the nature of language acquisition are just as critical as attempts to specify what is meant by the phrase *d/Deaf and hard of hearing*. In fact, the lack of specificity with terminologies not only has led to misinterpretations and misunderstandings of the development of language in d/Dhh children and adolescents (e.g., see Blamey & Sarant, 2011) but also might have contributed to the contentious *What is/should be* perspective, pitting ASL against English.

With a basic understanding of English language acquisition, we can proceed to a brief examination of the relations between language and literacy (discussed briefly in Chapter 1 as well). Specifically, we mean the relations between through-the-air (primary) and the written (secondary) development of English. (Note: Chapter 3 provides much more detail on the development of English as a second language, and Chapter 4 presents additional information on English literacy.) One strong justification for this approach is that there is ample evidence that the English literacy process contains English language-based underpinnings. Reflections on both language and literacy acquisition and their relations should yield a better understanding of the development in each domain as well as the contributions of one domain to the development of the other one.

To put it one way, at least with respect to English language and reading (Kamhi & Catts, 2012), "knowledge of the similarities and differences between spoken language and reading is critical for understanding how children learn to read and why some children have difficulty learning to read" (p. 1). The application of the construct of *spoken language*, in this passage, to d/Dhh children and adolescents is complicated and controversial (e.g., see Blamey & Sarant, 2011; Marschark & Spencer, 2010; Paul, 2009). However, Kamhi and Catts (2012) are focused on the relationships between the primary (through-the-air) and secondary (in this case, reading) forms of English. They are not referring to *speech* per se in the construct of spoken language. Their emphasis is on listening or language comprehension of English and the relation to English literacy development.

It would be difficult to find any current scholarly book or textbook on English language disorder/delay or development that does not also explore, sometimes in depth, the subsequent effects on English literacy or the emergence and subsequent development of English literacy (e.g., Bernstein & Tiegerman-Farber, 2009; Kaderavek, 2011; Kuder, 2013; Owens, 2010; Pence & Justice, 2008; Reed, 2012). There are specific, critical differences between the primary (i.e., through-the-air) and secondary (written) forms of English, mainly because the development of English literacy skills requires much more than proficiency in through-the-air English language development. Without a working knowledge (intuitive) in the primary form of English, progress in English literacy, especially during the period when children are learning to read and write, will be impeded and in some cases will plateau for a number of d/Dhh children and adolescents (Paul, 1998; Trezek, Wang, & Paul, 2011). As mentioned later, it is quite a challenge to learn to read and write and, simultaneously, to continue to acquire an understanding of the basic components (e.g., phonology, syntax, semantics, etc.) of the English language (e.g., see various chapters in Cain & Oakhill, 2007, and McGill-Franzen & Arlington, 2011; for d/Dhh children and adolescents, see Mayer, 2010; Trezek et al., 2011).

We are not suggesting that it is *necessary* to hear and speak adequately a spoken language such as English in order to learn to read and write in that language (Shull & Crain, 2010; Trezek, Wang, & Paul, 2010; Wang, Trezek, Luckner, & Paul, 2008). We are suggesting (and reiterating) that children need (1) to acquire fundamental aspects of the components of English to use English in the through-the-air mode,

(2) to apply this intuitive knowledge in learning to read and write, and (3) to use this knowledge in reading and writing to learn more about other content areas such as science and mathematics. These assertions should become clearer later in this chapter, in Chapter 3, and elsewhere and should provide additional perspectives on the validity of the QSH.

In this chapter we present a synthesis of the research on English language development for both children with typical hearing and those who are d/Dhh and we compare both developmental trajectories. The research literature on hearing children is voluminous, and only major highlights are listed. On the other hand, the research literature on d/Dhh children is not as extensive because of not only the low incidence of hearing loss but also the difficulty of obtaining an adequate understanding of through-the-air knowledge of English in any form—speech, Cued Speech/Language, English sign, or any combination—especially for individuals with severe to profound hearing loss (Moores, 2001; Paul, 2009; Quigley & Kretschmer, 1982; Rose, McAnally, & Quigley, 2004).

There is a basis to compare the development of English language by d/Dhh children and adolescents with that of individuals who have typical hearing. This comparison should provide a context for using effective or evidence-based practices in developing English language and literacy skills (Easterbrooks, 2010; Schirmer & Williams, 2011; see also Chapter 6 of this book). We also proffer a perspective on one of the *broken promises* (e.g., Marschark & Spencer, 2010) related to the development of English in d/Dhh children and adolescents.

It has been interpreted that Alexander Graham Bell (as discussed in Marschark & Spencer, 2010) stated that spoken language is not appropriate for all deaf children (presumably those with a profound hearing loss and, perhaps, some with a severe hearing loss). We can accept this assertion somewhat if it means that not all "deaf" children can learn to speak English proficiently, albeit we should acknowledge that there is a range of proficiency in spoken English (i.e., reception and expression of intelligible speech) (see also the discussion in Bernstein & Auer, 2011). Setting aside the complex relationship between speaking (i.e., production) and understanding (i.e., comprehension) English, Bell's statement needs to be reformulated and reinterpreted in light of our emerging understanding of the connection between English language and English literacy—as per, for example, the previously quoted passage by Kamhi and Catts (2012). Our next focus is what it means to understand English.

PERSPECTIVES ON ENGLISH LANGUAGE DEVELOPMENT AND PROFICIENCY

A synthesis of descriptions of English language acquisition models should demonstrate why a certain level of proficiency in English is necessary, albeit not sufficient, for the development of English literacy skills (Cain & Oakhill, 2007; Kamhi & Catts, 2012; McGill-Franzen & Arlington, 2011; for deafness, see Mayer & Trezek, 2011; Paul, 2011; Trezek, Wang, & Paul, 2010). In addition, this rendition should elucidate the problems with current ASL–English bilingual models, particularly those that attempt to bypass the *form* components of English such as, for example, English phonology, for the development of English literacy skills (Mayer & Wells, 1996; Paul, 2009, 2010, 2011; Paul & Wang, 2012).

What does it means to provide a synthesis of descriptions? Or, perhaps, the better question is, What does it mean to *know* English? It is unsurprising that there is no consensus on the best model of English language acquisition (Lund, 2003; Paul, 2009; Pence & Justice, 2008). There is not even a consensus on the manner in which to group or categorize the various English language theories or models. In fact, there are as many *language models* as there are different types of theorists, who have a vested interest in this endeavor (Lund, 2003; Owens, 2010; Pence & Justice, 2008).

Without oversimplifying, language can be viewed broadly as a learned behavior, a cognitive activity, a social activity, or combinations of these constructs and more. A perusal of recent books on language reveals an array of models. For example, Pence and Justice (2008) employed the following categories: behaviorist, social-interactionist, cognitive, intentionality model, competition model, usage-based theory, modularity, universal grammar, syntactic bootstrapping, semantic bootstrapping, and connectionist theories. Bernstein and Tiegerman-Farber (2009) mentioned approaches such as behavioral, psycholinguistic/syntactic, semantic/cognitive, and pragmatic. Kaderavek (2011) focuses on behavioral, cognitive, nativist, social interaction, sociocultural, and systems/ecological approach theories as well as research from neurobiology and neurocognition. Reed (2012) discusses the biological, cognitive, and social bases of language and communication and incorporates within each category some of the terms listed previously such as social interaction and information processing. Kuder (2013) proffered models such as behavioral, semantic–cognitive, social interactionist, information processing, and emergentist.

Attempts to synthesize these theories and models and to demonstrate the connections between the different frameworks are nothing short of complex or intricate or, perhaps, convoluted. We take the easy way out and defer to the broad but integrative definition provided about 30 years ago by the American Speech-Language-Hearing Association (ASHA) (1983), which is still relevant today:

> Language is a complex and dynamic system of conventional symbols that is used in various modes for thought and communication. Contemporary views of human language hold that: (a) language evolves within specific historical, social, and cultural contexts; (b) language, as rule-governed behavior, is described by at least five parameters—phonologic, morphologic, syntactic, semantic, and pragmatic; (c) language learning and use are determined by the interaction of biological, cognitive, psychosocial, and environmental factors; and (d) effective use of language for communication requires a broad understanding of human interaction including such associated factors as nonverbal cues, motivation, and sociocultural roles. (p. 44)

It can be argued that the four aspects above (letters a to d) are interrelated and form the basis for the various language acquisition models. One critical implication of the ASHA definition (i.e., letter b) is the assertion that individuals who know a language are able to demonstrate a level of proficiency in the five parameters (also known as components or elements or aspects) such as phonology (sounds), morphology (word parts), syntax (word order), semantics (meaning), and pragmatics (function or use). From another perspective, (b) of the ASHA definition can be related to Bloom's and Lahey's (1978) oft-cited model of *form* (phonology, morphology, syntax), *content* (semantics), and *use* (pragmatics).

In the various language texts, mentioned previously, on *language delays or language disorders*, it is not uncommon to find explanations of the delay or disorder in individuals related to problems in one or more of the components of language, despite the various approaches or interventions advocated, which often attempt to incorporate (a), (c), and (d) of the ASHA definition (Bernstein & Tiegerman-Farber, 2009; Kaderavek, 2011; Kuder, 2013; Owens, 2010; Pence & Justice, 2008; Reed, 2012). A further discussion of the constructs of *language delay* and *language disorder* (or disability) appears later in this chapter. We provide brief descriptions of the components of English and relate them to the development of English literacy, particularly reading, and to through-the-air English via oralism and the English sign systems for d/Dhh children and adolescents.

We assert that if individuals are proficient in a bona fide language such as English, then they have developed a level of proficiency in the integrative use of *all* major language parameters. The debate on which parameter is paramount has led to the different foci in the variety of language acquisition models as well as in the range of language teaching or intervention approaches (e.g., Owens, 2010; Pence & Justice, 2008; Reed, 2012). Nevertheless, it is still critical for individuals to obtain a threshold of proficiency in each language parameter to reap the benefits of the integrative use of the entire language for communication and thought. The contributions of affective, biological, cognitive, environmental, social, and other factors to the language learning process are acknowledged—even if the nature of these contributions is not clearly understood.

English language proficiency entails the development of precursors for all parameters during the prelinguistic period. This process continues with the mature development of the linguistic period, which commences with the production of the first words. It is axiomatic to remark that the first few years of life are essential for language development (Crystal, 2006). O'Grady (2005) stated that

> Within three years of birth, children acquire several thousand words, figure out how to build and understand complex sentences, and master the sound [or phonological] system of their language—all before they can tie their shoes. (n.p)

The major developmental milestones of the prelinguistic and linguistic periods are highlighted in the ensuing paragraphs.

Prelinguistic Period

This is a critical period of language development and, in general, it entails the first 12 months of life. Disruptions or delays during this period have a deleterious effect on the subsequent development of the parameters, let alone typical language development, during the linguistic period (Bernstein & Tiegerman-Farber, 2009; Crystal,

2006; Kaderavek, 2011; Kuder, 2013; Reed, 2012). Although the prelinguistic period is said to *end* with the production of the first words (i.e., real intelligible words), the demarcation between prelinguistic and linguistic periods may be fluid for a time after the first words (which can actually occur earlier than 12 months for a number of children) (Crystal, 1997, 2006; Gerken, Jusczyk, & Mandel, 1994; O'Grady, 2005; Reed, 2012).

The progression of sounds produced by infants during this period proceeds from reflexive vocalizations (birth to about 2 months) to a range of babbling (4 months to about 10 months) to the concatenation of sounds in the first words (Crystal, 2006; Gerken et al., 1994; O'Grady, 2005; Reed, 2012). By 3 months, infants can perceive differences between speech sounds and can distinguish their mother's voice from other voices. Infants are also sensitive to the suprasegmental aspects of speech such as intonation, pause, and rhythm prior to the segmental ones—vowels and consonants—during the production stage.

Infants learn very early—during the first few months—about the power of language, even with the use of sounds, which is a precursor for pragmatics development (Crystal, 2006; Gerken et al., 1994; O'Grady, 2005; Reed, 2012). They use their voices to express their moods and to elicit responses from others, particularly their caregivers. There are specific concatenations of sounds associated with hunger, pain, discomfort, sleepiness, tiredness, and boredom or, perhaps, a need for a different type of stimulation. The rise–fall contour of the infant's voice and those of others that the infant hears is a critical precursor for the subsequent development of sentence types such as a statement, question, or exclamation.

In a nutshell, the development of phonology entails both suprasegmentals and segmentals during the prelinguistic (and part of the linguistic) period (Crystal, 2006; Gerken et al., 1994; O'Grady, 2005; Reed, 2012). Thus, it should not be surprising that the foundation for this development during the prelinguistic time frame requires the use of an adequate articulatory–auditory feedback loop (or a close alternative representation) (for a discussion of this construct, see Paul, 2009). The problem with spoken language for many d/D and some hh children is not intelligible speech per se but the lack of an intuitive understanding or internalization of phonology (suprasegmentals and segmentals) for the development of English and, as we also argue later, for the use of English, particularly phonology, during the English literacy process.

With respect to the subsequent development of literacy, the prelinguistic period is important for the development of the various representations related to phonology—which forms the basis for the manifestations of speech perception, speech production, and other areas related to understanding the phoneme–grapheme links (e.g., phonemic awareness). Without an adequate representation of phonology and the associated connections to other parameters/components (e.g., semantics, morphology), the d/Dhh child may be able to pronounce a word but will have no or few cognitive representations to access (from long-term memory) (see discussions in Ehri, 1991; Paul, 1998). This is what is meant by the prelinguistic period (and subsequently, the early linguistic period) providing the foundations for the development of the auditory–articulatory feedback loop and especially the phonological loop in working memory (Baddeley, 1990).

Linguistic Period

Regardless of when it occurs, the linguistic phase of the child's development begins with the production of the first words (Crystal, 2006; Gerken et al., 1994; O'Grady, 2005; Reed, 2012). A word is a word when it is used consistently in a specific context or situation and exhibits a fairly ordered intelligible (phonetic) form. It does not (and will not) sound like an adult word, but it is discernible or recognizable.

The action really begins or takes off when the child has a working vocabulary of 50 words (i.e., single words around 18 months or so). The child begins to develop a more efficient strategy of considering the words as composed of individual sounds and learning about the phonological rules of English sounds (i.e., phonological awareness). A few of these first words represent labels (or, perhaps, concepts), but a number of others reflect what can be called sentencelike commentaries (Crystal, 2006; Gerken et al., 1994; O'Grady, 2005; Reed, 2012).

The synergism between the precursors for phonology and semantics (again, with respect to the "sounds" of English) also emerges during the first-word phase. Children learn more quickly words that begin with consonants similar to other words that they know than they learn words that begin with unfamiliar consonants (Crystal, 2006; Gerken et al., 1994; O'Grady, 2005; Reed, 2012). This can be considered the precursor for metaphonological awareness, which is relevant for the development of subsequent phonemic awareness.

For some children, there is no even progression from first to second to third words (Crystal, 2006; Gerken et al., 1994; O'Grady, 2005; Reed, 2012). Some children jump from first to third and then back to first to second, and so on. When children use two-word utterances consistently (about 18 to 26 months), this can be considered the beginning of the syntactic phase of the linguistic period (Crystal, 2006; Gerken et al., 1994; O'Grady, 2005; Reed, 2012). A vocabulary of 50 words seems to be necessary to commence the two-word stage, but from here on, the number of words begins to increase dramatically.

Detailed descriptions of the early development of all parameters of language, particularly the English language, can be found elsewhere (e.g., Bloom & Lahey, 1978; Brown, 1973; Crystal, 1997, 2006). Despite the controversies of the production–comprehension constructs, it is possible to describe this early language development via observations of language use. Complex language use (i.e., morphology, syntax, etc.) commences with the consistent use of three words (and beyond). Whether one focuses on the growth of vocabulary in the semantic domains (e.g., multimeanings and nuances of words, relational categories; Bloom & Lahey, 1978) or in the syntactic domain (e.g., negation, question formation, relativization; C. Chomsky, 1969), it is important to remember the contributions of the synergistic integrations of all parameters based on English as a sound-based language. Whether this type of development in English is possible via a visual–motor representation only as evident by the English sign systems (with d/D children having little or no access to phonology) or via explanations from a language not based on sound, such as ASL, for the purposes of acquiring English proficiently might be considered an open question; however, the evidence is not robust (e.g., see discussions in Paul, 2009; Paul & Wang, 2012; Trezek et al., 2010, 2011).

There is much more to relate concerning the linguistic period; we have only scratched the surface here (for further details, see Bernstein & Tiegerman-Farber, 2009; Crystal, 2006; Gerken et al., 1994; O'Grady, 2005; Reed, 2012). The last major construct that should be covered (albeit briefly) is metalinguistic awareness. Although it might be the case that true metalinguistic awareness does not emerge until the early school years or when a child is about 7 to 8 years old, the basics can be seen in children as early as 3 years old (as most TV viewers of *Blue's Clues* can attest) and much younger (e.g., see the learning of new words beginning with the same sounds during the prelinguistic period). Examples of premetalinguistic awareness include the playing with sounds and words. By age 4 or 5 years (the preschool years), a number of children have begun to understand the concepts of word, sentence, and speech sounds, which are important for early development of phonemic awareness and literacy. Of course, there are children who continue to have difficulties even throughout grade 1 (see various chapters in McGill-Franzen & Arlington, 2011). Metalinguistic development and, particularly, metacognitive development continues throughout the elementary years with adult-like skills emerging during early adolescence (Bernstein & Tiegerman-Farber, 2009; Crystal, 1997, 2006; Kamhi & Catts, 2012; Kuder, 2013; Reed, 2012).

Table 2.1 illustrates a few highlights of the early development of English during the prelinguistic and linguistic phases with a focus on the parameters (e.g., phonology, etc.).

Table 2.1. **Brief Highlights of Prelinguistic and Linguistic Development**

Prelinguistic Development

- In the first few months of life, infants use their voices to influence others and to get them to do things.
- Prior to the emergence of intentional and meaningful communicative acts, children explore the environment for about 12 months. Children come to realize that persons, objects, and events are separate from their selves.
- During the first year, children develop the precursors for the major language parameters—phonology, morphology, syntax, semantics, and pragmatics.

Linguistic Development

- There are wide variations in early phonologic development. Most phonologic rules are acquired by around 6 to 8 years of age.
- Vocabulary growth is rapid throughout the preschool and early school years. This growth is highly variable among individual children. The acquisition of new words and meanings are not simply added in a serial, cumulative fashion. Exposure to new words changes and refines the current semantic representations of words and meanings and the relationships between words in children's lexicon.
- Beyond the three-word stage, children begin to experiment and learn the major syntactic transformations of language (question formation, relativization, passive voice).
- Most children internalize much of the grammar of language by age 4 or 5 years and master nearly all of the grammar by age 9 or 10.

LANGUAGE DELAY AND LANGUAGE DISORDER/DISABILITY

After that brief overview of typical English language development, we can begin a discussion of the constructs of language delay and language disorder/disability. The discussion of these constructs is similar to that in Chapter 1 regarding reading difficulty versus reading disability (Bernstein & Tiegerman-Farber, 2009; Kamhi & Catts, 2012; Kaderavek, 2011; Kuder, 2013; Reed, 2012). Again, there is no consensus or broad agreement on the use of these terminologies. However, it might be that these constructs are also socially constructed with respect to ideological (or power) issues or the types of assessment employed to measure language development.

Language disorder, language disability, and language impairment are fairly synonymous. Kaderavek (2011) avers that

> A language disorder is impaired comprehension and/or use of spoken, written, and/or other symbol systems. A language disorder can represent a deficit in receptive language, expressive language, or a combined expressive–receptive deficit. (p. 2)

Similar to the tenets of the term *reading disability*, a language disorder or disability typically has underlying biological–psychological or neuropsychological conditions. Although there might be little disagreement in applying this term to children with autism or those with cognitive or intellectual disabilities, it is not clear that this term can be easily applied to other areas such as children who are d/Dhh or to those with learning disabilities.

The use of the term *language delay* is also not clear other than to state that the development of language problems cannot be diagnosed reliably (in young children) in the absence of a specific disorder (autism, etc.) (Bernstein & Tiegerman-Farber, 2009; Kamhi & Catts, 2012; Kaderavek, 2011; Kuder, 2013; Reed, 2012). Whether the delay is due to factors outside the child (e.g., home environment, teaching, etc.) is not explicitly discussed, but it seems to be implied. If the language development is characterized as a *developmental lag* (as in late talkers), *language delay* is the term used. However, *late talkers* may be a function of internal (affective domain, etc.) as well as external (e.g., hostile environment, etc.) factors. In any case, language delay can be used to state that there is a difference between the levels of language, prelinguistic and linguistic, associated with the chronological age of the child as compared to the expected or general language development at that age.

It might not be productive to make a strong distinction between language disorder/disability and language delay, especially if one subscribes to the basic tenets of the QSH regarding developmental similarities. A similar argument can be inferred from the comments of Kaderavek (2011) to the readers of her book:

> much of what you will learn about language disorders applies across disability categories. Rather than focusing on a child's diagnostic category (e.g., autism, specific learning disability), skilled practitioners use a descriptive–developmental framework . . . [which] focuses on a student's language development and function in a variety of natural contexts. . . . I continually clarify descriptive and developmental

similarities between disability groups and highlight connections between intervention approaches across disability types. (p. 3)

RELATIONS BETWEEN THROUGH-THE-AIR AND WRITTEN FORMS OF ENGLISH

In Chapter 1, we mentioned that English literacy requires an understanding of or a working level of proficiency in the English language (see also Chapters 3 and 4). The relative contributions of through-the-air English language parameters to the development of early English literacy development continue to be debated (Cain & Oakhill, 2007; Israel & Duffy, 2009; Shanahan, 2006; Whitehurst & Lonigan, 2002). Several scholars (e.g., Kamhi & Catts, 2012; McGuinness, 2005; Shanahan, 2006) have argued that the effects of language competencies on reading and writing are much more pronounced than previously thought and should be explored in greater detail in research on the development of early and advanced English literacy skills. In the research literature on children with typical hearing, it has been argued that oral English language skills, albeit critical for emergent literacy, are connected more strongly to later conventional reading than to emergent or early reading (McGuinness, 2004, 2005; National Early Literacy Panel, 2008; Whitehurst & Lonigan, 2002).

The nature of these complex relations between English language and English literacy are influenced by perspectives on the nature or definitions of English reading and writing (as well by the nature or definitions of English language proficiency, as discussed previously). Consider, for example, that a broad view of reading is adopted—that is, reading comprehension requires higher-level social, cognitive, and knowledge-based skills such as making inferences, applying background knowledge, and understanding the influences of the home environment (e.g., see discussions in Israel & Duffy, 2009; Perfetti, 1986). Within this context, it might be that the effects of through-the-air English language competencies are *more critical* for advanced English reading levels because of the increased linguistic and cognitive demands of the texts (McGuinness, 2004, 2005; Whitehurst & Lonigan, 2002). On the other hand, it is also possible that phonological processing skills are a strong primary mediator between language (and cognitive) capacity and the development of English reading comprehension skills. This assumes an intricate connection between word identification and text comprehension as is often stated by scholars who favor a narrow (or simple) view of literacy (particularly, reading) (Crowder, 1982; Gough & Tunmer, 1986; see also the discussion in Chapter 1 and in Perfetti, 1985, 1986).

Regardless of whether English literacy is considered within a narrow or broad view, many d/Dhh children begin their formal schooling period (kindergarten or grade 1) with inadequate levels of *English* language development for engaging in the English literacy learning process (Mayer, 2007, 2009; Mayer & Trezek, 2011; Paul, 2009, 2012; Trezek et al., 2010, 2011). Thus, these children are simultaneously learning to communicate and think in the language (e.g., English) while attempting to learn to read and write in the same language; d/Dhh children need to develop proficiency in the use of the English language to decode print as part of the processes of constructing meaning from print (i.e., comprehending the text) and constructing meaning with print (i.e., writing). These processes take into account the strong overlapping interrelations among language (e.g., speaking, listening), reading, and writing, particularly in the emergent literacy years (Bear, Invernizzi, Templeton, & Johnston, 2007; Cain & Oakhill, 2007; Paul, 2009; Shanahan, 2006; Shanahan & Lomax, 1986, 1988; Williams, 2004, 2011). There is research documenting the effects of the English language, particularly vocabulary, syntax, and semantics, on the reading (and writing) development of d/Dhh children (Mayer, 2007, 2010; Moores & Sweet, 1990; Paul, 2009, 2012; Perfetti & Sandak, 2000; Trezek et al., 2010, 2011; Williams, 2004, 2011; see also Chapters 3 and 4).

A perspective on these findings can be gleaned from an understanding (albeit incomplete) of the contributions of through-the-air or "oral" comprehension of English to the literacy process (see also Chapter 1). Through-the-air English language comprehension is facilitated by access to the phonological component of English. A working knowledge of phonology, including the suprasegmental (i.e., prosodic) aspects, provides the foundation for the development of the other components (parameters) of English. It should be added that prosodic features such as stress, intonation, and rhythm are critical for the perception of speech (Crystal, 1997, 2006; Goodluck, 1991).

Phonological knowledge facilitates the development of early English literacy foundational elements such as phonemic awareness, which is instrumental for learning phoneme–grapheme relations (Adams, 1990; 1994; National Early Literacy Panel, 2008; National Reading Panel, 2000). In conjunction with phonology, morphology also contributes to the development of conventional spelling skills and reading (e.g., see Stahl & Nagy, 2006). In fact, the contributions of syntax and semantics also can be seen for the comprehension of sentences and for the development of vocabulary knowledge.

The nature of children's lexical access processes has determined the importance of phonemic awareness in English reading and has led to the debate on how and if phonemic awareness can and should be taught. This debate is also applicable to d/Dhh children, and it offers a compelling argument for the difficulty that many of these children have in learning to read and write well. Good language users as well as good readers and writers need to be aware of more than just the semantic features of words to develop rapid, automatic, word identification skills or to use their mental lexicon as a major source of comprehension in language use.

RESEARCH SYNTHESIS ON ENGLISH LANGUAGE DEVELOPMENT

In this section, we present a synthesis of major findings on the development of through-the-air English for children with slight to profound hearing loss (see also Blamey & Sarant, 2011; Dettman & Dowell, 2010; Leybaert, Aparicio, & Alegria, 2011; Paul, 2009). Our focus is on children for whom English is a first language or, specifically, for whom English is the language of the home. Although establishing a line of demarcation is disputable and somewhat arbitrary, we contend that this discussion, commencing with the beginning of the 20th century and the use of standardized assessments, should entail two major phases with a third one that is emerging. One phase covers the period up until the advent of modern amplification systems such as the use of digital hearing aids and cochlear implants. The second phase, essentially the current one, covers the past 20 years or so with the use of the current amplification systems by d/Dhh children, adolescents, and adults. It is premature to state that there is (or will be) a third phase; nevertheless, the future is always full of surprises as we obtain a better understanding of the auditory system and of our attempts to improve audition and its relation to the development of a spoken language (e.g., Paul & Whitelaw, 2011; Plack, 2005).

It is tempting—but a gross oversimplification—to characterize these phases as different renditions of the oral–manual controversy (e.g., Miller & Clark, 2011), which has been raging for more than 200 years (Moores, 2010). In our view, the temptation was greater during phase 1 in light of the uneven progress or fairly inconsistent patterns regarding the prelinguistic and linguistic developments of a number of d/Dhh children as compared to the English language development of children who are native, typical learners of English. Our emerging understanding of the complex intertwinement of the sensory, cognitive, and motor domains related to language development during phase 2 has clarified the picture somewhat, albeit there is still much more work to be done.

Phase 1: General Issues and Findings

Much of the effort and research associated with phase 1 have been focused on describing the merits of developing English either via an oral mode (i.e., speech, speech reading, audition) or what should be labeled as a combined or simultaneous mode—namely, speaking and signing English at the same time (Moores, 2010; Paul, 2009). To facilitate the development of English as a first language, it has been asserted that there needs to be a fluent and intelligible communication system between the child and his or her significant caregivers (Quigley & Kretschmer, 1982).

There have been two major avenues for developing this type of system (Moores, 2010; Paul, 2009; Quigley & Paul, 2004). One avenue has been to foster better access to the articulatory–auditory feedback loop via the enhancement of speech, speech reading, and audition. This avenue is constrained, for the most part, by the limits of amplification systems and the challenges of developing speech and speech reading skills, especially for children with severe to profound hearing loss. The second avenue entails an improvement in the representation and delivery of English visually, particularly via the use of sign systems or Cued Speech/Language (CSL). Along with the condition of hearing loss, there are additional factors to consider such as the demands of the types of assessments (e.g., those requiring speech perception and production), cognitive and affective aspects, family/caregiver environment, and so on, which make it difficult to understand adequately the patterns of language development (see discussions in Blamey & Sarant, 2011; Paul, 2009).

Despite the imperfections of the specific avenue (oral, sign, or combined), it has been shown that the development of English is qualitatively similar to but quantitatively delayed for a number of children with a range of hearing loss when compared to the development of children with typical hearing or who are native learners of English and often younger than children with hearing loss (see reviews in Paul, 2009; Trezek et al., 2010, 2011; Wang, Trezek, Luckner, & Paul, 2008). It also has been averred that even a slight hearing loss (up to 26 dB for adults and up to 15 dB for children) can have deleterious effects on English language development (Kodman, 1963; Marschark, Sapere, Convertino, Mayer, Wauters, & Sarchet, 2009; Pintner & Lev, 1939; Quigley & Thomure, 1968; see review in Paul, 2009). It is important to examine the language (and literacy) development of children in the slight to moderately severe range because this group represents the majority of children with hearing loss in educational programs (e.g., Marschark, 2007; Moores, 2001; Paul & Whitelaw, 2011). In any case, these negative effects can become more pronounced (i.e., consistent and inconsistent delays) with the increase in hearing loss and advancing age (Quigley & Thomure, 1968; Ross, Brackett, & Maxon, 1982).

Pressnell (1973) and Wilcox and Tobin (1974), for example, examined the performances of children with moderate or greater hearing loss on aspects of the verb system of English (e.g., tense, number, active/passive, etc.). Based on the analyses of spontaneous language samples and the results of the Northwestern Syntax Screening Test, Pressnell (1973) reported that the performances of the children were similar in manner (i.e., developmentally) but different in rate when compared to the norms of the assessments for children who were developing English in a typical or chronological age manner. Using a sentence repetition task, Wilcox and Tobin (1974) reported similar findings.

Davis and Blasdell (1975) studied the syntactic ability of young children, 6 to 9 years old, whose degree of hearing loss ranged from 35 to 75 dB. Specifically, they examined the ability of the children to comprehend medially embedded relative clauses (e.g., *The girl who kissed the boy ran away*). The children with hearing loss produced more errors, but these errors were similar in kind—that is, developmentally—to those of typical young native learners of English.

Although the assessment was conducted via written English (i.e., a written test of syntactic ability), the longitudinal work of Quigley and his collaborators (mentioned in Chapter 1) has provided the most extensive documentation on the comprehension of nine major English syntactic structures (Russell, Quigley, & Power, 1976; see review in Paul, 2009). This was a national stratified study of children, age 10 to 18 years inclusive, whose hearing loss was profound (90 dB or greater, preamplification, better ear average). For all nine structures examined, children with profound hearing loss made more errors than children with typical hearing or who were typical learners of English, but these errors were similar and followed developmental patterns of learning English.

Regardless of the type of assessment (e.g., analysis of language samples, language comprehension tasks—oral or via signing, or written language tests), there is support for the QSH via the acquisition or comprehension of morphological elements (e.g., Cooper, 1967; Crandall, 1978; Raffin, Davis, & Gilman, 1978), verb–particles (Payne & Quigley, 1987), expressive vocabulary development (e.g., Griswold & Cummings, 1974), multiple meanings of words (Paul & Gustafson, 1991), and emergence of semantic relations (e.g., Layton, Holmes, & Bradley, 1979). As an example, Raffin and collaborators (Gilman, Davis, & Raffin, 1980; Raffin, 1976; Raffin et al., 1978; see also, Crandall, 1978) examined the development of selected English morphemes (e.g., plurality, past tense) in children who were exposed to a system labeled Seeing Essential English (SEE I). These researchers reported that the order of acquisition of the markers were qualitatively similar to the order of acquisition by students who were hearing and typical learners of English (e.g., Brown, 1973). Specifically, the children exposed to SEE I proceeded through developmental stages at a slower pace and produced errors that were similar to those of younger, native learners of English.

Phase 2: Issues and Findings

It should be noted that there was a range of variability in performance due to the individual situations or differences associated with a number of individuals who are d/Dhh in the studies cited previously and in others for our phase 1 era. The possible reasons for this state of affairs may include any of the following factors or combinations:

- An inadequate representation or reception of the form or structure of English, including phonology and morphology, by d/Dhh individuals.
- The inconsistent use (i.e., execution or production) of the English sign systems by practitioners, due to the cumbersomeness and the difficulty of speaking and signing simultaneously.
- The learnability of the sign systems or skills such as speech and speech reading by d/Dhh children.
- Specific social, cognitive, or environmental factors such as working memory capacity, motivation or interest, poor or inadequate teacher–learner interactions, impoverished or disadvantaged home situations associated with children with hearing loss.
- Shortsighted or limited research designs that undermine the complexity of learning either the language of English or its representation in print.
- Lack of or limited understanding of the nature of assessing language through the air and interpreting the findings (Blamey & Sarant, 2011; LaSasso, Crain, & Leybaert, 2010; Paul, 2009, 2010, 2011; Wang et al., 2008).

English Sign Systems   Much has been written about the shortcomings of the use of the various English sign communication modes or specific systems such as Signed English (Bornstein & Saulnier, 1981; Bornstein, Saulnier, & Hamiliton, 1980), Signing Exact English (Gustason, Pfetzing, & Zawolkow, 1980), and Seeing Essential English (Anthony, 1966) (see critiques in Dragsow & Paul, 1995; LaSasso et al., 2010; Paul, 2009; Paul & Dragsow, 1998; Schick, 2011; Wilbur, 2011). It should be highlighted that there are somewhat arbitrary and idealized descriptions of these systems with respect to their representation of English. The major rationale for their development and use is to represent the form or structure of English, specifically morphology and syntax, in a visual manner. When the signs are executed in conjunction with speech (i.e., simultaneous communication), it is purported that the phonology of English can be represented as well, assuming that children with hearing loss can learn to speech read adequately with or without amplification (e.g., Moores, 2001; Paul, 2009).

It is possible to find empirical evidence for success for some children and adolescents exposed to one or more of the English sign systems (Luetke-Stahlman, 1988a, 1988b; Luetke-Stahlman & Milburn, 1996; Schick & Moeller, 1992; Washburn, 1983; see critiques in Paul, 2009). This success might be related to the level of achievement in English reading or academic achievement in general (cf., Dragsow & Paul, 1995; Paul & Dragsow, 1998). Nevertheless, the level of success seems to be pervasively contingent on the individual's ability to access the form or structure of the English language—again, via phonology and morphology. Confounding our understanding is the fact that a number of individuals might have abstracted morphological and orthographic information from engaging with English print materials. This emphasizes the facilitative, reciprocal effects of both through-the-air and written forms of English—if there is a threshold of proficiency within each domain (e.g., see discussion in Cain & Oakhill, 2007).

Several scholars have asserted that the function of hearing might have a diminished influence on English language development when a threshold of English literacy proficiency (i.e., reading and writing) has been reached (e.g., Blamey & Sarant, 2011; Paul & Whitelaw, 2011). Until more efficient and comprehensive research paradigms are utilized, especially for children involved in early intervention and the use of modern amplification devices (e.g., cochlear implants), the list of reasons is endless and/or might be unsystematically delineated, making it difficult for researchers and scholars to reach a consensus on the merits of the various English sign systems.

The manner of the representation of English by the use of sign systems by practitioners and the naturalness of the systems themselves are the most contentious topics (LaSasso et al., 2010; Paul, 2009, 2010, 2011; Wilbur, 2011). It seems to be clear that the sign systems convey, albeit imperfectly and grossly, only partial information about the morphological and syntactic structures of English (LaSasso et al., 2010; Paul, 2009, 2010, 2011). In addition, even with the avenue of speech reading, there is not an adequate acquisition of phonology when signing is accompanied by speech (e.g., Wang et al., 2008). Ironically, none of the research on the English sign systems has examined the acquisition or importance of the suprasegmental aspects of phonology discussed previously. We are inclined to agree with LaSasso et al. (2010) that these systems, even when used simultaneously with speech, provide a degraded representation of English, especially English phonology, for a large number of d/Dhh children and adolescents.

The second major issue with the use of the systems is that they are not natural communication modes in light of the traditional phrase of fluent and intelligible use (Quigley & Kretschmer, 1982) or even a community of users (Paul, 2009; Schick, 2011; Wilbur, 2011). However, in our view, the more critical issue might be the learnability of the systems with respect to the structure of English (Gee & Goodhart, 1988; Maxwell, 1983, 1987; Supalla, 1991). Despite being exposed systematically and consistently to any of the sign systems, it still might be difficult for d/Dhh children to learn or internalize via social interactions the rules of the systems and, subsequently, the language that the systems purportedly represent—that is, English. These studies indicate that the execution of signing by the users is incompatible with the perception or production capabilities of the receivers. The d/Dhh receivers are altering the morphological and syntactic elements and producing odd sequences of signing or simply omitting the salient features of the form of English. Strong proponents of ASL have argued that the alterations of English signing reflect the processing capabilities of the eye (e.g., Supalla, 1991; see perspectives in Paul, 2009, and Wilbur, 2011) and have concluded that ASL is or should be the *natural* language of most or all children with severe to profound hearing loss.

There might be some truth to these assertions; however, much more research is needed. Remarks on the use of limited research designs, involving the English sign systems (and even ASL) have been proffered (Paul, 2010):

> Most of the existing research on the sign systems, including ASL, is focused on establishing a correlational link between the use and/or exposure of a specific sign system or language and the subsequent development of English language or literacy. Establishing a correlation is a necessary first step—albeit it is a narrow one. Specifically, it does not provide deep insights that often result from the use of painstaking, systematic, creative experimental research designs. Furthermore, conducting these simple correlational studies undermines the complexity of the language process and, even more so, the literacy process. (pp. 13–14)

Another perspective on the need for research can be gleaned by returning to the ASHA's (1983) definition of language, particularly the mention of proficiency in the various language parameters (e.g., phonology, etc.). In essence, it seems that future research endeavors should examine the contributions of a sign system (or ASL) to the specific development of an English parameter or component, rather than focusing on the global correlational effects on English proficiency or literacy (Paul, 2009, 2011).

Table 2.2 depicts the major findings of a representative, but not exhaustive, sample of research studies cited during this discussion.

Table 2.2. Summaries of Selected Major Studies

Studies	Highlights
Kodman (1963)	Reported the academic performance of students with hearing loss from 20 to 65 dB. The average achievement level of these students (in sixth grade) was 3.8 years, which was more than two grades lower than that of their peers with typical hearing. Kodman also reported that only a third of these students wore hearing aids and only one-fourth received speech, hearing, and language services.
Quigley & Thomure (1968)	Found an inverse relationship between degree of hearing loss and academic achievement. Students with a slight hearing loss (from 27 dB to about 40 dB in this study) demonstrated a 1-year lag; students with a moderate hearing loss (from 55 to about 69 dB) were 3 years lower in achievement. Quigley and Thomure were the first researchers to document the negative effects of even a slight hearing loss. In fact, students with losses up to 14 dB exhibited a delay of about 1 year on a vocabulary subtest (i.e., word meaning).

(continued)

Table 2.2. Summaries of Selected Major Studies (*continued*)

Studies	Highlights
Pressnell (1973)	Reported that the rate (quantitative) of syntactic development in children with hearing loss was slower than that of comparable children without hearing loss. The examination of spontaneous language samples showed that there was no significant improvement of syntactic knowledge associated with age (i.e., as the children with hearing loss became older). Pressnell provided evidence for the QSH for the order of acquisition of the examined syntactic structures. However, it was documented that a few verb constructions seem to be acquired in a different order than that reported for children with typical hearing. Pressnell conjectured that this was due to the unnatural order of teaching verbs by instructors. This is a theme that will be reiterated in a number of subsequent studies examining the order of acquisition of English language structures (e.g., see discussion in Paul, 2009).
Davis & Blasdell (1975)	Syntactic development of students with hearing loss was quantitatively slower or delayed, but qualitatively similar to that of students who had typical hearing and were younger. Students with hearing loss made more errors at all age levels compared, and the gap between students with hearing loss and their hearing counterparts increased with age. The errors of the students with hearing loss were similar to those made by students with typical hearing.
Gilman, Davis, & Raffin (1980); Raffin (1976); Raffin, Davis, & Gilman (1978)	Examined the acquisition and use of markers (e.g., morphological markers such as *–ed*, etc.) in children exposed to a system called Seeing Essential English (SEE 1). The researchers reported that the use of the SEE 1 markers by children were influenced markedly by teachers' use of the markers. As teachers were more systematic and consistent in executing the sign markers, students became more likely to acquire and use them. It was noted that the acquisition of the morphological markers were developmentally similar to younger children with typical hearing (e.g., Brown, 1973).
Bornstein, Saulnier, & Hamilton (1980); Bornstein & Saulnier (1981)	Examined the acquisition and use of Signed English (SE) markers (e.g., morphological markers) for a 5-year period. The researchers reported that few students were using the markers consistently and most were using only half of the 14 SE sign markers.
Washburn (1983)	Examined the achievement of students exposed to SEE 1 in grades 11 and 12 of one program. These students scored in the top 20% of all students taking a reading comprehension subtest of the Stanford Achievement Test.

Luetke-Stahlman (1988a, 1988b)	Investigated the performances of students with hearing loss exposed to two groups of language/communication approaches. One group consisted of approaches that reflected either a language (ASL) or a fairly complete representation of a language (e.g., via a signed system such as Signing Exact English [SEE 2]). The second group consists of approaches not considered to be a complete representation of a language (via a signed system such as English sign or manual English). Luetke-Stahlman reported that the students exposed to forms representative of a language performed significantly better than students in the other group. Students exposed to SEE 2 performed significantly better than students exposed to signed/manual English, or pidgin sign English (i.e., English sign).

Note. Adapted from Paul (2009). Further information on these studies can also be found in Paul (2009).

Spoken Language and the Use of Amplification   Despite the risks of oversimplification and bias, a better understanding of the English developmental process might emerge from the ongoing research on the effects of cochlear implantation (CI), including its use by children exposed to CSL (Blamey & Sarant, 2011; Leybaert et al., 2011; Paul & Whitelaw, 2011; Spencer, Marschark, & Spencer, 2011). Examination of the range of access, particularly the increase or improvement of access to English phonology, should produce clearer findings with respect to the basic tenets of the QSH as long as there is consideration of other additional social, cognitive, and affective factors. It is best to discuss this issue with respect to the findings on the use of CIs and on individuals who are exposed to CSL with or without CIs.

Cochlear Implantations.   Wilson and Dorman (2008) remarked that CIs are "among the great success stories of modern medicine" (p. 695). Despite the medical, political, and ideological controversies (Blume, 2010) surrounding the use of this amplification system, there is research that documents benefits, especially via longitudinal data. For example, with respect to adult users, there are reports of significant increases in speech reception and understanding (Palmer, Niparko, Wyatt, Rothman, & de Lissovoy, 1999). Other studies have proffered greater quality of life benefits for adults with severe to profound hearing loss who use either hearing aids or CI versus no amplification with the more significant results noted for CI users (Cohen, Labadie, Dietrich, & Haynes, 2004). Some benefits have also been reported for adults with prelinguistic hearing loss, typically in the severe to profound range. Researchers have documented significant improvements in speech understanding, speech production, and quality of life (Klop, Briaire, Stiggelbout, & Frijns, 2009; see discussions in Paul & Whitelaw, 2011; Spencer et al., 2011).

The findings for children, particularly those with prelinguistic severe to profound hearing loss, with CIs continue to be debated (Spencer et al., 2011). There has been an increase in the number of young children receiving CIs at 12 months of age or earlier (as early as 6 months). This clearly represents a marked shift in the educational landscape in the field of education and d/Dhh children (e.g., Mayer & Leigh,

2010; Paul & Whitelaw, 2011). Evidence indicates that a number of children with CIs develop near age-appropriate speech and language when compared to peers with typical hearing (Archbold, 2010; Paul, 2009). It has been argued that an increased access to phonological aspects, including a stronger development of the auditory–articulatory feedback loop, is a major contributor to the successes of these children (Paul, 2009; Paul & Whitelaw, 2011).

The findings on the development of English literacy are not straightforward or unequivocal. Children may progress quantitatively similar (i.e., same rate) in the beginning, but there are quantitative delays in the later grades (Archbold, 2010; Marschark, Sarchet, Rhoten, & Zupan, 2010; Paul, 2009). The variability (and even validity) of these findings might be due to factors such as age at onset of the hearing loss, age at implantation, the quality of early intervention, mode of communication used (i.e., speech, sign, etc.), consistency in the use of the device, and even attitudes (e.g., motivation, etc.) of the users or parents (Spencer & Marschark, 2003; Spencer et al., 2011; Spencer & Oleson, 2008). Thus, there is a need to provide adequate descriptions of the samples of children with CIs to identify the benefits in a particular program or in a particular set of circumstances and to document the progress of these learners over time. Such investigations are necessary to better understand the factors that impact both the English language and literacy development in these young d/Dhh children. Nevertheless, it is clear that CIs have provided improved access to auditory information for d/Dhh children when the research is well designed and conducted.

Overall, these positive findings should be viewed with caution and should not be interpreted to mean that the CI is an all-encompassing factor even if it seems to assist with the development of speech, language, and literacy in a number of d/Dhh children and adolescents. There is much more to consider in the development of English language and literacy than just the ability to perceive the speech signal either auditorily, visually, or both. The development of language and literacy skills is not due *solely* to the use of CIs or any other assistive device.

Cued Speech/Language (CSL).   There is some evidence that CSL, a language/communication approach, also might provide complete, adequate access to the English language by rendering the phonological component more accessible (Cornett, 1967, 1991; LaSasso et al., 2010; Leybaert et al., 2011; Paul, 2009). This *complete, adequate access* was posed in a question quite some time ago: "Can a language that has traditionally been spoken and heard remain intact when conveyed with different articulators and in a different medium?" (Fleetwood & Metzger, 1998, p. 10). It has been argued that an affirmative answer to this question requires the acquisition of the phonological component of a language (Paul, 2009). Indeed, the question has now become, Can a complete phonological representation of English (or any spoken language) be rendered visually to match what is typically rendered via speech? (e.g., see LaSasso et al., 2010; Leybaert et al., 2011).

Comprehensive reviews of the development and research on CSL can be found in the work of LaSasso et al. (2010) and Leybaert et al. (2011). Early research demonstrated improvements in speech reception and production. By far, the more interesting results are those associated with the contributions of CSL to the development of English language and English reading. It seems that CSL is related to the development of aspects of phonology and perhaps subsequently to morphology, syntax, and semantics (e.g., word knowledge), and this, in turn, assists with the development of early English reading skills. With respect to reading, the development of rapid word identification skills in English is dependent, in part, on the cognitive representation of the phonological and morphological properties of English.

Research has shown that d/Dhh children who are exposed to CSL early in life, particularly before learning to read, seem to rely on internal phonological representations to perform tasks involving rhyming, remembering, and spelling, and this reliance is *qualitatively similar* to that noted for children with typical hearing. Children who have a hearing loss and are exposed to CSL can use language and phonologically related skills during the emergent and conventional reading stages with impressive results (LaSasso et al., 2010; Leybaert et al., 2011; Paul, 2009).

CSL is highlighted here because it may be the most viable language/communication mode of all created systems, including the English sign systems, that can be used to develop fluent and intelligible interactions between caregivers and children. This is especially the case for children who have CIs and need something more to assist in the development of receptive and expressive English language skills. With rigorous research designs, we might be able to address and clarify the mixed findings for d/Dhh children with CIs with respect to English literacy development that have been reported in the literature (e.g., Paul, 2009; Spencer et al., 2011).

More research is needed to ascertain whether the acquisition of phonology is not dependent on the rendering of acoustic information as via CSL. This line of research should also provide further evidence for the claim that CSL can develop the use of a phonological code in short-term memory and permit representations of phonological information cognitively (Leybaert et al., 2011; Paul, 2009). This will require that information rendered in CSL should represent the same range of abstract phonemic values as does speech in any spoken language.

Table 2.3 provides a few brief highlights of the research findings on children with CIs and those exposed to CSL.

Phase 3: The Future

If there is a phase 3, what would be the expectations or trends for research? One challenge is for investigators to obtain a better understanding of individual differences, particularly the presence of deviant structures (i.e., errors) in the language development of d/Dhh children and adolescents. As argued long ago by Pressnell (1973) and others (e.g., see discussion in Paul, 2009), the existence of these structures might be due predominantly to external or sociocultural factors such as inadequate instructional strategies or exposure to an incomplete or degraded model of English (e.g., LaSasso et al., 2010; Wang et al., 2008). This also has been the case for children and adolescents learning English as a second language (see Chapter 3; Paul & Wang, 2012, Chapter 9). Regardless of the reasons for the deviant structures, most of the documented errors of d/Dhh children (and even individuals learning English as a second language) are still developmental in nature (Paul, 2012; Paul & Wang, 2012).

Table 2.3. **Remarks on Cochlear Implantation and Cued Speech/Language**

Cochlear Implantation (CI)

- Researchers have reported the beneficial effects of CI on speech production, speech perception, various aspects of the English language including through the air (i.e., knowledge and use of English components/parameters) and English literacy (e.g., phonological awareness, vocabulary, working memory, suprasegmentals, and comprehension).

- For the past 20 years or more, there has been evidence relating to the positive development of oral (through-the-air) English and subsequent English literacy skills in children and quality-of-life benefits in adults.

- The variability of results across children is attributed to factors such as age at onset of the hearing loss, age at implementation of the CI, the quality of the auditory management program, mode of communication (sign, oral, etc.) of the children, consistency in the use of the CI, and attitudes of the CI users or parents. This variability in research results is most likely due to the inadequate control of critical factors in the investigations.

- Despite the impressiveness of the results, there needs to be caution and restraint in interpreting the findings. As argued in this chapter and elsewhere, there is much more to consider than just the ability to hear the speech signal for the development of language (and literacy) skills.

Cued Speech/Language (CSL)

- The use of cues in CSL has not been found to affect negatively the ability to speech read or to use residual hearing for d/Dhh children, adolescents, or adults. CSL, in conjunction with modern devices such as digital hearing aids or CIs, should result in even more impressive findings.

- CSL might play a major role in the development of reading skills, particularly via the development of phonological and phonemic awareness. More research is needed to determine if the acquisition of phonology is not dependent on the rendering of acoustic information as via CSL. This line of research should also provide further evidence for the claim that CSL can develop the use of a phonological code in short-term memory and permit representations of phonological information cognitively.

- A number of d/Dhh children exposed to CSL early in life and prior to the beginning formal reading period seem to rely on internal phonological representations to perform tasks such as rhyming, remembering, and spelling. This reliance is *qualitatively* similar to that noted for children with typical hearing.

Similar to the discussion of reading (and writing) in Chapter 1, it might be necessary to construct individual cognitive profiles to obtain a better understanding of the English language development of d/Dhh children. These profiles should consider the wide array of linguistic (e.g., language parameters/components), cognitive (e.g., working memory), social (e.g., home environment), and affective (e.g., motivation) variables. In short, we agree with Blamey and Sarant (2011) that hearing loss by itself might not be sufficient to account for the developmental trajectory of English language development, both receptive and expressive. We add that hearing loss might not even pertain to the so-called line of demarcation between hard of hearing and deaf, which historically has been at the profound level (about 90 to 92 dB)—at least for adolescents and adults—especially for the acquisition of a spoken language such as English (Quigley & Kretschmer, 1982). The continuing improvements associated with early intervention and early amplification should contribute to the altered landscape of the demographics and achievement of children and adolescents who are d/Dhh (e.g., see Mayer & Leigh, 2010; Easterbrooks & Beal-Alvarez, 2012). This might result in a line of demarcation in which hearing loss plays only a minor role in the development of English.

Considering this discussion, research in phase 3 might also clarify the distinction, if any, between *language delay* (external to the individual) and *language disability* (internal). As with reading delay/difficulty and reading disability, it is often difficult to discern these constructs for d/Dhh children and adolescents, even for many other children with special-education labels. The fact that some d/Dhh children might possess a language disability (e.g., dyslexia) in addition to possessing a hearing loss should not come as a surprise. Clarifying this distinction is useful for developing and implementing an effective instructional program and will contribute to the refinement of theory (and research). Progress is contingent on the construction of adequate language assessments and being cautious about the constraints and interpretations of specific assessments with respect to, for example, the cognitive demands for perception and production aspects of the tests (e.g., see Blamey & Sarant, 2011; Paul, 2009, Chapter 11).

CONCLUSION

In this chapter, we focused on the development of through-the-air English as a first language for children and adolescents with hearing loss and compared this development to that of typical learners of English. We also discussed the nature of English language acquisition and related this to the subsequent acquisition of English literacy skills. Our interpretation of the research findings indicates that the development of English in individuals with hearing loss is qualitatively similar but might be quantitatively delayed when compared to counterparts who are typical or native learners of English. This interpretation pertains to individuals with all degrees of hearing loss and who have been exposed to signing and/or oral forms of English. In essence, we provided both empirical and reason-based evidence for the QSH.

We also address one of the *broken promises* of Marschark and Spencer (2010) with respect to English language development, both through the air and English literacy. Part of our response is similar to the assertion of these investigators and others about the need for rigorous, comprehensive research designs that consider and control for the array of significant factors (demographic and achievement) that impact the interpretation and generalization of findings. Other issues, discussed by Blamey and Sarant (2011), are the need to understand the requirements and constraints of current language assessments and the need to develop and use more comprehensive language tests. This is in line with researchers (outside of deafness) who have argued that English language proficiency plays a greater role in English literacy development than previously thought (e.g., McGuiness, 2005; Shanahan, 2006). Considering these factors, we might be able to obtain a stronger perspective on the individual differences and the uneven progress of children and adolescents with hearing loss.

Finally, to adequately address this broken promise, there is a need for investigators to ascribe to a model of English language development based on an in-depth analysis of extant theory and research. Setting aside the nature of current language tests, we argue that English language proficiency means, at the least, a threshold of competence in each language parameter or component (e.g., phonology, morphology, etc.) and in the integrative use of these components. In our view, phonology represents the building blocks of learning the English language (actually, any language). This working threshold knowledge of phonology entails not only the segmentals such as consonants and vowels but also the suprasegmental aspects such as intonation, stress, and rhythm. If the development of English literacy depends in part on English language proficiency, then English language proficiency—even as part of the ASHA definition cited in this chapter—must be related to the use of the various parameters. This more complete understanding of English language acquisition should engender the development and implementation of effective English language instructional/ intervention practices for individuals with hearing loss.

REFERENCES

Adams, M. (1990). *Beginning to read: Thinking and learning about print.* Cambridge, MA: MIT Press.

Adams, M. (1994). Phonics and beginning reading instruction. In F. Lehr & J. Osborn (Eds.), *Reading, language, and literacy: Instruction for the 21st century* (pp. 3–23). Hillsdale, NJ: Erlbaum.

American Speech–Language–Hearing Association (ASHA) Committee on Language. (1983, June). Definition of language. *ASHA, 25,* 44.

Anthony, D. (1966). *Seeing essential English.* Unpublished master's thesis, Eastern Michigan University, Ypsilanti.

Archbold, S. (2010). *Deaf education: Changed by cochlear implantation?* Nijmegen, the Netherlands: University of Nijmegen Medical Centre.

Baddeley, A. (1990). *Human memory: Theory and practice.* Hillsdale, NJ: Erlbaum.

Bear, D., Invernizzi, M., Templeton, S., & Johnston, F. (2007). *Words their way: Words study for phonics, vocabulary, and spelling instruction* (4th ed). Upper Saddle River, NJ: Pearson.

Bernstein, L., & Auer, E. (2011). Speech perception and spoken word recognition. In M. Marschark & P. Spencer (Eds.). *The Oxford handbook of deaf studies, language, and education* (2nd ed., Vol. 1, pp. 399–411). New York, NY: Oxford University Press.

Bernstein, D., & Tiegerman-Farber, E. (2009). *Language and communication disorders in children* (6th ed.). Boston, MA: Pearson.

Blamey, P., & Sarant, J. (2011). Development of spoken language by deaf children. In M. Marschark & P. Spencer (Eds.), *The Oxford handbook of deaf studies, language, and education* (2nd ed., Vol. 1, pp. 241–257). New York, NY: Oxford University Press.

Bloom, L., & Lahey, M. (1978). *Language development and language disorders.* New York, NY: Wiley.

Blume, S. (2010). *The artificial ear:Cochlear implants and the culture of deafness.* New Brunswick, NJ: Rutgers University Press.

Bornstein, H., & Saulnier, K. (1981). Signed English: A brief follow-up to the first evaluation. *American Annals of the Deaf, 126,* 69–72.

Bornstein, H., Saulnier, K., & Hamilton, L. (1980). Signed English: A first evaluation. *American Annals of the Deaf, 125,* 467–481.

Brown, R. (1973). *A first language: The early stages.* Cambridge, MA: Harvard University Press.

Cain, K., & Oakhill, J. (2007). Cognitive bases of children's language comprehension difficulties: Where do we go from here? In K. Cain & J. Oakhill (Eds.), *Children's comprehension problems in oral and written language: A cognitive perspective* (pp. 283–295). New York, NY: Guilford Press.

Chomsky, C. (1969). *The acquisition of syntax in children from 5 to 10.* Cambridge, MA: MIT Press.

Chomsky, N. (2006). *Language and mind* (3rd ed.). New York, NY: Cambridge University Press.

Cohen, S., Labadie, R., Dietrich, M., & Haynes, D. (2004). Quality of life in hearing-impaired adults: The role of cochlear implants and hearing aids. *Otolaryngology—Head and Neck Surgery, 131*(4), 413–422.

Cooper, R. (1967). The ability of deaf and hearing children to apply morphological rules. *Journal of Speech and Hearing Research, 10,* 77–86.

Cornett, R. O. (1967). Cued speech. *American Annals of the Deaf, 112,* 3–13.

Cornett, R. O. (1991). A model for ASL/English bilingualism. In S. Polowe-Aldersley, P. Schragle, V. Armour, & J. Polowe (Eds.), *Proceedings of the 55th Biennial Meeting of CAID and the 63rd Annual Meeting of CEASD* (pp. 33–39). New Orleans, LA: Convention of American Instructors of the Deaf.

Crandall, K. (1978). Inflectional morphemes in the manual English of young hearing impaired children and their mothers. *Journal of Speech and Hearing Research, 21,* 372–386.

Crowder, R. (1982). *The psychology of reading.* New York, NY: Oxford University Press.

Crystal, D. (1997). *The Cambridge encyclopedia of language* (2nd ed). New York, NY: Cambridge University Press.

Crystal, D. (2006). *How language works.* London, England: Penguin.

Davis, J., & Blasdell, R. (1975). Perceptual strategies employed by normal-hearing and hearing-impaired children in the comprehension of sentences containing relative clauses. *Journal of Speech and Hearing Research, 18,* 281–295.

Dettman, S., & Dowell, R. (2010). Language acquisition and critical periods for children using cochlear implants. In M. Marschark & P. Spencer (Eds.), *The Oxford handbook of deaf studies, language, and education* (Vol. 2, pp. 331–342). New York, NY: Oxford University Press.

Drasgow, E., & Paul, P. (1995). A critical analysis of the use of MCE systems with deaf students: A review of the literature. *ACEHI/ACEDA, 21*(2/3), 80–93.

Easterbrooks, S. (2010). Evidence-based curricula and practices that support development of reading skills. In M. Marschark & P. Spencer (Eds.), *The Oxford handbook of deaf studies, language, and education* (Vol. 2, pp. 111–126). New York, NY: Oxford University Press.

Easterbrooks, S., & Beal-Alvarez, J. (2012). States' reading outcomes of students who are d/Deaf and hard of hearing. *American Annals of the Deaf, 157*(1), 27–40.

Ehri, L. (1991). Development of the ability to read words. In R. Barr, M. Kamil, P. Mosenthal, & P. D. Pearson (Eds.), *Handbook of reading research* (2nd ed., pp. 383–417). White Plains, NY: Longman.

Fleetwood, E., & Metzger, M. (1998). *Cued language structure: An analysis of cued American English based on linguistic principles.* Silver Spring, MD: Calliope Press.

Gee, J., & Goodhart, W. (1988). American Sign Language and the human biological capacity for language. In M. Strong (Ed.), *Language learning and deafness* (pp. 49–74). New York, NY: Cambridge University Press.

Gerken, L., Jusczyk, P., & Mandel, D. (1994). When prosody fails to cue syntactic structure: Nine-month-olds' sensitivity to phonological versus syntactic phrases. *Cognition, 51*(3), 237–265.

Gilman, L., Davis, J., & Raffin, M. (1980). Use of common morphemes by hearing impaired children exposed to a system of manual English. *Journal of Auditory Research, 20,* 57–69.

Goodluck, H. (1991). *Language acquisition: A linguistic introduction.* Cambridge, MA: Blackwell.

Gough, P., & Tunmer, W. (1986). Decoding, reading, and reading disability. *Remedial and Special Education, 7,* 6–10.

Griswold, E., & Cummings, J. (1974). The expressive vocabulary of preschool deaf children. *American Annals of the Deaf, 119,* 16–28.

Gustason, G., Pfetzing, D., & Zawolkow, E. (1980). *Signing exact English.* Los Alamitos, CA: Modern Signs Press.

Israel, S., & Duffy, G. (Eds.). (2009). *Handbook of research on reading comprehension.* New York, NY: Routledge.

Kaderavek, J. (2011). *Language disorders in children: Fundamental concepts of assessment and intervention.* Boston, MA: Pearson.

Kamhi, A., & Catts, H. (2012). *Language and reading disabilities* (3rd ed.). Boston, MA: Pearson Education.

King, C. (1981). *An investigation of similarities and differences in the syntactic abilities of deaf and hearing children learning English as a first or second language.* Unpublished doctoral dissertation, University of Illinois, Champaign-Urbana.

Klop, W. M., Briaire, J. J., Stiggelbout, A. M., & Frijns, J. H. (2009). Cochlear implant outcomes and quality of life in adults with prelingual deafness. *Laryngoscope, 117*(11), 1982–1987.

Kodman, F. (1963). Educational status of hard-of-hearing children in the classroom. *Journal of Speech and Hearing Disorders, 28,* 297–299.

Kuder, S. J. (2013). *Teaching students with language and communication disabilities* (4th ed.). Boston, MA: Pearson.

LaSasso, C., Crain, K., & Leybaert, J. (Eds.). (2010). *Cued speech and cued language for deaf and hard of hearing children.* San Diego, CA: Plural.

Layton, T., Holmes, D., & Bradley, P. (1979). A description of pedagogically imposed signed semantic–syntactic relationships in deaf children. *Sign Language Studies, 23,* 137–160.

Leybaert, J., Aparicio, M., & Alegria, J. (2011). The role of cued speech in language development of deaf children. In M. Marschark & P. Spencer (Eds.), *The Oxford handbook of deaf studies, language, and education* (2nd ed., Vol. 1, pp. 276–289). New York, NY: Oxford University Press.

Luetke-Stahlman, B. (1988a). The benefit of oral-English-only as compared with signed input to hearing-impaired students. *Volta Review, 90,* 349–361.

Luetke-Stahlman, B. (1988b). Documenting syntactically and semantically incomplete bimodal input to hearing-impaired subjects. *American Annals of the Deaf, 133,* 230–234.

Luetke-Stahlman, B., & Milburn, W. (1996). Seeing essential English. *American Annals of the Deaf, 141,* 29–33.

Lund, N. (2003). *Language and thought.* New York, NY: Routledge.

Marschark, M. (2007). *Raising and educating a deaf child: A comprehensive guide to the choices, controversies, and decisions faced by parents and educators* (2nd ed.). New York, NY: Oxford University Press.

Marschark, M., Sapere, P., Convertino, C. M., Mayer, C., Wauters, L., & Sarchet, T. (2009). Are deaf students' reading challenges really about reading? *American Annals of the Deaf, 154*(4), 357–376.

Marschark, M., Sarchet, T., Rhoten, C., & Zupan, M. (2010). In M. Marschark & P. Spencer (Eds.), *The Oxford handbook of deaf studies, language, and education* (Vol. 2, pp. 127–143). New York. NY: Oxford University Press.

Marschark, M., & Spencer, P. (2010). The promises(?) of deaf education: From research to practice and back again. In M. Marschark & P. Spencer (Eds.), *The Oxford handbook of deaf studies, language, and education* (Vol. 2, pp. 1–14). New York, NY: Oxford University Press.

Maxwell, M. (1983). Language acquisition in a deaf child of deaf parents: Speech, sign variations, and print variations. In K. Nelson (Ed.), *Children's language* (Vol. 4, pp. 283–313). Hillsdale, NJ: Erlbaum.

Maxwell, M. (1987). The acquisition of English bound morphemes in sign form. *Sign Language Studies, 57,* 323–352.

Mayer, C. (2007). What really matters in the early literacy development of deaf children. *Journal of Deaf Studies and Deaf Education, 12*(4), 411–431.

Mayer, C. (2009). Issues in second language literacy education for learners who are deaf. *International Journal of Bilingual Education and Bilingualism, 12*(3), 325–334.

Mayer, C. (2010). The demands of writing and the deaf writer. In M. Marschark & P. Spencer (Eds.), *Oxford handbook of deaf studies, language, and education* (Vol. 2, pp. 144–155). New York, NY: Oxford University Press.

Mayer, C., & Leigh, G. (2010). The changing context for sign bilingual education programs: Issues in language and the development of literacy. *International Journal of Bilingual Education and Bilingualism, 13*(2), 175–186.

Mayer, C., & Trezek, B. J. (2011). New (?) answers to old questions: Literacy development in D/HH learners. In D. Moores (Ed.), *Partners in education: Issues and trends from the 21st International Congress on Education of the Deaf Conference Proceedings* (62–74). Washington, DC: Gallaudet University Press.

Mayer, C., & Wells, G. (1996). Can the linguistic interdependence theory support a bilingual–bicultural model of literacy education for deaf students? *Journal of Deaf Studies and Deaf Education, 1*(2), 93–107.

McGill-Franzen, A., & Allington, R. (Eds.). (2011). *Handbook of reading disability research.* New York, NY: Routledge.

McGuinness, D. (2004). *Early reading instruction: What science really tells us about how to teach reading.* Cambridge, MA: MIT Press.

McGuinness, D. (2005). *Language development and learning to read: The scientific study of how language development affects reading skill.* Cambridge, MA: MIT Press.

Miller, P., & Clark, D. (2011). Phonemic awareness is not necessary to become a skilled deaf reader. *Journal of Developmental Physical Disabilities, 23,* 459–476.

Moores, D. (2001). *Educating the deaf: Psychology, principles, and practices* (5th ed.). Boston, MA: Houghton-Mifflin.

Moores, D. (2010). The history of language and communication issues in deaf education. In M. Marschark & P. Spencer (Eds.), *The Oxford handbook of deaf studies, language, and education* (Vol. 2, pp. 17–30). New York, NY: Oxford University Press.

Moores, D., & Sweet, C. (1990). Factors predictive of school achievement. In D. Moores & K. Meadows-Orlans (Eds.), *Educational and developmental aspects of deafness* (pp. 154–201). Washington, DC: Gallaudet University Press.

National Early Literacy Panel. (2008). *Developing early literacy: Report of the National Early Literacy Panel.* Washington, DC: National Institute for Literacy. Retrieved from http://www.nifl.gov/earlychildhood/NELP/NELPreport.html.

National Reading Panel. (2000). *Report of the National Reading Panel: Teaching children to read—An evidence-based assessment of the scientific research literature on reading and its implications for reading instruction.* Jessup, MD: National Institute for Literacy at EDPubs.

O'Grady, W. (2005). *How children learn language.* New York, NY: Cambridge University Press.

Owens, R. (2010). *Language disorders: A functional approach to assessment and intervention* (5th ed.). Boston, MA: Pearson Education.

Palmer, C. S., Niparko, J. K., Wyatt, J. R., Rothman, M., & de Lissovoy, G. (1999). A prospective study of the cost–utility of the multichannel cochlear implant. *Archives of Otolaryngology Head Neck Surgery, 125*(11), 1221–1228.

Paul, P. (1998). *Literacy and deafness: The development of reading, writing, and literate thought.* Needham Heights, MA: Allyn & Bacon.

Paul, P. (2009). *Language and deafness* (4th ed.). Sudbury, MA: Jason & Bartlett.

Paul, P. (2010). Qualitative–similarity hypothesis. In R. Nata (Ed.), *Progress in education* (Vol. 20, pp. 1–31). New York, NY: Nova Science.

Paul, P. (2011). A perspective on language and literacy issues. In D. Moores (Ed.), *Partners in education: Issues and trends from the 21st International Congress on the Education of the Deaf* (pp. 51–61). Washington, DC: Gallaudet University Press.

Paul, P. (2012). Qualitative similarity hypothesis. In P. Paul and D. Moores (Eds.), *Deaf epistemologies: Multiple perspectives on the acquisition of knowledge* (pp. 179–198). Washington, DC: Gallaudet University Press.

Paul, P., & Drasgow, E. (1998). The great ASL–MCE debate: A rejoinder. *CAEDHH Journal/La Revue ACESM, 24*(1), 5–15.

Paul, P., & Gustafson, G. (1991). Hearing-impaired students' comprehension of high-frequency multimeaning words. *Remedial and Special Education (RASE), 12*(4), 52–62.

Paul, P., & Wang, Y. (2012). *Literate thought: Understanding comprehension and literacy.* Sudbury, MA: Jason & Barlett Learning.

Paul, P., & Whitelaw, G. (2011). *Hearing and deafness: An introduction for health and educational professionals.* Sudbury, MA: Jason & Bartlett Learning.

Payne, J.-A., & Quigley, S. (1987). Hearing-impaired children's comprehension of verb–particle combinations. *Volta Review, 89,* 133–143.

Pence, K., & Justice, L. (2008). *Language development from theory to practice.* Upper Saddle River, NJ: Pearson/Merrill Prentice Hall.

Perfetti, C. (1985). *Reading ability.* New York, NY: Oxford University Press.

Perfetti, C. (1986). Cognitive and linguistic components of reading ability. In B. Foorman & A. Siegel (Eds.), *Acquisition of reading skills* (pp. 1–41). Hillsdale, NJ: Erlbaum.

Perfetti, C., & Sandak, R. (2000). Reading optimally builds on spoken language: Implications for deaf readers. *Journal of Deaf Studies and Deaf Education, 5,* 32–50.

Pintner, R., & Lev, J. (1939). The intelligence of the hard-of-hearing school child. *Journal of Genetic Psychology, 55,* 31–48.

Plack, C. (2005). *The sense of hearing.* Mahwah, NJ: Erlbaum.

Pressnell, L. (1973). Hearing-impaired children's comprehension and production of syntax in oral language. *Journal of Speech and Hearing Research, 16,* 12–21.

Quigley, S., & Kretschmer, R. E. (1982). *The education of deaf children: Issues, theory, and practice.* Austin, TX: Pro-Ed.

Quigley, S., & Paul, P. (2004). Reflections. In Rose, S., McAnally, P., & Quigley, S., *Language learning practices with deaf children* (3rd ed., pp. 227–242). Austin, TX: Pro-Ed.

Quigley, S., & Thomure, R. (1968). *Some effects of hearing impairment upon school performance.* Urbana, IL: University of Illinois, Institute for Research on Exceptional Children.

Raffin, M. (1976). *The acquisition of inflectional morphemes by deaf children using seeing essential English.* Unpublished doctoral dissertation, University of Iowa, Iowa City.

Raffin, M., Davis, J., & Gilman, L. (1978). Comprehension of inflectional morphemes by deaf children exposed to a visual English sign system. *Journal of Speech and Hearing Research, 21,* 387–400.

Reed, V. (2012). *An introduction to children with language disorders* (4th ed.). Boston, MA: Pearson.

Rose, S., McAnally, P., & Quigley, S. (2004). *Language learning practices with deaf children* (3rd ed.). Austin, TX: Pro-ed.

Ross, M., Brackett, D., & Maxon, A. (1982). *Hard of hearing children in regular schools.* Englewood Cliffs, NJ: Prentice-Hall.

Russell, W., Quigley, S., & Power, D. (1976). *Linguistics and deaf children.* Washington, DC: Alexander Graham Bell Association for the Deaf.

Schick, B. (2011). The development of American Sign Language and manually coded English systems. In M. Marschark & P. Spencer (Eds.). *The Oxford handbook of deaf studies, language, and education* (Vol. 1, 2nd ed., 229–240). New York, NY: Oxford University Press.

Schick, B., & Moeller, M. (1992). What is learnable in manually coded English sign systems? *Applied Psycholinguistics, 13,* 313–340.

Schirmer, B. R., & Williams, C. (2011). Approaches to reading instruction. In M. Marschark & P. Spencer (Eds.), *Oxford handbook of deaf studies, language, and education* (2nd ed., Vol. 1, pp. 115–129). New York, NY: Oxford University Press.

Shanahan, T. (2006). Relations among oral language, reading, and writing development. In C. MacArthur, S. Graham & J. Fitzgerald (Eds.), *Handbook of writing research* (pp. 171–183). New York, NY: Guilford Press.

Shanahan, T., & Lomax, R. (1986). An analysis and comparison of theoretical models of the reading–writing relationship. *Journal of Educational Psychology, 78*(2), 116–123.

Shanahan, T., & Lomax, R. (1988). A developmental comparison of three theoretical models of the reading–writing relationship. *Research in the Teaching of English, 22*(2), 196–212.

Shull, T., & Crain, K. (2010). Fundamental principles of cued speech and cued language. In C. LaSasso, K. Crain, & J. Leybaert (Eds.), *Cued speech and cued language for deaf and hard of hearing children* (pp. 27–51). San Diego, CA: Plural.

Spencer, L., & Oleson, J. (2008). Early listening and speaking skills predict later reading proficiency in pediatric cochlear implant users. *Ear and Hearing, 29,* 270–280.

Spencer, P., & Marschark, M. (2003). Cochlear implants: Issues and implications. In M. Marschark & P. E. Spencer (Eds.), *Oxford handbook of deaf studies, language, and education* (pp. 434–448). New York, NY: Oxford University Press.

Spencer, P., Marschark, M., & Spencer, L. (2011). Cochlear implants: Advances, issues, and implications. In M. Marschark & P. Spencer (Eds.). *The Oxford handbook of deaf studies, language, and education* (Vol. 1, 2nd ed., pp. 452–470). New York, NY: Oxford University Press.

Stahl, S., & Nagy, W. (2006). *Teaching word meanings.* Mahwah, NJ: Erlbaum.

Supalla, S. (1991). Manually coded English: The modality question in signed language development. In P. Siple & S. Fischer (Eds.), *Theoretical issues in sign language research: Vol. 2. Psychology* (pp. 85–109). Chicago, IL: University of Chicago Press.

Trezek, B. J., Wang, Y., & Paul, P. V. (2010). *Reading and deafness: Theory, research, and practice.* Clifton Park, NY: Delmar/Cengage Learning.

Trezek, B., Wang, Y., & Paul, P. (2011). Processes and components of reading. In M. Marschark & P. Spencer (Eds.), *Handbook of deaf studies, language, and education* (2nd ed., Vol. 1, pp. 99–114). New York, NY: Oxford University Press.

Washburn, A. (1983). Seeing essential English: The development and use of a sign system over two decades. *Teaching English to Deaf and Second-Language Students, 2*(1), 26–30.

Wang, Y., Trezek, B., Luckner, J., & Paul, P. (2008). The role of phonology and phonological-related skills in reading instruction for students who are deaf or hard of hearing. *American Annals of the Deaf, 153*(4), 396–407.

Whitehurst, G., & Lonigan, C. (2002). Emergent literacy: Development from preschoolers to readers. In S. Neuman & D. Dickinson (Eds.), *Handbook of early literacy research* (pp. 11–29). New York, NY: Guilford Press.

Wilbur, R. (2011). Modality and the structure of language: Sign languages versus signed systems. In M. Marschark & P. Spencer (Eds.), *The Oxford handbook of deaf studies, language, and education* (2nd ed., Vol. 1, pp. 350–366). New York, NY: Oxford University Press.

Wilcox, J., & Tobin, H. (1974). Linguistic performance of hard-of-hearing and normal hearing children. *Journal of Speech and Hearing Research, 17,* 286–293.

Williams, C. (2004). Emergent literacy of deaf children. *Journal of Deaf Studies and Deaf Education, 9*(4), 352–365.

Williams, C. (2011). Adapted interactive writing instruction with kindergarten children who are deaf or hard of hearing. *American Annals of the Deaf, 156*(1), 23–34.

Wilson, B. S., & Dorman, M. F. (2008). Cochlear implants: Current designs and future possibilities. *Journal of Rehabilitation Research & Development, 45*(5), 695–730.

3

English Language Learners

The U.S. Department of Education report, the *Condition of Education 2011* (Aud et al., 2011), estimates that, in 2009, approximately 21% (or 11.2 million) of children ages 5 to 17 years spoke a language other than English at home (i.e., language minority learners), and 5% (or 2.7 million) spoke English with difficulty (i.e., English language learners [ELLs]; see a review of the different terms associated with ELLs in Paul & Wang, 2012, Chapter 9). Seventy-three percent of those children speaking English with difficulty spoke Spanish. Although ELLs are a heterogeneous group with a wide range of individual differences (e.g., many children who are d/Deaf and hard of hearing are also ELLs), in general, 71% of ELLs from 2004 to 2007 were performing below grade level, and they continue to be among the nation's lowest achieving students (Short & Fitzsimmons, 2007). Improving the literacy skills of ELLs is critical, particularly considering the increasing prevalence of ELLs in U.S. school-age children. For example, based on the most recent data from the National Clearinghouse for English Language Acquisition (NCELA) (2009), in 2008–2009, the P–12 growth in the United States since 1997–1998 was 7.22%, whereas the ELL growth was 51.01%.

In this chapter, we compare and contrast the program models, theory, and research on both hearing and d/Deaf ELLs to identify the similarities and differences between these two populations. We assert that both hearing and d/Deaf ELLs learn to read and write English (as a second language) in a way qualitatively similar to that of their typically developing monolingual English-speaking peers, but at a quantitatively different—that is, slower—rate.

NATIONAL LITERACY PANEL FOR ELLS

In 2002, the U.S. Department of Education charged a panel of 13 experts with the task of reviewing the literature on the literacy development of ELLs. The published report of the National Literacy Panel on Language Minority Children and Youth (August & Shanahan, 2006) examined quantitative and qualitative research in each of the five components of effective reading instruction identified by the National Reading Panel

(2000): phonemic awareness, phonics, fluency, vocabulary, and text comprehension. Approximately 1,800 studies from 1980 to 2003 were initially identified through the literature, and 293 of those met the methodological criteria established by the panel and thus were included in the report.

The report concludes that effective instructional techniques for monolingual English-speaking students (e.g., Adams, 1990; Chall, 1983, 1996; McGuinness, 2004, 2005; National Early Literacy Panel, 2008; National Reading Panel, 2000) are also applicable to ELLs, although modifications and accommodations are needed for maximum results. For example, certain components of literacy, such as efficient word recognition and satisfactory levels of reading comprehension, cannot be fully developed until precursor skills, such as proficient decoding and orthographic skills, are acquired. Particularly, the importance of oral English proficiency is highlighted. In this chapter we summarize the panel's report and review the literature written from the publication of the report to the present.

PROGRAM MODELS

In the United States, Arizona was the first state to offer bilingual education in the 1960s. Bilingual education was favored by policies and practice in the 1970s and 1980s, during which many ELLs were taught partially or entirely in their native language and transitioned into English-only instruction in elementary grades (see the review by Salvin & Cheung, 2005). In 1998, Proposition 227 was passed in California to replace existing bilingual instruction with a structured English immersion for a period of no more than one year. Similar legislation went into effect in Arizona and Massachusetts. The passage of No Child Left Behind by the U.S. Congress in 2001 emphasized accountability in English only and offered no support for native language learning for ELLs.

Other than the heritage language programs, in which bilingual education is designed as a way to preserve or show respect for a given language, bilingual education is typically offered to help ELLs who are genuinely struggling with English. Currently, there are two major strategies for teaching ELLs in the United States: English immersion and bilingual education (Office for Civil Rights, 2012; Salvin & Cheung, 2005). At times, newcomer programs are offered for newly arrived immigrants in self-contained classrooms before they enter traditional English immersion or bilingual education classrooms.

There are different forms of English immersion programs: Some place ELLs immediately in classes with monolingual English speaking students (i.e., submersion) whereas others use structured English immersion in which English instruction in a separate class is gradually phased in for a period of time until the ELLs are ready to be mainstreamed. The majority of the bilingual education programs in the U.S. offer Spanish along with English.

Of bilingual education programs, one form is transitional bilingual instruction, in which ELLs are taught to read entirely in their native language in the primary grades and transitioned to English later. It includes early-exit models, in which transition happens in grade 2 or 3, and late-exit models, or maintenance bilingual education (MBE), in which the transition does not occur until the completion of elementary school. Another form is paired bilingual, or alternative immersion, in which ELLs are taught in both English and their native language at different times of each day or on alternative days. A special form of paired bilingual is two-way bilingual, or dual language/ dual immersion, in which reading instruction in the native language and English is provided for both ELLs and English speakers.

Table 3.1 provides a summary of the different programs for ELLs.

Salvin and Cheung (2005) conducted a best-evidence synthesis of experimental studies comparing bilingual and English-only reading programs for ELLs. They identified 17 studies that met the inclusion criteria. Of the 13 studies on elementary reading for Spanish-speaking students, nine favored bilingual programs on English reading measurements and four reported no differences. Bilingual programs were also favored in one of two studies on heritage languages (French and Choctaw) and two secondary studies. The authors concluded that existing evidence favored bilingual programs, particularly the ones with paired bilingual strategies that teach reading in the native language and English at different times each day.

Recent studies confirmed the conclusions drawn by Salvin and Cheung (2005). For example, in a longitudinal, experimental study conducted by Duran, Roseth, and Hoffman (2010), 31 Spanish-speaking preschoolers were randomly assigned to two Head Start classrooms differing only in the language of instruction (English vs. Spanish).

Table 3.1. **Summary of Different Programs for English Language Learners**

		English instruction	L1 instruction	Share classrooms with native English speakers
English immersion	Structured English immersion	Yes	No	No
	Submersion	Yes	No	Yes
Bilingual education	Paired bilingual/ alternative Immersion	Yes	Yes	Varies[a]
	Transitional bilingual Education	Yes	Yes	No
Special programs	Newcomer program	Yes	Varies	No
	Heritage language program	Yes	Yes	Yes

[a]As a special form of paired bilingual, two-way bilingual or dual language/dual immersion programs include both ELLs and native English speakers.

Sources: Office for Civil Rights (2012); Paul & Wang (2012).

After one year of implementation, students in the transitional bilingual program with Spanish language instruction outperformed their peers in the English-only program in both Spanish oral vocabulary and letter–word identification measures, whereas there were no significant differences between these two groups on the same measures in English.

Similarly, Farver, Lonigan, and Eppe (2009) randomly assigned 94 Spanish-speaking preschoolers into one control group ($n = 32$) and two groups receiving small-group interventions: a targeted early literacy intervention in English only ($n = 31$) or initially in Spanish transitioning to English after approximately 14 weeks ($n = 31$). After one year of implementation, children in the two intervention groups made significant gains in emergent literacy skills in both Spanish and English compared to their peers in the control group. The two intervention groups were equally effective for English language outcomes; however, only the transitional model was effective for Spanish language outcomes.

Proctor, August, Carlo, and Snow (2006) investigated English reading comprehension among a sample of 135 Spanish–English bilingual Latino/a grade 4 students, 69% of whom received initial literacy instruction in Spanish only for between two and to three years before they exited from the Spanish program, whereas 31% of whom were first taught to read in English only. Both groups used the same literacy curriculum with the only difference being the language of instruction. Consistent with the findings of Carlisle and Beeman (2001), the study authors reported significant differences between the two groups for Spanish alphabetic knowledge and fluency, in favor of the Spanish-instructed students, but no significant differences between the groups for the same measures in English.

In brief, one of the consistent findings of the panel (August & Shanahan, 2006) and other research studies is that ELLs who receive reading instruction in their first language are more likely to be successful in English literacy acquisition. It is highly possible that ELLs learn to read best when taught in both their native language and English from early in the process of formal schooling because reading instruction in a familiar language serves as a bridge to English literacy proficiency, especially when the native language is Spanish or French, which entails a phonetic orthography similar to that of English. The decoding, sound blending, and generic comprehension *strategies* are clearly transferable between languages (see the review in Paul & Wang, 2012). However, current practices in the field are driven more by politics than by empirical data.

THEORY AND RESEARCH SYNTHESIS

Cummins's linguistic interdependence theory (1978, 1979, 1980, 1984) proposes a common proficiency underlying all languages, allowing for transferring cognitive–academic or literacy-related skills from the first language (i.e., L1) to related skills in the second language (i.e., L2). According to Cummins, automatic linguistic transfer in surface aspects of dissimilar languages (e.g., lexical and grammatical knowledge) might be impossible, whereas the possibility of automatic transfer of conceptual knowledge as well as metalinguistic and metacognitive strategies (e.g., phonological awareness, comprehension monitoring, etc.) between dissimilar languages is much greater.

For example, studies on English word reading skills of ELLs with different L1 backgrounds have suggested that the L1 orthographic features (alphabetic vs. nonalphabetic) might affect phonological awareness skills (Holm & Dodd, 1996), orthographic coding mechanism (i.e., sensitivity to the case alternation effect in a naming task) (Akamatsu, 1999), or intraword structural sensitivity (i.e., understanding of the internal orthographic structure of words) of English (Koda, 1999; although Koda's 2000 study found similar intraword structural sensitivity among ELLs with alphabetic and nonalphabetic L1 literacies). However, as a whole, the literature suggests that differences in word reading of ELLs, if there are any, are associated less with type of L1 orthography than with history of exposure to English (Jackson, Chen, Goldsberry, Kim & Vanderwerff, 1999). For example, although students with nonalphabetic L1 literacy experienced difficulties processing nonwords, which might be due to their poor phonological awareness skills, they did not perform differently from students with alphabetic L1 literacy on real word decoding performance (Holm & Dodd, 1996; Koda, 1999). Many researchers suggest an interactive view of L2 reading, in which properties of both L1 and L2 interact with each other, jointly contributing to L2 reading process (Wang & Koda, 2007).

Research on Spanish-speaking children has shown evidence of cross-linguistic transfer of early literacy skills. For example, Spanish phonological processing, decoding, and print awareness are associated with improved English early reading skills (see the review in Duran, Roseth, & Hoffman, 2010), and Spanish vocabulary knowledge has a significant effect on English reading fluency for older children (e.g., grade 4) when decoding skills played a less predictive role than oral language proficiency (Proctor et al., 2006; Proctor, Carlo, August, & Snow, 2005). In a recent study, Proctor and Silverman (2011) assessed various language and literacy indicators in both English and Spanish for a group of 118 Latino/a students in second grade through fourth grade. They found that biliterate Spanish–English bilinguals outperformed their English monoliterate Spanish–English bilinguals on, not surprisingly, the Spanish language and literacy measures but also English literacy, although no significant differences were identified for English language proficiency between these two groups. They suggest that because of the similar orthographies of Spanish and English, the following is possible:

> Many of the bilingual children were actually monoliterate in English but possessed reasonable Spanish language skills and were able to work through reading Spanish words such that they were categorized as biliterate. The ability to do that, however, is precisely the metalinguistic skill that researchers argue is predictive of strong literacy outcomes. (p. 64)

In short, research evidence has supported Cummins's linguistic interdependence theory that certain metalinguistic conceptual knowledge (e.g., phonological processing, decoding and print awareness, and vocabulary knowledge) might be transferable from L1 to L2. Meanwhile, there has been no evidence for the transferring of surface aspects of languages (e.g., lexical and grammatical knowledge) in dissimilar languages.

Early Language Development of ELLs

Pearson and Fernandez (1994) investigated the lexical development of 20 English–Spanish bilingual infants, ages 10 to 30 months, on the patterns of growth in one language related to the growth in the other as well as the growth in both languages combined. They reported that the rate and pace of language development as a whole for these bilingual children were similar to those observed in monolinguals. Furthermore, the observed vocabulary spurt occurred in approximately the same percentage of bilingual children as what was reported for monolingual children.

The similar vocabulary-learning trajectory was observed not only for infants and toddlers but also for preschool-age bilingual and monolingual children. Leung, Silverman, Nandakumar, Qian, and Hines (2011) administered a researcher-developed receptive picture vocabulary assessment to 238 preschool-age ELLs and monolinguals. They found that although ELLs and monolinguals differed in mastery of target words (e.g., it is possible that *all* monolinguals know the word *night* whereas *many* ELLs know it, so the difficulty level of the item can be different for the two groups), the ranking of target words by difficulty was similar for both groups (i.e., words that are less difficult for ELLs are also less difficult for monolinguals). Therefore, the researchers suggested that ELLs and monolinguals might learn English words in a qualitatively similar order with a quantitatively different rate, and they called for further research to support this conclusion. Such a conclusion actually concurs with studies on monolinguals, that is, "the order of word difficulty remained much the same as overall levels of word knowledge increased" (Biemiller & Slonim, 2001, p. 499). Leung and colleagues propose that if ELLs and monolinguals learn most words in the same order, the same curriculum may be used in inclusive classrooms for both groups, but a different starting place in the curriculum may be used for these two groups, and ELLs and monolinguals may progress at different rates. They suggest the practice of small homogenous grouping for targeted vocabulary instruction in heterogeneous classrooms.

In sum, the early language development of ELLs, particularly the vocabulary-learning trajectory, is qualitatively similar to that of their monolingual English-speaking age peers. Thus, the same curriculum with accommodations and adaptations for ELLs is recommended in inclusive classrooms with both ELLs and their monolingual English-speaking peers.

Reading Development of ELLs

In the beginning stages of learning to read, similar skills, especially phonological awareness skills, are predictors of word reading ability for both ELLs and their monolingual peers (Chiappe, Siegel, & Wade-Woolley, 2002; Geva & Zadeh, 2006; Gottardo, 2002; Manis, Lindsey, & Bailey, 2004). For example, in a study investigating the phonological development of monolingual English, bilingual Chinese–English, and bilingual Spanish–English children in kindergarten through second grade, Bialystok,

Majumder, and Martin (2003) found that there were minimal differences between bilinguals and monolinguals.

For older ELLs, Garcia's (2003) review found that they need the similar knowledge (e.g., lexical, syntactic, semantic, background, and textual), cognitive strategies, and processes required in first-language reading comprehension, although they might also face more unfamiliar English vocabulary and topics than their monolingual peers and utilize some unique cognitive strategies developed in their first language. That is, English vocabulary and spoken English listening comprehension (e.g., syntactic, semantic, background, and verbal working memory) play a critical role in English reading comprehension for ELLs in the upper elementary and middle school ages (Garcia, 1991; Lesaux, Crosson, Kieffer, & Pierce, 2010; Lesaux & Kieffer, 2010; Mancilla- Martinez, Kieffer, Biancarosa, Christodoulou, & Snow, 2011; Proctor, August, et al., 2006; Proctor, Carlo, et al., 2005; Reese, Garnier, Gallimore, & Goldenberg, 2000).

Vocabulary is widely considered as the single most encountered obstacle ELLs face in learning to read because they are less able to exploit context clues to figure out unfamiliar words while reading. ELLs might encounter a greater proportion of unknown words and lack full command of the English grammar to use linguistic cues (Carlo et al., 2004; Jimenez, Garcia, & Pearson, 1996; Silverman, 2007; Swanson, Rosston, Gerber, & Solari, 2008; Taffe, Blachowicz, & Fisher, 2009). Even though many ELLs might be familiar with the vocabularies involving basic interpersonal communication skills (BICS), they often have less exposure to and experiences with written English involving cognitive academic language proficiency (CALP) (Cummins, 1978, 1979, 1980, 1984). In general, ELLs know less about topics included in English texts (Garcia, 2000) as well as the academic language used to express these topics (Birch, 2007).

Other skills, such as syntactic awareness and verbal working memory, might also require different amounts of exposure to English before ELLs are capable of performing at similar levels as those of their monolingual peers (e.g., Lipka, Siegel & Vukovic, 2005; Swanson et al., 2008). Furthermore, Kieffer and Lesaux (2008) found that the relationship between morphological awareness and reading comprehension strengthened between grades 4 and 5 for ELLs, and morphological awareness became a significant predictor of reading comprehension in grade 5.

Another difficulty in closing the English literacy skill gaps between typically developing monolinguals and many ELLs is the different catch-up trajectories for decoding (i.e., word-level) and language comprehension (i.e., text-level) skills. It has been stated that five or more years is typically required for ELLs to catch up in English vocabulary and language comprehension (if they ever catch up), compared with one to two years generally required for word-level decoding skills (Cummins, 2009).

A number of studies have confirmed the different trajectories of word-level and text-level skills for ELLs (e.g., Lipka & Siegel, 2007; Mancilla-Martinez & Lesaux, 2010; Mancilla-Martinez & Lesaux, 2011; see also the review in Lesaux, 2006). For example, Chiappe et al. (2002) examined the basic literacy skills of 727 native English speakers and 131 ELLs in kindergarten and first grade. They found that the phonological abilities of the ELLs had increased so much in one year that their performance in first grade was indistinguishable from that of monolingual children; however, their performance on syntactic and verbal memory measures were still behind. In another example, following a cohort of Spanish-speaking ELLs from grades 1 through 6, Nakamoto, Lindsey, and Manis (2007) found that English reading comprehension scores of ELLs at the first and second grades were near national norms for monolinguals; however, the scores rapidly fell below the norms beginning in third grade and reached approximately the 20th percentile by sixth grade. Meanwhile, the word reading skills of ELLs remained close to the national norms.

The comparison of reading comprehension difficulties among early adolescent ELLs and their monolingual peers also proved to be more similar than different. For example, Lesaux and Kieffer (2010) measured the reading comprehension skills of 399 ELLs and 182 monolinguals in grade 6. More ELLs (60%) than their monolingual peers (40%) were below the 35th percentile and classified as struggling readers. The majority of struggling readers had developed basic fluency skills, and for all the struggling readers, there were no statistically significant differences between ELLs and their monolingual peers on eight measures of language and reading, but a statistically significant difference existed between the two groups on general vocabulary. Furthermore, the ELLs and their monolingual peers were evenly distributed among three skill profiles of struggling readers (i.e., slow word callers, automatic word callers, and globally impaired readers), and each profile was characterized by low vocabulary knowledge, although there were differences in word reading accuracy and fluency. The apparent trend of well-developed word reading skills and underdeveloped vocabulary for both groups suggests that the different catch-up trajectories for decoding and language comprehension skills might be applicable for not only ELLs but also their monolingual peers who are struggling readers, that is, there might be "the heterogeneity of reading comprehension difficulties" (Lesaux & Kieffer, 2010, p. 620).

Echoing the findings of previous studies at various grade levels, Kieffer (2011) suggested that limited English proficiency, rather than ELL status per se, might be a more powerful risk factor for the reading difficulties of many ELLs. Similarly, Lipka and colleagues (2005) reviewed the published studies on ELLs in Canada to investigate the reading development of ELLs and characteristics of reading disabilities (RD) in this population. They found that "ELLs with RD experienced reading difficulties similar to those of L1 students with RD. On the basis of the evidence, ELLs are not at greater risk for RD than their native English-speaking peers" (p. 39). Many researchers (e.g., Lesaux & Kieffer, 2010; Leung et al., 2011) criticized the practice of grouping ELLs by their ELL status, which might lead to receiving fewer resources, being taught by less qualified teachers, spending less time on quality literacy tasks, and in turn, worsen the negative consequences.

In short, the literature suggests that the reading development of ELLs might proceed through similar stages as those of their English monolingual peers, although the rates might progress differently and the patterns of strengths and weakness might vary (August & Shanahan, 2006; Garcia, 2003; Grabe, 2009; Kieffer, 2011; Lipka et al., 2005).

Other Challenges in Reading Development of ELLs

The low socioeconomic status of many ELLs often confounds the language- and literacy-learning situation. In the United States, ELLs, especially the ones entering kindergarten with limited English proficiency, are more likely than their monolingual peers to come from low-income families and to attend schools in the underfunded districts (Garcia, 2003; Kieffer, 2008, 2011). For example, based on nine years of longitudinal data from the Early Childhood Longitudinal Study—Kindergarten, 1998 (ECLS-K), Kieffer (2011) found that ELLs who entered kindergarten with spoken English proficiency caught up with monolinguals nationally by first grade and maintained national average levels through eighth grade. On the other hand, those with initially limited spoken English proficiency demonstrated substantially below national average English reading trajectories, but these trajectories converged with those of their peers from similar socioeconomic backgrounds during middle school.

There are many factors associated with the socioeconomic backgrounds of the students, and teacher quality in their neighborhood schools is one of them (Garcia, 2003). For instance, Haager and Windmueller (2001) found that in an urban school with 98% of the students being Hispanic, nine out of 17 first and second grade teachers were teaching without full certification. "Without project support, these teachers would typically have little ongoing contact with master teachers and would receive little supervision beyond periodic mandatory evaluations" (p. 249).

Garcia (2000) also suspected that the literal thinking skills of low- and average-performing ELLs might be related to the type of instruction that they had received. For example, Ramirez, Yuen, and Ramey (1991) found that regardless of the language of instruction, Spanish-speaking ELLs received passive, teacher-directed instruction, which did not promote the development of complex language and higher-order thinking skills. Researchers have called for a developmentally sensitive and mediated learning instruction in academic English to prepare culturally and linguistically diverse ELLs to comprehend conceptually complex texts, particularly for higher grades (Birch, 2007; Collier, 1987; Coulter & Smith, 2006; Jimenez & Teague, 2009; Portes & Salas, 2009).

In brief, socially related factors such as low socioeconomic status and type of instruction have contributed to the quantitative delays of many ELLs in reading development.

Interventions for Improving Reading Skills of ELLs

Direct instruction on early literacy skills, particularly those related to phonological skills, have proved to be effective for both ELLs and their monolingual peers in elementary grades (e.g., Denton, Anthony, Parker, & Hasbrouck, 2004; Gunn, Biglan, Smolkowski, & Ary, 2000; Kamps et al., 2007; Leafstedt, Richards & Gerber, 2004; Linan-Thompson, Vaughn, Hickman-Davis, & Kouzekanani, 2003; Vaughn et al., 2006). For example, 790 monolingual English speakers and 188 ELLs participated in a longitudinal study conducted by Lesaux and Siegel (2003) from kindergarten to second grade. All participants received direct phonological awareness instruction in kindergarten and targeted phonics instruction in first grade. Although the ELLs entered kindergarten with little or no English, by second grade, they were able to demonstrate comparable reading and spelling skills to that of their monolingual peers. The authors concluded that "the development of reading skills in children who speak English as a second language is very similar to the development of reading skills in native English speakers" (p. 1018).

In another example, Gunn and colleagues (2000) randomly assigned 256 students (158 Hispanic and 98 non-Hispanic) in kindergarten through second grade to a control group and an intervention group receiving supplemental reading instruction focused on phonological awareness and decoding skills. Along with the follow-up study (Gunn, Smolkowski, Biglan, & Black, 2002), Gunn and colleagues reported that students in the intervention group performed significantly better than the control group on measures of word attack, word identification, oral reading fluency, vocabulary, and reading comprehension at the end of the two-year intervention, and the greater improvement in word attack and oral reading fluency were still evident one year after the intervention.

Similarly, a Canadian study (Lovett et al., 2008) investigated the efficiency of an intervention program providing 105 hours of remedial instruction with a central emphasis on phonologically based word attack and word identification for 166 children with reading disabilities, ranging from 6 to 13 years old (90 monolingual English speakers and 76 ELLs). It was found that students in the intervention group outperformed those in the control group on both reading outcomes and rate of growth. Furthermore, there were no differences between ELLs and their monolingual peers in intervention outcomes or growth during intervention. Instead of the primary language, it was the level of oral (i.e., through-the-air) language ability at entry that proved to be highly predictive of final outcomes and of reading growth during intervention; that is, greater language impairment at entry was associated with greater growth.

Interventions on teaching word analysis and vocabulary learning strategies to improve comprehension outcomes have proved to be efficient for both ELLs and their monolingual peers (see the review in Taffe et al., 2009). For example, Carlo and colleagues (2004) conducted a 15-week intervention with 142 ELLs and 112 monolingual students in grade 5. Students in the intervention group (94 ELLs and 75 monolinguals) were taught meanings of academically useful words together with strategies for utilizing information from context, morphology, knowledge of multimeaning words, and cognates to infer word meaning. The students in the intervention group demonstrated greater growth than the comparison group on knowledge of the words taught, depth of vocabulary knowledge, understanding of multimeaning words, and reading comprehension. Within the intervention group, although the ELLs scored lower on all pre- and posttest measures, the effects were as large for the ELLs as for the monolinguals. The authors concluded that direct vocabulary instruction is effective for both ELLs and monolingual students in the inclusive classroom, if it incorporates the well-verified principles from previous work on monolingual English speakers and ELLs. Research also suggests that ELLs learn better when vocabulary is taught explicitly, including cross-linguistic relationships such as cognates and multimeaning words (Carlo et al.,

2004), and a significant amount of reading practice is incorporated (Zimmerman, 1997).

Similar to the research on English monolingual students, reading engagement has been shown to be a powerful factor in promoting English reading comprehension of ELLs (e.g., Reese et al., 2000; Roessingh, 2011). For example, working with fourth- and fifth-grade ELLs in Fiji, Elley and Mangubhai (1983) reported that ELLs who were in the Book Flood program during their 30-minute daily English as a second language class, in which they participated in either silent reading alone or guided reading, significantly outperformed their peers in the traditional classes after two years of intervention.

Other reading instructional strategies proven to be effective for monolingual English speakers have also been reported as successful in improving the reading skills of ELLs such as peer-assisted learning (Saenz, Fuchs, & Fuchs, 2005), direct teaching and mastery learning on vocabulary instruction, error correction and fluency building (Tam, Heward, & Heng, 2006), multidimensional vocabulary intervention through reading storybooks aloud (Silverman, 2007), and utilizing technology (e.g., computers, Internet, universal design for learning; audiotapes, iPod, DVDs, etc.) to improve the accessibility and comprehension of information (Blum, Koskinen, Tennant, Parker, Straub, & Curry, 1995; Solomon & Schrum, 2007).

REFLECTIONS

A comprehensive review of the theory and research on language and literacy development of ELLs reveals that their development is actually more similar to than different from that of their monolingual peers, particularly the ones who are identified as having language and/or reading disabilities (or delays). The effective interventions for both ELLs and their monolingual peers, especially the ones with language and/or reading disabilities or delays, have been proven to be explicit and systematic instruction on phonologically based skills, word analysis and vocabulary learning strategies, and reading comprehension, as well as the emphasis on reading engagement, peer-assisted learning, utilizing technology, and so on. Certain adjustments might be necessary for ELLs to accommodate their sometimes different progress rates in language and reading development, particularly in understanding unfamiliar vocabulary and topics. Meanwhile, when learning the English language and/or trying to read and write English, many ELLs are confronting unique challenges, many of which are more socially related (e.g., socioeconomic status and type of instruction) rather than developmentally related. All of these should be taken into consideration when designing program models for ELLs.

ELLs Who Are d/Deaf and Hard of Hearing

In 1847, T. H. Gallaudet first discussed the benefits of a natural sign language for individuals who are d/Deaf and hard of hearing in the debut issue of the *American Annals of the Deaf*. However, the modern-day official validation of sign language as a bona fide language (Stokoe, Casterline, & Croneberg, 1965) did not occur until the late 1960s, and the first formal bilingual–bicultural (BiBi) education for students who are d/Dhh was not established until the early 1980s.

Today, the 2009–2010 regional and national summary conducted by Gallaudet Research Institute (GRI) (2011) states that, based on the reported data on a national sample of 37,828 children who are d/Dhh in the United States, 22.8% of them are categorized as ELLs (17.5% of the sample did not report the information). However, as discussed later, the number of d/Dhh students whose native language is American Sign Language (ASL) is actually low, and the practice of ASL/English bilingualism–biculturalism is extremely complicated.

ASL/English Bilingualism–Biculturalism

The predominant theoretical framework for and, interestingly, against using ASL to teach English as a second language or ASL/English bilingualism–biculturalism has been Cummins's linguistic interdependence theory (see the discussion in the section Theory and Research Synthesis for ELLs). The field is divided on the assertion that English literacy could be developed through reading and writing the print without exposure to, or proficiency in, the through-the-air (i.e., spoken or signed) form of the primary language (e.g., English). That is, the meaning of words or sentences can be explained or negotiated via the use of ASL only in conjunction with English print without either spoken or signed English (see the review in Trezek, Wang, & Paul, 2010; Wang, 2012; Wang, Trezek, Luckner, & Paul, 2008).

Even Cummins (2000) acknowledges bilingual education for d/Deaf and hard of hearing children as "high stakes, complex and controversial" (p. 29). As discussed previously, Cummins maintains that there is the possibility of automatic transfer of conceptual knowledge and metalinguistic/metacognitive strategies (e.g., pragmatics) between dissimilar languages such as a sign language and a spoken/written language while rejecting that possibility for the surface aspects of dissimilar languages such as lexical and grammatical knowledge. That is, he suggests that the lexical and grammatical knowledge in a sign language (e.g., ASL) might not directly facilitate the acquisition of the lexical and grammatical knowledge in a spoken/written language (e.g., English). Quoting Cummins's well-known words, "To the extent that instruction in Lx is effective in promoting proficiency in Lx, transfer of this proficiency to Ly will occur provided there is adequate exposure to Ly and adequate motivation to learn Ly" (Cummins, 1981, p. 29).

Mayer and colleagues (Mayer, 2009; Mayer & Akamatsu, 2003, 2011; Mayer & Leigh, 2010; Mayer & Wells, 1996) published extensively on the implications of Cummins's linguistic interdependence theory for BiBi education for children who are d/Dhh. First, accentuating the importance of a threshold level L2 proficiency for mediating L2 literacy development, Mayer asserts that the fundamental and crucial difference between hearing and d/Deaf L2 literacy learners is the various levels of L2 through-the-air or conversational (spoken or signed) proficiency that have been acquired before they have to use L2 in more cognitively and linguistically demanding situations (e.g., written form in academic settings). That is, it is difficult if not impossible for d/Deaf individuals, or any individual, to make extensive use of L2 print in academic settings without a basic conversational knowledge of the surface aspects of L2 (i.e., phonology, morphology, and syntax). The second major obstacle to developing L2 literacy skills for many d/Deaf students, Mayer believes, is their inadequate proficiency in L1, as discussed later in the section Other Home or First Languages of d/DHH Students, and most important, learning opportunities and quality of literacy instruction for children who are d/Dhh are often restricted in academic settings, even in the BiBi programs (see the review in Wang, 2012).

COMPARISON WITH PROGRAMS/ MODELS FOR ELLs

In the United States, most of the BiBi programs for students who are d/Deaf and hard of hearing are within state-funded residential schools for the d/Dhh. Some programs are self-contained classrooms within public schools, and a few are separate public schools, such as P.S. 47/347 in New York City (i.e., the ASL and English Dual Language School), which serves students who are d/Dhh, students of d/Dhh parents or siblings, and nondeaf students who want to be fluent in sign language from prekindergarten to grade 12.

Compared with the educational programs/models for hearing ELLs, the BiBi programs for students who are d/Dhh are most closely related to paired bilingual programs, in which students who are d/Dhh are taught in ASL (or other ASL-based sign systems) and English (mostly written English). Dual-language programs that also enroll hearing students are mostly at the early childhood or early elementary grades and P–12 programs such as that at P.S. 47/347 are rare.

The BiBi programs in the United States vary significantly from program to program, particularly in the language of instruction. Supported by the strongest advocates of Deaf culture, some programs exclude the use of voice, including sign and voice simultaneously, as well as any artificial manually coded English (MCE) systems with signs that are considered ungrammatical and phonologically impossible in natural sign languages (Chamberlain & Mayberry, 2008). These BiBi programs advocate that d/Deaf students should be taught mostly by Deaf teachers and that Deaf history as well as Deaf culture should be important parts of the curricula for d/Deaf students (Gertz, 2008; Humphries, 2008).

However, in practice, since Strong's (1995) pioneer study profiling BiBi programs in the United States, the difficulties of finding qualified personnel who were fluent in ASL and the absence of formulated BiBi curricula and teaching methods have been reported repeatedly. For example, LaSasso and Lollis (2003) conducted a survey study on 78 day and residential schools for d/Dhh students in the United States. Nineteen schools self-identified as BiBi programs. Based on the self-reports of these BiBi programs, 47% had no more than half of the instructional staff members fluent in ASL, and 68% had no more than half of the support staff members fluent in ASL. Furthermore, only 21% of the programs reported having an official BiBi curriculum with annual goals as well as recommended instructional materials and procedures for teachers. Even in the programs where a Deaf studies curriculum had been established, the teachers did not implement it because academic subjects took precedence (Evans, 2004).

In terms of instructional practice, the strongest advocates of Deaf culture believe that d/Deaf students are visual learners with brains wired differently from those of hearing students (and even hard of hearing students) and that they learn differently than hearing students. Therefore, general theories of instruction and research for hearing students do not apply to d/Deaf students (Hauser, O'Hearn, McKee, Steider, & Thew, 2010). Such a practice is very different from the practice in teaching hearing ELLs, in which general theories of instruction and research for monolingual English speakers are typically considered the starting points for educating ELLs despite the varying conditions of gender, sexual orientation, ethnicity, and even disability.

In spite of variations, one consistent theme at many BiBi programs in the United States is using ASL to teach written English directly without exposure to, or proficiency in, spoken or signed English. Furthermore, some researchers (e.g., Evans, 2004) believe that a BiBi approach to educate students who are d/Dhh entails discourse-based language structure instruction, which excludes word-based language structure instruction and any explicit teaching of grammatical structures and rules.

OTHER HOME OR FIRST LANGUAGES OF d/Dhh STUDENTS

Despite the widely divided disagreement on the practice of BiBi education for d/Deaf (and hh) students, researchers generally agree that the reported low reading achievement of d/Deaf students is primarily a result of incomplete language acquisition, signed or spoken (e.g., Chamberlain & Mayberry, 2008; Mayer, 2009).

The language development of children who are d/Dhh varies significantly, particularly in the early ages. An older individual with linguistic competence who misses communication due to a slight or mild hearing loss (between 15 and 40 dB) should have more skills at their disposal to gain access to the parts of the communication that were missed through the utilization of contextual cues, linguistic knowledge, and communication repair strategies. However, for infants and young children, even a slight or mild hearing loss may adversely affect language development because they typically do not have the linguistic competence or attending skills of older individuals (Flexer, 1994; see also the discussion in Chapter 2).

Ninety-five percent of children who are d/Dhh in the United States are born to hearing parent(s) utilizing spoken communication (Mitchell & Karchmer, 2004). Currently, all states in the United States have initiated early hearing detection and intervention (EHDI) (initially referred to as universal newborn hearing screening [UNHS]) programs providing early intervention services to infants and their families, which includes screening, diagnosis, early intervention services, family support, and long-term goal setting (White, 2008). However, the effectiveness of the EHDI programs varies, and many children who are d/Dhh fall between the cracks in the system (Wang & Engler, 2010). In extreme cases, a child with a profound hearing loss born to hearing parents who do not use any form of a sign language or other meaningful communication methods at home might enter school with extremely limited language skills. Thus, for this child, there is a dual task: Learning the English language and learning to read and write English. Nevertheless, English, to some degree, is the first language for this child.

According to the 2009–2010 Regional and National Summary (GRI, 2011), 82.3% of the 37,828 national sample of children who are d/Dhh in the United States have English as one of the languages regularly used at home (2.4% of the sample did not report the information and multiple responses are allowed for this question). English can be used via the form of spoken English, and/or Cued Speech/Language, manually coded English systems (e.g., Signed English, Signing Exact English, etc.), or the combination of speech and manually coded English systems simultaneously. Unsurprisingly, the quality and quantity of exposure to English varies considerably. Meanwhile, although 21.9% of children who are d/Dhh reported Spanish as the home language and 25.2% reported *other*, only 5.8% reported using ASL at home. In brief, the home or first languages of children who are d/Dhh vary significantly, and only a small percentage of the families actually use ASL at home.

SYNTHESIS OF RESEARCH

To date, limited research is available in the United States to document the BiBi practice for educating students who are d/Dhh, and there are no experimental studies directly assessing its effectiveness (see the review in Moores, 2008; Spencer & Marschark, 2010; Wang, 2012). However, some correlational studies on sign language and written language proficiency have been used to support the practice of using ASL to teach English as a second language or ASL/English bilingualism–biculturalism.

For example, in a pioneer study on the correlations between linguistic proficiency in sign language and English written language, Strong and Prinz (1997) assessed the proficiency in ASL and written English of 160 d/Deaf students, ages eight to 15 years. They found that, after controlling for age and nonverbal intelligence, the written English skills of d/Deaf children with higher levels of ASL were significantly greater than those with the lowest ASL ability levels. However, it was not clear if the higher levels of English literacy skills compared favorably with hearing age peers (Mayer & Akamatsu 2003; Mayer & Leigh, 2010). Furthermore, the authors did not explain the reason(s) for excluding subsequent analysis on the subgroup of older children (aged 12–15 years) with d/Deaf mothers, in which there was no significant correlation between ASL level and English literacy.

Similarly, English reading achievement was found to be positively correlated with proficiency in ASL plural markers as well as knowledge of synonyms and antonyms (Hoffmeister, 2000), recognition and memory of fingerspelled initialized signs within ASL sentences (Padden & Ramsey, 2000), both ASL and MCE narrative comprehension (Chamberlain & Mayberry, 2000), and ASL syntactic ability and narrative comprehension (Chamberlain & Mayberry, 2008). However, few of these studies reported the reading levels of the participants compared with their hearing peers (eighth-grade reading level was used to distinguish skilled adult d/Deaf readers from less skilled adult d/Deaf readers in the study conducted by Chamberlain & Mayberry, 2008), and all had small samples of participants.

With a relatively larger sample, Singleton, Morgan, DiGello, Wiles, and Rivers (2004) compared the written English vocabulary of 72 d/Deaf elementary school students of various proficiency levels in ASL with those of 60 hearing ELL peers and 61 hearing monolingual English speaking peers. They found that neither of the deaf groups was commensurate with either the monolingual or ELL hearing peers although strong ASL signers outperformed the weaker signers in the quality of their written texts.

In another study with a relatively larger sample, Moores and Sweet (1990) found no correlation between English reading skills and ASL proficiency for two groups of congenitally deaf students 16 to 18 years of age, 65 of whom had hearing parents ($r = .04$) and 65 of whom had d/Deaf parents ($r = .06$). However, high correlations between reading and two measures of English syntax and morphology were identified.

Research studies on correlations among morphological, syntactical, and/or lexical knowledge of L1 sign language and L2 written or spoken language other than English have found them to be positive in German (Mann, 2007), French (Niederberger, 2008), Dutch (Hermans, Knoors, Ormel, & Verhoeven, 2008; Hermans, Ormel, & Knoors, 2010) and Spanish (Menendez, 2010). The direction and sufficiency of the linguistic transfer cannot be answered because of the limitation of the correlational design (see the review in Wang, 2012, and Chapter 7 of this text).

SIMILARITIES AND DIFFERENCES: d/Dhh AND HEARING STUDENTS

On the surface, hearing and d/Dhh ELLs appear to be two different populations with diverse language and literacy backgrounds and development. Let us investigate the consensus and dissension of the performances of these two populations.

Consensus and Dissension

The National Literacy Panel on Language-Minority Children and Youth (August & Shanahan, 2006) concludes that vocabulary knowledge, particularly school-based academic vocabulary, poses one of the biggest challenges for ELLs to achieve reading comprehension skills comparable with those of their monolingual English speaking peers. In addition, the best predictors of English reading comprehension skills of ELLs also include metalinguistic competence and other English oral proficiency variables such as listening comprehension, syntactic skills, and oral storytelling skills. Other contributing factors include exposure to print, learning opportunities and quality of literacy instruction, first-language literacy development, the ability to navigate complex text and utilize prior knowledge to draw inferences, and use of cross-linguistic transfer strategies, particularly cognitive and metacognitive strategies.

For children who are d/Dhh, the task of learning to read and write English, a language unfamiliar to many of them, is similarly challenging as for hearing ELLs. In fact, the reading difficulties of ELLs identified by the panel (August & Shanahan, 2006) have been documented in many research investigations on reading difficulties of children who are d/Dhh (see the review in Trezek et al., 2010, and Chapter 4, specifically, of this book). Some might argue that the task of learning to read is more demanding for children who are d/Dhh. For example, acquiring school-based academic vocabulary knowledge might be even more challenging for children who are d/Dhh because approximately 60% of the words considered important from a science curriculum review do not have sign representations (Lang, Hupper, Monte, Brown, Babb, & Scheifele, 2007). Another obvious difference between hearing ELLs and many children who are d/Dhh is the differential access to the phonology of English, a phonemic language that is more than 80% phonetic (Moats, 2001), although the role of which in literacy development is still controversial (see the discussions in Allen et al. 2009; Mayberry, del Giudice, & Lieberman, 2011; Paul, Wang, Trezek, & Luckner, 2009; Wang et al., 2008).

One outstanding difference between hearing ELLs and many d/Deaf ELLs is the quality of their first or home languages. As discussed previously, many children who are d/Dhh might not have a complete first or home language before they start the demanding task of learning to read and write in English.

DIRECTIONS FOR FURTHER RESEARCH

In sum, children who are d/Dhh experience reading difficulties similar to hearing ELLs with the exception of the unique characteristics of sign languages, different exposure to phonology of English, and varied first or home language competency. As advocated by many studies on hearing ELLs, the practice of teaching language and literacy for children who are d/Dhh should start from the best practices for language and literacy instruction for typically developing monolingual English-speaking children with some accommodations and adaptations.

Furthermore, based on Cummins's linguistic interdependence theory, phonology, morphology, and syntax are language specific; that is, it is almost impossible to develop knowledge of these forms of English via the use of another language such as ASL (see the review in Wang, 2012). The content (i.e., semantics) and use (i.e., pragmatics) of English may be acquired via explanations in another language, but not the forms. A rigid BiBi sign program without any exposure to the signed or spoken form of English might deprive the students of a required proficiency in the morphology and syntax of the language that they are trying to read. Through-the-air English-based systems, primarily MCE systems, have been proposed to bridge the gap between ASL and written English (Stewart, 2006). For example, spoken or signed English should be used in discussing English morphology and syntax, even in a BiBi sign program. Furthermore, the use of other approaches such as Cued Speech/Language and Visual Phonics can and should be used to provide students, who are d/Dhh, access to the phonology of English (see also Paul et al., 2009; Trezek et al., 2010, Wang et al., 2008; Wang, 2012).

It is naïve to believe that complete sign language acquisition is sufficient for automatic transferring from a L1 sign language to a L2 written language, just as proficiency in written Chinese cannot automatically transfer to proficiency in written English. This is the case, particularly, considering the fact that a L1 sign language does not have a well-recognized written form, and many d/Deaf children do not have a fully developed L1 sign language in the first place. There is much more to English literacy than just knowledge or proficiency in a sign language.

CONCLUSION

The available literature suggests that the language and literacy development of hearing ELLs might go through similar stages as those of their English monolingual peers with different progress rates and varying patterns of strengths and weakness. Furthermore, their development is more similar to than different from that of their monolingual peers, particularly those who are identified as having language and/or reading disabilities or delays, and the differences are more socially related rather than developmentally related. Similar intervention strategies have been identified as effective for both ELLs and their monolingual peers, especially those with language and/or reading disabilities or delays, for example, explicit and systematic instruction on phonologically based skills, word analysis and vocabulary learning strategies, and reading comprehension, as well as the emphasis on reading engagement, peer-assisted learning, and utilizing technology. Some accommodations and adaptations might be necessary for a number of ELLs.

Students who are d/Dhh learn to read English in a way similar to that of hearing ELLs with two major exceptions. First, a number of students who are d/Dhh have not acquired the level of proficiency in surface aspects of L2 (e.g., phonology, morphology, and syntax of English) in the through-the-air or conversational (spoken or signed) form before they have to use L2 in more cognitively and linguistically demanding situations such as the written form in academic settings. Research on hearing ELLs has demonstrated that oral English proficiency is one of the best predictors of English reading skills, particularly for older children. Many students who are d/Dhh are attempting to learn written English directly without a sufficient exposure to the spoken or signed form of English. Second, many children who are d/Dhh do not acquire a proficiency level in L1 (e.g., ASL), partially because only a low percentage of them actually use ASL at home, and learning opportunities and quality of literacy instruction are often restricted in academic settings, even in the BiBi programs.

Similar to their typically developing, hearing, monolingual, English-speaking peers, hearing ELLs and children who are d/Dhh, including many d/Deaf ELLs, are climbing the same mountain when learning how to read and write English. They might carry extra packages (e.g., unfamiliar English vocabulary and topics), which impede or slow down their progress when compared to that of children who are typically developing in this area. Nevertheless, the bumps and glitches that they encounter along the way are similar, and with the use of different transportation tools (e.g., effective interventions accommodating their special needs), most of them can and should eventually reach the peak of proficiency, like everyone else.

REFERENCES

Adams, M. (1990). *Beginning to read: Thinking and learning about print.* Cambridge, MA: MIT Press.

Akamatsu, N. (1999). The effects of first language orthographic features on word recognition processing in English as a second language. *Reading and Writing: An Interdisciplinary Journal, 11,* 381–403.

Allen, T., Clark, M. D., del Giudice, A., Koo, D., Lieberman, A., Mayberry, R., & Miller, P. (2009). Phonology and reading: A response to Wang, Trezek, Luckner, and Paul. *American Annals of the Deaf, 154*(4), 338–345.

Aud, S., Hussar, W., Kena, G., Bianco, K., Frohlich, L., Kemp, J., Tahan, K., Mallory, K., Nachazel, T., & Hannes, G. (2011). *The condition of education 2010.* Washington, DC: National Center for Education Statistics, Institute of Education Sciences, U.S. Department of Education.

August, D., & Shanahan, T. (Eds.). (2006). *Developing literacy in second-language learners: Report of the National Literacy Panel on Language-Minority Children and Youth.* Mahwah, NJ: Erlbaum.

Bialystok, E., Majumder, S., & Martin, M. M. (2003). Developing phonological awareness: Is there a bilingual advantage? *Applied Psycholinguistics, 24,* 27–44.

Biemiller, A., & Slonim, N. (2001). Estimating root word vocabulary growth in normative and advantaged populations: Evidence for a common sequence of vocabulary acquisition. *Journal of Educational Psychology, 93,* 498–520.

Birch, B. (2007). *English L2 reading: Getting to the bottom* (2nd ed.). Mahwah, NJ: Erlbaum.

Blum, I. H., Koskinen, P. S., Tennant, N., Parker, E. M., Straub, M., & Curry, C. (1995). Using audiotaped books to extend classroom literacy instruction into the homes of second-language learners. *Journal of Reading Behavior, 27*(4), 535–563.

Carlisle, J. F., & Beeman, M. M. (2001). The effects of language of instruction on the reading and writing achievement of first-grade Hispanic children. *Scientific Studies of Reading, 4,* 331–353.

Carlo, M. S., August, D., McLaughlin, B., Snow, C. E., Dressler, C., Lippman, D. N., et al. (2004). Closing the gap: Addressing the vocabulary needs of English language learners in bilingual and mainstream classrooms. *Reading Research Quarterly, 39,* 188–215.

Chall, J. S. (1983). *Stages of reading development.* New York, NY: McGraw-Hill.

Chall, J. S. (1996). *Stages of reading development* (2nd ed.). New York, NY: McGraw-Hill.

Chamberlain, C., & Mayberry, R. I. (2000). Theorizing about the relationship between ASL and reading. In C. Chamberlain, J. Morford, & R. I. Mayberry (Eds.), *Language acquisition by eye* (pp. 221–260). Mahwah, NJ: Erlbaum.

Chamberlain, C., & Mayberry, R. I. (2008). American Sign Language syntactic and narrative comprehension in skilled and less skilled readers: Bilingual and bimodal evidence for the linguistic basis of reading. *Applied Psycholinguistics, 29,* 367–388.

Chiappe, P., Siegel, L. S., & Wade-Woolley, L. (2002). Linguistic diversity and the development of reading skills: A longitudinal study. *Scientific Studies of Reading, 6,* 369–400.

Collier, V. P. (1987). Age and rate of acquisition of second language for academic purposes. *TESOL Quarterly, 21*(4), 617–641.

Coulter, C., & Smith, M. L. (2006). English language learners in a comprehensive high school. *Bilingual Research Journal, 30*(2), 309–335.

Cummins, J. (1978). Educational implications of mother tongue maintenance in minority language groups. *Canadian Modern Language Review, 35,* 395–416.

Cummins, J. (1979). Linguistic interdependence and the educational development of bilingual children. *Review of Educational Research, 49*(2), 222–251.

Cummins, J. (1980). The crosslingual dimensions of language proficiency: Implications for bilingual education and the optimal age issue. *TESOL Quarterly, 14*(2), 175–187.

Cummins, J. (1981). The role of primary language development in promoting educational success for language minority students. In *Schooling and language minority students: A theoretical framework* (pp. 3–49). Los Angeles, CA: Education, Dissemination, and Assessment Center, California State University.

Cummins, J. (1984). *Bilingual and special education: Issues in assessment and pedagogy.* San Diego, CA: College Hill Press.

Cummins, J. (2000). *Language, power, and pedagogy: Bilingual children in the crossfire.* Clevedon, UK: Multilingual Matters.

Cummins, J. (2009). Literacy and English-language learners: A shifting landscape for students, teachers, researchers, and policy makers. *Educational Researcher, 38*(5), 382–394.

Denton, C. A., Anthony, J. L., Parker, R., & Hasbrouck, J. (2004). Effects of two tutoring programs on the English reading development of Spanish–English bilingual students. *Elementary School Journal, 104*(4), 289–305.

Duran, L. K., Roseth C. J., & Hoffman, P. (2010). An experimental study comparing English-only and transitional bilingual education on Spanish-speaking preschoolers' early literacy development. *Early Childhood Research Quarterly, 25,* 207–217.

Elley, W. B., & Mangubhai, F. (1983). The impact of reading on second language learning. *Reading Research Quarterly, 19*(1), 53–67.

Evans, C. J. (2004). Literacy development in deaf students: Case studies in bilingual teaching and learning. *American Annals of the Deaf, 149*(1), 17–27.

Farver, J. M., Lonigan, C. J., & Eppe, S. (2009). Effective early literacy skill development for young Spanish-speaking English language learners: An experimental study of two methods. *Child Development, 80*(3), 703–719.

Flexer, C. (1994). *Facilitating hearing and listening in young children.* San Diego, CA: Singular.

Gallaudet Research Institute. (2011). *Regional and national summary report of data from the 2009–10 annual survey of deaf and hard of hearing children and youth.* Washington, DC: GRI, Gallaudet University.

Garcia, G. E. (1991). Factors influencing the English reading test performance of Spanish-speaking Hispanic children. *Reading Research Quarterly, 26,* 371–392.

Garcia, G. E. (2000). Bilingual children's reading. In M. L. Kamil, P. B. Mosenthal, P. D. Pearson, & R. Barr (Eds.), *Handbook of reading research: Vol. 3* (pp. 813–834). Mahwah, NJ: Erlbaum.

Garcia, G. E. (2003). The reading comprehension development and instruction of English-language learners. In C. E. Snow & A. Sweet (Eds.), *Rethinking reading comprehension* (pp. 30–50). New York, NY: Guilford.

Gertz, G. (2008). Dysconscious audism: A theoretical proposition. In H.-D. Bauman (Ed.), *Open your eyes: Deaf studies talking* (pp. 219–234). Minneapolis, MN: University of Minnesota Press.

Geva, E., & Zadeh, Z. Y. (2006). Reading efficiency in native English-speaking and English-as-a-second language children: The role of oral proficiency and underlying cognitive–linguistic process. *Scientific Studies of Reading, 10*(1), 31–57.

Gottardo, A. (2002). The relationship between language and reading skills in bilingual Spanish–English speakers. *Topics in Language Disorders, 22*(5), 46–70.

Grabe, W. (2009). *Reading in a second language: Moving from theory to practice.* Cambridge, UK: Cambridge University Press.

Gunn, B., Biglan, A., Smolkowski, K., & Ary, D. (2000). The efficacy of supplemental instruction in decoding skills for Hispanic and non-Hispanic students in early elementary school. *Journal of Special Education, 34*(2), 90–103.

Gunn, B., Smolkowski, K., Biglan, A., & Black, C. (2002). Supplemental instruction in decoding skills for Hispanic and non-Hispanic students in early elementary school—A follow-up. *Journal of Special Education, 36*(2), 69–79.

Haager, D., & Windmueller, M. P. (2001). Early reading intervention for English language learners at risk for learning disabilities: Student and teacher outcomes in an urban school. *Learning Disability Quarterly, 24,* 235–250.

Hauser, P. C., O'Hearn, A., McKee, M., Steider, A., & Thew, D. (2010). Deaf epistemology: Deafhood and deafness. *American Annals of the Deaf, 154*(5), 486–492.

Hermans, D., Knoors, H., Ormel, E., & Verhoeven, L. (2008). The relationship between the reading and signing skills of deaf children in bilingual education programs. *Journal of Deaf Studies and Deaf Education, 13*(4), 518–530.

Hermans, D., Ormel, E., & Knoors, H. (2010). On the relation between the signing and reading skills of deaf bilinguals. *International Journal of Bilingual Education and Bilingualism, 13*(2), 187–199.

Hoffmeister, R. (2000). A piece of the puzzle: ASL and reading comprehension in deaf children. In C. Chamberlain, J. Monford, & R. Mayberry (Eds.), *Language acquisition by eye* (pp. 143–164). Mahwah, NJ: Erlbaum.

Holm, A., & Dodd, B. (1996). The effect of first written language on the acquisition of English literacy. *Cognition, 59*, 119–147.

Humphries, T. (2008). Talking culture and culture talking. In H.-D. Bauman (Ed.), *Open your eyes: Deaf studies talking* (pp. 35–41). Minneapolis, MN: University of Minnesota Press.

Jackson, N. E., Chen, H., Goldsberry, L., Kim, A., & Vanderwerff, C. (1999). Effects of variations in orthographic information on Asian and American readers' English text reading. *Reading and Writing: An Interdisciplinary Journal, 11*, 345–379.

Jimenez, R. T., Garcia, G. E., & Pearson, P. D. (1996). The reading strategies of bilingual Latina/o students who are successful English readers: Opportunities and obstacles. *Reading Research Quarterly, 31*, 90–112.

Jimenez, R. T., & Teague, B. L. (2009). Language, literacy, and content: Adolescent English language learners. In L. M. Morrow, R. Rueda, & D. Lapp (Eds.), *Handbook of research on literacy and diversity* (pp. 114–134). New York, NY: Guilford Press.

Kamps, D., Abbott, M., Greenwood, C., Arreaga-Mayer, C., Wills, H., Longstaff, J., Culpepper, M., & Walton, C. (2007). Use of evidence-based, small-group reading instruction for English language learners in elementary grades: Secondary-tier intervention. *Learning Disability Quarterly, 30*, 153–168.

Kieffer, M. J. (2008). Catching up or falling behind? Initial English proficiency, concentrated poverty, and the reading growth of language minority learners in the United States. *Journal of Educational Psychology, 100*, 851–868.

Kieffer, M. J. (2011). Converging trajectories: Reading growth in language minority learners and their classmates, kindergarten to grade 8. *American Educational Research Journal, 48*(5), 1187–1225.

Kieffer, M. J., & Lesaux, N. K. (2008). The role of morphology in the reading comprehension of Spanish-speaking English language learners. *Reading and Writing: An Interdisciplinary Journal, 21*, 783–804.

Koda, K. (1999). Development of L2 intraword orthographic sensitivity and decoding skills. *Modern Language Journal, 83*, 51–64.

Koda, K. (2000). Cross-linguistic variations in L2 morphological awareness. *Applied Psycholinguistics, 21*, 297–320.

Lang, H., Hupper, M., Monte, D., Brown, S., Babb, I., & Scheifele, P. (2007). A study of technical signs in science: Implications for lexical database development. *Journal of Deaf Studies and Deaf Education, 12*(I), 65–79.

LaSasso, C., & Lollis, J. (2003). Survey of residential and day schools for deaf students in the United States that identify themselves as bilingual–bicultural programs. *Journal of Deaf Studies and Deaf Education, 8*(I), 79–91.

Leafstedt, J. M., Richards C. R., & Gerber, M. M. (2004). Effectiveness of explicit phonological-awareness instruction for at-risk English learners. *Learning Disabilities Research and Practice, 19*(4), 252–261.

Lesaux, N. K., Crosson, A., Kieffer, M. J., & Pierce, M. (2010). Uneven profiles: Language minority learners' word reading, vocabulary, and reading comprehension skills. *Journal of Applied Developmental Psychology, 31*, 475–483.

Lesaux, N. K., & Kieffer, M. J. (2010). Exploring sources of reading comprehension difficulties among language minority learners and their classmates in early adolescence. *American Educational Research Journal, 47*(3), 596–632.

Lesaux, N. K., Koda, K., Siegel, L. S., & Shanahan, T. (2006). Development of literacy in language-minority students. In D. August & T. Shanahan (Eds.), *Developing literacy in second-language learners: Report of the National Literacy Panel on Language-Minority Children and Youth* (pp. 75–122). Mahwah, NJ: Erlbaum.

Lesaux, N. K., & Siegel, L. S. (2003). The development of reading in children who speak English as a second language. *Developmental Psychology, 39*(6), 1005–1019.

Leung, C. B., Silverman, R., Nandakumar, R., Qian, X., & Hines, S. (2011). A comparison of difficulty levels of vocabulary in first grade basal readers for preschool dual language learners and monolingual English learners. *American Educational Research Journal, 48*(2), 421–461.

Linan-Thompson, S., Vaughn, S., Hickman-Davis, P., & Kouzekanani, K. (2003). Effectiveness of supplemental reading instruction of English language learners with reading difficulties. *Elementary School Journal, 103*(3), 221–238.

Lipka, O., & Siegel, L. S. (2007). The development of reading skills in children with English as a second language. *Scientific Studies of Reading, 11*(2), 105–131.

Lipka, O., Siegel, L. S., & Vukovic, R. (2005). The literacy skills of English language learners in Canada. *Learning Disabilities Research and Practice, 20*(1), 39–49.

Lovett, M. W., Palma, M. D., Frijters, J., Steinbach, K., Temple, M., Benson, N., & Lacerenza, L. (2008). Interventions for reading difficulties: A comparison of response to intervention by ELL and EFL struggling readers. *Journal of Learning Disabilities, 41*(4), 333–352.

Mancilla-Martinez, J., Kieffer, M. J., Biancarosa, G., Christodoulou, J., & Snow, C. E. (2011). Investigating English reading comprehension growth in adolescent language minority learners: Some insights from the simple view. *Reading and Writing: An Interdisciplinary Journal, 24,* 339–354.

Mancilla-Martinez, J., & Lesaux, N. K. (2010). Predictors of reading comprehension for struggling readers: The case of Spanish-speaking language minority learners. *Journal of Educational Psychology, 102,* 701–711.

Mancilla-Martinez, J., & Lesaux, N. K. (2011). The gap between Spanish speakers' word reading and word knowledge: A longitudinal study. *Child Development, 82*(5), 1544–1560.

Manis, F., Lindsey, K., & Bailey, A. (2004). Development of reading in grades K-2 in Spanish-speaking English-language learners. *Learning Disabilities Research and Practice, 19*(4), 214–224.

Mann, W. (2007). German deaf children's understanding of referential distinction in written German and German Sign Language. *Educational and Child Psychology, 24*(4), 59–76.

Mayberry, R. I., del Giudice, A. A., & Lieberman, A. M. (2011). Reading achievement in relation to phonological coding and awareness in deaf readers: A meta-analysis. *Journal of Deaf Studies and Deaf Education, 16*(2), 164–188.

Mayer, C. (2009). Issues in second language literacy education with learners who are deaf. *International Journal of Bilingualism and Bilingual Education, 12*(3), 325–334.

Mayer, C., & Akamatsu, C. T. (2003). Bilingualism and literacy. In M. Marschark & P. Spencer (Eds.), *Oxford handbook of deaf studies, language, and education* (Vol. 1, pp. 136–147). New York, NY: Oxford University Press.

Mayer, C., & Akamatsu, C. T. (2011). Bilingualism and literacy. In M. Marschark & P. Spencer (Eds.), *Oxford handbook of deaf studies, language, and education* (2nd ed., Vol. 1, Part 2, pp. 144–157). New York, NY: Oxford University Press.

Mayer, C., & Leigh, G. (2010). The changing context for sign bilingual education programs: Issues in language and the development of literacy. *International Journal of Bilingual Education and Bilingualism, 13*(2), 175–186.

Mayer, C., & Wells, G. (1996). Can the linguistic interdependence theory support a bilingual–bicultural model of literacy education for deaf students? *Journal of Deaf Studies and Deaf Education, 1*(2), 93–107.

Menendez, B. (2010). Cross-modal bilingualism: Language contact as evidence of linguistic transfer in sign bilingual education. *International Journal of Bilingual Education and Bilingualism, 13*(2), 201–223.

McGuinness, D. (2004). *Early reading instruction: What science really tells us about how to teach reading.* Cambridge, MA: MIT Press.

McGuinness, D. (2005). *Language development and learning to read: The scientific study of how language development affects reading skill.* Cambridge, MA: MIT Press.

Mitchell, R. E., & Karchmer, M. A. (2004). Chasing the mythical 10%: Parental hearing status of deaf and hard of hearing students in the United States. *Sign Language Studies, 4,* 138–163.

Moats, L. M. (2001). *Speech to print: Language essentials for teachers.* Baltimore, MD: Paul H. Brookes.

Moores, D. (2008). Research on bi–bi instruction. *American Annals of the Deaf, 153*(1), 3–4.

Moores, D., & Sweet, C. (1990). Relationships of English grammar and communicative fluency in reading in deaf adolescents. *Exceptionality, 1,* 97–106.

Nakamoto, J., Lindsey, K. A., & Manis, F. R. (2007). A longitudinal analysis of English language learners' word decoding and reading comprehension. *Reading and Writing: An Interdisciplinary Journal, 20,* 691–719.

National Clearinghouse for English Language Acquisition. (2009). *The growing number of English learner students.* Washington, DC: NCELA.

National Early Literacy Panel. (2008). *Developing early literacy: Report of the National Early Literacy Panel.* Washington, DC: National Institute for Literacy. Retrieved from http://www.nifl.gov/earlychildhood/NELP/NELPreport.html

National Reading Panel. (2000). *Report of the National Reading Panel: Teaching children to read— An evidence-based assessment of the scientific research literature on reading and its implications for reading instruction.* Jessup, MD: National Institute for Literacy at EDPubs.

Niederberger, N. (2008). Does the knowledge of a natural sign language facilitate Deaf children's learning to read and write? Insights from French Sign Language and written French data. In C. Plaza-Pust & E. Morales-Lopez (Eds.), *Sign bilingualism: Language development, interaction, and maintenance in sign language contact situations* (pp. 29–50). Amsterdam, the Netherlands: John Benjamins.

Office for Civil Rights. (2012). *Developing programs for English language learners: Glossary.* Retrieved January 9, 2012 from http://www2.ed.gov/about/offices/list/ocr/ell/glossary.html

Padden, C., & Ramsey, C. (2000). American Sign Language and reading ability in deaf children. In C. Chamberlain, J. Morford, & R. Mayberry (Eds.), *Language acquisition by eye* (pp. 165–189). Mahwah, NJ: Erlbaum.

Paul, P., & Wang, Y. (2012). *Literate thought: Understanding comprehension and literacy.* Sudbury, MA: Jones & Bartlett.

Paul, P., Wang, Y., Trezek, B., & Luckner, J. (2009). Phonology is necessary, but not sufficient: A rejoinder. *American Annals of the Deaf, 154*(4), 346–356.

Pearson, B. Z., & Fernandez, S. C. (1994). Patterns of interaction in the lexical growth in two languages of bilingual infants and toddlers. *Language Learning, 44*(4), 617–653.

Portes, P., & Salas, S. (2009). Poverty and its relation to development and literacy. In L. M. Morrow, R. Rueda, & D. Lapp (Eds.), *Handbook of research on literacy and diversity* (pp. 97–113). New York, NY: Guilford Press.

Proctor, C. P., August, D., Carlo, M. S., & Snow, C. E. (2006). The intriguing role of Spanish language vocabulary knowledge in predicting English reading comprehension. *Journal of Educational Psychology, 98*(1), 159–169.

Proctor, C. P., Carlo, M., August, D., & Snow, C. E. (2005). Native Spanish-speaking children reading in English: Toward a model of comprehension. *Journal of Educational Psychology, 97,* 246–256.

Proctor, C. P., & Silverman, R. D. (2011). Confounds in assessing the associations between biliteracy and English language proficiency. *Educational Researcher, 40*(2), 62–64.

Ramirez, J. D., Yuen, S. D., & Ramey, D. R. (1991). *Executive summary: Final report—Longitudinal study of structured English immersion strategy, early-exit and late-exit transitional bilingual education programs for language minority children.* San Mateo, CA: Aguirre.

Reese, L., Garnier, H., Gallimore, R., & Goldenberg, C. (2000). Longitudinal analysis of the antecedents of emergent Spanish literacy and middle-school English reading achievement of Spanish-speaking students. *American Educational Research Journal, 37*, 633–662.

Roessingh, H. (2011). Family treasures: A dual-language book project for negotiating language, literacy, culture, and identity. *Canadian Modern Language Review, 67*(1), 123–148.

Saenz, L. M., Fuchs, L. S., & Fuchs, D. (2005). Peer-assisted learning strategies for English language learners with learning disabilities. *Exceptional Children, 71*(3), 231–247.

Salvin, R. E., & Cheung, A. (2005). A synthesis of research on language of reading instruction for English language learners. *Review of Educational Research, 75*, 247–284.

Short, D., & Fitzsimmons, S. (2007). *Double the work: Challenges and solutions to acquiring language and academic literacy for adolescent English language learners—A report to Carnegie Corporation of New York.* Washington, DC: Alliance for Excellent Education.

Silverman, R. D. (2007). Vocabulary development of English-language and English-only learners in kindergarten. *Elementary School Journal, 107*, 365–384.

Singleton, J. L., Morgan, D., DiGello, E., Wiles, J., & Rivers, R. (2004). Vocabulary use by low, moderate, and high ASL-proficient writers compared to hearing ESL and monolingual speakers. *Journal of Deaf Studies and Deaf Education, 9*(1), 86–103.

Solomon, G., & Schrum, L. (2007). *Web 2.0: New tools, new schools.* Eugene, OR: International Society for Technology in Education.

Spencer, P. E., & Marschark, M. (2010). *Evidence-based practice in educating deaf and hard-of-hearing students.* New York, NY: Oxford University Press.

Stewart, D. (2006). Instructional and practical communication: ASL and English-based signing in the classroom. In D. Moores & D. Martin (Eds.), *Deaf learners: Developments in curriculum and instruction* (pp. 207–220). Washington, DC: Gallaudet University Press.

Stokoe, W., Casterline, D., & Croneberg, C. (1965). *A dictionary of American Sign Language on linguistic principles.* Washington, DC: Gallaudet College Press.

Strong, M. (1995). A review of bilingual–bicultural programs for deaf children in North America. *American Annals of the Deaf, 140*(2), 84–94.

Strong, M., & Prinz, P. M. (1997). A study of the relationship between ASL and English literacy. *Journal of Deaf Studies and Deaf Education, 2*(1), 37–46.

Swanson, H. L., Rosston, K., Gerber, M., & Solari, E. (2008). Influence of oral language and phonological awareness on children's bilingual reading. *Journal of School Psychology, 46*, 413–429.

Taffe, S. W., Blachowicz, C. L. Z., & Fisher, P. J. (2009). Vocabulary instruction for diverse students. In L. M. Morrow, R. Rueda, & D. Lapp (Eds.), *Handbook of research on literacy and diversity* (pp. 320–336). New York, NY: Guilford Press.

Tam, K. Y., Heward, W. L., & Heng, M. A. (2006). A reading instruction intervention program for English-language learners who are struggling readers. *Journal of Special Education, 40*(2), 79–93.

Trezek, B., Wang, Y., & Paul, P. (2010). *Reading and deafness: Theory, research and practice.* Clifton Park, NY: Cengage Learning.

Vaughn, S., Mathes, P., Linan-Thompson, S., Cirino, P., Carlson, C., Pollard-Durodola, S., Cardenas-Hagan, E., & Francis, D. (2006). Effectiveness of an English intervention for first-grade English language learners at risk for reading problems. *Elementary School Journal, 107*(2), 153–180.

Wang, M., & Koda, K. (2007). Commonalities and differences in word identification skills among learners of English as a second language. *Language Learning, 57*(1), 201–222.

Wang, Y. (2012). Educators without borders: A metaparadigm for literacy instruction in bilingual–bicultural education. In P. Paul & D. Moores (Eds.), *Deaf epistemologies: Multiple perspectives on the acquisition of knowledge* (pp. 199–217). Washington, DC: Gallaudet University Press.

Wang, Y., & Engler, K. (2010). Early intervention. In P. Paul & G. Whitelaw, *Hearing and deafness* (pp. 241–268). Sudbury, MA: Jones & Bartlett.

Wang, Y., Trezek, B., Luckner, J., & Paul, P. (2008). The role of phonology and phonological-related skills in reading instruction for students who are deaf or hard of hearing. *American Annals of the Deaf, 153*(4), 396–407.

White, K. R. (2008). Newborn hearing screening. In J. Madell & C. Flexer (Eds.), *Pediatric audiology diagnosis, technology, and management* (pp. 31–41). New York, NY: Thieme.

Zimmerman, C. (1997). Do reading and interactive vocabulary instruction make a difference? An empirical study. *TESOL Quarterly, 31*(1), 121–140.

4

English Literacy Development

English language development is our first and by far our most important intellectual accomplishment. *English literacy development* is our second. The development of English literacy is a lifelong intellectual process of gaining meaning from written language. The key to literacy in English is learning to read, a complex process that begins with through-the-air language proficiency and culminates in deep understanding and critical interpretation of written text. Learning to read and the development of reading (and writing) involves a range of complex language components including phonology, orthography, semantics, syntax, and morphology, all of which provide an essential foundation for reading fluency and comprehension. The acquisition and development of these components of language allows us to achieve English literacy.

In this chapter, we discuss current empirical research on two major constructs, *emergent literacy*, where the roots of English literacy are first apparent, and *conventional literacy*, the continuation of a lifelong process of developing competence in the components of English. For each construct, we review current research on English literacy in students who are hearing (i.e., typical literacy learners) and students who are d/Deaf and hard of hearing (d/Dhh). We also describe the similarities and differences between English literacy in these two groups of learners and assert that the basic tenets of the qualitative similarity hypothesis (QSH) are viable. The chapter concludes with a few implications for instruction (expanded in Chapter 6) and directions for further research.

EMERGENT LITERACY

Emergent literacy is the understanding that English literacy development begins long before children commence formal schooling. It is a widely accepted theoretical conceptualization of young children's initial encounters with print and their early reading and writing development. There is now consensus among educators, scholars, and researchers that children engage in significant cognitive and social work in literacy during the preschool years, if provided with conceptually rich and meaningful experiences with print. High-quality instructional support from caretakers and early childhood educators can make a critical contribution to young children's emergent literacy learning. Most researchers agree that supporting literacy learning in the preschool years plays a critical role in children's long-term English literacy achievement. In fact, scholars have accumulated significant evidence of enduring stability in children's literacy-related abilities from preschool through high school.

Emergent literacy has been investigated from a number of theoretical perspectives (e.g., cognitive, sociocultural, ecological, critical) and diverse disciplines (e.g., psychology, linguistics, education, child development) that explicate the nature of emergent literacy learning, underscore its complexity, and provide important insights on how caretakers and early childhood educators can nurture its growth and development. Several strands of emergent literacy research have been examined, including emergent reading (e.g., Elster, 1994; Segel-Drori, Korat, Shamir, & Klein, 2010; Sulzby, 1985), emergent writing (e.g., Clay, 1975; Dyson, 2010; Saracho, 1990), home and school influences (e.g., Neumann, Hood, & Neuman, 2009; Smith & Dickinson, 1994; Sylva, Melhuish, Sammons, Siraj-Blatchford, & Taggart, 2010), instructional practices (e.g., Connor, Morrison, & Slominski, 2006; Morrow & Gambrell, 2001), and emergent literacy development among diverse populations (e.g. Araujo, 2002; Travers, Higgins, Pierce, Boone, Miller, & Tandy, 2011). In addition, several core theoretical constructs have been investigated extensively, including, in particular, spoken language, phonological awareness, and alphabetic knowledge and skills. Researchers believe that these precursor abilities serve as cognitive and linguistic building blocks that shape later English literacy abilities.

Spoken Language

A substantial body of research among children who have typical hearing has documented the importance of spoken (i.e., through-the-air) language to emergent literacy (e.g., Dyson, 1983; Heath, 1983; Snow, 1983; Wells, 1981) as well as to later reading proficiency (e.g., Senechal, Ouellette, & Rodney, 2006; Wells, 1986). Early experience with spoken language, particularly the language of print, promotes growth in vocabulary (Farkas & Beron, 2004; Hart & Risley, 1995). Children who have more experiences with rich spoken language are provided more practice in the skills that are directly associated with English word learning (Beck & McKeown, 2007). Exposure to varied vocabulary in the context of the spoken language in use gives way to a richer stock of lexical, morphological, and syntactic cues to support fluency in understanding (Fernald & Weisleder, 2011). In general, children who have larger English speaking vocabularies and greater understanding of English spoken language (i.e., listening vocabularies) attain higher achievement in English reading.

The role of shared storybook reading in supporting young children's spoken language acquisition and early literacy development has been widely investigated for decades. Book sharing provides for rich and extended spoken language input from parents as well as opportunities for children's contributions to become increasingly more sophisticated, especially when there is repeated exposure to the same book. For example, through their investigations of parent–child storybook readings, Snow and

Ninio (1986) illustrated the ways in which repeated shared readings contributed both to the child's early literacy and to spoken language development through dialogic interactions having a structured turn-taking sequence. Whitehurst and colleagues were among the first researchers to demonstrate experimentally the effectiveness of dialogic shared reading in supporting children's growth in English vocabulary and syntax (Whitehurst, Arnold, et al., 1994; Whitehurst, Falco, et al., 1988; Whitehurst & Lonigan, 1998). More recently, a number of meta-analyses of this significant body of work have demonstrated strong links between storybook reading and early literacy (Bus, van Ijzendoorn, & Pellegrini, 1995), spoken language outcomes (Mol, Bus, de Jong, & Smeets, 2008; National Early Literacy Panel [NELP], 2008) including vocabulary development (Marulis & Neuman, 2010) and print knowledge (NELP, 2008). The research also indicates that parent involvement in shared reading activities has a positive impact on children's reading acquisition (Senechal & Young, 2008). Moreover, individual studies indicate that shared storybook reading may also contribute to later reading, spelling, and writing development of English (e.g., Dickinson & McCabe, 2001; Justice & Ezell, 2002). Current research continues to examine the efficacy of shared storybook reading in supporting children's spoken language and early literacy outcomes, particularly for preschool children at risk for reading difficulties (e.g., Goldfeld et al., 2011; Lefebvre, Trudeau, & Sutton, 2011).

Phonological Awareness

The role of phonological awareness in early English reading also has been well documented among children who have typical hearing (e.g., Ehri et al., 2001). Phonological awareness is a language- and code-related skill that facilitates the mapping of phonemes onto graphemes. Children who can detect and manipulate phonemes, rhymes, and syllables learn to read more quickly, whereas children who lack phonological sensitivity have difficulty learning to read (Wagner et al., 1997). In fact, poor phonological processing skills appear to be the core deficit in English reading disability (National Reading Panel, 2000; Scarborough, 1998).

The development of phonological processing skills is believed to be related to spoken language acquisition. Phonological processing requires young children to make implicit comparisons between similar-sounding words in their mental lexicons and then restructure that lexicon so that their phonological representations become increasingly segmented and distinct in terms of phonetic features (Metsala & Walley, 1998). With continued vocabulary growth, the lexicon becomes crowded and needs to be reorganized so that more segmental representations can emerge (Metsala, 2011). In addition to its links with early spoken language, phonological awareness is also strongly associated with later English word-reading skills (Stanovich, 2000) and predicts later English reading achievement (Brunswick, Martin, & Rippon, 2012; Lonigan et al., 2009; for a review, see the National Early Literacy Panel, 2008). Given the importance of phonological processing to both early literacy and later reading success, a number of approaches to phonological awareness training have been investigated, including metalinguistic games and activities (e.g., Gonzalez & Nelson, 2003; Treutlein, Zöller, Roos, & Schöler, 2008), the use of invented spelling (e.g., Craig, 2006), and

Web-based computer interventions (e.g., Segers & Verhoeven, 2005; van der Kooy-Hofland, Kegel, & Bus, 2011).

Additionally, there is also growing evidence for the importance of phonological naming—the ability to name a set of items (often numerals, colors, pictures) as quickly as possible. Phonological naming skill appears to reflect a child's ability to retrieve phonological information associated with letters and words, which is crucial to the development of fluent, automatic word identification skills. Naming speed, or speed of lexical access (also known as rapid automatized naming [RAN]), has been causally linked to English reading development as well as reading disability (van den Bos, Zijlstra, & lutje Spelberg, 2002; Wolf et al., 2000).

Alphabetic Knowledge

Alphabetic knowledge—the knowledge of letter forms, letter names, and the sounds those letters represent—is also of primary importance to early literacy and the development of reading and writing skills. Young children's alphabetic knowledge is a strong predictor of later English reading and spelling ability (Evans, Bell, Shaw, Moretti, & Page, 2006; Parilla, Kirby, & McQuarrie, 2004; Schatschneider, Flectcher, Francis, Carolson, & Forman, 2004). Preschool and kindergarten children who have limited knowledge of letter names and letter sounds are more likely to have difficulty learning to read (Gallagher, Frith, & Snowling, 2000; Torppa, Poikkeus, Laakso, Eklund, & Lyytinen, 2006) and tend to fall further behind their peers in reading and spelling skills, reading fluency and comprehension, and vocabulary development (Torgesen, 2002). Alphabetic knowledge is related to children's acquisition of the alphabetic principle, the understanding that sounds of the spoken language are represented by letters of the alphabet. Acquisition of the alphabetic principle is crucial to children's learning to read and write. Facilitating children's development of alphabetic knowledge and acquisition of the alphabetic principle has become a primary feature of instruction and intervention in early childhood programs.

The impact of instructional efforts to support the development of alphabetic knowledge has been examined in two recent meta-analyses. In the first, a synthesis of the results of 24 code-focused intervention studies in preschool and kindergarten, NELP (2008) reported favorable alphabetic knowledge outcomes. Studies of phonological awareness training, phonological awareness and alphabet knowledge training, and phonological and phonics training each demonstrated small to modest effects on alphabetic knowledge. In the second meta-analysis, Piasta and Wagner (2010) synthesized more than 60 studies and reported effects for five distinct alphabet outcomes (letter name knowledge, letter sound knowledge, letter name fluency, letter sound fluency, letter writing). In the studies providing instruction in several early literacy domains (including alphabetic knowledge), instruction had a significant impact on every alphabet outcome except letter name fluency, lending support to conceptualizations of emergent literacy skills as reciprocal and mutually reinforcing (Lonigan, Burgess, & Anthony, 2000; National Reading Panel [NRP], 2000). In studies providing only alphabet instruction, however, only letter sound knowledge showed a significant overall effect. Moreover, results provided minimal evidence for transfer of alphabet instruction to early phonological, reading, or spelling skills. These findings conflicted with previous meta-analytic work, which demonstrated strong relationships among early literacy skills (e.g., NELP, 2008; NRP, 2000; see also Bus & van IJzendoorn, 1999).

Recent research has investigated the use of shared storybook reading to promote English alphabetic knowledge. Using an instructional technique called *print referencing*, parents and early childhood educators drew children's attention to print during shared storybook readings by pointing to and then making comments and asking questions about print within the text. Print referencing occurred alongside other facilitative practices that support spoken language and early literacy learning among young children who have typical hearing. Short-term studies indicated that children experienced significant gains on measures of alphabetic knowledge when adults utilized print references (Justice & Piasta, 2011; Lovelace & Stewart, 2007). Longitudinal results demonstrated that the use of print referencing had significant impacts on children's reading, spelling, and comprehension for two years after the intervention, suggesting a causal relation between early print knowledge and later literacy skills (Piasta, Justice, McGinty, & Kaderavek, 2012).

Early Intervention

As researchers have underscored the importance of emergent literacy for early conventional literacy and future literacy achievement, research on innovative approaches to early literacy intervention and, most recently, targeted professional development of early childhood educators has burgeoned. For example, *Reach Out and Read* is an evidence-based pediatric approach to supporting emergent literacy among low-income families. A primary goal of the intervention is to help ameliorate the achievement gap between children growing up in poverty and their middle-class peers. Physicians trained in promoting early literacy give new, culturally relevant picture books to children at every checkup from six months to five years of age and offer their parents specific guidance about reading aloud, often modeling specific read-aloud techniques. Numerous studies demonstrate the effectiveness of the intervention for supporting children's receptive and expressive language and vocabulary development and increasing the frequency of reading aloud in the home (e.g., Mendelsohn, et al., 2001; Needlman, Toker, Dreyer, Klass, & Mendelsohn, 2005; Silverstein, Iverson, & Lorzano, 2002; Zuckerman, 2009).

The goal of high-quality early literacy intervention is to draw on current understandings of the cognitive and linguistic dimensions of literacy, as well as understandings of the sociocultural context, to provide young children the emotional, instructional, and environmental supports necessary to develop the essential knowledge, skills, and dispositions that are critical for early conventional literacy and later literacy success. To support the development and implementation of these types of early literacy interventions, early childhood educators engage in ongoing professional development that supports their use of evidence-based instructional practices within their immediate classroom contexts (Sigel, 2006). Preliminary research on intensive professional development for early childhood educators indicates that coaching-based interventions, including those that are delivered remotely through various forms of technology, hold promise for improving literacy teaching practices in the preschool program as well as supporting the spoken language and early literacy outcomes of young children who are at risk for reading difficulty (Hsieh, Hemmeter, McCollum, & Ostrosky, 2009; Powell & Diamond, 2011; Powell, Diamond, Burchinal, & Koehler, 2010; Wasik & Hindman, 2011).

EMERGENT LITERACY IN d/DEAF AND HARD OF HEARING CHILDREN

While the emergent literacy of children with typical hearing has been explicated comprehensibly, there is yet no coherent framework for emergent literacy in young children who are d/Dhh. Considerably less research attention has been focused on d/Dhh children's emergent literacy, and scholars have yet to identify clearly the core theoretical constructs that predict early literacy and shape later literacy success. Pioneering research was guided by emergent literacy research more generally, as scholars sought to determine if *emergent literacy*, as a theoretical construct, was viable for conceptualizing d/Dhh children's initial encounters with reading and writing and their nascent understandings about print. Given the primacy of spoken language in the emergent literacy of young hearing children, researchers wondered, in particular, whether the lack of a strong through-the-air language, particularly English, would prevent young d/Dhh children from learning about the nature of written language and participating in literacy events in the preschool years in ways that were similar (i.e., quantitatively and qualitatively) to those of their hearing peers (see, e.g., Rottenberg & Searfoss, 1992; Williams, 1994). Interestingly, these initial studies indicated that the children's through-the-air language delay was not an issue in their emergent literacy; the children's emergent reading and writing knowledge and behaviors were similar to that of children with typical hearing (Conway, 1985; Ewoldt, 1985; Maxwell, 1984; Ruiz, 1995, 1996; Rottenberg & Searfoss, 1992; Williams, 1994, 1999; see Williams, 2004, for a review).

This early evidence led scholars to predict similar literacy learning trajectories, and researchers began to investigate instructional approaches that had proven effective in supporting the emergent literacy learning of young hearing children. In particular, researchers examined the impact of shared storybook reading on d/Dhh children's word recognition skills (Andrews, 1988; Andrews & Mason, 1986), engagement with, interest in, and responses to storybooks read (Gillespie &Twardosz, 1997; Rowe & Allen, 1995; Williams & McLean, 1997), and teachers' techniques for shared reading events (Rowe & Allen, 1995; Williams & McLean, 1997). Researchers also investigated young d/Dhh children's emergent writing in the context of open-ended composing periods in their preschool classrooms. These studies examined the children's emerging concepts about print (Ewoldt, 1985; Andrews & Gonzales, 1991), purposes for which children used written language (Conway, 1985), and the role of sign language in supporting d/Dhh children's emergent writing (Williams, 1999). Again, both the storybook reading and the writing research suggested that these children's emergent literacy was similar to that of hearing children as documented in the general literature on emergent literacy.

Over time, however, a quantitative delay in most d/Dhh children's literacy development became clear. In the early phases of emergent literacy, that is, when children learn to distinguish between drawing and writing, come to understand that the print (not the pictures) carries the message, and acquire fundamental concepts about print, most d/Dhh children's literacy trajectories were both qualitatively and quantitatively similar to those of their hearing peers. However, at the point in development when literacy learning required an understanding of the alphabetic principle and an ability to use letter–sound relationships to encode language—a developmental milestone that is crucial to the movement from emergent to early conventional literacy—the trajectories of hearing and d/Dhh children began to diverge (Allman, 2002; Mayer, 2007). Apparently, the d/Dhh children's lack of phonological processing skills and an overall unfamiliarity with the lexicon and syntax of English prevented them from moving into early conventional literacy. These findings led a number of researchers to assert that, like children with typical hearing, d/Dhh children must develop proficiency in the phonology, vocabulary, and syntax of the English language if they are to acquire conventional reading and writing abilities (e.g., LaSasso, Crain, & Leybaert, 2010; Mayer, 2007; Paul, 2009; Trezek, Wang, & Paul, 2011).

These assertions came in the wake of two significant advances in the field: universal newborn hearing screening (now early hearing detection and intervention [EHDI]), which allows earlier identification of children with hearing loss and thus earlier intervention (Leigh, 2008; Mayer & Leigh, 2010), and progress in amplification technologies, especially cochlear implants, which allow many d/Dhh children considerably improved access to the speech spectrum (Archbold, 2010). As a consequence of earlier intervention and better access to spoken language, there are increased expectations that many d/Dhh children will develop age-appropriate literacy outcomes (DesJardin, Ambrose, & Eisenberg, 2009; Marschark, Rhoten, & Fabich, 2007; Spencer & Oleson, 2008; see also, Chapter 2). Within this context, researchers are now seeking to document through-the-air language development and the emergent literacy learning of d/Dhh children, particularly those who benefit from these technological advances, and to determine the precise ways in which their literacy learning trajectories are similar to and different from those of their hearing peers (e.g., Ruggirello & Mayer, 2010; Spencer, Barker, & Tomblin, 2003; Watson, 2002, 2009). Doing so may lead to identification of the core theoretical constructs that predict early literacy and shape later literacy success in this new generation of d/Dhh children.

A Closer Look

Current emergent literacy research with children who are d/Dhh now examines the ways in which these children's knowledge and skills compares to those of their hearing peers with respect to the core theoretical constructs of emergent literacy, as described in the general research literature. For example, Colin, Magnan, Ecalle, and Leybaert (2007) wanted to know whether deaf children's phonological skills in kindergarten would predict word recognition in first grade, as is the case for hearing children. A group of 21 deaf children and 21 hearing peers participated in the study. The deaf children had severe-to-profound hearing losses and wore hearing aids; eight of the children had cochlear implants. The researchers assessed the 6-year-old deaf and hearing children on two phonological tasks, rhyme decision and rhyme generation. Children were reassessed 12 months later and also presented with a written word choice test. Results indicated that the deaf children had lower performances on the rhyme decision and rhyme generation tasks in kindergarten and achieved lower word recognition scores in first grade than did the hearing children. However, the deaf children's early and implicit phonological skills in kindergarten predicted their written word recognition skills in first grade, accounting for 28% of the variance in later reading scores. The researchers argue that deaf children who develop phonological knowledge before learning to read will be better readers when this knowledge has been exploited through reading instruction (see also the discussion in Chapter 2).

More recently, in a 2-year longitudinal study, Kyle and Harris (2011) compared the emergent literacy of 5- and 6-year-old hearing and deaf children. All 24 deaf children had severe to profound hearing losses; 17 wore digital hearing aids and 7 were fitted with cochlear implants. They used a range of communication modalities. The hearing and deaf children were given a battery of literacy-related assessments over the 2-year period. Results indicated the deaf and hearing children utilized slightly different reading strategies during the first 2 years of reading instruction. Initially, the deaf children used a logographic, or whole-word, strategy to read, despite severe vocabulary delay. After 2 years of reading instruction, however, they used a more alphabetic strategy that tapped into underlying phonological representations derived from speech reading input. In contrast, the hearing children used an alphabetic strategy from the start. Unsurprisingly, for the hearing children, speech reading, phonological awareness, and letter name knowledge were strong correlates of later reading. For the deaf children, earlier vocabulary, speech reading, and letter–sound knowledge predicted later reading ability, although early vocabulary was the most consistent correlate of later reading ability across the study. Phonological awareness was not longitudinally predictive of later reading ability. Kyle and Harris (2011) wondered whether deaf children might develop phonological skills through learning to read rather than as a prerequisite to beginning reading—unlike hearing children's typical route. However, no definitive conclusions were possible.

Given these contrasting findings, current research continues to compare the emergent literacy of d/Dhh children to that of their typically hearing peers in an effort to explicate the ways in which the children's learning trajectories are similar and different. At the same time, researchers are also exploring other aspects of emergent literacy among d/Dhh children, including emergent literacy development in home, school, and early intervention settings.

Emergent Literacy in the Home

In light of earlier identification and intervention, and increased access to spoken language for many d/Dhh children, researchers have turned their attention to the home environment as a critical setting for supporting emergent literacy, particularly among the pediatric implant population. Given the prominence of shared storybook reading in the general research literature, several researchers have investigated early book sharing between mothers and their d/Dhh children. Aram, Most, and Mayafit (2006), for example, investigated the dialogic storytelling of 30 mothers and their kindergarten children around a wordless picture book, focusing specifically on the mothers' use of *wh-* questions to monitor their child's comprehension. All of the children used spoken language to communicate and wore hearing aids or utilized a cochlear implant. Results of the study indicated that the book-sharing activity showed significant positive correlations with children's phonological awareness, general knowledge, and receptive vocabulary. Higher levels of mother–child interactivity yielded greater child outcomes. These findings reflected those for hearing children as documented in the general research literature.

Similarly, in their longitudinal research on children with cochlear implants, DesJardin and colleagues (DesJardin, Ambrose, & Eisenberg, 2009; DesJardin & Eisenberg, 2007) found that mothers' uses of open-ended questions and recasts during interactive storybook reading with their preschool children were positively related to phonological awareness, expressive vocabulary, reading vocabulary, and reading comprehension 3 years later. Again, greater levels of interactivity yielded greater child outcomes. The researchers followed the children into the primary grades and used joint storybook reading to examine the mothers' instructional responses to their children's reading miscues (DesJardin et al., 2011). Results indicated that mothers most often provided the word or ignored the child's miscue. Mothers often referred to characters in the book or asked comprehension questions but rarely focused on vocabulary or related the story to children's prior experiences. Not surprisingly, the mothers' techniques were not positively associated with the children's early literacy skills. Research among hearing children also demonstrates that mothers' interactions with children during joint storybook reading emerge as predictor variables for children's later literacy skills (e.g., Ezell & Justice, 2005).

Research on emergent literacy in the home also has examined joint mother–child writing activities. Aram, Most, and Ben Simon (2008) investigated mothers' mediation of writing tasks with their kindergarten children. All of the children used spoken language to communicate and wore hearing aids or had a cochlear implant. The researchers asked children to write the names of nouns pictured on cards; the mothers were asked to help the children write the words. Researchers identified the mothers' cognitive (graphophonemic, printing, demand for precision, task perception, reference to orthography) and emotional (atmosphere, cooperation, conduct-related, physical contact) mediation of the joint writing tasks. Results indicated that the mothers' guidance correlated positively and significantly with word writing, word recognition, and, in particular, letter knowledge. None of mothers' mediation measures correlated with phonological awareness. Mothers typically dictated letter names and helped with letter shape but did not address sound. Similar research on joint writing activities between mothers and their hearing children indicates that mothers provide support for both orthographic and phonological aspects of word writing (Aram & Levin, 2001).

The findings of these studies suggest that parents of young d/Dhh children may benefit from early intervention programs that provide guidance on the ways in which parents can enhance their children's early reading and writing development in the home. Such programs would need to be culturally relevant and provide practical support for parent implementation of evidence-based practices (see, e.g., Aram & Levin, 2011; Ezell & Justice, 2000; see also Senechal & Young, 2008). Moreover, parent–school liaisons must be strengthened, and parents and teachers of young d/Dhh children need to understand each other's perspectives and expectations (Watson & Swanwick, 2008).

Emergent Literacy in School

Easterbrooks and colleagues (Easterbrooks, Lederberg, Miller, Bergeron, & Connor, 2008; Easterbrooks, Lederberg, & Connor, 2010) were among the first researchers to examine emergent literacy in the pediatric implant population within the context of early childhood school settings. The researchers assessed the emergent literacy skills of 44 d/Dhh children, ages 3–6 years, who had developed speech perception skills. The majority of the children had cochlear implants and attended oral-only classes. The researchers assessed the children's phonological awareness, vocabulary, letter–sound knowledge, letter–word identification, and passage comprehension in the fall and spring and also examined specific characteristics of the children's classrooms (e.g., literacy centers, numerous books, repeated readings, environmental print, literacy-related play) that have been proven to support emergent literacy in children with typical hearing (see Wayne, DiCarlo, Burts, & Benedict, 2007). Results indicated that the classroom environments did not optimally support the children's emergent literacy. On average, the children learned only four new letter–sound correspondences across the school year. Although they showed growth in all phonological tasks except rhyming, their phonological skills were considerably delayed compared to those of hearing children. The d/Dhh children's performance on letter recognition and word recognition tasks was similar to that of hearing children, but there was a negative correlation with age, suggesting an increasing gap in literacy skills between children with and without hearing loss.

Easterbrook and colleagues argue that this gap may develop as reading depends more on acquisition of the alphabetic principle. An important finding of the study was that the children did not make progress in vocabulary, which the researchers attribute to a lack of explicit instruction. The children's phonological awareness and vocabulary in the fall predicted early reading in spring, and letter–sound knowledge strongly correlated with literacy skills and phonological awareness concurrently and over time. These findings highlight the importance of both early phonological processing skills and English vocabulary development to later English literacy achievement. The study also emphasizes the importance of a literacy-rich classroom and explicit early literacy instruction. Professional development among early childhood educators of d/Dhh children will need to address these instructional issues.

A number of intervention studies designed to support d/Dhh children's emergent literacy development have been examined within both home and school settings (Beal-Alvarez, Lederberg, & Easterbrooks, 2011; Bergeron, Lederberg, Easterbrooks,

Miller, & Connor, 2009; Fung, Chow, & McBride-Chang, 2005). These intervention studies are examined in detail in Chapter 6.

A summary of major points on the construct of and research associated with emergent literacy is provided in Table 4.1.

Table 4.1. Emergent Literacy

Emergent literacy among children with typically developing literacy skills

- Emergent literacy is a widely accepted theoretical conceptualization of young children's initial encounters with print and their early reading and writing development.

- It has been investigated from a number of theoretical perspectives (e.g., cognitive, sociocultural, critical) and diverse disciplines (e.g., psychology, education, linguistics).

- Several strands of research have been examined, including emergent reading, emergent writing, home and school influences, instructional practices, and emergent literacy among diverse populations.

- Core theoretical constructs have been identified and investigated extensively, in particular, spoken language, phonological awareness, and alphabetic knowledge and skills, which have been demonstrated to predict early literacy and shape later literacy achievement.

- Recent research has investigated innovative approaches to early literacy intervention and professional development of early childhood educators.

Emergent literacy among children who are d/Deaf and hard of hearing

- There is yet no coherent theoretical framework guiding the research.

- Core theoretical constructs have not been clearly identified empirically but may be inferred, tentatively, from the research on children with typically developing literacy skills.

- In the early phases of emergent literacy, most d/Dhh children's literacy trajectories are qualitatively and quantitatively similar to those of children with typically developing literacy skills.

- The literacy trajectories of d/Dhh children diverge from those of their typically developing peers when an understanding of and ability to use the alphabetic principle becomes essential for the transition from emergent literacy to early conventional literacy.

- Advances in amplification technologies may allow many d/Dhh children considerably improved access to spoken English and support their development of proficiency with the phonology, vocabulary, and syntax of English.

- Researchers are now investigating whether the core theoretical constructs of emergent literacy predict early literacy and shape later literacy success in this new generation of d/Dhh children.

- Current research suggests that parents and early childhood educators might not be adequately supporting d/Dhh children's development of the foundational constructs that are essential to emergent literacy learning and the transition into early conventional literacy.

- The absence of parental scaffolding that reflects evidence-based practices, the lack of literacy-rich classrooms, and the paucity of explicit early literacy instruction needs to be addressed.

CONVENTIONAL LITERACY

Conventional literacy, the ability to decode and encode written language to attain or construct meaning, requires an understanding of the alphabetic principle, growth in the ability to process and use print (e.g., letters, words), and development of the ability to comprehend, interpret, and construct comprehensible text. Specifically, the development of conventional literacy requires deeper understanding and greater control of phonology, syntax, vocabulary, morphology, and the pragmatics of use in particular sociocultural contexts as well as strategic control and use of comprehension strategies and skills (e.g., summarizing, making inferences, regulating, repairing). The reciprocity between these print processing skills and comprehension strategies also supports the development of conventional literacy.

While emergent literacy is the guiding theoretical framework for research on children's initial understandings of written language and experiences with print, a number of contemporary theories ground current research on conventional literacy learning and development among children who are typical learners, including a range of perspectives within *constructivism* (e.g., Anderson & Pearson, 1984; Dewey, 1916), *cognitivism* (e.g., Chall, 1983; Piaget & Inhelder, 1969), *cognitive-processing* (e.g., LaBerge & Samuels, 1974; Stanovich, 1980), and *social learning theories* (e.g., Bronfenbrenner, 1979; Gee, 1990; Vygotsky, 1978). These theories explicate the nature of conventional reading and writing development from varying vantage points, which can provide guidance to educators in helping students learn to read and write.

Recent research on conventional literacy learning and development continues to examine the component processes of reading, particularly since the findings of the National Reading Panel (2000) highlighted the importance of phonemic awareness, phonics, fluency, vocabulary, and text comprehension in skilled reading. More recently, scholars have focused specific attention on word recognition and orthographic processing. Vocabulary development continues to receive investigative attention, as does fluency and reading comprehension instruction.

Word Recognition

Accurate, automatic word recognition is foundational to proficient reading (Ehri, 2005). The ability to read words quickly, accurately, and effortlessly (i.e., without conscious attention to the process) allows a reader's cognitive resources in working memory to be allocated almost entirely to reading comprehension and comprehension monitoring (Muter, Hulme, Snowling, & Stevenson, 2004; Schwanenflugel et al., 2006). Automaticity frees up a reader's mental capabilities for thinking about the writer's intent and the meaning the reader is constructing of the text rather than what word is represented by the printed letters. As students progress through schooling, conceptually more demanding texts require higher-level processes and greater use of cognitive resources in working memory, and so it is necessary to reduce the conscious attention a reader gives to word identification. In fact, as a reader's facility with word recognition is greater, that reader's chances to comprehend the text improve. To this end, readers must acquire overt knowledge and effortless use of the alphabetic code (Vellutino, Tunmer, Jaccard, & Chen, 2007).

Perfetti (2007) argues that word recognition is facilitated by *lexical representations*, knowledge a reader has about the features of words. High-quality lexical representations include well-specified knowledge of phonology and orthography and flexible semantic representations, allowing the reader rapid and reliable retrieval of meaning in a given context. Perfetti's (2007) lexical quality hypothesis (LQH) claims that the quality of a reader's word representations (i.e., knowledge of both form and meaning) has consequences for reading proficiency and comprehension. Proficient readers have high-quality representations of words; less skilled readers have low-quality lexical representations (see also Perfetti & Hart, 2001).

Recent evidence for the LQH was demonstrated by Verhoeven, van Leeuwe, and Vermeer (2011) in a longitudinal study of vocabulary, word decoding, and reading comprehension in Dutch children. The Dutch orthography is very consistent in the mapping between phonemes and graphemes, allowing for highly phonology-based word decoding. Thus, measures of word decoding and vocabulary depicted form and meaning aspects of lexical quality. Findings of the study indicated that children made significant progress in vocabulary, word decoding, and reading comprehension from one grade to the next, and the quality of children's lexical representations, along with the total number of words they knew, directly affected reading comprehension. More lexical entries, and the more fully these were specified in memory, made the child's word identification and reading comprehension more successful. As specified in the LQH, knowledge of word forms and word meanings predicted the development of reading comprehension.

The LQH, with its emphasis on the quality of lexical representations (i.e., phonological, orthographic, and semantic information), contrasts with core deficit models of reading that focus on a reader's difficulties with phonological processing (e.g., Snowling, 1995), naming speed (see Wolfe, Bowers, & Biddle, 2000 for a review), or semantic processing (e.g., Berends & Reitsma, 2006; see also Dickenson, McCabe, Anastasopoulos, Peisner-Feinberg, & Poe, 2003). Perfetti (2007) argues that reading problems "cut across meaning, orthographic, and phonological knowledge," and so the LQH emphasizes "knowledge that has not been acquired or practiced to a high-enough level" (p. 380). Perfetti's theory portends the importance of instructional activities that support learners' engagement with specific concepts and their corresponding language forms, extensive practice in reading and writing, learning to decode print, and the development of visual, orthographic processing skills.

Orthographic Processing

It is evident now that in addition to acquisition of the alphabetic principle and development of phonological processes, progress in reading also requires the development of *orthographic* (or visual) processing, the ability to construct, store, and access visual or *orthographic representations,* "rich lexical instantiations of orthographic patterns and their associated pronunciations" (Cunningham, Nathan, & Raher, 2011, p. 273; see also Ehri, 2005; Perfetti, 2007). Orthographic representations specify permissible letter patterns within the orthography and are closely linked to phonological, semantic, morphological, and syntactic information. Although the development of visual, orthographic processing skills is to some extent dependent on phonological processing abilities, recent research provides some evidence that orthographic processing is a distinctive and separate construct that contributes to word recognition skill beyond the contributions of phonological skills and alphabetic knowledge (Cunningham, Perry, & Stanovich, 2001; Hagiliassis, Pratt, & Johnston, 2006).

Orthographic learning, the development of orthographic representations and orthographic processing skills, has been examined extensively by Share (1995, 1999, 2004, 2008) and is explicated in his *self-teaching hypothesis,* a theoretical framework that proposes that the well-specified orthographic representations necessary for automatic word recognition are developed both through self-teaching during independent reading and by means of skilled word identification. When a reader encounters an unfamiliar word in text, he or she "self-teaches" by using current knowledge of phoneme–grapheme correspondences to construct a pronunciation, which is then matched to words in the reader's oral vocabulary (Share, 1995). If the reader is successful at identifying the unfamiliar word, specific orthographic information about that word, such as the identity and order of the letters, is acquired. After a few subsequent successes with that same word, it will be added to the reader's orthographic lexicon (Share, 1999, 2004). Over time, the reader's store of orthographic representations in memory promotes automatic word recognition. Importantly, as a reader reads more, he or she has more opportunities to learn higher-order regularities in the orthography, such as morphemic constraints (*missed* rather than *mist; magician* rather than *magishin*). Share (2008) suggests that the process is a two-way interchange between decoding abilities and orthographic knowledge, which is at first slow and laborious, but over time transitions to automaticity.

Recent empirical investigations have provided evidence for Share's self-teaching model by demonstrating a decisive relationship between phonological processing and orthographic learning (Bowey & Muller, 2005; de Jong & Share, 2007; Kyte & Johnson, 2006; Wesseling & Reitsma, 2000). Some studies have served to refine the self-teaching hypothesis. For example, Cunningham and colleagues (Cunningham, 2006; Cunningham, Perry, Stanovich, & Share, 2002) demonstrated that *prior* orthographic knowledge contributes uniquely to a reader's ability to self-teach, beyond what is accounted for by phonological processing. A study by Chateau and Jared (2000) suggested that knowledge gained from exposure to print also contributes to orthographic learning beyond the self-teaching accounted for by phonological processing of text. Both prior orthographic knowledge and print exposure likely offer learners opportunities to develop sensitivity to larger orthographic units. Print exposure in particular may allow students the opportunity to acquire morphologic and syntactic knowledge (Chliounaki & Bryant, 2007).

To promote orthographic learning, students need frequent opportunities to self-teach, that is, to decode words without immediate assistance from teachers or peers during group reading activities. Even singular attempts to phonologically code an unfamiliar word may facilitate orthographic learning (Cunningham et al., 2011). Students also need ample time to read, which can afford increased opportunities to encounter unfamiliar words that can be incorporated into their lexicon. Explicit spelling instruction and related activities also may improve the quality of students' orthographic representations of words.

Vocabulary Development

Beyond automatic word recognition and orthographic processing, word-specific knowledge of word meanings, or vocabulary, is critical to reading comprehension. It is only when word forms are readily identified and word meanings are easily accessed that English reading comprehension can be successful. As readers engage with text, reading vocabulary is mapped onto speaking or listening vocabulary. When a word encountered in text is not in the reader's speaking or listening vocabulary, comprehension suffers. In fact, reading comprehension is compromised if a reader does not know between 90 and 95% of the words in the text (Nagy & Scott, 2000). Moreover, readers who know more words often find it easier to integrate information from the text into coherent concepts (Senechal, Ouellette, & Rodney, 2006).

To be proficient readers, students continually must build their speaking and listening vocabularies. In fact, the size of students' *meaning vocabularies*—that is, the number of words they have meanings for in their speaking and listening vocabularies—is strongly associated with reading comprehension (Stahl & Nagy, 2006; Verhoeven & van Leeuwe, 2008). Perfetti (2007) argues that word meanings are the "interface between word identification and comprehension" (p. 380). A large and rich vocabulary is essential if students are to understand the variety of books they will read in school, especially given the vocabulary demands of content-area texts.

While students learn the majority of vocabulary words indirectly through conversation, independent reading, and being read to (Landry & Smith, 2006), direct instruction also is highly effective for vocabulary development (Baumann, Edwards, Boland, Olejnik, & Kame'enui, 2003; Beck & McKeown, 2007), particularly for content-based words (National Reading Panel, 2000). In fact, vocabulary development in the upper elementary grades and beyond requires instruction in general academic vocabulary, words that are needed and can be taught across content areas (e.g., *disproportionate, contrast, integrate*), as well as domain-specific academic vocabulary (e.g., in mathematics, words such as *absolute value, bisect, coefficient*) (see Bailey, 2007). Hiebert and Lubliner (2008) suggest that academic vocabulary also includes words related to specific school tasks (i.e., *learning log*) and literary vocabulary (i.e., *flustered, rambunctious*).

Since the National Reading Panel's (2000) call for research on the ways in which vocabulary growth is fostered within instructional contexts—"in authentic school contexts, with real teachers, under real conditions" (p. 4.27)—scholars have investigated a number of classroom-based vocabulary interventions, in particular, those that focus on supporting students' development of academic vocabulary. Lesaux, Kieffer, Faller, and Kelley (2010), for example, designed, implemented, and evaluated the effectiveness of an academic vocabulary program used in sixth-grade classrooms. The 18-week intervention utilized short informational texts from *Time for Kids* magazine. From each text, the researchers chose eight or nine high-utility academic words, which were taught repeatedly across the intervention. Results demonstrated significant effects on students' knowledge of words taught, morphological awareness, and word meanings as presented in expository text. The program also yielded marginally significant effects on a depth of word knowledge measure and a norm-referenced reading comprehension test.

Shook, Hazelkorn, and Lozano (2011) examined the effectiveness of a vocabulary intervention that utilized expository, content-area text and collaborative learning. Specifically, the researchers investigated the *collaborative strategic reading* (CSR) approach to vocabulary instruction on ninth-grade biology students' learning of science vocabulary. CSR supports vocabulary development through comprehension strategies that also facilitate students' learning from expository texts. In small groups, students preview the content-area material to be read. As they read, they label vocabulary and concepts they know and understand. They also identify vocabulary and concepts they do not know or understand and seek to construct provisional meanings of those words/concepts from the context of the passage. Finally, they summarize the passage and make connections to previous knowledge on the topic. Findings of study indicated that students significantly improved their science vocabulary scores after the 5-week intervention. Previous research also has demonstrated the effectiveness of contextual analysis in supporting vocabulary development (Bauman et al., 2003; Harmon, Hedrick, & Wood, 2005).

Vocabulary is a key mechanism in the reading comprehension process; students who know more words have more conceptual language at their disposal with which to be strategic while reading, and students who know more academic vocabulary are better prepared to meet the demands of disciplinary learning. Further research on vocabulary learning within the context of classroom instruction is needed.

Fluency

When a reader's cognitive and linguistic abilities are developed to the degree that he or she can read with sufficient accuracy and rate to both understand the text and reflect the text's prosodic features, the reading can be characterized as fluent (Rasinski, Reutzel, Chard, & Linan-Thompson, 2011). Fluent reading has two features, automaticity and prosody. Automaticity is the ability to read words quickly, accurately, and effortlessly, without conscious attention to the process. Prosodic reading is the ability to read in such a way that one's oral reading sounds like authentic spoken language, where the reader segments text into meaningful, syntactically appropriate phrases. Rasinski (2004) suggests that when readers embed appropriate volume, tone, emphasis, phrasing, and expression in oral reading, they are demonstrating comprehension of the text.

Fluent reading and reading comprehension go hand in hand (Fuchs, Fuchs, Hosp, & Jenkins, 2001). Fluent readers are able to process text effortlessly, which frees up cognitive resources in working memory to attend to higher level reading processes, such as analyzing syntax, making inferences, and evaluative or critical reading. In contrast, nonfluent readers tend to read laboriously; they focus significantly more conscious attention and cognitive resources on lower-level skills such as decoding and word recognition. Thus, fluent reading contributes to reading proficiency and lack of fluency contributes to reading difficulty (Rasinski, Rikli, & Johnston, 2009).

Fortunately, fluency in reading is a skill that can be learned, practiced, and improved (Gersten, Fuchs, Williams, & Baker, 2001; Therrien, 2004). Since the National Reading Panel's report (2000), fluency has taken center stage in classroom reading instruction (Pikulski & Chard, 2005), and researchers have investigated a number of approaches to supporting fluent reading, in particular, repeated readings of text. Repeated readings of the same text increase reading rate, accuracy, and comprehension (Schwanenflugel et al., 2006; Vadasy & Sanders, 2009). Typically, students reread the same selection until they achieve the criterion (Rasinski & Padak, 2008), which is generally between three and five repetitions. Various techniques are used to engage students in repeated readings of text, including choral, echo, teacher–student, and partner reading.

One approach to repeated reading, fluency-oriented reading instruction (FORI), was designed for primary-grade reading instruction as well as content-area reading instruction using a school's core (i.e., basal) reading program (Kuhn & Schwanenflugel, 2006; Stahl & Heubach, 2005). In the first FORI lesson, the teacher reads the selection orally while students follow along in their books, and then a follow-up discussion highlights the central concepts in the text. Over the week, students repeatedly read the selected text orally, using a variety of assisted reading techniques, including partner, choral, and echo reading, and also read the text at home each evening. Kuhn and colleagues (Kuhn et al., 2006) compared the effects of FORI to traditional reading instruction and to wide reading (discussed later in this chapter; Kuhn, 2004), also a repeated-readings approach. Results indicated that FORI and wide reading were similarly effective in promoting reading fluency, and long-term use of both approaches significantly increased students' sight word reading and reading comprehension as compared to the traditional reading approach. Stahl and Heubach (2005) also demonstrated positive outcomes with a FORI intervention in the primary grades.

Wide reading approaches to fluency instruction (Kuhn, 2004, 2005) engage students in reading more books per week with fewer repeated readings of each book. Choral reading, partner reading, echo reading, and other forms of assisted reading with teachers and peers are also used. The wide reading approach is based on the assertion that improvements in reading fluency may derive more from the scaffolding of oral reading practice than repetition (see Kuhn & Stahl, 2003). Kuhn (2005) compared wide reading to repeated readings of the same story, listening to stories read aloud, and traditional reading instruction. Results indicated that the wide reading and repeated-readings groups made greater gains on word recognition, words correct per minute, and prosody when compared to the listening-only and traditional instruction groups. However, only the wide reading group made comprehension gains.

Readers' theater also has been investigated as an approach to supporting students' reading fluency, especially with respect to prosody. Students adapt a literature selection into a reader's theater script, or rehearse a previously designed script, to prepare for a performance. Students are assigned roles for the oral reading. Prosodic reading is emphasized; minimal props and scenery are used (Rasinski, 2008). This method of repeated readings offers students an authentic reason to repeatedly read the same text and practice fluent, expressive reading. Griffith and Rasinski (2004) found that fourth-grade students made more than 2 years of reading achievement gains, including gains in reading fluency, during one academic year when reader's theater was a regular part of the reading program. Students found the reader's theater approach to be an engaging and motivating technique for developing fluent reading.

The results of these studies indicate that fluency instruction that emphasizes extensive oral reading of grade-level texts using repeated readings and assisted, scaffolded reading techniques is effective for promoting reading fluency. However, despite the National Reading Panel's (2000) plea, what is missing still is an extensive and robust body of experimental research examining the effects of *independent reading practice* on the development of reading fluency. Conventional wisdom assumes that fluent reading is developed primarily through extensive independent practice, but studies are needed to test this assertion experimentally.

Reading Comprehension Instruction

Reading comprehension involves simultaneously gaining meaning and constructing meaning from text. It involves an interaction between the knowledge and abilities of the reader, the demands of the text, the activities engaged in by the reader, and the sociocultural context in which the reading occurs (McNamara, Miller, & Bransford, 2000; RAND Reading Study Group, 2002). Reading comprehension is a dynamic and context-sensitive process; changing one element changes the interaction, thus changing the meaning that is constructed (Wilkinson & Son, 2011).

As readers engage with text, the active and intentional use of cognitive strategies can help to monitor comprehension or circumvent or repair a breakdown in comprehension (Graesser, 2007). It is therefore essential that students know and be able to use these comprehension-monitoring tools as they read. Explicit instruction in comprehension strategies can significantly improve students' reading comprehension skills (Gajria, Jitendra, Sood, & Sacks, 2007). The importance of comprehension strategy instruction to reading comprehension was highlighted by the National Reading Panel's (2000) decision to focus on comprehension strategy instruction in its report.

The goal of comprehension strategy instruction is to encourage students to self-monitor their meaning construction and to execute specific strategies as they interact with text (McKeown, Beck, & Blake, 2009). Gunning (2013) recommends the teaching of four major categories of comprehension strategies, including preparational (e.g., predicting; activating prior knowledge), organizational (e.g., determining the main idea; summarizing), elaboration (e.g., making inferences; critical evaluation), and metacognitive (e.g., regulating; repairing). To these print-based comprehension strategies, readers also must add cognitive and physical strategies specific to reading in Web-based contexts, particularly when the goal of online reading is to seek information (Coiro & Schmar-Dobler, 2007).

The National Reading Panel (2000) identified specific types of instruction that improve comprehension, including the use of graphic and semantic organizers, question answering, question generation, teaching comprehension monitoring and summarization skills, and utilizing cooperative learning. Many of these strategies have also been used effectively in combination, leading to a multiple-strategy approach to instruction.

In recent years, there has been increasing interest in comprehension strategy instruction that is embedded in the content areas to promote understanding of domain-specific content. For example, *concept-oriented reading instruction* (CORI; Guthrie, Wigfield, & Perencevich, 2004) teaches comprehension strategies within the context of hands-on, collaborative inquiry in science. Guthrie and colleagues conducted a series of quasi-experimental studies comparing the effects of CORI with the effects of traditional approaches to strategy instruction in the upper elementary grades, and in a meta-analysis of those studies, Guthrie, McRae, and Klaudia (2007) reported a mean effect size in favor of CORI on standardized tests of comprehension and on measures of students' science knowledge.

Similarly, *in-depth expanded application of science* (IDEAS; Romance & Vitale, 2001) embeds reading and language arts instruction within a daily 2-hour block of science instruction in the upper elementary grades. Students are taught comprehension strategies that relate directly to the knowledge-building activities of science (e.g., concept-mapping, relating prior knowledge to new concepts). Results of four quasi-experimental studies comparing the effects of IDEAS with those of traditional instruction showed significantly greater performance in both comprehension and science achievement in favor of IDEAS (Romance & Vitale, 2001).

Finally, *reading apprenticeship* (Jordon & Schoenbach, 2003; Schoenbach, Braunger, Greenleaf, & Litman, 2003) is an instructional framework that provides content-rich comprehension strategy instruction in science, social studies, math, or English in the middle and high school grades. Teachers apprentice students in the reading of subject-area texts by modeling their own use of discipline-based comprehension strategies and processes and then providing sufficient opportunities for students to practice using those strategies during authentic content-area reading activities. During group discussions, teachers and students engage in "metacognitive conversations" that make explicit the specific strategies that were used while reading challenging texts. In a year-long study, Greenleaf and Mueller (2003) found that ninth-grade students who engaged in an academic literacy course based on reading apprenticeship made greater than expected gains on a standardized test of reading comprehension.

The findings of this research attest to the educational benefits both for students' reading comprehension as well as discipline-specific knowledge of bringing comprehension strategy instruction into content-area teaching. Despite the demonstrated benefits of comprehension strategy instruction, however, research continues to demonstrate that this instruction is rare and often rudimentary (Vaughn, Levy, Coleman, & Bos, 2002). For example, Ness (2011) found that in 3000 minutes of direct classroom observation of elementary school language arts instruction, teachers spent 25% of instructional time on explicit reading comprehension instruction. The most frequently taught strategies were predicting, activating prior knowledge, and summarization. Although these teachers spent considerably more time teaching comprehension strategies than did teachers in Durkin's (1978–1979) seminal study (25% compared to 1%), in both investigations, teacher-generated questions (i.e., comprehension assessment) dominated instructional time allotted for reading comprehension instruction.

Given the importance of comprehension strategies to students' reading comprehension in particular, and academic achievement more generally, further research is needed to identify instructional frameworks that are straightforwardly implemented and appealing to classroom teachers. Approaches that integrate comprehension strategy instruction into content-area subjects may be easier to put into practice and more sustainable than isolated strategy instruction.

CONVENTIONAL LITERACY IN d/DEAF AND HARD OF HEARING STUDENTS

Research on conventional literacy learning and development among d/Dhh students also has been influenced by the National Reading Panel's (2000) report. Recent research has investigated, most particularly the role of phonology and phonological processing in word recognition. Other major reading components and processes have also been examined, including vocabulary, fluency, and reading comprehension.

Phonology and Phonological Processing

The role and importance of phonology and phonological processing in word recognition among d/Dhh students has received considerable research attention in recent years. Evidence from the more general research literature indicates that the use of a *phonological code* in working memory is the most efficient code for processing English print (McGuinness, 2005; Snowling & Hulme, 2005). Consequently, researchers are particularly interested in the ability of d/Dhh readers to use phonological processing skills to cognitively code printed words in working memory. Working memory provides the cognitive resources that help a reader store words long enough to process a complete sentence. If a reader's strategies for processing words place considerable demands on working memory, then fewer words can be retained and comprehension of the sentence is compromised. Thus, the development of phonological processing skills supports word recognition skills. Some researchers, however, question whether the use of phonological processing is necessary for d/Dhh readers' development of age-appropriate reading skills (e.g., Harris & Moreno, 2004). We have argued throughout this book that phonological skills are fundamental to the acquisition of literacy in English, but the role and importance of phonological skills among d/Dhh readers, specifically d/D readers, is ardently debated, as illustrated in the findings reported here.

Since Conrad's (1979) seminal study on deaf adolescent readers who used phonological codes, or what he termed "internal speech," to identify words, evidence for phonological coding among readers who are d/Dhh has accumulated (e.g., Charlier & Leybaert, 2000; Dyer, MacSweeney, Szczerbinski, Green, & Campbell, 2003; LaSasso, Crain, & Leybaert, 2003; Luetke-Stahlman & Nielsen, 2003; see also Perfetti & Sandak, 2000, for a review of earlier work). Results of these studies indicated that participants used phonological information during reading, particularly the better readers.

More recently, research conducted by Kyle and Harris (2006) also provided evidence for phonological processing among young deaf children. The researchers compared the performance of 7- and 8-year-old deaf and hearing children on a number of literacy-related tasks to examine similarities and differences in levels of performance and in predictors of literacy. All 29 children had severe to profound hearing losses and wore hearing aids; seven children were fitted with cochlear implants. Results of the study demonstrated qualitative similarities but quantitative differences (i.e., rates of acquisition) between the two groups on all measures. The deaf children were significantly delayed in reading, spelling, and productive vocabulary and demonstrated less detailed phonological awareness and knowledge compared to the hearing children. Nevertheless, the deaf children's knowledge of phoneme–grapheme correspondences suggested either an implicit sensitivity to phonological information or the use of an explicit phonological coding strategy. Kyle and Harris argue that the deaf children's phonological representations were derived from speech reading input. In this study, speech reading was the strongest predictor of single-word reading ability. Productive vocabulary explained 28% of the variance in children's comprehension.

Kyle and Harris (2010) followed the deaf children's reading development for three years and found that while both speech reading and vocabulary showed longitudinal relationships with word reading, only vocabulary knowledge was longitudinally related to both word reading and sentence and text comprehension. Earlier reading ability was predominately associated with later phonological awareness, rather than the other way around. That is, the deaf children's phonological abilities developed mainly as a consequence of learning to read, rather than being a prerequisite to reading. These findings contrast with those of Colin et al. (2007) and Easterbrooks et al. (2008), who reported positive longitudinal relations between phonological awareness and later reading.

Some studies have reported no strong relationship between phonological coding and reading achievement in d/Dhh learners. Miller and Clark (2011) recently conducted a review of the research investigating word reading skills, phonemic awareness, and reading comprehension and argued that the empirical evidence indicated that d/Dhh readers benefit from the development of orthographic knowledge in conjunction with syntactic awareness and metacognitive skills rather than development of phonological processing skills. Mayberry, del Giudice, and Lieberman (2011) conducted a meta-analysis of 57 studies that experimentally tested phonological coding and awareness skills in 2,078 participants who had severe to profound hearing loss. Results of the meta-analysis indicated that half of the studies found statistically significant evidence for phonological coding and awareness skills and half of the studies did not. Overall, phonological processing predicted 11% of the variance in reading proficiency. Language ability was measured in seven studies and predicted 35% of the variance in reading proficiency. The researchers argue that phonological awareness and coding skills are a low to moderate predictor of reading achievement in deaf individuals and that language ability has a greater influence on reading development.

The conflicting findings reported across these studies highlight the need for continued research on the relationship between phonological ability and reading achievement in d/Dhh learners. However, the considerable evidence for phonological processing among many of the d/Dhh participants in these studies demonstrates its role in reading development and highlights the need for researchers to identify the ways in which phonological information can be provided to d/Dhh students who have limited access to the phonology of English.

Alternative Means of Acquiring Phonology

The lack of access to the phonology of English puts d/Dhh readers at a disadvantage for acquiring phonological representations, but alternative means of acquiring English phonology have been identified, including speech reading and articulatory feedback. Two additional mechanisms, Cued Speech and Visual Phonics, have received recent research attention.

Cued Speech/Language   Cued Speech/Language (CSL) is a sound-based, visual communication system that uses eight handshapes in four different locations around the mouth to convey phonological information. Sets of consonants are represented by handshapes and sets of vowels are represented by hand positions (and sometimes movement). CSL is used in combination with the natural movements of the mouth during speech. For instructional purposes, CSL is used at the phoneme level. Recent research on the use of CSL demonstrates its effectiveness in promoting phonological skills, acquisition of the alphabetic principle, word recognition, and invented spelling (Colin et al., 2007; LaSasso et al., 2003; Sirois, Boisclair & Giasson, 2008; see also Chapter 2).

Visual Phonics   Visual Phonics (or "See the Sound–Visual Phonics") is a multisensory system that uses hand cues and written graphemes to teach each of the 46 phonemes of English. The hand cues represent individual phonemes and mirror the articulatory features of the sound. The written symbols reflect the gestures used in the cues and provide visual discrimination between the letter and the sound it makes, which helps students to understand that a letter may represent more than one sound. Recent research demonstrates the effectiveness of Visual Phonics used in conjunction with phonics-based reading programs in promoting phonological awareness, speech production, phonics skills, and beginning reading skills (Narr, 2008; Smith & Wang, 2010; Trezek & Malmgren, 2005; Trezek & Wang, 2006; Trezek, Wang, Woods, Gampp, & Paul, 2007).

If readers who are d/Dhh are able to code phonologically while reading, as the evidence suggests, then mechanisms such as CSL and Visual Phonics can be used as instructional tools to support these students' phonological processing skills. Given that phonological awareness and phonological processing skills have been shown repeatedly to be important to beginning reading in hearing children (e.g., Caravolas, Hulme, & Snowling, 2001; Muter et al., 2004), the development of phonological coding abilities undoubtedly will lead to increased reading achievement among students who are d/Dhh.

Vocabulary

The National Reading Panel (2000) suggested that in the more general field of literacy, empirically based knowledge about vocabulary acquisition exceeds knowledge of pedagogy, and, consequently, the panel specifically called for research on vocabulary instruction within the classroom context. However, among d/Dhh learners, research on vocabulary development continues to examine vocabulary acquisition and word learning; investigations of instructional interventions are rare.

Cochlear Implantation   Research on the impact of cochlear implantation on vocabulary learning among d/Dhh learners has taken center stage. Overall, the body of work suggests that age at implantation might be the most important factor for vocabulary growth (Hayes, Geers, Treiman, & Moog, 2009; James, Rajput, Brinton, & Goswami, 2008; Johnson & Goswami, 2010; Willstedt-Svensson, Lofqvist, Almqvist, & Sahlen, 2004). Children who were implanted before 2.5 years of age showed greater rates of vocabulary growth (Hayes et al. 2009; Connor, Craig, Raudenbush, Heavner, & Zwolan, 2006; Fagan, Pisoni, Horn, & Dillon, 2007) and greater reading comprehension scores (Fagan et al., 2007) than children who were implanted later, and some early-implant children showed a burst of vocabulary growth immediately after implantation (Connor et al., 2006). Children who received their cochlear implants during the preschool years achieved better vocabulary outcomes over time than children who were implanted during the elementary school years (Connor, Hieber, Arts, & Zwolan, 2000), but even children who were fitted with a cochlear implant at a later age also demonstrated vocabulary growth (James et al., 2008). Children may benefit from using cochlear implants regardless of communication mode or teaching approach used in their classrooms (Connor et al., 2000). In fact, Connor and Zwolan (2004) found that children who used Total Communication (speaking and signing simultaneously) and received a cochlear implant at an earlier age showed stronger vocabulary skills after implant than did children who used oral communication and were implanted at a later age.

In general, the body of work indicates that many children who utilize cochlear implants demonstrate substantial vocabulary growth after implantation. Increased access to spoken language supports their English vocabulary acquisition and development. However, even when the children's vocabulary knowledge is commensurate with years of cochlear implant experience (e.g., Fagan & Pisoni, 2010), these children's scores on vocabulary measures are still lower than the scores of children with typical hearing (Hayes et al., 2009; Fagan et al. 2007; Schorr, Roth, & Fox, 2008; see also, the discussion in Chapter 2).

Novel Word Learning   Recent research on novel word learning among d/Dhh students demonstrates that a student's ability to learn new words is influenced by the number of words the student already knows and the number of exposures to a new word the student experiences. Students with larger vocabularies learn new words more easily, and this is the case regardless of the language-learning environment—that is, whether children are acquiring language through speech, sign, or both, in children with cochlear implants, and among children who have d/Deaf parents (Lederberg & Spencer, 2009). Students who are d/Dhh might have significantly smaller vocabularies than their hearing peers and less in-depth knowledge of words and might require more exposures to learn new words (Coppens, Tellings, Verhoeven, & Schreuder, 2011; Pittman, 2008; Pittman, Lewis, Hoover, & Stelmachowicz, 2005; Stelmachowicz, Pittman, Hoover, & Lewis, 2004). On word learning tasks, hearing students performed significantly better and retained almost twice as many new words as did many students who were d/Dhh (Pittman et al., 2005; Stelmachowicz et al., 2004). Scores on the Peabody Picture Vocabulary Test were highly predictive of novel word learning scores (Pittman et al., 2005; Stelmachowicz et al., 2004). Pittman (2008) found that d/Dhh students performed better on word learning tasks that were presented in extended bandwidth (i.e., high-frequency amplification), suggesting that hearing aids with frequency transposition may improve speech perception and word learning.

Although children with typical hearing acquire a large portion of their vocabularies incidentally (Landry & Smith, 2006), that is often not the case for many children who are d/Dhh (Easterbrooks & Baker, 2002; Paul, 2009). Children who are d/Dhh are exposed to fewer words and experience those words less often; as a result they acquire vocabulary knowledge more slowly (Lederberg & Spencer, 2009). In fact, Easterbrooks et al. (2008) found that 3- to 6-year old d/Dhh children who had a pure tone average of more than 50dB and demonstrated speech perception skills did not make progress in vocabulary across the 1-year duration of the study (see also, Paul, 2009, for a review of studies on vocabulary acquisition). Many of the children scored below the normal range on vocabulary measures. The researchers contend that most children who are d/Dhh will require explicit instruction to support vocabulary development.

These findings corroborate a long line of empirical work, which has consistently demonstrated that the acquisition of vocabulary knowledge is delayed for students who are d/Dhh. They have considerably smaller lexicons compared to their hearing agemates due to a slower rate of new word acquisition and a narrower range of word learning experiences (Lederberg & Beal-Alvarez, 2011; Paul, 2009; Pittman, 2008; Marschark & Wauters, 2008). However, the research also demonstrates that d/Dhh students can and do acquire new vocabulary and word-learning strategies, despite severe language delay (Lederberg, Prezbindowski, & Spencer, 2000; Lederberg & Spencer, 2009).

Writing Vocabulary   One study examined writing vocabulary among elementary d/Dhh students (see also Chapter 3). Singleton, Morgan, DiGello, Wiles, and Rivers (2004) examined English vocabulary use in the writing of 72 deaf students. Sixty-six monolingual hearing and 60 English-as-a-second-language (ESL) hearing students served as comparison groups. To elicit the writing sample, students were shown a 3-minute silent cartoon of "The Tortoise and the Hare." Results indicated that the deaf students wrote fewer words in their written retellings than did the hearing students; they also used significantly fewer function words. Deaf students with moderate to high ASL proficiency used the same percentage of frequently used words and unique words as hearing students and performed better on both measures than the hearing ESL group and low-ASL groups. The moderate- and high-ASL groups used more diverse vocabulary than the low-ASL group and the ESL group. The study highlights the importance of a strong foundation in through-the-air language as a prerequisite for literacy acquisition. Findings also emphasize the need for explicit instruction in English function words, which pose particular challenges for d/Dhh learners in general and users of ASL in particular, as many function words do not exist in ASL. Function words provide clues to the semantic and syntactic relationships between content words and play a significant role in comprehension of text. An effective vocabulary program for d/Dhh learners must include instruction in both content and function words (Trezek, Wang, & Paul, 2010).

The research on vocabulary development continues to demonstrate that most children who are d/Dhh experience significant delay in vocabulary learning and have smaller vocabularies than their hearing peers, even with the benefits of cochlear implants, enhanced amplification, and the support of American Sign Language. The recent research also suggests that incidental learning of vocabulary is rare; most d/Dhh students require direct and explicit instruction to support vocabulary development. In five recent investigations (Barker, 2003; Cannon, Fredrick, & Easterbrooks, 2010; Massaro & Light, 2004; Paatsch, Blarney, Sarant, & Bow, 2006), researchers examined instructional interventions designed to support vocabulary learning among d/Dhh students; these studies are reviewed in detailed in Chapter 6.

Fluency

As mentioned previously, since the National Reading Panel's report (2000), research on fluency among readers with typical hearing has taken center stage in reading instruction and garnered considerable research attention. In contrast, however, during that same time period, research on fluency among d/Dhh readers has been rare. We identified only four investigations, three of which were intervention studies (Enns & Lafond, 2007; Schirmer, Schaffer, Therrien, & Schirmer, 2012; Schirmer, Therrien, Schaffer, & Schirmer, 2009), which are discussed in detail in Chapter 6.

Most measures of reading fluency require students to read aloud, and those measures can be used with d/Dhh students who communicate primarily through spoken language. For students using a manual mode of communication, however, evaluations of signed reading fluency are more appropriate. Easterbrooks and Huston (2008) recently introduced the construct of *signed reading fluency*, the ability of a reader to form a mental visualization of the printed English text and then render it expressively in some form of sign, whether English-like signing, American Sign Language, or a combination of the two. Signed reading fluency involves three components: (1) accuracy, the ability to render the concepts expressed in English words into a signed format that has equivalent conceptual meaning; (2) fluency envelope, the ability to convey prosodic and pragmatic features of the text; and (3) visual grammar, the ability to convey syntactic elements of the passage. These three aspects of signed reading fluency encompass skills that parallel automaticity and prosodic reading in measures of reading fluency for hearing children.

Easterbrooks and Huston (2008) developed the Signed Reading Fluency Rubric for Deaf Children, which measures two aspects of signed reading fluency: fluency envelope and visual grammar. They used the rubric to evaluate the signed reading fluency of 29 d/Dhh students ranging in age from 9 to 16 years. Results of the study demonstrated a positive correlation between signed reading fluency and both word reading and reading comprehension. Greater scores on the signed reading fluency rubric were associated with greater word comprehension and reading comprehension scores.

Reading Comprehension

Recent research on reading comprehension among readers who are d/Dhh examines several aspects of text comprehension, including mode of word acquisition, syntactic knowledge, and use of metacognitive strategies to comprehend text. Intervention studies examining aspects of reading comprehension have been rare; in fact, we identified only three studies (Al-Hilawani, 2003; Gentry, Chinn, & Moulton, 2004; Pakulski & Kaderavek, 2001), which are discussed in detail in Chapter 6.

Mode of Acquisition   A relatively new construct in the research on reading comprehension among d/Dhh students is mode of word acquisition. Wauters and colleagues (Wauters, Tellings, van Bon, & Mak, 2008; Wauters, van Bon, Tellings, & van Leeuwe, 2006) argue that *mode of acquisition* or the way in which a student acquires the meaning of a word—through perception, linguistic information, or both—will influence comprehension of text. Word meanings learned through perception are acquired through seeing, smelling, or hearing the referents of the words. For example, the word *green* is learned through perception because no verbal description is possible. Words learned through linguistic information are acquired through verbal or written descriptions, explanations, or discussions of referents, as in the word *century*. Acquiring word meanings through linguistic information requires access to both through-the-air and written language, which for many d/Dhh children is scarce.

Knowledge of a word's meaning can be understood as the interrelated array of various linguistic and perceptual experiences one has with a word (e.g., the smell and taste of freshly baked bread along with an explanation of its ingredients: "Bread is made of flour and yeast"). Both types of associations are necessary to develop rich word meanings. Students learn the meanings of words, however, as a consequence of time and place, experience, culture, and socioeconomic status, and so mode of word acquisition is environmentally dependent.

Wauters and colleagues argue that mode of word acquisition influences comprehension of text. In a recent investigation that examined students' understanding of items on a reading comprehension test, Wauters et al. (2006) found that mode of word acquisition influenced 7- to 20-year-old d/Dhh students' performance. Students gave fewer correct answers when the words of a test item were typically acquired through linguistic information. In a subsequent study which engaged 7- to 15-year-old d/Dhh students in a self-paced reading task, Wauters et al. (2008) found that reading times on linguistically acquired words were longer than on perceptually acquired words.

Moreover, comprehension scores were lower on linguistic items than on perceptual items although the students showed difficulty on both perceptual and linguistic items. Further, in both investigations, the d/Dhh students scored lower than hearing students participating in the studies. The researchers argue that words that are acquired primarily through linguistic information might be more difficult for d/Dhh students to learn; therefore, classroom instruction should focus first on building a foundation in perceptually acquired words. Using these perceptual words as a basis, linguistic word meanings can be built.

Syntactic Knowledge   To comprehend a text, a reader must understand the syntax or word order of the sentences within that text. Syntactic knowledge has been one of the most researched areas in literacy and deafness because of the difficulties English syntax poses for many students who are d/Dhh (see review in Paul, 2009). Current research continues to examine the role of syntactic knowledge in the reading comprehension of these students. Miller (2000, 2005), for example, has studied the topic extensively and argues that d/Dhh students' difficulties with reading comprehension is primarily due to a lack of syntactic knowledge necessary for processing words at the sentence level. In two separate studies, Miller (2000, 2005) found that many d/Dhh students in grades 4 through 11 had remarkably poor understanding of syntactic rules. They relied on a "semantic reading strategy" to make sense of text. That is, they generated sentence meaning by interpreting the meaning of content words using their prior knowledge and experience. They did not process syntactic information conveyed by word order or sentence structure. The evidence suggested that students did not have difficulty processing words at the lexical level but had not internalized the syntactic knowledge crucial for processing words at the sentence level. Neither degree of hearing loss nor communication mode was a factor in the students' performance.

In a subsequent study using a sentence comprehension test, Miller (2010) identified d/Dhh students as either "syntactic readers," those who relied on syntactic knowledge for comprehension; "semantic readers," those who applied a semantic reading strategy; or "anomalous readers," those who appeared unable to use either processing strategy effectively. Students in grades 3 through 11 and university students 21–29 years of age participated in the study. The majority of primary-school students were anomalous readers; they had yet to internalize sufficient syntactic knowledge or developed the ability to use prior knowledge to make sense of text. Half of the high school students were syntactic readers and half were semantic readers. The vast majority of university students were syntactic readers. Students with anomalous reader profiles demonstrated low comprehension (60% or less) whereas students with syntactic reader profiles demonstrated greater comprehension (85% or more). Students with semantic reader profiles demonstrated a range of comprehension scores (67–89%). These findings indicate that deafness can delay, but does not preclude, the acquisition, internalization, and application of syntactic knowledge necessary for English reading comprehension. Findings also suggest that the semantic reading strategy may be transitional in nature. Given that the meaning of a sentence is ultimately determined by the way words are structured within that sentence, processing at the structural level is crucial to English text comprehension.

Metacognitive Strategies Metacognition, self-awareness of a reader's own cognitive processes and strategies, plays a crucial role in reading comprehension. Skilled readers are able to monitor their comprehension and use a range of metacognitive strategies to repair or circumvent a breakdown in comprehension. A student's ability to engage in metacognitive processing makes a significant difference in text comprehension.

Recent research has examined d/Dhh readers' use of metacognitive strategies while reading. Schirmer (2003) used verbal or signed protocols to investigate self-reported metacognitive strategy use among elementary students attending a residential state school for d/Dhh students. Analysis of the protocols indicated that the students used specific metacognitive strategies to construct meaning, monitor and improve comprehension, and evaluate texts that were read. Strategies for constructing meaning were used most. Evaluative responses were primarily affective. Students did not predict the meaning of a text based on their knowledge of text genre nor did they use text structure for monitoring comprehension. Students were not aware of their own strategies, which may have led to an inability to vary strategy use to improve comprehension. In a subsequent replication study in a sited-based classroom for d/Dhh students at a public elementary school, Schirmer, Bailey, and Schirmer Lockman (2004) demonstrated similar results.

More recently, Ducharme and Arcand (2010) examined d/Dhh students' use of metacognitive strategies while reading one on one with their teachers. The students were considered developing readers, with reading levels ranging from grades 2 through 4. The researchers documented use of "global meaning" (e.g., prior knowledge, imagery, illustrations) strategies as well as word attack (e.g., decoding, fingerspelling) strategies. Less-skilled readers used more word attack strategies whereas more-skilled readers used more global meaning strategies, suggesting that as reading proficiency increases more global meaning strategies are used.

A recent investigation by Banner and Wang (2010) examined the metacognitive strategies used by adult and student readers, ages 16 to 36, who were d/Dhh. Findings of the study indicated that all of the readers demonstrated use of several metacognitive strategies, regardless of reading level, including mental imagery, summarizing or paraphrasing, and use of prior knowledge. Unlike the students in the Schirmer (2003) and Schirmer et al. (2004) studies, these participants were capable of talking about their strategy use. Among both the adult and student participants, the researchers identified skilled readers who effectively employed multiple reading strategies, as well as less-skilled readers who employed limited use of reading strategies. The most skilled reader, a deaf adult, demonstrated a range of metacognitive strategies that supported constructing meaning, monitoring and improving comprehension, and evaluating the quality of a text. An important finding of the study was that none of the student readers demonstrated the use of evaluative strategies and not all adult readers did so. Banner and Wang suggest that only a reader who is highly skilled at activating reading strategies will be able to assign a text a subjective evaluation.

The current research, as discussed here, demonstrates that d/Dhh readers can and do use metacognitive strategies to comprehend text, but with varying degrees of success. However, the knowledge base is still inconclusive: Other language-related factors also are involved in reading comprehension (e.g., knowledge of figurative language, efficient use of prior knowledge) and these factors need to be addressed in future research.

A summary of major points on the construct of and research associated with conventional literacy is provided in Table 4.2.

Table 4.2. Conventional Literacy

Conventional literacy among children with typically developing literacy skills

- Conventional literacy is the ability to decode and encode written language to construct meaning; it requires proficiency with the phonology, vocabulary, syntax, morphology, and pragmatics of English, as well as strategic use of comprehension strategies and skills.

- A number of theories frame current research on conventional literacy learning, including constructivism, cognitivism, cognitive processing, and a range of social learning theories.

- Recent research reflects the results of the National Reading Panel (2000) in continuing to examine the component processes of reading, including phonemic awareness, phonics, fluency, vocabulary, and text comprehension.

- The most current research has focused particular attention on word recognition and orthographic processing.

- Word recognition is facilitated by *lexical representations,* the knowledge a reader has about the features of words. High-quality lexical representations include well-specified knowledge of phonology and orthography and flexible semantic representations, allowing the reader rapid and reliable retrieval of meaning in a given context.

- In addition to acquisition of the alphabetic principle and phonological processing skills, reading development also requires *orthographic processing,* the ability to construct, store, and access visual or orthographic representations of patterns and pronunciations.

Conventional literacy among children who are d/Deaf and hard of hearing

- Research has been influenced by the results of the National Reading Panel (2000). Investigators continue to examine the component processes of reading, including phonemic awareness, phonics, fluency, vocabulary, and text comprehension.

- The role and importance of phonological skills among d/Deaf readers have received considerable research attention; the evidence repeatedly demonstrates that d/Dhh students often lack the phonological skills necessary for literacy in English.

- Alternative means of acquiring phonology have been examined, specifically the instructional use of Cued Speech/Language and Visual Phonics, which can support the development of phonological processing skills.

- Children who utilize cochlear implants demonstrate substantial vocabulary growth after implantation, regardless of communication mode used. Nevertheless, vocabulary development in d/Dhh children is quantitatively delayed and not commensurate with peers with typically developing literacy skills.

- Incidental vocabulary learning is rare; most d/Dhh children will require explicit vocabulary instruction. Novel word learning also will be influenced by the size of a student's current lexicon and the number of exposures to a new word.

(continued)

Table 4.2. **Conventional Literacy** (*continued*)

- Although research on fluency has been rare, researchers have examined the construct of *signed reading fluency,* which may support both word reading and reading comprehension. Signed reading fluency is the ability of a reader to form a mental visualization of a printed English text and render it expressively in English signs, American Sign Language, or a combination of the two.

- Mode of word acquisition—the way in which a student acquires the meaning of a specific word (through perception, linguistic information, or both)—will influence comprehension of text; d/Dhh students will benefit most from explicit instruction on words that are learned perceptually followed by instruction on words that are learned through linguistic information.

- Difficulties with reading comprehension may be due primarily to students' insufficient knowledge of the syntax of English, which is necessary for processing words at the structural level.

- Many d/Dhh readers use metacognitive strategies to construct meaning of text, but their use of strategies to monitor and improve comprehension or evaluate texts is less sophisticated.

SIMILARITIES AND DIFFERENCES

The research reviewed in this chapter on emergent and conventional literacy learning among children and adolescents who have typical hearing and those who are d/Dhh reveals a number of qualitative similarities and quantitative differences between the two groups. These similarities and differences hold important implications for improving pedagogy and informing future research.

Emergent Literacy

The research on emergent literacy demonstrates that both groups of children engage purposefully in emergent reading and emergent writing activities in the preschool years and that their emergent literacy development is influenced by a variety of interactions in both home and school settings. Instructional interactions that support emergent literacy learning in young hearing children also hold promise for supporting emergent literacy in children who are d/Dhh.

The evidence also demonstrates that during the earliest phases of emergent literacy learning—that is, when children distinguish between drawing and writing, come to understand that print rather than pictures carries the meaning, and acquire fundamental concepts about print—d/Dhh and hearing children's development is remarkably similar. However, the research also indicates that in the final phase of emergent literacy, when acquisition of the alphabetic principle and use of letter–sound relationships is essential for movement into early conventional literacy, the literacy learning trajectories of most d/Dhh children diverge from those of their hearing peers. While most hearing children acquire these fundamental constructs and transition from emergent literacy into early conventional literacy, many d/Dhh children do not.

The evidence on emergent literacy also suggests that parents and early childhood educators might not be supporting adequately young d/Dhh children's development of the foundational constructs that are essential to these children's emergent literacy learning and, specifically, their transition into early conventional literacy. In particular, the absence of parental scaffolding that reflects evidence-based practices, the lack of literacy-rich classrooms, and the paucity of explicit early literacy instruction for d/Dhh children need to be addressed.

Phonology

A significant portion of the research reviewed in this chapter focuses on the role of phonology and phonological processing skills in the literacy development of d/Dhh children and adolescents. The evidence repeatedly demonstrates that these students often lack sufficient phonological awareness, knowledge, and processing skills to acquire literacy in English. That is not the case for hearing children, for whom it has been firmly established that phonological awareness and phonological processing skills strongly predict later reading achievement. In fact, for this group, researchers have turned their attention to other constructs that work alongside phonological processing skills (i.e., orthographic processing) to support the acquisition of literacy in English. This represents a major difference, then, between the two groups. While most hearing children acquire phonological awareness and phonological processing skills early, most d/Dhh, and particularly d/D, children do not. We argue that this is not a developmental difference—it is a quantitative difference due to insufficient access to the phonological components (e.g., segmentals and suprasegmentals) of spoken English (see also the discussion in Chapter 2).

Vocabulary

Researchers also have devoted considerable attention to d/Dhh students' English vocabulary development. The research repeatedly demonstrates that the acquisition of vocabulary knowledge is delayed for students who are d/Dhh. Consequently, they have considerably smaller lexicons than those of their hearing peers. This is another quantitative difference between the two groups. Although hearing students acquire a large portion of their vocabularies incidentally, that is often not the case for students who are d/Dhh. Students who are d/Dhh are exposed to fewer words and experience those words less often, and they have a narrower range of word learning experiences. Again, this is not a developmental difference—it is a quantitative difference due to insufficient access to through-the-air language, particularly via English.

However, these circumstances are changing for the d/Dhh students who benefit from recent advances in amplification technologies, including cochlear implants. These technologies provide considerably improved access to spoken English, which has supported students' vocabulary development as well as their acquisition of phonological knowledge and processing skills. For many students who take a predominantly nonauditory path to literacy in English, instructional mechanisms such as Cued Speech/Language and Visual Phonics have provided sufficient access to the phonology of spoken English to support their development of phonological knowledge and skills, as well. Given these advancements, we are hopeful that the quantitative differences with respect to the development of both vocabulary and phonology between students who have typical hearing and students who are d/Dhh will be reduced considerably in the days ahead. The research presented in this chapter strengthens that hope by offering considerable evidence that, when provided sufficient access to spoken English, many d/Dhh students demonstrate vocabulary growth and acquire phonological knowledge and skills similar to those of their hearing peers.

Yet, we also know this: Explicit instruction on these important literacy-related constructs will be necessary. The evidence reviewed here suggests that even with the benefits afforded by advancements in amplification technologies, d/Dhh students need explicit instruction to support their development of English vocabulary and phonological skills. At this point in time, the empirical evidence suggests that incidental learning is not the norm. Identifying instructional approaches that integrate explicit instruction on these foundational constructs into authentic reading and writing activities is the challenge before us.

Fluency

Research on reading fluency among students with typical hearing has garnered considerable research attention in recent years. The body of work focuses on repeated readings and demonstrates the effectiveness of this instructional approach for supporting reading fluency among students who have typical hearing. Among students who are d/Dhh, research on reading fluency has been rare. The Signed Reading Fluency Rubric for Deaf Children (Easterbrooks & Huston, 2008) holds promise for the assessment of reading fluency but needs to be investigated with larger populations of d/Dhh students and in diverse educational settings. The paucity of research on this crucial component of reading hinders our ability to provide students the instructional support they need and may contribute to the difficulties d/Dhh students experience in becoming skilled readers and writers.

Reading Comprehension

A primary focus of recent research on reading comprehension among students who have typical hearing is comprehension strategy instruction using content-area texts to promote students' understanding of domain-specific information. By contrast, however, in literacy and deafness, much of the recent research is still examining specific aspects of the reading comprehension process, in particular, mode of word acquisition, syntactic knowledge, and the use of metacognitive strategies in understanding text.

Research on mode of acquisition proposes that how students learn words (i.e., perceptually or through linguistic information) influences their reading comprehension. The pedagogical implication is that d/Dhh students will benefit most from explicit instruction on words that are learned perceptually followed by instruction on words that are learned through linguistic information. The hypothesis is that a strong foundation in perceptually learned words may facilitate students' learning of linguistically learned word meanings.

Recent research on syntactic knowledge highlights d/Dhh readers' use of an ineffective approach to comprehension—a semantic reading strategy—whereby the reader adds up the meanings of individual content words to construct meaning of the sentence. However, by ignoring the syntax—the order of the words in that sentence—the reader's comprehension is severely compromised. The importance of syntactic knowledge and the processing of syntactic information in a text cannot be underestimated, but scholars have provided little insight into how teachers might address this important issue. The field is desperate for intervention studies that will shed light on how to support students' development of syntactic knowledge.

Recent research on metacognition suggests that for all except the most skilled readers, application of metacognitive strategies is at a basic level—that is, many d/Dhh readers use metacognitive strategies to construct meaning but their use of strategies to monitor or improve comprehension or evaluate texts they have read is less sophisticated. Many readers are not metacognitively aware of the strategies they employ. The empirical evidence suggests that many d/Dhh readers would benefit from explicit instruction in the application of a range of metacognitive strategies. Given the importance of reading comprehension to students' overall academic achievement, intervention studies that examine specific factors related to reading comprehension among d/Dhh readers, as well as identifying effective practices for comprehension strategy instruction, must be a top priority among researchers.

CONCLUSION

In this chapter, we have reviewed current research on emergent literacy and conventional literacy learning in children and adolescents who have typical hearing and compared the findings of that investigative work to research on emergent and conventional literacy learning in children and adolescents who are d/Dhh. Together, the body of work supports a major premise of the qualitative similarity hypothesis—that the acquisition of English literacy by d/Dhh students is developmentally similar to that of typical literacy learners. Although there are quantitative differences in progress and growth, the empirical evidence demonstrates that d/Dhh students' development of both emergent and conventional literacy is qualitatively similar to that of their hearing peers. We argue that the evidence compels us to build on the knowledge gained from research and scholarship in the general field of literacy education as we strive to support both emergent and conventional literacy learning among children and adolescents who are d/Dhh.

REFERENCES

Al-Hilawani, Y. A. (2003). Clinical examination of three methods of teaching reading comprehension to deaf and hard-of-hearing students: From research to classroom applications. *Journal of Deaf Studies and Deaf Education, 8*(2), 146–156.

Allman, T. M. (2002). Patterns of spelling in young deaf and hard of hearing students. *American Annals of the Deaf, 147*(1), 46–64.

Anderson, R. C., & Pearson, P. D. (1984). A schema-theoretic view of basic processes in reading. In P. D. Pearson (Ed.), *Handbook of reading research* (Vol. 1, pp. 185–224). New York, NY: Longman.

Andrews, J. F. (1988). Deaf children's acquisition of prereading skills using the reciprocal teaching procedure. *Exceptional Children, 54*(4), 349–355.

Andrews, J. F., & Mason, J. (1986). How do deaf children learn about prereading? *American Annals of the Deaf, 131*(3), 210–217.

Aram, D., & Levin, I. (2001). Mother–child joint writing in low SES: Sociocultural factors, maternal mediation, and emergent literacy. *Cognitive Development, 16*(3), 831–852.

Aram, D., & Levin, I. (2011). Home support of children in the writing process: Contributions to early literacy. In S. Neuman & D. Dickinson (Eds.), *Handbook of early literacy research* (Vol. 3, pp. 189–199). New York, NY: Guilford Press.

Aram, D., Most, T., & Mayafit, H. (2006). Contributions of mother–child storybook retelling and joint writing to literacy development in kindergarteners with hearing loss. *Language, Speech, and Hearing Sciences in Schools, 37*, 209–223.

Aram, D., Most, T., & Ben Simon, A. (2008). Early literacy of kindergartners with hearing impairment: The role of mother–child collaborative writing. *Topics in Early Childhood Special Education, 28*(1), 31–41.

Araujo, L. (2002). The literacy development of kindergarten English language learners. *Journal of Research in Childhood Education, 16*(2), 232–247.

Archbold, S. (2010). *Deaf education: Changed by cochlear implantation?* Nijmegen, the Netherlands: University of Nijmegen Medical Center.

Bailey, A. L. (2007). *The language demands of school: Putting academic English to the test.* New Haven, CT: Yale University Press.

Banner, A., & Wang, Y. (2010). An analysis of the reading strategies used by adult and student deaf readers. *Journal of Deaf Studies and Deaf Education, 16*(1), 2–23.

Barker, L. (2003). Computer-assisted vocabulary acquisition: The CSLU vocabulary tutor in oral-deaf education. *Journal of Deaf Studies and Deaf Education, 8*(2), 187–197.

Baumann, J. F., Edwards, E. C., Boland, E. M., Olejnik, S., & Kame'enui, E. J. (2003). Vocabulary tricks: Effects of instruction in morphology and context on fifth-grade students' ability to derive and infer word meanings. *American Educational Research Journal, 40*, 447–494.

Beal-Alvarez, J. S., Lederberg, A. R., & Easterbrooks, S. R. (2011). Grapheme–phoneme acquisition of deaf preschoolers. *Journal of Deaf Studies and Deaf Education, 17*(1), 39–60.

Beck, I., & McKeown, M. (2007). Increasing young low income children's oral vocabulary repertories through rich and focused instruction. *Elementary School Journal, 107*(3), 251–271.

Berends, I. E., & Reitsma, P. (2006). Addressing semantics promotes the development of reading fluency. *Applied Psycholinguistics, 27*(2), 247–265.

Bergeron, J. P., Lederberg, A. R., Easterbrooks, S. R., Miller, E. M., & Connor, C. M. (2009). Building the alphabetic principle in young children who are deaf or hard of hearing. *Volta Review, 109*(2–3), 87–119.

Bowey, J. A., & Muller, D. (2005). Phonological recoding and rapid orthographic learning in third-graders' silent reading: A critical test of the self-teaching hypothesis. *Journal of Experimental Child Psychology, 92*, 203–219.

Bronfenbrenner, U. (1979). *The ecology of human development: Experiments by nature and design.* Cambridge, MA: Harvard University Press.

Brunswick, N., Martin, N. G., & Rippon, G. (2012). Early cognitive profiles of emergent readers: A longitudinal study. *Journal of Experimental Child Psychology, 111*(2), 268–285.

Bus, A. G., & van Ijzendoorn, M. H. (1999). Phonological awareness and early reading: A meta-analysis of experimental training studies. *Journal of Educational Psychology, 91*(3), 403–414.

Bus, A. G., van Ijzendoorn, M. H., & Pellegrini, A. (1995). Joint book reading makes for success in learning to read: A meta-analysis on intergenerational transmission of literacy. *Review of Educational Research, 65*(1), 1–21.

Cannon, J. E., Fredrick, L. D., & Easterbrooks, S. R. (2010). Vocabulary instruction through books read in American Sign Language for English language learners with hearing loss. *Communication Disorders Quarterly, 31*(2), 98–112.

Caravolas, M., Hulme, C., & Snowling, M. J. (2001). The foundations of spelling ability: Evidence from a 3-year longitudinal study. *Journal of Memory and Language, 45,* 751–774.

Chall, J. S. (1983). *Stages of reading development.* New York, NY: McGraw-Hill.

Charlier, B. L., & Leybaert, J. (2000). The rhyming skills of deaf children educated with phonetically augmented speechreading. *Quarterly Journal of Experimental Psychology, 53A,* 349–375.

Chateau, D., & Jared, D. (2000). Exposure to print and word recognition process. *Memory and Cognition, 28,* 143–153.

Chliounaki, K., & Bryant, P. (2007). How children learn about morphological spelling rules. *Child Development, 78,* 1360–1373.

Clay, M. M. (1975). *What did I write?* Auckland, New Zealand: Heinemann.

Coiro, J., & Schmar-Dobler, E. (2007). Exploring the online reading comprehension strategies used by sixth-grade skilled readers to search for and locate information on the internet. *Reading Research Quarterly, 42,* 214–257.

Colin, S., Magnan, A., Ecalle, J., & Leybaert, J. (2007). Relation between deaf children's phonological skills in kindergarten and word recognition performance in first grade. *Journal of Child Psychology and Psychiatry, 48,* 139–146.

Connor, C., Craig, H., Raudenbush, S., Heavner, K., & Zwolan, T. (2006). The age at which young deaf children receive cochlear implants and their vocabulary and speech-production growth: Is there an added value for early implantation? *Ear and Hearing, 27*(6), 628–644.

Connor, C., Hieber, S., Arts, H., & Zwolan, T. (2000). Speech, vocabulary, and the education of children using cochlear implants: Oral or Total Communication? *Journal of Speech, Language, and Hearing Research, 43*(5), 1185–1204.

Connor, C., Morrison, F., & Slominski, L. (2006). Preschool instruction and children's emergent literacy growth. *Journal of Educational Psychology, 98*(4), 665–689.

Connor, C., & Zwolan, T. A. (2004). Examining multiple sources of influence on the reading comprehension skills of children who use cochlear implants. *Journal of Speech, Language, and Hearing Research, 47*(3), 509–526.

Conway, D. (1985). Children (re)creating writing: A preliminary look at the purposes of free-choice writing of hearing-impaired kindergarteners. *Volta Review, 87*(5), 91–107.

Coppens, K. M., Tellings, A., Verhoeven, L., & Schreuder, R. (2011). Depth of reading vocabulary in hearing and hearing-impaired children. *Reading and Writing, 24,* 463–477.

Craig, S. (2006). The effects of an adapted interactive writing intervention on kindergarten children's phonological awareness, spelling, and early reading development: A contextualized approach to instruction. *Journal of Educational Psychology, 98*(4), 714–731.

Cunningham, A. E., Nathan, R. G., & Raher, K. S. (2011). Orthographic processing in models of word recognition. In M. Kamil, P. D. Pearson, E. Moje, & P. Afflerbach (Eds.), *Handbook of reading research* (Vol. 4, pp. 259–285). New York, NY: Routledge.

Cunningham, A. E., Perry, K. E., & Stanovich, K. E. (2001). Converging evidence for the concept of orthographic processing. *Reading and Writing, 14,* 549–568.

Cunningham, A. E., Perry, K. E., Stanovich, K. E., & Share, D. L. (2002). Orthographic learning during reading: Examining the role of self-teaching. *Journal of Experimental Child Psychology, 82,* 185–199.

de Jong, P. F., & Share, D. L. (2007). Orthographic learning during oral and silent reading. *Scientific Studies of Reading, 11,* 55–71.

DesJardin, J. L., Ambrose, S. E., & Eisenberg, L. S. (2009). Literacy skills in children with cochlear implants: The importance of early oral language and joint storybook reading. *Journal of Deaf Studies and Deaf Education, 14*(1), 22–43.

DesJardin, J. L., Ambrose, S. E., & Eisenberg, L. S. (2011). Maternal involvement in the home literacy environment: Supporting literacy skills in children with cochlear implants. *Communication Disorders Quarterly, 32*(3), 135–150.

DesJardin, J. L., & Eisenberg, L. (2007). Maternal contributions: Supporting language development in children with cochlear implants. *Ear and Hearing, 28,* 456–469.

Dewey, J. (1916). *Democracy and education.* New York, NY: Macmillan.

Diamond, K. E., & Powell, D. R. (2011). An iterative approach to the development of a professional development intervention for Head Start teachers. *Journal of Early Intervention, 33*(1), 75–93.

Dickinson, D. K., & McCabe, A. (2001). Bringing it all together: The multiple origins, skills, and environmental supports of early literacy. *Learning Disabilities Research and Practice, 16*(4), 186–202.

Dickinson, D. K., McCabe, A. L., Anastasopoulos, L., Peisner-Feinberg, E. S., & Poe, M. D. (2003). The comprehensive language approach to early literacy: The interrelationships among vocabulary, phonological sensitivity, and print knowledge among preschool-aged children. *Journal of Educational Psychology, 95,* 465–481.

Ducharme, D. A., & Arcand, I. (2010). How do deaf signers of LSQ and their teachers construct the meaning of a text? *Journal of Deaf Studies and Deaf Education, 16*(1), 47–65.

Durkin, D. (1978–1979). What classroom observation reveals about reading comprehension instruction. *Reading Research Quarterly, 14,* 481–533.

Dyer, A., MacSweeney, M., Szczerbinski, M., Green, L., & Campbell, R. (2003). Predictor of reading delay in deaf adolescents: The relative contribution of rapid automatized naming speed and phonological awareness and decoding. *Journal of Deaf Studies and Deaf Education, 9*(3), 215–220.

Dyson, A. H. (1983). The role of oral language in early writing processes. *Research in the Teaching of English, 17*(1), 1–30.

Dyson, A. H. (2010). Writing childhoods under construction: Re-visioning "copying" in early childhood. *Journal of Early Childhood Literacy, 10*(1), 7–31.

Easterbrooks, S. R., & Baker, S. (2002). *Language learning in children who are deaf and hard of hearing.* Boston, MA: Allyn and Bacon.

Easterbrooks, S. R., & Huston, S. G. (2008). The signed reading fluency of students who deaf/hard of hearing. *Journal of Deaf Studies and Deaf Education, 13*(1), 37–54.

Easterbrooks, S. R., Lederberg, A., Miller, E., Bergeron, J., & McDonald-Connor, C. (2008). Emergent literacy skills during early childhood in children with hearing loss: Strengths and weaknesses. *Volta Review, 108*(2), 91–114.

Easterbrooks, S. R., Lederberg, A., & Connor, C. (2010). Contributions of the emergent literacy environment to literacy outcomes for young children who are deaf. *American Annals of the Deaf, 155*(4), 467–480.

Ehri, L. C. (2005). Learning to read words: Theory, findings, and issues. *Scientific Studies of Reading, 9*(2), 167–188.

Ehri, L. C., Nunes, S., Willows, D., Schuster, B., Yaghoub-Zadeh, Z., & Shanahan, T. (2001). Phoneme awareness instruction helps children learn to read: Evidence from the National Reading Panel's meta-analysis. *Reading Research Quarterly, 36*(3), 250–287.

Elster, C. (1994). Patterns within preschoolers' emergent readings. *Reading Research Quarterly, 29*(4), 402–418.

Enns, C., & Lafond, L. D. (2007). Reading against all odds: A pilot study of two deaf students with dyslexia. *American Annals of the Deaf, 152,* 63–72.

Evans, M. A., Bell, M., Shaw, D., Moretti, S., & Page, J. (2006). Letter names, letter sounds, and phonological awareness: An examination of kindergarten children across letters and of letters across children. *Reading and Writing: An Interdisciplinary Journal, 19*(9), 959–989.

Ewoldt, C. (1985). A descriptive study of the developing literacy of young hearing-impaired children. *Volta Review, 87*(5), 109–126.

Ezell, H. K., & Justice, L. M. (2000). Increasing the print focus of adult–child shared book reading through observational learning. *American Journal of Speech-Language Pathology, 9*, 36–47.

Ezell, H. K., & Justice, L. M. (2005). *Shared storybook reading: Building young children's language and emergent literacy skills.* Baltimore, MD: Brookes.

Fagan, M. K., & Pisoni, D. (2010). Hearing experience and receptive vocabulary development in deaf children with cochlear implants. *Journal of Deaf Studies and Deaf Education, 15*(2), 149–161.

Fagan, M. K., Pisoni, D. B., Horn, D. L., & Dillon, C. M. (2007). Neuropsychological correlates of vocabulary, reading, and working memory in deaf children with cochlear implants. *Journal of Deaf Studies and Deaf Education, 12*(4), 461–471.

Farkas, G., & Beron, K. (2004). The detailed age trajectory of vocabulary knowledge: Differences by class and race. *Social Science Research, 33*(3), 464–497.

Fernald, A., & Weisleder, A. (2011). Early language experience is vital to developing fluency in understanding. In S. Neuman & D. Dickinson (Eds.), *Handbook of early literacy research* (Vol. 3, pp. 3–19). New York, NY: Guilford Press.

Fuchs, L. S., Fuchs, D., Hosp, M. K., & Jenkins, J. R. (2001). Oral reading fluency as an indicator of reading competence: A theoretical, empirical, and historical analysis. *Scientific Studies of Reading, 5*(3), 239–256.

Fung, P., Chow, B. W., & McBride-Chang, C. (2005). The impact of a dialogic reading program on deaf and hard-of-hearing and early primary school-aged students in Hong Kong. *Journal of Deaf Studies and Deaf Education, 10*(1), 82–95.

Gajria, M., Jitendra, A. K., Sood, S., & Sacks, G. (2007). Improving comprehension of expository text in students with LD: A research synthesis. *Journal of Learning Disabilities, 40*, 210–225.

Gallagher, A., Frith, U., & Snowling, M. J. (2000). Precursors of literacy delay among children at genetic risk of dyslexia. *Journal of Child Psychology and Psychiatry, and Allied Disciplines, 41*(2), 203–213.

Gee, J. (1990). *Sociolinguistics and literacies.* London, England: Falmer Press.

Gentry, M. M., Chinn, K. M., & Moulton, R. D. (2004). Effectiveness of multimedia reading materials when used with children who are deaf. *American Annals of the Deaf, 149*(5), 394–403.

Gersten, R., Fuchs, L. S., Williams, J. P., & Baker, S. (2001).Teaching reading comprehension strategies to students with learning disabilities: A review of the research. *Review of Educational Research, 71*(1), 279–320.

Gillespie, C. W., & Twardosz, S. (1997). A group storybook-reading intervention with children at a residential school for the deaf. *American Annals of the Deaf, 141*(4), 320–332.

Goldfeld, S., Napiza, N., Quach, J., Reilly, S., Ukoumunne, O., & Wake, M. (2011). Outcomes of a universal shared reading intervention by 2 years of age: The Let's Read Trial. *Pediatrics, 127*(3), 445–453.

Gonzalez, J. E., & Nelson, R. (2003). Stepping stones to literacy: A prevention-oriented phonological awareness training program. *Reading and Writing Quarterly, 19*(4), 393–398.

Graesser, A. C. (2007). An introduction to strategic reading comprehension. In D. D. McNamara (Ed.), *Reading comprehension strategies, theories, interventions, and technologies* (pp. 3–26). New York, NY: Erlbaum.

Greenleaf, C. L., & Mueller, F. L. (2003). *Impact of the pilot academic literacy course on ninth grade students' reading development: Academic year 1996–1997.* San Francisco, CA: Stuart Foundation.

Griffith, L. W., & Rasinski, T. V. (2004). A focus on fluency: How one teacher incorporated fluency with her reading curriculum. *Reading Teacher, 58*(2), 126–137.

Guthrie, J. T., McRae, A., & Klauda, S. L. (2007). Contributions of concept-oriented reading instruction to knowledge about interventions for motivations in reading. *Educational Psychologist, 42*(4), 237–250.

Guthrie, J. T., Wigfield, A., & Perencevich, K. C. (Eds.). (2004). *Motivating reading comprehension: Concept-oriented reading instruction.* Mahwah, NJ: Erlbaum.

Hagiliassis, N., Pratt, C., & Johnston, M. (2006). Orthographic and phonological processes in reading. *Reading and Writing, 19*, 235–263.

Harmon, J. M., Hedrick, W. B., & Wood, K. D. (2005). Research on vocabulary instruction in the content areas: Implications for struggling readers. *Reading and Writing Quarterly, 21*, 261–280.

Hart, B., & Risley, T. (1995). *Meaningful differences in the everyday experience of young American children.* Baltimore, MD: Brookes.

Hayes, H., Geers, A. E., Treiman, R., & Moog, J. S. (2009). Receptive vocabulary development in deaf children with cochlear implants: Achievement in an intensive auditory–oral educational setting. *Ear and Hearing, 30*(1), 128–135.

Heath, S. B. (1983). *Ways with words: Language, life, and work in communities and classrooms.* Cambridge, MA: Cambridge University Press.

Hiebert, E. H., & Lubliner, S. (2008). The nature, learning, and instruction of general academic vocabulary. In A.E. Farstrup & S.J. Samuels (Eds.), *What research has to say about vocabulary instruction* (pp. 106–129). Newark, DE: International Reading Association.

Howell, J. J., & Luckner, J. L. (2003). Helping one deaf student develop content literacy skills: An action research report. *Communication Disorders Quarterly, 25*(1), 23–27.

Hsieh, W. Y., Hemmeter, M. L., McCollum, J. A., & Ostrosky, M. M. (2009). Using coaching to increase preschool teachers' use of emergent literacy teaching strategies. *Early Childhood Research Quarterly, 24*(3), 229–247.

International Communication Learning Institute. (1996). *See the sound: Visual phonics.* Webster, WI: ICLI.

James, D., Rajput, K., Brinton, J., & Goswami, U. (2008). Phonological awareness, vocabulary, and word reading in children who use cochlear implants: Does age of implantation explain individual variability in performance outcomes and growth? *Journal of Deaf Studies and Deaf Education, 13*(1), 117–137.

Johnson, C., & Goswami, U. (2010). Phonological awareness, vocabulary, and reading in deaf children with cochlear implants. *Journal of Speech, Language, and Hearing Research, 53*, 237–261.

Jordan, M., & Schoenbach, R. (2003). Breaking through the literacy ceiling: Reading is demystified for secondary students in reading apprenticeship classrooms, where students "can read to learn" in all their subject areas. *Leadership, 33*(2), 8–13.

Justice, L. M., & Ezell, H. (2002). Use of storybook reading to increase print awareness in at-risk children. *American Journal of Speech-Language Pathology, 11*(1), 17–29.

Justice, L. M., & Piasta, S. (2011). Developing children's print knowledge through adult–child storybook reading interactions: Print referencing as an instructional practice. In S. Neuman & D. Dickinson (Eds.), *Handbook of early literacy research* (Vol. 3, pp. 200–213). New York, NY: Guilford Press.

Kuhn, M. R. (2004). Helping students become accurate, expressive reads: Fluency instruction for small groups. *Reading Teacher, 58*(4), 338–344.

Kuhn, M. R. (2005). A comparative study of small group fluency instruction. *Reading Psychology, 26*(2), 127–146.

Kuhn, M. R., & Schwanenflugel, P. J. (2006). Fluency-oriented reading instruction: A merging of theory and practice. In K. A. D. Stahl & M. C. McKenna (Eds.), *Reading research at work: Foundations of effective practice* (pp. 205–213). New York, NY: Guilford.

Kuhn, M. R., Schwanenflugel, P. J., Morris, R. D., Morrow, L. M., Woo, D. G., Meisinger, E. B., et al. (2006). Teaching children to become fluent and automatic readers. *Journal of Literacy Research, 38*(4), 357–387.

Kuhn, M. R., & Stahl, S. A. (2003). Fluency: A review of developmental and remedial practices. *Journal of Educational Psychology, 95*, 3–22.

Kyle, F. E., & Harris, M. (2006). Concurrent correlates and predictors of reading and spelling achievement in deaf and hearing school children. *Journal of Deaf Studies and Deaf Education, 22*(3), 273–288.

Kyle, F. E., & Harris, M. (2010). Predictors of reading development in deaf children: A 3-year longitudinal study. *Journal of Experimental Child Psychology, 107*, 229–243.

Kyle, F. E., & Harris, M. (2011). Longitudinal patterns of emergent literacy in beginning deaf and hearing readers. *Journal of Deaf Studies and Deaf Education, 16*(3), 289–304.

Kyte, C. S., & Johnson, C. J. (2006). The role of phonological recoding in orthographic learning. *Journal of Experimental Child Psychology, 93*, 166–185.

LaBerge, D., & Samuels, S. J. (1974). Toward a theory of automatic information processing in reading. *Cognitive Psychology, 6*, 293–323.

Landry, S. H., & Smith, K. E. (2006). The influence of parenting on emerging literacy skills. In D. Dickinson & S. Neuman (Eds.), *Handbook of early literacy research* (Vol. 2, pp. 135–148). New York, NY: Guilford Press.

LaSasso, C., Crain, K., & Leybaert, J. (2003). Rhyme generation in deaf students: The effect of exposure to Cued Speech. *Journal of Deaf Studies and Deaf Education, 8*, 250–270.

LaSasso, C., Crain, K., & Leybaert, J. (Eds.). (2010). *Cued Speech and cued language for deaf and hard of hearing children.* San Diego, CA: Plural Publishing.

Lederberg, A. R., & Beal-Alvarez, J. S. (2011). Expressing meaning: From prelinguistic communication to building vocabulary. In M. Marschark & P. Spencer (Eds.), *The Oxford handbook of deaf studies, language, and education* (2nd ed., Vol. 1, pp. 258–275). New York, NY: Oxford University Press.

Lederberg, A. R., Miller, E. M., Easterbrooks, S. R., & Connor, C. M. (2011). *Foundations for literacy.* Unpublished curriculum. Atlanta, GA: Georgia State University.

Lederberg, A. R., Prezbindowski, A. K., & Spencer, P. E. (2000). Word-learning skills of deaf preschoolers: The development of novel mapping and rapid word-learning strategies. *Child Development, 71*(6), 1571–1585.

Lederberg, A. R., & Spencer, P. E. (2009). Word-learning abilities in deaf and hard-of-hearing preschoolers: Effect of lexicon size and language modality. *Journal of Deaf Studies and Deaf Education, 14*(1), 44–62.

Lefebvre, P., Trudeau, N., & Sutton, A. (2011). Enhancing vocabulary, print awareness, and phonological awareness through shared storybook reading with low-income preschoolers. *Journal of Early Childhood Literacy, 11*(4), 453–479.

Leigh, G. (2008). Changing parameters in deafness and deaf education. In M. Marschark & P. Hauser (Eds.), *Deaf cognition: Foundations and outcomes* (pp. 24–51). New York, NY: Oxford University Press.

Lesaux, N. K., Kieffer, M. J., Faller, S. E., & Kelley, J. G. (2010). The effectiveness and ease of implementation of an academic vocabulary intervention for linguistically diverse students in urban middle schools. *Reading Research Quarterly, 45*(2), 196–228.

Lonigan, C. J., Anthony, J. L., Phillips, B. M., Purpura, D. J., Wilson, S. B., & McQueen, J. D. (2009). The nature of preschool phonological processing abilities and their relations to vocabulary, general cognitive abilities, and print knowledge. *Journal of Educational Psychology, 101*(2), 345–358.

Lonigan, C. J., Burgess, S. R., & Anthony, J. L. (2000). Development of emergent literacy and early reading skills in preschool children: Evidence from a latent-variable longitudinal study. *Developmental Psychology, 36*(5), 596–613.

Lovelace, S., & Stewart, S. R. (2007). Increasing print awareness in preschoolers with language impairment using non-evocative print referencing. *Language, Speech, and Hearing Services in Schools, 38*(1), 16–30.

Luckner, J. L., & Urbach, J. (2012). Reading fluency and students who are deaf or hard of hearing: Synthesis of the research. *Communication Disorders Quarterly, 33*(4), 230–241.

Luetke-Stahlman, B., & Nielsen, D. C. (2003). The contribution of phonological awareness and receptive and expressive English to the reading ability of deaf students with varying degree of exposure to accurate English. *Journal of Deaf Studies and Deaf Education, 8*(4), 464–484.

Marschark, M., Rhoten, C., & Fabich, M. (2007). Effects of cochlear implants on children's reading and academic achievement. *Journal of Deaf Studies and Deaf Education, 12*(3), 269–282.

Marschark, M., & Wauters, L. (2008). Language comprehension and learning by deaf students. In M. Marschark & P. C. Hauser (Eds.), *Deaf cognition: Foundations and outcomes* (pp. 309–350). New York, NY: Oxford University Press.

Marulis, L. M., & Neuman, S. B. (2010). The effects of vocabulary intervention on young children's word learning: A meta-analysis. *Review of Educational Research, 80*(3), 300–335.

Massaro, D., & Light, J. (2004). Improving the vocabulary of children with hearing loss. *Volta Review, 104*(3), 141–174.

Maxwell, M. (1984). A deaf child's natural development of literacy. *Sign Language Studies, 44,* 191–224.

Mayberry, R. I., del Giudice, A. A., & Lieberman, A. M. (2011). Reading achievement in relation to phonological coding and awareness in deaf readers: A meta-analysis. *Journal of Deaf Studies and Deaf Education, 16*(2), 164–188.

Mayer, C. (2007). What matters in the early literacy development of deaf children. *Journal of Deaf Studies and Deaf Education, 12*(4), 411–431.

Mayer, C., & Leigh, G. (2010). The changing context for sign bilingual education programs: Issues in language and the development of literacy. *International Journal of Bilingual Education and Bilingualism, 13*(2), 175–186.

McKeown, M. G., Beck, I. L., & Blake, R. K. (2009). Rethinking reading comprehension instruction: A comparison of instruction for strategies and content approaches. *Reading Research Quarterly, 44,* 218–253.

McNamara, T., Miller, D., & Bransford, J. D. (2000). Mental models and reading comprehension. In R. Barr, M. L. Kamil, P. D. Mosenthal, & P. D. Pearson (Eds.), *Handbook of reading research* (Vol. 2, pp. 490–511). New York, NY: Longman.

Mendelsohn, A., Mogliner, L., Dreyer, B. P., Forman, J. A., Weinstein, S. C., Broderick, M., et al. (2001). The impact of a clinic-based literacy intervention on language development in inner-city preschool children. *Pediatrics, 107*(1), 130–134.

Metsala, J. L., & Walley, A. C. (1998). Spoken vocabulary growth and the segmental restructuring of lexical representations: Precursors to phonemic awareness and early reading ability. In J. L. Metsala & L. C. Ehri (Eds.), *Word recognition in beginning literacy* (pp. 89–120). Hillsdale, NJ: Erlbaum.

Miller, P. (2000). Syntactic and semantic processing in Hebrew readers with prelingual deafness. *American Annals of the Deaf, 145*(5), 436–451.

Miller, P. (2005). Reading comprehension and its relation to the quality of functional hearing: Evidence from readers with different functional hearing abilities. *American Annals of the Deaf, 150*(3), 305–323.

Miller, P. (2010). Phonological, orthographic, and syntactic awareness and their relation to reading comprehension in prelingually deaf individuals: What can we learn from skilled readers? *Journal of Developmental and Physical Disabilities, 22,* 549–580.

Miller, P., & Clark, M. D. (2010). Phonemic awareness is not necessary to become a skilled reader. *Journal of Developmental and Physical Disabilities, 23,* 459–476.

Moll, S. E., Bus, A. G., de Jong, M. T., & Smeets, D. (2008). Added value of dialogic parent–child book readings: A meta-analysis. *Early Education and Development, 19*(1), 7–26.

Morrow, L. M., & Gambrell, L. B. (2001). Literature-based instruction in the early years. In S. Neuman & D. Dickinson (Eds.), *Handbook of early literacy research* (pp. 348–360). New York, NY: Guilford.

Muter, V., Hulme, C., Snowling, M. J., & Stevenson, J. (2004). Phonemes, rimes, vocabulary, and grammatical skills as foundations of early reading development: Evidence from a longitudinal study. *Developmental Psychology, 40,* 665–681.

Nagy, W. E., & Scott, J. A. (2000). Vocabulary process. In M. L. Kamil, P. B. Mosenthal, P. D. Pearson, & R. Barr (Eds.), *Handbook of reading research* (Vol. 3, pp. 269–284). Mahwah, NJ: Erlbaum.

Narr, R. F. (2008). Phonological awareness and decoding in deaf/hard-of-hearing students who use visual phonics. *Journal of Deaf Studies and Deaf Education, 13*(3), 405–416.

National Early Literacy Panel. (2008). *Developing early literacy: Report of the National Early Literacy Panel.* Washington, DC: National Institute for Literacy.

National Reading Panel. (2000). *Teaching children to read: An evidence-based assessment of the scientific research literature on reading and its implications for reading instruction* (NIH Publication No. 00-4769). Washington, DC: U.S. Government Printing Office.

Needlman, R., Toker, K. H., Dreyer, B. P., Klass, P., & Mendelsohn, A. L. (2005). Effectiveness of a primary care intervention to support reading aloud: A multicenter evaluation. *Ambulatory Pediatrics, 5*(4), 209–215.

Ness, M. (2011). Explicit reading comprehension instruction in elementary classrooms: Teacher use of reading comprehension strategies. *Journal of Research in Childhood Education, 25*(1), 98–117.

Neumann, M. M., Hood, M., & Neuman, D. (2009). The scaffolding of emergent literacy skills in the home environment: A case study. *Early Childhood Education Journal, 36*(4), 313–319.

Paatsch, L., Blamey, P., Sarant, J., & Bow, C. (2006). The effects of speech production and vocabulary training on different components of spoken-language performance. *Journal of Deaf Studies and Deaf Education, 11*(1), 39–55.

Pakulski, L. A., & Kaderavek, J. N. (2001). Narrative production by children who are deaf or hard of hearing: The effect of role play. *Volta Review, 103*(3), 127–139.

Parilla, R., Kirby, J., & McQuarrie, L. (2004). Articulation rate, naming speed, verbal short-term memory and phonological awareness: Longitudinal predictors of early reading development. *Scientific Studies of Reading, 8*(1), 3–26.

Paul, P. (2009). *Language and deafness* (4th ed.). Sudbury, MA: Jason & Bartlett.

Perfetti, C. A. (2007). Reading ability: Lexical quality to comprehension. *Scientific Studies of Reading, 11*(4), 357–383.

Perfetti, C. A., & Hart, L. (2001). The lexical quality hypothesis. In L. Verhoeven, C. Elbro, & P. Reitsma (Eds.), *Precursors of functional literacy* (pp. 189–214). Amsterdam, the Netherlands: John Benjamins.

Perfetti, C. A., & Sandak, R. (2000). Reading optimally builds on spoken language: Implications for deaf readers. *Journal of Deaf Studies and Deaf Education, 5*(1), 32–50.

Piaget, J., & Inhelder, B. (1969). *The psychology of the child* (H. Weaver, Trans.). New York, NY: Basic Books.

Piasta, S., Justice, L., McGinty, A., & Kaderavek, J. (2012). Increasing young children's contact with print during shared reading: Longitudinal effects on literacy achievement. *Child Development, 83*(3), 810–820.

Piasta, S., & Wagner, R. (2010). Developing early literacy skills: A meta-analysis of alphabet learning and instruction. *Reading Research Quarterly, 45*(1), 8–38.

Pikulski, J. J., & Chard, D.J. (2005). Fluency: Bridge between decoding and reading comprehension. *Reading Teacher, 58*(6), 510–519.

Pittman, A. L. (2008). Short-term word-learning rate in children with normal hearing and children with hearing loss in limited and extended high-frequency bandwidths. *Journal of Speech, Language, and Hearing Research, 51,* 785–797.

Pittman, A. L., Lewis, D. E., Hoover, B. M., & Stelmachowicz, P. G. (2005). Rapid word-learning in normal hearing and hearing impaired children: Effects of age, receptive vocabulary, and high-frequency amplification. *Ear and Hearing, 26,* 619–629.

Powell, D. R., Diamond, K. E., Burchinal, M. R., & Koehler, M. J. (2010). Effects of an early literacy professional development intervention on Head Start teachers and children. *Journal of Educational Psychology, 102*(2), 239–312.

RAND Reading Study Group. (2002). *Reading for understanding: Toward an R&D program in reading comprehension.* Santa Monica, CA: RAND.

Rasinski, T. V. (2004). *Assessing reading fluency*. Honolulu, HI: Pacific Resources for Education and Learning.

Rasinski, T. V. (2008). Teaching fluency artfully. In R. Fink & S.J. Samuels (Eds.), *Inspiring reading success: Interest and motivation in an age of high-stakes testing* (pp. 117–140). Newark, DE: International Reading Association.

Rasinski, T. V., & Padak, N. D. (2008). *From phonics to fluency: Effective teaching of decoding and reading fluency in the elementary school* (2nd ed.). Boston, MA: Allyn & Bacon.

Rasinski, T. V., Reutzel, D. R., Chard, D., & Linan-Thompson, S. (2011). Reading fluency. In M. Kamil, P. D. Pearson, E. Moje, & P. Afflerbach (Eds.), *Handbook of reading research* (Vol. 4, pp. 286–319). New York, NY: Routledge.

Rasinski, T. V., Rikli, A., & Johnston, S. (2009). Reading fluency: More than automaticity? More than a concern for the primary grades? *Literacy Research and Instruction, 48*(4), 350–361.

Romance, N. R., & Vitale, M. R. (2001). Implementing an in-depth expanded science model in elementary schools: Multi-year findings, research issues, and policy implications. *International Journal of Science Education, 23*(4), 373–404.

Rottenberg, C., & Searfoss, L. (1992). Becoming literate in a preschool class: Literacy development of hearing-impaired children. *Journal of Reading Behavior, 24*(4), 463–479.

Rowe, L., & Allen, B. (1995). Interactive storybook reading with young deaf children in school and home settings. In P. Dreyer (Ed.), *Towards multiple perspectives on literacy: Fifty-ninth yearbook of the Claremont Reading Conference* (pp. 170–182). Claremont, CA: Claremont Reading Conference.

Ruggirello, C., & Mayer, C. (2010). Language development in a hearing and a deaf twin with simultaneous bilateral cochlear implants. *Journal of Deaf Studies and Deaf Education, 15*(3), 274–286.

Ruiz, N. (1995). A young deaf child learns to write: Implications for literacy development. *Reading Teacher, 49*(3), 206–217.

Ruiz, N. (1996). A young deaf child explores punctuation. In N. Hall & A. Robinson (Eds.), *Learning about punctuation* (pp. 109–127). Portsmouth, NH: Heinemann.

Saracho, O. (1990). Developmental sequences in three-year-old children's writing. *Early Childhood Development, 56*, 1–10.

Scarborough, H. S. (1998a). Early identification of children at risk for reading disabilities: Phonological awareness and some other promising predictors. In B. K. Shapiro, P. J. Accardo, & A. J. Capute (Eds.), *Specific reading disability: A view of the spectrum* (pp. 75–119). Timonium, MD: York Press.

Scarborough, H. S. (2005). Developmental relationships between language and reading: Reconciling a beautiful hypothesis with some ugly facts. In H.W. Catts & A. G. Kamhi (Eds.), *The connections between language and reading disabilities* (pp. 3–24). Mahwah, NJ: Erlbaum.

Schatschneider, C., Flectcher, K. M., Francis, D. J., Carolson, S. D., & Forman, B. R. (2004). Kindergarten prediction of reading skills: A longitudinal comparative analysis. *Journal of Educational Psychology, 96*(2), 265–282.

Schickedanz, J., & Dickinson, D. K. (2005). *Opening the world of learning: A comprehensive literacy program*. Parsippany, NJ: Pearson Early Learning.

Schirmer, B. (2003). Using verbal protocols to identify the reading strategies of students who are deaf. *Journal of Deaf Studies and Deaf Education, 8*(2), 157–170.

Schirmer, B. R., Bailey, J., & Schirmer Lockman, A. (2004). What verbal protocols reveal about the reading strategies of deaf students: A replication study. *American Annals of the Deaf, 149*(1), 5–16.

Schirmer, B. R., Schaffer, L., Therrien, W. J., & Schirmer, T. N. (2012). Reread–adapt and answer–comprehend intervention with deaf and hard of hearing readers: Effect on fluency and reading achievement. *American Annals of the Deaf, 156*(5), 469–475.

Schirmer, B. R., Therrien, W. J., Schaffer, L., & Schirmer, T. N. (2009). Repeated reading as an instructional intervention with deaf readers: Effect on fluency and reading achievement. *Reading Improvement, 46*, 168–177.

Schoenbach, R., Braunger, J., Greenleaf, C., & Litman, C. (2003). Apprenticing adolescents to reading in subject-area classrooms. *Phi Delta Kappan, 85*(2), 133–138.

Schorr, E., Roth, F., & Fox, N. (2008). A comparison of the speech and language skills of children with cochlear implants and children with normal hearing. *Communication Disorders Quarterly, 29*(4), 195–210.

Schwanenflugel, P. J., Meisinger, E. B., Wisenbaker, J. M., Kuhn, M. R., Strauss, G. P., & Morris, R. D. (2006). Becoming a fluent and automatic reader in the early elementary school years. *Reading Research Quarterly, 41*, 496–522.

Segal-Drori, O., Korat, O., Shamir, A., & Klein, P. S. (2010). Reading electronic and printed books with and without adult instruction: Effects on emergent reading. *Reading and Writing, 23*(8), 913–930.

Segers, E., & Verhoeven, L. (2005). Long-term effects of computer training of phonological awareness in kindergarten. *Journal of Computer Assisted Learning, 21*(1), 17–27.

Senechal, M., Ouellette, G., & Rodney, D. (2006). The misunderstood giant: On the predictive role of early vocabulary to future reading. In D. Dickinson & S. Newman (Eds.), *Handbook of early literacy research* (Vol. 2, pp. 173–182). New York, NY: Guilford Press.

Senechal, M., & Young, L. (2008). The effect of family literacy interventions on children's acquisition of reading from kindergarten to grade 3: A meta-analytic review. *Review of Educational Research, 78*(4), 880–907.

Share, D. L. (1995). Phonological recoding and self-teaching: Sine qua non of reading acquisition. *Cognition, 55*, 151–218.

Share, D. L. (1999). Phonological recoding and orthographic learning: A direct test of the self-teaching hypothesis. *Journal of Experimental Child Psychology, 72*, 95–129.

Share, D. L. (2004). Orthographic learning at a glance: On the time course and developmental onset of self-teaching. *Journal of Experimental Child Psychology, 87*, 267–298.

Share, D. L. (2008). Orthographic learning, phonological recoding, and self-teaching. In R. Kail (Ed.), *Advances in child behavior and development* (Vol. 36, pp. 31–82). San Diego, CA: Elsevier Academic Press.

Shook, A. C., Hazelkorn, M., & Lozano, E. R. (2011). Science vocabulary for all. *Science Teacher, 78*(3), 45–49.

Sigel, I. E. (2006). Research to practice redefined. In W. Damon & R. M. Lerner (Series Eds.) & K. A. Renninger & I. E. Sigel (Vol. Eds.), *Handbook of child psychology: Vol. 4, Child psychology in practice* (6th ed., pp. 1017–1023). Hoboken, NJ: Wiley.

Silverstein, M., Iverson, L., & Lorzano, P. (2002). An English-language clinic-based literacy program is effective for a multilingual population. *Pediatrics, 109*(5), e76, 1–6.

Singleton, J. L., Morgan, D., DiGello, E., Wiles, J., & Rivers, R. (2004). Vocabulary use by low, moderate, and high ASL-proficient writers compared to hearing ESL and monolingual speakers. *Journal of Deaf Studies and Deaf Education, 9*(1), 86–103.

Sirois, P., Boisclair, A., & Giasson, J. (2008). Understanding of the alphabetic principle through invented spelling among hearing-impaired children learning to read and write: Experimentation with a pedagogical approach. *Journal of Research in Reading, 31*(4), 339–358.

Smith, A., & Wang, Y. (2010). The impact of visual phonics on the phonological awareness and speech production of a student who is deaf: A case study. *American Annals of the Deaf, 155*(2), 124–130.

Smith, M. W., & Dickinson, D. K. (1994). Describing oral language opportunities and environments in Head Start and other preschool classrooms. *Early Childhood Research Quarterly, 9*(3), 345–366.

Snow, C. E. (1983). Literacy and language: Relationships during the preschool years. *Harvard Educational Review, 53*(2), 165–189.

Snow, C. E., & Ninio, A. (1986). The contracts of literacy: What children learn from learning to read books. In W. Teale & E. Sulzby (Eds.), *Emergent literacy* (pp. 116–138). Norwood, NJ: Ablex.

Snowling, M. J. (1995). Phonological processing and developmental dyslexia. *Journal of Research in Reading, 18,* 132–138.

Spencer, L. J, Barker, B. A., & Tomblin, J. B. (2003). Exploring the language and literacy outcomes of pediatric cochlear implant users. *Ear and Hearing, 24*(3), 236–247.

Stahl, S., & Heubach, K. (2005). Fluency-oriented reading instruction. *Journal of Literacy Research, 37*(1), 25–60.

Stahl, S., & Nagy, W. (2006). *Teaching word meanings.* Mahwah, NJ: Erlbaum.

Stanovich, K. E. (1980). Toward an interactive-compensatory model of individual differences in the development of reading fluency. *Reading Research Quarterly, 16,* 32–71.

Stanovich, K. E. (2000). *Progress in understanding reading: Scientific foundations and new frontiers.* New York, NY: Guilford Press.

Stelmachowicz, P. G., Pittman, A. L., Hoover, B. M., & Lewis, D. E. (2004). Novel-word learning in children with normal hearing and hearing loss. *Ear and Hearing, 25,* 47–56.

Sulzby, E. (1995). Children's emergent reading of favorite storybooks: A developmental study. *Reading Research Quarterly, 20*(4), 458–481.

Sylva, K., Melhuish, E., Sammons, P., Siraj-Blatchford, I., & Taggart, B. (2010). *Early childhood matters: Evidence from the Effective Pre-School and Primary Education project.* London, England: Routledge.

Therrien, W. J. (2004). Fluency and comprehension gains as a result of repeated reading: A meta-analysis. *Remedial and Special Education, 25,* 252–261.

Torgesen, J. K. (2002). The prevention of reading difficulties. *Journal of School Psychology, 40*(1), 7–26.

Torppa, M., Poikkeus, A.-M., Laakso, M.-L., Eklund, K., & Lyytinen, H. (2006). Predicting delayed letter knowledge development and its relation to grade 1 reading achievement among children with and without familial risk for dyslexia. *Developmental Psychology, 42*(6), 1128–1142.

Travers, J. C., Higgins, K., Pierce, T., Boone, R., Miller, S., & Tandy, R. (2011). Emergent literacy skills of preschool students with autism: A comparison of teacher-led and computer-assisted instruction. *Education and Training in Autism and Developmental Disabilities, 46*(3), 326–338.

Treutlein, A., Zöller, I., Roos, J., & Schöler, H. (2008). Effects of phonological awareness training on reading achievement. *Written Language and Literacy, 11*(2), 147–166.

Trezek, B., & Malmgren, K. (2005). The efficacy of utilizing a phonics treatment package with middle school deaf and hard of hearing students. *Journal of Deaf Studies and Deaf Education, 10,* 256–271.

Trezek, B. J., & Wang, Y. (2006). Implications of utilizing a phonics-based reading curriculum with children who are deaf or hard of hearing. *Journal of Deaf Studies and Deaf Education, 11,* 202–213.

Trezek, B. J., Wang, Y., & Paul, P. V. (2010). *Reading and deafness: Theory, research, and practice.* Clifton Park, NY: Delmar, Cengage Learning.

Trezek, B., Wang, Y., & Paul, P. (2011). Processes and components of reading. In M. Marschark & P. Spencer (Eds.), *Handbook of deaf studies, language, and education* (2nd ed., Vol. 1, pp. 99–114). New York, NY: Oxford University Press.

Trezek, B. J., Wang, Y., Woods, D. G., Gampp, T. L., & Paul, P. V. (2007). Using visual phonics to supplement beginning reading instruction for students who are deaf or hard of hearing. *Journal of Deaf Studies and Deaf Education, 12,* 373–384.

Vadasy, P. F., & Sanders, E. A. (2009). Supplemental fluency intervention and determinants of reading outcomes. *Scientific Studies of Reading, 13,* 383–425.

van den Bos, K. P., Zijlstra, B. J., & lutje Spelberg, H. C. (2002). Life-span data on continuous-naming speeds of numbers, letters, colors, and pictured objects, and word-reading speed. *Scientific Studies of Reading, 6*(1), 25–49.

van der Kooy-Hofland, V., Kegel, C., & Bus, A. (2011). Evidence-based computer interventions targeting phonological awareness to prevent reading problems in at-risk young students. In

S. Neuman & D. Dickinson (Eds.), *Handbook of early literacy research* (Vol. 3, pp. 214–227). New York, NY: Guilford Press.

Vaughn, S., Levy, S., Coleman, M., & Bos, G. (2002). Reading instruction for students with LD and EBD: A synthesis of observation studies. *Journal of Special Education, 36*, 2–13.

Vellutino, F. R., Tunmer, W. E., Jaccard, J. J., & Chen, R. (2007). Components of reading ability: Multivariate evidence for a convergent skills model of reading development. *Scientific Studies of Reading, 11*, 3–32.

Verhoeven, L., & van Leeuwe, J. (2008). Prediction of the development of reading comprehension: A longitudinal study. *Applied Cognitive Psychology, 22*, 407–423.

Verhoeven, L., van Leeuwe, J., & Vermeer, A. (2011). Vocabulary growth and reading development across the elementary school years. *Scientific Studies of Reading, 15*(1), 8–25

Vygotsky, L. S. (1978). *Mind in society: The development of higher psychological processes.* Cambridge, MA: MIT Press.

Wagner, R., Torgesen, J., Rashotte, C. A., Hecht, S., Barker, T. A., Burgess, S. R., et al. (1997). Changing relations between phonological processing abilities and word-level reading as children develop from beginning to skilled readers. *Developmental Psychology, 33*(3), 468–479.

Wasik, B. A., & Hindman, A. H. (2011). Identifying critical components of an effective preschool language and literacy coaching intervention. In S. Neuman & D. Dickinson (Eds.), *Handbook of early literacy research* (Vol. 3, pp. 322–336). New York, NY: Guilford Press.

Watson, L. M. (2002). The literacy development of children with cochlear implants at age seven. *Deafness and Education International, 4*(2), 84–98.

Watson, L. M. (2009). Early print concepts: Insights from work with young deaf children. *Deafness and Education International, 11*(4), 191–209.

Watson, L. M., & Swanwick, R. (2008). Parents' and teachers' views on deaf children's literacy at home: Do they agree? *Deafness and Education International, 10*(1), 22–39.

Wauters, L. N., Tellings, A. E., van Bon, W. H., & Mak, W. M. (2008). Mode of acquisition as a factor in deaf children's reading comprehension. *Journal of Deaf Studies and Deaf Education, 13*(2), 175–192.

Wauters, L. N., van Bon, W. H., Tellings, A. E., & van Leeuwe, J. F. (2006). In search of factors in deaf and hearing children's reading comprehension. *American Annals of the Deaf, 151*(3), 371–380.

Wayne, A., DiCarlo, C., Burts, D., & Benedict, J. (2007). Increasing literacy behaviors of preschool children through environmental modification and teacher mediation. *Journal of Research in Childhood Education, 22*(1), 5–12.

Wells, G. (1981). *Learning through interaction.* Cambridge, UK: Cambridge University Press.

Wells, G. (1986). *The meaning makers: Children learning language and using language to learn.* Portsmouth, NH: Heinemann.

Wesseling, R., & Reitsma, P. (2000). The transient role of explicit phonological recoding for reading acquisition. *Reading and Writing, 13*, 313–336.

Whitehurst, G. J., Arnold, D. S., Epstein, J. N., Angell, A. L., Smith, M., & Fischel, J. E. (1994). A picture book reading intervention in day care and home for children from low-income families. *Developmental Psychology, 30*(5), 679–689.

Whitehurst, G. J., Falco, F. L., Lonigan, C. J., Fischel, J. E., BeBaryshe, B. D., Valdez-Menchaca, M. C., & Caulfield, M. (1988). Accelerating language development through picture book reading. *Developmental Psychology, 24*(4), 552–559.

Whitehurst, G. J., & Lonigan, C. J. (1998). Child development and emergent literacy. *Child Development, 69*(3), 848–872.

Wilkinson, I. A. G., & Son, E. H. (2011). A dialogic turn in research on learning and teaching to comprehend. In M. Kamil, P. D. Pearson, E. Moje, & P. Afflerbach (Eds.), *Handbook of reading research* (Vol. 4, pp. 359–387). New York, NY: Routledge.

Williams, C. (1994). The language and literacy worlds of three profoundly deaf preschool children. *Reading Research Quarterly, 29*(2), 125–155.

Williams, C. (1999). Preschool deaf children's use of signed language during writing events. *Journal of Literacy Research, 31*(2), 183–212.

Williams, C., & McLean, M. M. (1997). Young deaf children's response to picture book reading in a preschool setting. *Research in the Teaching of English, 31*(3), 59–88.

Willstedt-Svensson, U., Lofqvist, A., Almqvist, B., & Sahlen, B. (2004). Is age at implant the only factor that counts? The influence of working memory on lexical and grammatical development in children with cochlear implants. *International Journal of Audiology, 43,* 506–515.

Wolfe, M., Bowers, P. G., & Biddle, K. (2000). Naming-speed processes, timing, and reading: A conceptual review. *Journal of Learning Disabilities, 33*(4), 387–407.

Wolf, M., Miller, L., & Donnelly, K. (2000). Retrieval, automaticity, vocabulary, elaboration, orthography (RAVE-O): A comprehensive, fluency-based reading intervention program. *Journal of Learning Disabilities, 33*(4), 375–386.

Zuckerman, B. (2009). Promoting early literacy in pediatric practice: Twenty years of reach out and read. *Pediatrics, 124*(6), 1660–1665.

5

Research on Children With Language/ Literacy Difficulties

As reiterated throughout this book, literacy is a language-based skill, and thus difficulties in language development can negatively affect literacy achievement. Numerous studies have supported the correlation between language difficulties and literacy difficulties (e.g., Bishop & Adams, 1990; Catts, 1993; Catts, Fey, Tomblin, & Zhang, 2002; Hall & Tomblin, 1978; Silva, McGee, & Williams, 1987; Tomblin et al., 1997). It should also be emphasized that literacy, particularly reading, is not a simple derivative of through-the-air language (spoken or signed). Accordingly, reading abilities cannot be easily predicted by language skills alone. Learning to read involves learning to identify printed words and making sense of how they are combined in a particular context to convey an author's intent. Perhaps the most basic assumption about learning to read is that first and foremost it requires familiarity with the language to be read. Without knowledge of the language and all that entails, one cannot learn to read. Beyond knowing the language, a potential reader must then learn how that language is represented in print.

Almost all humans are reared in environments in which through-the-air language is the primary means of communication. Within a language-rich environment, most people learn through-the-air language effortlessly because we are biologically endowed to learn language and socialized to use language to communicate. However, it is almost impossible to expect a child to be able to read and writing automatically, simply by surrounding the child with a literacy-rich environment without any explicit and direct instruction. It is like taking a child to the local public library every day and expecting the child to be able to read on her or his own without any guidance.

In many cases, this discussion pertains strongly to children who possess language and literacy difficulties, the topic of this chapter. We examine the following questions: Who are children with language/literacy difficulties? What does theory and research say about the development of English language and literacy in these children? How can these issues be applied (i.e., for comparison purposes) to children who are d/Deaf and hard of hearing (d/Dhh)? In addressing these questions, we reiterate several of the major constructs and findings of studies discussed previously in this book. By providing additional details and perspectives, our goal is to emphasize that the main tenets of the qualitative similarity hypothesis (QSH) also apply to children with language/learning difficulties (indeed, to all children who are labeled as struggling readers and writers). We begin by discussing some background and brief descriptions of the constructs of reading difficulty and reading disability.

HISTORICAL BACKGROUND AND DESCRIPTION

As discussed in Chapter 1 of this book, *reading difficulty* and *garden-variety poor readers* (Gough & Tunmer, 1986; Stanovich, 1988) are typically used as generic terms to describe any individual or group who is below the reading (or writing) achievement level of typical chronological peers. *Reading disability*, sometimes interchangeable with *dyslexia*, is generally reserved for individuals or groups whose reading *difficulties* are related to biological, psychological, or neuropsychological conditions. In this chapter, *language/literacy difficulty* is used as an even broader term for individuals or groups whose language and literacy skills (e.g., spoken, written, or signing) are not commensurate with those of typical chronological peers.

Like the analogy used by Ellis (1985) and Stanovich (1988), language/literacy difficulty is not a discrete entity but a continuum; it is not like *measles* but is like *obesity*. Instead of a discontinuous hump near the bottom of the distribution for a discrete pathology, as suggested by Rutter and Yule (1975), language/literacy difficulty is a graded, uninterrupted continuum where it is operationally defined in an arbitrary way. Consider the following passage as an example (Ellis, 1985):

> For people of any given age and height there will be an uninterrupted continuum from painfully thin to inordinately fat. It is entirely arbitrary where we draw the line between "normal" and "obese", but that does not prevent obesity being a real and worrying condition, nor does it prevent research into the causes and cures of obesity being both valuable and necessary. (p. 172)

The severity of language/literacy difficulty that leads to reading difficulty or disability depends on the state, school district, and school community in which individuals live. Historically, reading disability is defined as a psychometric construct emphasizing norm-referenced discrepancy. That is, it reflects the discrepancy between, one, one-and-a-half, or two standard deviations from the mean on standardized, norm-referenced reading achievement tests compared to chronological peers with average intelligence (i.e., IQ). However, the method is widely criticized because the measurement of intelligence, which is not free of culture or language, is neither reliable nor valid, particularly for children with language/literacy difficulties (Gunderson, D'Silva, & Chen, 2011).

Since the approval of the Individual With Disabilities Education Improvement Act of 2004 (IDEA), reading disability or difficulty is increasingly defined by a child's performance on response to intervention (RtI) on a standard treatment protocol. Nevertheless, the RtI model also suffers from reliability issues because different researchers use a variety of different measures of reading. Gunderson and colleagues (2011) proffer three features of the definition of reading disability: (1) the notion of discrepancy, (2) the notion that the discrepancy is not wholly a result of intellectual, physical, emotional, or environmental features, and (3) the notion that the causal variables are likely genetic, neurological, biochemical, or some combination of these factors.

CONTRIBUTION OF STANOVICH'S DEVELOPMENT LAG HYPOTHESIS

As introduced in Chapter 1 of this book, Stanovich's developmental lag hypothesis (DLH; Stanovich, Nathan, & Zolman, 1988; Stanovich, Nathan, & Vala-Rossi, 1986) is similar to our construct of the QSH. In general, the DLH, a construct first applied to garden-variety poor readers (Gough & Tunmer, 1986) and later to children with language/reading disabilities (or difficulties), states that skilled and less skilled readers go through the same developmental sequence of reading stages; however, there are differences in reading acquisition rates among children of differing literacy skills. Furthermore, if children do not learn to read by the end of an optimal period, typically second or third grade, they might experience greater difficulties in reading to learn effectively, and this negatively affects their subsequent language and cognitive development. The accumulated effects might be that they will read less and begin to lag behind their typical peers, and become poorer as described by the Matthew effects (Stanovich, 1986, 1991, 1992, 2000; Stanovich et al., 1988). Both versions of the DLH, strong and weak, maintain that children proceed through similar developmental stages and will continue to make progress in literacy at varying rates.

Two of the most cited studies on testing the DLH were a study on a comparison of two groups of reading-level matched children in third and fifth grades (Stanovich et al., 1986) and its longitudinal follow-up after a 2-year interval (now fifth and seventh grade) with a third group (third grade) (Stanovich et al., 1988). The original study (Stanovich et al., 1986) found that older less-skilled readers were remarkably similar to their younger counterparts matched on reading ability in both general cognitive performance and specifically reading-related processes. The follow-up study (Stanovich et al., 1988) further confirmed the hypothesis that the younger skilled readers demonstrated more growth in reading than the older less skilled readers, although the groups were matched on grade-equivalent scores at the first testing.

In short, instead of highlighting qualitative differences, the DLH predicts that when older children with language and literacy difficulties and younger typically developing children are matched on reading level, their performance should not differ on any cognitive tasks causally related to reading. Furthermore, the reading development of the younger, typically developing children will progress at a faster rate than that of the older children with language and literacy difficulties.

RELATION TO THE QSH AND d/Dhh
INDIVIDUALS

In a study on large-scale academic achievement testing of students who are d/Dhh in the United States, Qi and Mitchell (2012) report that student performance levels on reading comprehension tests over three decades are slightly higher for each age cohort from age 8 to 17, but the median performance never exceeds the fourth-grade equivalent for any cohort. This finding confirms the troubling phenomenon that has been reported for years: On average, students with severe to profound hearing loss leave the educational system reading at the beginning of the fourth grade level, and more than 90% of students with severe to profound hearing loss are reading at the sixth grade level or less. Furthermore, compared with their hearing peers, many students who are d/Dhh generally make progress at 0.3–0.4 reading grade level per year (see reviews in Allen, 1986; Luckner, Sebald, Cooney, Young, & Goodwin Muir, 2005/2006; Paul, 2003, 2009; Paul & Wang, 2012; Schirmer & McGough, 2005; Traxler, 2000; Trezek, Wang, & Paul, 2010, 2011).

Several explanations have been offered for this reading achievement lag of students who are d/Dhh. Examples include the following:

- Artifacts associated with the types of assessments used to measure reading achievement.
- Inferential and language demands of reading materials increased dramatically after the third-grade level.
- Marked difficulty of many students with severe to profound hearing losses in developing or acquiring the language of written (print) English.
- The unpreparedness of the teachers of the d/Dhh in their teacher education program to teach literacy skills (Paul, 2003, 2009; Trezek et al., 2010).

Furthermore, Trezek et al. (2011) suggested that the proliferation of reading theories provides numerous, sometimes conflicting, views, and there seem to be misinterpretations of these theories, which are associated with the ongoing debates of whether the reading (and writing) development of students who are d/Dhh is qualitatively similar to that of their hearing peers, thereby validating the use of mainstream literacy models for understanding and improving reading and writing.

Similar to the assertions of Lenneberg (1967) and Stanovich et al. (1986, 1988) about children with language/literacy difficulties or disabilities, the main thesis of the QSH (Paul, 2010, 2012; Paul & Lee, 2010; Paul & Wang, 2012) is that the acquisition of English by any individual is developmentally similar to that of native speakers and to that of typical literacy learners of English. Children who are d/Dhh performed similarly to their younger hearing peers matched on reading ability in both general cognitive performance and specifically reading-related processes. This developmental similarity suggests that there are certain critical fundamentals that facilitate and enhance the acquisition process, whether one is learning English as either a first or second language.

In Chapter 2, we presented general findings on the performance of children who are d/Dhh on aspects of syntax, for example, relative clauses and negation (Davis & Blasdell, 1975; Quigley, Wilbur, Power, Montanelli, & Steinkamp, 1976; Russell, Quigley, & Power, 1976), verb system such as tense agreement (Payne & Quigley, 1987; Pressnell, 1973; Wilcox & Tobin, 1974), and morphology (Cooper, 1967; Crandall, 1978; Gilman, Davis, & Raffin, 1980; Raffin, Davis, & Gilman, 1978). It was reported that these children produce more errors than their hearing peers matched with age, and the gap increased with age. However, the errors that they made were comparable to the ones made by their younger hearing peers. In general, the acquisition of the examined language variables was qualitatively similar to that of the younger hearing children with comparable production of errors and use of strategies, but many d/Dhh children proceeded at a slower rate through the developmental stages than the younger hearing children (see also the reviews in Paul, 2009, 2012).

The pattern appears to be applicable to d/Deaf children who know Spanish as a first language and are English language learners (ELLs). For example, King (1981) conducted a comparison of two groups of children on syntactic tasks: (1) d/Deaf children with profound hearing losses and hearing students who were English native speakers; and (2) Spanish d/Deaf children with profound hearing losses and hearing students who were ELLs. The results showed that both groups of children demonstrated a similar order of difficulties on examined syntactic tasks, and these error types seemed similar for both groups as well.

Although more research evidence is needed, along with the DLH, the QSH is a feasible model for understanding the language and literacy difficulties of many students who are d/Dhh. Similar to children with language/literacy difficulties, many children who are d/Dhh might proceed through the developmental stages at a slower rate than their typically developing peers—nevertheless, the developmental pattern is qualitatively similar for anyone who is developing or acquiring English language/literacy. We demonstrate the applicability of the QSH to the larger population of children with language/literacy difficulties in the remainder of this chapter.

RESEARCH ON THE DEVELOPMENT OF
ENGLISH LANGUAGE AND LITERACY

Children with language/literacy difficulties (or disabilities) are often served at school by different professionals, for example, general education teachers, special education teachers, reading specialists, and speech-language pathologists. The development of English language and literacy for children with language/literacy difficulties has also been investigated by researchers in various fields, such as education, psychology, speech-language pathology, neuroscience, and child development. With slightly different emphases, a number of scholars in various fields have investigated the development of English language and literacy mainly in the following areas: phonology and other components, decoding, comprehension, and written language. This section synthesizes research in these four areas and connects the research to the findings of the National Reading Panel (2000) and the National Early Literacy Panel (2008).

Synthesis of Research on Phonology and Other Components

"English is the most difficult language to learn to read, and there appears to be more individuals who have trouble learning to read it" (Gunderson et al., 2011, p. 17). Ziegler and Goswami (2005) suggest: "The slower average rate of learning to read in English does not seem to occur because of variations in teaching method. . . . Rather, it seems due to the relatively low orthographic consistency of English" (p. 13). English is considered to possess a deep, perhaps the deepest, orthography, based on its inconsistent orthographic representations of the phonemes.

Based on the *grain size* or *granularity* model proposed by Ziegler and Goswami (2005), there are differences within and between orthographies in the size of the units represented: whole words, syllables, onset rimes, phonemes, and letters. The primary difficulty for all readers with dyslexia is the establishment of efficient processing at a small grain size (i.e., the phoneme level). Ziegler and Goswami further propose that smaller grain sizes are less consistent than larger ones and English has a wider variety of grain sizes than other orthographies, which makes it even harder to learn. Thus, in English reading instruction, explicit teaching of grapheme–phoneme correspondence (e.g., phonics) is not sufficient, and learning additional correspondences for larger orthographic units, such as syllables, rimes, or whole words, may be required for such a deep orthography.

Together with morphology, syntax, semantics, and pragmatics, phonology is considered an essential component of a language (as discussed in Chapter 2). Phonological mediation is an obligatory component of lexical access during reading (Perfetti, 1992; see also Chapter 4). Decoding problems of many children with language/literacy difficulties (discussed next) is often associated with problems in *phonological awareness*, which is the general understanding of and access to the sound structure of spoken language. *Phonemic awareness* is the ability to understand how the sounds/phonemes of spoken language work together to form words, whereas phonological awareness is a broader term that also includes the understanding of syllables and rhyming. Children with language difficulties are often at risk for poorly developed phonological and phonemic awareness (see the review in Verhoeven, 2011).

Phonological awareness typically develops before or along with the development of phonemic awareness and phonics skills in preschool and kindergarten. Preschoolers and kindergarteners start out with the least phonological awareness and gain the most from phonological awareness training. Again, although phonological awareness is necessary, it is not sufficient for learning to read. For example, Bus and van Ijzendoorn (1999) reported that although "phonological awareness affects learning-to-read processes in a positive and substantial way" (p. 405), the overall variance in reading skills explained by phonological awareness was approximately 12%. In a more detailed analysis, Ehri and colleagues (2001) calculated that phonological awareness explained approximately 6.5% of the variance in reading outcomes for all age groups, rising to 10% when letters were added, and to 28% for preschoolers. Therefore, in spite of its critical role, phonological awareness is only one component among a complex array of skills in helping children learn to read. "In sum, it must be remembered that phonics instruction is a means to an end, that being the ability not just to decode but to comprehend and interpret written text" (Phillips, Hayward, & Norris, 2011, p. 115).

Research studies on phonological awareness, and the meta-analyses of these studies, suggest that not only is phonological awareness related to reading success but also learning to read assists children's phonological awareness development (see the review in Phillips et al., 2011; see also Chapter 4). Additional research on phonology and other components is discussed later in this chapter in relation to the National Reading Panel and the National Early Literacy Panel. The research on phonology and other components is closely related to the research on decoding, which is introduced next.

Synthesis of Research on Decoding

Decoding is also referred to as *word recognition*, which can either go from part to whole as emphasized in phonemic awareness and phonics instruction or from whole to part as emphasized in sight word reading. Based on the so-called simple view of reading (Gough & Tunmer, 1986; Hoover & Gough, 1990), decoding and linguistic (or language) comprehension (i.e., listening or through-the-air comprehension) are the two basic, independent components of reading comprehension. Although it is an oversimplified model that does not take into account the various task, text, reader, and other factors (see Chapter 7), the emphasis on decoding and language comprehension seems to be relevant. For example, Catts, Hogan, and Fey (2003) investigated decoding and listening comprehension skills of a group of second-grade poor readers. They found that approximately one-third of the students had good or adequate listening comprehension but poor decoding skills; one-sixth of them had poor listening comprehension but good or adequate decoding skills; and one-third of them had both poor listening comprehension and decoding skills. The role of decoding in understanding reading development, particularly English reading development, is unquestionable.

Children are able to read words they know but have never seen in print by decoding printed words phonologically and activating their lexical access through this phonological mediation. Share (1995) and Share and Stanovich (1995) referred to this process as a *self-teaching hypothesis* (as discussed in Chapter 4), which suggests that phonological decoding functions as a self-teaching mechanism enabling children to acquire the orthographic representations necessary for fast and accurate visual word recognition and for proficient spelling (see the review in Kamhi & Catts, 2012a). Furthermore, through this self-teaching process, as the child is exposed to a printed word more frequently, he or she becomes more likely to use a visual approach (whole-word reading) to recognize the word. Phonological decoding skills are the means of adding new words to the body of words that individuals can recognize promptly by sight as a whole; that is, the new words that are initially recognized by phonological decoding skills eventually should be read quickly by sight. Phonological mediation thus plays a role similar to that of training wheels on a bicycle: Once the child reads fluently, the wheels can be taken off. A skillful reader should be able to acquire several skills in decoding: to attach sounds to letters and to blend letter sounds into recognizable words, as well as to recognize the whole words by sight, particularly in the case of irregularly spelled words.

The self-teaching hypothesis (Share, 1995; Share & Stanovich, 1995) suggests that phonological decoding provides opportunities for self-teaching rather than guarantees. Other factors will determine the extent to which these opportunities are exploited, for example, the quantity and quality of exposure to print, and the ability and/or inclination to attend to and remember orthographic details. In short, phonological decoding is the primary self-teaching mechanism for fluent word recognition, whereas the contribution of visual/orthographic factors is secondary. Share (1999) further found that pure visual exposure to a novel word did not facilitate orthographic learning because phonological decoding was essential to the acquisition of word-specific orthographic representations.

Decoding skills have been explicitly and directly taught to children with language/literacy difficulties, particularly in the early school years. For example, combining natural classroom observations with assessments of students' reading abilities, Juel and Minden-Cupp (2000) identified important interactions between first-grade students' profiles of phonologically related skills and the type of instruction they received, even within the same classroom. The researchers found that students entering first grade with middle-range literacy skills in alphabetic knowledge and spelling–sound knowledge were more likely to make significant growth in classrooms using a less-structured phonics curriculum, more reading of chapter books, and more time for writing. On the other hand, students entering first grade with a low-range of phonology-based literacy skills benefited most from phonics instruction, emphasizing writing for sounds, comparing and contrasting sounds and spelling patterns, and other activities involving letter–sound decoding. In addition, these low-ability students, who made substantial progress in decoding by the middle of the year, also benefited from the same type of increased attention to meaning-based activities as did their more skilled peers.

In short, decoding skills play an indispensable role in reading development, particularly for the early years, and phonological decoding is the primary self-teaching mechanism in fluent word recognition, whereas visual/orthographic decoding is secondary. Many children will need explicit and direct training in phonological decoding skills, especially those with language/literacy difficulties (McGill-Franzen & Allington, 2011; see also Paul & Wang, 2012, Chapter 6, and Chapter 4 of this book). When these skills are adequately developed, more attention can be directed to comprehension, which is discussed next.

Synthesis of Research on Comprehension

Reading is a meaning-making activity whose central purpose is comprehension. Fluent readers can decode and comprehend simultaneously because the word recognition process reaches an automaticity level, which enables them to focus their attention more on the meaning(s) of the text instead of on figuring out the words. However, being able to decode the text does not necessarily mean that a child can comprehend the text. For example, children with Williams syndrome and many children with autism spectrum disorders (ASD) have been reported to have well-developed decoding skills but severely impaired reading comprehension, which, although controversial, is similar to *hyperlexia* (e.g., Laing, Hulme, Grant, & Karmiloff-Smith, 2001; Nation, Clarke, Wright, & Williams, 2006; Snowling & Hulme, 2007). That is, although they might acquire letter–sound correspondences fairly effortlessly and utilize phonological processing during reading, they have been reported to be overly dependent on phonological decoding and might not process semantic information in the typical way. Thus, their comprehension of what they read is impaired (see also the review in Paul & Wang, 2012, Chapter 8).

Decoding is closely related to semantic access. The *bottleneck hypothesis*, proposed in Perfetti's verbal efficiency model (1992), has been proffered to explain comprehension failure by emphasizing the central role of speed and automaticity of decoding and semantic access. Later on, the model was refined in the *lexical quality hypothesis* (Perfetti & Hart, 2001; see also Chapter 4) to highlight not only the quality of the readers' lexical representations but also the quantity of available vocabulary (i.e., size or breath of vocabulary or word knowledge).

The Research and Development (RAND) Reading Study Group (RRSG, 2002) defines *comprehension* as the process of concurrently constructing and extracting meaning through interaction and engagement with print. Snow (2010) suggests three key components in comprehension: (1) accurate word-level decoding, (2) constructing knowledge through integrating inferences and information not in the text (i.e., world knowledge) with text information, and (3) an active, engaged reader. She further proposes a model of comprehension that includes a set of four concentric circles: (1) a center circle on basic word-level reading processes, (2) a second circle on the core comprehension processes constructing text-based inferences and linking text information to world knowledge, (3) a third circle on elaborated comprehension processes beyond text-based representations (e.g., visualizing, predicting, clarifying, summarizing, maintaining attention to extended discourse, monitoring comprehension and fixing up when comprehension fails, using author intention for critical response, generating questions while reading, and making text-to-text connections), and (4) an outermost and highest level circle on highly elaborated comprehension processes that are required for disciplinary studies and deep learning from texts.

Figure 5.1 provides a summary of the model of comprehension proposed by Snow (2010).

During reading, a child not only needs to crack the code (decode) by mapping letters to sounds and use phonological mediation to activate lexical access (the center circle) but also needs to make inferences, utilize the text structure, integrate information, and monitor her or his comprehension (mainly the second and third outer circles). While decoding plays a large role in explaining reading differences in beginner readers, comprehension is found to be more prominent for older, proficient readers (Catts, Hogan & Adlof, 2005; Chen & Vellutino, 1997; Tunmer & Hoover, 1993; Bast & Reitsma, 1998). For example, Jenkins, Fuchs, van den Broek, Espin, and Deno (2003) found that the most important factor distinguishing readers with low-level reading fluency was the ability to decode isolated words, whereas the largest share of variance in more fluent readers was their performance on reading comprehension measures.

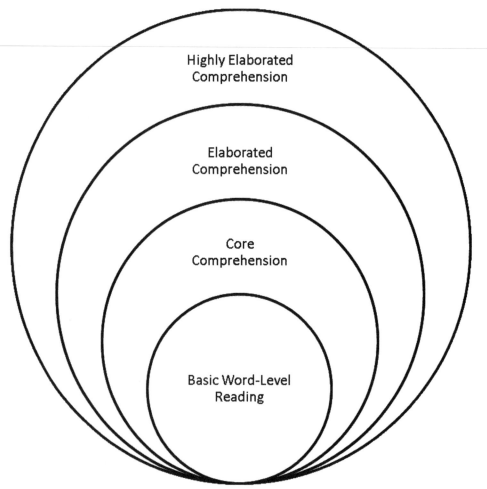

Figure 5.1. A summary of the model of comprehension proposed by Snow (2010).
Source: Based on the discussion in Snow (2010)

In another study, Kendeou, van den Broek, White, and Lynch (2009) used a cross-sequential design to examine the development of spoken (i.e., through-the-air) language and decoding skills from preschool to early elementary school and their correlation to beginning reading comprehension. Two cohorts of children, 113 four-year-olds and 108 six-year-olds, were tested on oral language and decoding skills and were retested again two years later when they were 6 and 8 years old, respectively. In both age groups, oral language and decoding skills formed distinct clusters which were related to each other in preschool, but the relationship became weaker in kindergarten and second grade. Structural equation modeling (SEM) demonstrated that both sets of skills in second grade independently predicted a child's reading comprehension. The authors concluded:

> Successful reading comprehension is the result of a confluence of elemental skills, each of which has its own developmental trajectory. The trajectories may intertwine

and influence each other at early stages (e.g., in the 4-year-old children in our study), but they also remain independent to a considerable degree. The risk of a child developing reading comprehension difficulties is smallest when he or she progresses appropriately along each trajectory. The more educational practice can help each child move forward along each dimension, the more it ensures the child against failure. This means that decoding skill development should be part of the curriculum—as it traditionally has—but so should oral language skill development including narrative comprehension. (p. 775)

Research indicates that both younger and poorer readers have more problems with higher level processing in reading comprehension. For example, in a longitudinal study of third- through fifth-grade children, Vauras, Kinnunen and Kuusela (1994) found that young children tended to process text in a linear element-by-element manner and the higher level processing skills increased with age. The specific developmental patterns depended on the initial listening comprehension skills of the children; that is, average and high-achieving children demonstrated clear progress whereas low-achieving children showed very low or no progress.

Effective instruction on comprehension is not easy to design. There are various reasons for the difficulties in comprehension intervention. First, the decoding process can be systematically taught, whereas comprehension is a complex higher-level mental process involving thinking, reasoning, imagining, and interpreting—not a skill with a well-defined scope of knowledge (Kamhi, 2009). Second, comprehension interventions are generally designed to improve the cognitive processes that occur *during* reading, whereas comprehension assessments and measurements of intervention effectiveness (e.g., recall or comprehension question-based tasks) occur *after* reading (Rapp, van den Broek, McMaster, Kendeou, & Espin, 2007). Third, the responses to interventions affecting different levels of comprehension are varied. Instruction targeting simpler, lower-level comprehension responses evidently demonstrates measurable gains much more quickly than those targeting deeper, higher-level comprehension.

Last, and most important, comprehension instruction should vary based on the children's language and literacy skills. For example, Cooner and colleagues (Cooner, Morrison, & Katch, 2004; Cooner, Morrison, & Petrella, 2004) investigated the effects of instruction on first- and third-grade students with varying language and literacy abilities. Similar to Juel and Minden-Cupp (2000), they used classroom observations to document the nature and amount of reading instruction in typical classrooms and administered various language and literacy measures. They found that children who began the school year with lower reading comprehension skills showed greater growth in comprehension when provided with teacher-managed, meaning-based activities such as reading comprehension strategies and vocabulary. Those with initial higher reading comprehension skills demonstrated greater gains in comprehension when engaging in child-managed comprehension activities such as silent reading, partner reading, and independent writing.

In sum, decoding without comprehension (i.e., constructing and extracting meaning) is not reading. While reading differences in beginner readers can be largely explained by different decoding skills, comprehension is found to be more prominent for older, more skilled readers. Furthermore, both younger and poorer readers demonstrate similar patterns in their difficulties of higher-level processing in reading comprehension. However, it is not easy to design effective comprehension intervention because of its nature as a complex higher-level mental process without a well-defined scope of knowledge, the imbalance between product-based assessment and process-based intervention, different response rates to different levels of comprehension, and different intervention effects on children with varying language and literacy abilities (or difficulties). Making matters more complicated, development in through-the-air (spoken or signed) language comprehension is not necessarily equal to written language comprehension. The differences and similarities between written language and through-the-air (mainly spoken) language are discussed in the next section.

Synthesis of Research on Written Language

Chapter 2 touches on the relations between spoken (through-the-air) and written (i.e., print) forms of a language, particularly English. We inquire further: Are the processes and knowledge involved in spoken and written language comprehension the same? The perspectives on the latter question have pervasive implications, especially for children with language and literacy difficulties (or disabilities).

At the word level, word meaning can only be activated through a word's phonological representation in processing speech. These phonological representations are directly linked to a word's meaning in the mental lexicon. In contrast, word meaning can be accessed through both ways in reading—a phonological representation and a visual representation (Kamhi & Catts, 2012b; see further discussion on dual-route model of word recognition in Stanovich, 1991).

In the *phonological* approach, also known as the *indirect* approach, it is asserted that children use knowledge of phoneme–grapheme correspondences to code the visually perceived letters into corresponding phonemes, blend the individual phonemes together, and form a phonological sequence that is matched to a similar sequence in the mental lexicon. Therefore, reading by the phonological route is similar to speech recognition because both approaches recognize a word by its phonological representation. However, one important difference between these two is that one must have explicit awareness of the phonological structure of words (e.g., the knowledge that words consist of discrete phonemic segments) to be able to successfully use the phonological route in reading. Thus, although speech recognition generally appears to be effortless, children typically require explicit instruction and practice on phonological awareness to become efficient in using the phonological approach in reading. In the *visual* approach, also referred to as *direct, look-and-say,* or *whole-word* approach, it is asserted that children match the perceived visual configuration with "a visual representation that is part of the mental lexicon for the particular word" (Kamhi & Catts, 2012b, p. 8).

At the discourse level, theoretically, the knowledge and strategies discussed previously in the synthesis of research on comprehension could apply to both spoken and written discourse. However, in practice, they rarely do. There are many similarities and differences in the knowledge and processes underlying spoken and written language. The most obvious similarity between them is the vocabulary that they share; however, they have some distinct differences, as suggested by Kamhi and Catts (2012b):

> The most fundamental differences between spoken and written language involve the perceptual and biological/social bases of spoken language and the explicit phonological awareness required to become a proficient reader. Because reading is not a biologically endowed human ability, attentional, instructional, and motivational factors play a central role in learning to read. These differences explain to a large extent why learning to read is not a simple derivative of spoken language as well as why some children have difficulty learning to read. (p. 21)

Table 5.1 provides a summary of the differences between spoken and written language comprehension.

Table 5.1. Summary of Differences Between Written and Spoken Language

Differences	Written language	Spoken language
Physical	Relatively durable and can be read and reread	Ephemeral, unless it is recorded
Situational	Often individual endeavors with great care and precision to bear the whole burden of communication	Typically in face-to-face, interactive communication where contextual and nonverbal cues can be used to aid communication
Functional	Retaining accurate records, information labeling, communication, literature, exploring ideas at leisure and in private, as well as extending and clarifying one's thinking and ideas	Limited in these areas
Form	Consisting of letters; less representations of suprasegmental, paralinguistic, and prosodic features	Consisting of sounds; more representations of suprasegmental, paralinguistic, and prosodic features
Vocabulary	Using clearer, more unambiguous vocabulary with more variety and more literate lexicon (e.g., *therefore, hence,* and *thus*)	Allowing little opportunity to consider alternative word choices, limited in variety and more colloquial vocabulary (e.g., *hang out, wanna,* and *gonna*)
Grammatical	Generally high in lexical density and low in redundancy	Typically using high frequencies of coordination, repetition, and rephrasing
Processing	Fluent readers can identify written words out of context with near-perfect accuracy whereas poor readers rely more on contextual information	High-level contextual information plays a more important role because of ambiguity in decontextualized speech

Source: Adapted from Kamhi and Catts (2012b).

Relation to the National Reading Panel and the National Early Literacy Panel

Because of concerns that our nation's children were not making acceptable academic progress, particularly in reading, the National Institute of Health (NIH) was charged by Congress, in consultation with the secretary of education, to provide a foundation for what would be considered as *best practices* to meet the goals of the No Child Left Behind Act of 2001. Named by the director of the National Institute of Child Health and Human Development (NICHHD), the National Reading Panel (NRP, 2000) was established to identify the skills and methods of instruction consistently associated with reading achievement. After reviewing 450 studies on the teaching of reading in grades K–12, the panel published a comprehensive meta-analysis in five areas of effective reading instruction: phonemic awareness, phonics, fluency, vocabulary, and text comprehension (see also Chapter 4). Since its publication, the report has engendered both passionate critics (e.g., Allington, 2002) and strong advocates (e.g., Shanahan, 2004).

Later, in consultation with the NICHHD, the U.S. Department of Education, the Head Start Bureau, and the U.S. Department of Health and Human Services, the National Early Literacy Panel (NELP) was convened by the National Institute for Literacy and was directed to conduct a review on approximately 500 empirical studies of early literacy development using a methodology similar to the one used by NRP. The product was *Developing Early Literacy: Report of the National Early Literacy Panel* (NELP, 2008). The NELP identified six variables in predicting early literacy skills: (1) alphabetic knowledge, (2) phonological awareness, (3) rapid automatized naming of letters/digits, (4) rapid automatized naming of objects/colors, (5) writing/writing name, and (6) phonological memory. Five additional variables were identified as potentially important: (1) concepts about print, (2) print knowledge, (3) reading readiness, (4) oral language, and (5) visual processing.

One of the most interesting findings of the NELP (2008) is that oral (i.e., through-the-air) language is a weaker predictor of conventional literacy than originally thought. However, Shanahan and Lonigan (2010) explain:

> When the oral language category was broken down by the type of skill measured, the panel found that oral language played a larger role in later literacy achievement when it was measured using more complex or composite measures that included grammar, the ability to define words, and listening comprehension, rather than with measures of simple receptive or expressive vocabulary. (p. 281)

In terms of instructional practices, NELP (2008) reported the impact of code-focused interventions (e.g., phonological awareness and alphabetic knowledge) on the early literacy skills of young children as moderate to large. Accordingly, shared reading interventions produced statistically significant and moderate-size effects on children's oral language skills and print knowledge.

Similar to the responses to the NRP (2000) report, the NELP (2008) report has received wide attention in the field, and a special issue of *Educational Researcher* (vol. 39, no. 4), was devoted to the report with a presentation of strengths (e.g., Schickedanz & McGee, 2010) and criticisms (e.g., Dail & Payne, 2010). For both reports, one of the most controversial areas is the conclusion on the importance of phonologically based processing skills on reading outcomes and the implications for literacy practices. The NRP (2000) report asserted that effective phonemic awareness instruction entails directly teaching children to notice, think about, and work with the phonemes of English. These activities include phoneme (1) isolation, (2) identity, (3) categorization, (4) blending, (5) segmentation, (6) deletion, (7) addition, and (8) substitution. In addition, early and systematic instruction in phonics leads to better achievement in reading than later and less systematic phonics instruction (Armbruster, Lehr, & Osborn, 2001).

In systematic phonics programs, children receive explicit, systematic instruction in a set of prespecified associations between letters and sounds, and they are taught how to use them to read, typically in texts containing controlled vocabulary. Children are taught to decode unfamiliar words by sounding out the letters and blending them to pronounce a recognizable word. The controversy is not whether these strategies suggested by the NRP (and many are similar to the suggestions of the NELP) are effective in developing phonemic awareness and phonics, but whether phonemic awareness and phonics skills should be directly and explicitly taught to all children.

Other areas investigated by the NRP (2000) were for school-age children; thus, these were not specifically discussed in the NELP (2008) report. For example, *fluency*, the ability to read a text accurately and quickly with proper expression, is identified as the critical bridge between decoding and comprehension. Despite the near-universal recognition that fluency is one of several critical components of skilled reading, fluency is often given little attention in the classroom. The panel concluded that repeated guided oral reading has a significant and positive impact on overall reading achievement including word recognition, fluency, and comprehension. Specifically, the NRP recommended (1) modeling fluent reading and having the students reread the text themselves and (2) having students repeatedly read text aloud with guidance.

The NRP's suggestions on fluency are not without controversy either, especially its conclusion on independent silent reading programs: "Independent silent reading is not an effective practice when used as the *only* type of reading instruction to develop fluency and other reading skills, particularly with students who have not yet developed critical alphabetic and word reading skills" (NRP, 2000, p. 13). As discussed previously in this chapter, based on classroom observations, Cooner and colleagues (2004) found that children who began the school year with initially greater reading comprehension skills demonstrated greater gains in comprehension when engaging in child-managed comprehension activities such as silent reading; however, children with lower reading comprehension skills showed greater growth in comprehension when provided with teacher-managed/guided activities. Many children with language/literacy difficulties do not have fully developed alphabetic and word-reading skills; therefore, they need more modeling and guidance in fluent reading, instead of relying predominantly on independent silent reading. Once they become fluent readers, the use of silent reading might be more appropriate for them (see discussion in Kamhi & Catts, 2012c; see also McGill-Franzen & Allington, 2011; Paul & Wang, 2012, Chapter 6).

The scientific research on vocabulary instruction, as reported by the NRP (2000), concludes that vocabulary instruction, both explicit and implicit, is positively related to comprehension. In addition, it was asserted that a combination of instructional methods with emphasis on multimedia aspects of learning and richness of context is more effective in developing word knowledge than any one particular method. Similarly, the review regarding text comprehension instruction noted seven main strategies effective in developing comprehension: comprehension monitoring, cooperative learning, graphic and semantic organizers, story structure, question answering, question generating, and summarization. As with their findings in the other areas, the NRP noted that teaching a variety of reading comprehension strategies combined flexibly and appropriately is more effective than teaching any one alone.

In general, a combination of child-managed implicit learning and teacher-managed explicit teaching practices is more effective than any approach alone. However, many children with language/literacy difficulties might need more teacher-managed explicit and direct instruction practices (see discussions in Kamhi & Catts, 2012c; McGill-Franzen & Arlington, 2011; Paul & Wang, 2012, Chapter 6).

In short, we agree with the conclusion of the NELP: "Rarely did these metaanalyses identify differences in effectiveness due to race/ethnicity, age, family income, or disability status. . . . It is possible that what works in early literacy works for all children, no matter their status and background" (Shanahan & Lonigan, 2010, p. 284). The components for effective reading instruction are qualitatively similar for everyone who is learning to read, but the required quantity of each component needs to be differentiated, based on the needs of individuals. This is the case not because the effects of the components are different, but because individuals need differentiated quantities of the component based on what they have already possessed. For example, some children might not need explicit phonemic awareness and phonics instruction in learning to read, not because phonemic awareness and phonics skills are not important in early reading but simply because these children have already possessed these skills through implicit literacy activities such as "which one does not sound like the other" games with their family members or early childhood teachers. However, other children, including most children with language/literacy difficulties, need explicit and direct instruction on these skills. Echoing the suggestions by the NRP (2000), we believe that flexibility and appropriateness are more effective than any one reading instructional strategy alone.

SIMILARITIES AND DIFFERENCES: COMPARED TO d/Dhh STUDENTS

The most pervasive aspect of deafness is its adverse effect on aural/oral language acquisition. Most children who are d/Deaf or have severe hearing losses, even with the use of amplification, sign language, and special intervention, experience significant auditory/oral language delay and have smaller vocabularies than their hearing peers in that language (Paul, 2009). To a lesser extent this is true for hard of hearing children as well (i.e., children with hearing loss up to about the severe level; see Paul & Whitelaw, 2011). For d/Deaf children who communicate and learn in ASL, the issue concerns the fact that ASL is a different language. The syntax of ASL does not correspond to English word order, and its vocabulary is organized differently, incurring the additional challenging effort of forging a relationship between the two languages.

Educators of d/Dhh children and adolescents are foremost language teachers, because many of their students are struggling with English language and literacy. This leads to the question: What are the similarities and differences between the English language and literacy profiles of children who are d/Dhh and those of children with language/literacy difficulties?

CONSENSUS AND DISSENSION

The inability to hear does not, by itself, predict a child's cognitive ability or potential for learning. Nevertheless, because it severely limits access to spoken language, d/Dhh children have a much more difficult time learning words that will eventually appear in print, how words are organized syntactically in sentences, and how words are used idiomatically and figuratively. Naturally these deficits in oral (i.e., spoken) language affect English reading development. Because of their reduced access to auditory/oral language (which is related to the language of print), many d/Dhh children typically bring a partial and still evolving language system and an impoverished vocabulary to early reading instruction. In essence, they must learn the basis of the auditory/oral language and learn to read the language at the same time. Confounding this process is the fact that about 95% of children who are d/Dhh are born to parent(s) who are hearing, and of these hearing parents, only approximately 10% of them learn to sign (Mitchell & Karchmer, 2004). Many children with profound hearing losses show up in the school system with minimal language skills in either sign or spoken language.

Children with English language/literacy difficulties, on the other hand, generally do not experience the severely limited access to spoken language as do many children who are d/Dhh, particularly those with severe to profound hearing loss. They typically share the same language with their family members and are immersed, for the most part, in spoken language during their formative years. Based on studies developing "profiles" (e.g., Catts et al., 2003), many children with language/literacy difficulties have poor listening comprehension skills, which means that although they can access spoken English by being immersed in it, they might have difficulties comprehending what they are accessing.

Besides access to spoken English, different levels of vocabulary knowledge separate many children who are d/Dhh from children with language/literacy difficulties. Reading vocabulary, which encompasses the words one can recognize and understand in print, initially develops as young hearing readers make associations between the words they have heard and spoken and the words they see on a page; d/Deaf children in particular do not know as many words and do not have greatly expanded schemata for the words they do know. This is also true for a number of hard of hearing children, though to a lesser extent.

The situation is compounded as d/Dhh children attempt to read more advanced texts where they are confronted with an ever-increasing number of new words and more complicated syntax. Although many children with English language/literacy difficulties also might have a limited vocabulary pool, the situation is not as serious as it is for most children who are d/Dhh, particularly those who do not share the common language with other family members.

Many children who are d/Dhh have reduced vocabulary size overall, as well as in a particular category. The English language is composed of two major classifications of words: content words (e.g., nouns, verbs, adjectives, and most adverbs) and function words (determiners, prepositions, conjunctions, pronouns, auxiliary verbs, copulas, etc.). Function words have little lexical meaning or have ambiguous meaning on their own but carry specific meaning as they serve to express grammatical relationships with other words within a sentence by marking meaning units. Though there are far fewer function words than content words, they are common in content-area texts. Most speakers of a language, including children with language/literacy difficulties, learn function words without difficulty, beginning in the early stages of language development. By the time they see these words in print they have most likely heard and used these words thousands of times.

For d/Dhh children, though, function words are much harder to learn and to generalize. These words are generally unstressed in a spoken language, such as English, so most d/Deaf children do not hear them. Functions words also are not explicitly marked in a sign language such as ASL—albeit they are implied during a translation into another language (such as English). In addition, these functions words are often omitted in English sign systems (such as Signed English, Signing Exact English) during the use of the systems by teachers and practitioners (see discussion in Paul, 2009). Because function words often do not carry intonational emphasis or stress, they are frequently contracted and their identification is obscured even more (Weber, 2006). To further complicate the acquisition of these words, many function words have several different uses. All of these issues essentially amount to teaching through-the-air language while teaching students who are d/Dhh to read at the same time (see the review in Wang, Kretschmer, & Hartman, 2008).

Access to the phonology of English, obviously, is the most prominent difference between many children who are d/Dhh and children with language/literacy difficulties. As discussed previously in this book (see Chapters 1, 2, & 4), various researchers have explored the quantity and quality of phonemic awareness and phonics skills demonstrated by students who are d/Dhh. Several researchers have identified phonemic awareness and phonics skills as indicators of reading success (see the reviews in Perfetti & Sandak, 2000; Wang, Trezek, Luckner, & Paul, 2008; Paul, Wang, Trezek, & Luckner, 2009), whereas others have studied the amount of phonemic awareness and phonics skills used by d/Dhh students (mostly those with severe to profound loss) and have found the benefits to be minimal (e.g., Izzo, 2002; Mayberry, del Giudice, & Lieberman, 2011; Ormel, Hermans, Knoors, Hendriks, &Verhoeven, 2010; see also the review in Miller & Clark, 2011). Interestingly, Mayberry et al. (2011) reported that the overall phonological coding and awareness (PCA) skills predicted 11% of the variance in reading proficiency in the participants. This finding was similar to the 12% overall variance in reading skills explained by phonological awareness for early reading in general (Bus & van Ijzendoorn, 1999), discussed earlier in this chapter.

Although still controversial (Allen et al., 2009; Mayberry et al., 2011; Miller & Clark, 2011), ample evidence has suggested that d/Deaf readers, particularly skilled d/Deaf readers, use phonological information during reading, and the ability to use phonological processing is what distinguishes skilled d/Deaf readers from poor d/Deaf readers (Hanson, 1989; Paul, 2009; Paul et al., 2009; Perfetti & Sandak, 2000; Trezek et al., 2010, 2011; Wang et al., 2008). As discussed previously, phonological awareness and other related skills play critical roles in reading, although they are among a complex array of skills in helping children learn to read.

In essence, many children who are d/Dhh are struggling with reading in areas that are similar to those of children with language/literacy difficulties; however, there might be a variety of different reasons for these struggles. The major difference is the limited access to spoken (through-the-air) English, and, accordingly, many children who are d/Dhh might have a diminished vocabulary size overall and in content words particularly, as well as limited access to the phonology of English. Many children with English language/literacy difficulties also struggle with phonology and its components, decoding, comprehension, and written language but generally to a lesser extent. The differences between children who are d/Dhh and children with language/literacy difficulties in their struggles with English language/literacy are primarily due to the degree of severity, which impacts rate not *manner* of acquisition.

DIRECTIONS FOR FURTHER RESEARCH

There is an old saying in China: "You can't see the forest for the trees." If you are immersed in the details, you cannot see the big picture. You need to get out of the forest to enjoy it, because within the forest, you can see only the trees that comprise the forest but not the forest as a whole. There is little doubt that children who are d/Dhh have different reading profiles than children with language/literacy difficulties. Even within the two groups, there are various differences. In fact, each child might have her or his unique reading profile, regardless of whether he or she has disabilities or difficulties in language/literacy. If we are too immersed in these detailed differences, there will be no point conducting educational research on language/literacy because there will be millions of different ways of teaching language/literacy or explaining the acquisition of these entities.

As discussed in Chapter 1, there is a conceptual framework associated with disciplines such as language or literacy. Although there is no all-encompassing fundamental rule to account for one's entire language or literacy development, children generally acquire English language or literacy in a qualitatively similar way, in spite of (dis)ability, ethnic group, gender, language status (first vs. second or third language), socioeconomic status, and so on. This basic premise of the QSH should be considered as a guideline to avoid an oversimplification of the challenges associated with each population, for example, children who are d/Dhh or children with English language/literacy difficulties. Adaptations and accommodations associated with literacy practices should be based on the findings and applications of *mainstream* theory and research.

Wolbers and Dostal (2011) remarked:

> Whereas there are indeed significant challenges for the deaf that do not exist for others, *it can be argued that there are more similarities than differences.* Deaf education professionals are encouraged to apply their specialized knowledge to adapt and modify existing instructional interventions in ways that better suit the needs of deaf learners instead of discounting their applicability. (p. 403; emphasis added)

Clay's (1987) work has been widely interpreted as asserting that, unless high-quality and responsive instruction have been provided and failed to accelerate progress, children should not be considered for the *reading disability* category. Advocates of this assertion eventually pushed out the IQ–achievement–discrepancy (or "wait-to-fail") model in favor of the RtI model in identifying reading disability. However, the RtI model is not without controversy either, especially with its need to implement interventions with fidelity. For example, Scanlon (2011) suggested that the emphasis on fidelity limits teachers' ability to respond to the needs of individual child and when the child was identified as *unresponsive*, it might be due to the unresponsive instruction, not the fault of the child. Scanlon advocates an *interactive strategies approach* that "calls for the teacher to plan and deliver instruction that is responsive to the children by taking account of both what the children know and are able to do and by considering the characteristics and expectations of the classroom curriculum" (p. 141). Accordingly, the RtI model has evolved into a practice with five instructional principles (Frankel, Pearson, & Nair, 2011): (1) individualized instruction, (2) responsive assessment, (3) dynamic assessment, (4) "Goldilocks" pedagogy (i.e., just right materials and just in time scaffolding), and (5) programs fail; students do not.

Children with English language/literacy difficulties are not in a homogeneous group and do not need the same one-size-fits-all approach. Language/literacy development is not a monolithic process based on learning a single strategy such as phonics: "Children who experience difficulty will need particular interventions at particular points in the developmental process" (McGill-Franzen, 2011, p. xi).

We agree that instruction should be targeted to students' areas of need, as Valencia (2011) suggests: "High-quality instruction is a relative term. What is considered high-quality instruction for one child may be considered poor quality for another. Furthermore, when instructional time was spent on skills and abilities in which a student was strong, no additional growth was detected" (p. 31). We propose that an *interactive* model be used in unpacking the profiles of children with English language/literacy difficulties to design the best practice linking instruction to profiles and which considers the influences and interactions of various text, situational, and reader factors in language/literacy development. Profiling (or classifying, labeling) children with language/literacy difficulties is only the means to the end of designing "instruction that will make a difference" (Valencia, 2011, p. 31).

Juel's classic 1988 study, which calculated the probability of a poor reader in first grade becoming a poor reader in fourth grade as .88, has been frequently cited as evidence for the developmental trajectory of children with language/literacy difficulties. However, research has demonstrated that effective instructional practices can overcome the failing trajectory of these children and substantially reduce the number of children with reading disabilities (Pressley, Allington, Wharton-McDonald, Collins-Block, & Morrow, 2001; Wharton-McDonald, 2011; Wharton-McDonald, Pressley, & Hampton, 1998). For example, Pressley and colleagues (2000) found that the lowest-achieving first-grade students in classrooms with expert teachers achieved at the same level as their average peers in classrooms with typical teachers. In a commonly cited report by the National Research Council, Snow, Burns, and Griffin (1998) concluded that high-quality classroom instruction in the early grades is "the single best weapon against reading failure" (p. 343).

Wharton-McDonald (2011) proposed the following for students with reading disabilities: (1) *explicitness,* which means that teachers teach skills and strategies clearly and directly and (2) *intensity,* which is enhanced by increasing instructional time and decreasing group size. Wharton-McDonald further suggested that expert teachers provide (1) instruction matched to individual skills, understandings, and needs; (2) scaffolding; (3) appropriate level of challenge; (4) motivational learning environments; and (5) informed flexibility. We propose, based on the principles of the QSH, that these should be applicable for children with language/literacy difficulties in general, as well as many children who are d/Dhh, and, in fact, for anyone who is developing and acquiring English language/literacy. Children at the slower end of the developmental continuum might need more explicitness and intensity whereas those in the faster track might need less—nevertheless, the fundamentals should be the same or similar.

REFERENCES

Allen, T. (1986). Patterns of academic achievement among hearing impaired students: 1974 and 1983. In A. Schildroth & M. Karchmer (Eds.), *Deaf children in America* (pp. 161–206). San Diego, CA: Little, Brown.

Allen, T., Clark, M. D., del Giudice, A., Koo, D., Lieberman, A., Mayberry, R., & Miller, P. (2009). Phonology and reading: A response to Wang, Trezek, Luckner, and Paul. *American Annals of the Deaf, 154*(4), 338–345.

Allington, R. (2002). *Big brother and the national reading curriculum: How ideology trumped evidence.* Portsmouth, NH: Heinemann.

Armbruster, B. B., Lehr, F., & Osborn, J. (2001). *Put reading first: The research building blocks for teaching children to read kindergarten through grade 3.* Jessup, MD: National Institute for Literacy.

Bast, J., & Reitsma, P. (1998). Analyzing the development of individual differences in terms of Matthew effects in reading: Results from a Dutch longitudinal study. *Developmental Psychology, 34,* 1373–1399.

Bishop, D. V. M., & Adams, C. (1990). A prospective study of the relationship between specific language impairment, phonological disorders, and reading retardation. *Journal of Child Psychology and Psychiatry, 31,* 1027–1050.

Bus, A. G., & van Ijzendoorn, M. H. (1999). Phonological awareness and early reading: A meta-analysis of experimental training studies. *Journal of Educational Psychology, 91*(3), 403–414.

Catts, H. W. (1993). The relationship between speech language impairments and reading disabilities. *Journal of Speech and Hearing Research, 36,* 948–958.

Catts, H. W., Fey, M. E., Tomblin, J. B., & Zhang, X. (2002). A longitudinal investigation of reading outcomes in children with language impairments. *Journal of Speech, Language and Hearing Research, 45,* 1142–1157.

Catts, H. W., Hogan, T. P., & Adlof, A. M. (2005). Developmental changes in reading and reading disabilities. In H. W. Catts & A. G. Kamhi (Eds.), *Connections between language and reading disabilities* (pp. 25–40). Mahwah, NJ: Erlbaum.

Catts, H. W., Hogan, T., & Fey, M. E. (2003). Subgrouping poor readers on the basis of individual differences in reading-related abilities. *Journal of Learning Disabilities, 36*(2), 151–164.

Chen, R. S., & Vellutino, F. R. (1997). Prediction of reading ability: A cross-validation study of the simple view of reading. *Journal of Literacy Research, 29,* 1–24.

Clay, M. (1987). Learning to be learning disabled. *New Zealand Journal of Educational Studies, 22,* 155–173.

Cooner, C. M., Morrison, F. J., & Katch, E. L. (2004). Beyond the reading wars: Exploring the effect of child–instruction interactions on growth in early reading. *Scientific Studies of Reading, 8,* 305–336.

Cooner, C. M., Morrison, F. J., & Petrella, J. N. (2004). Effective reading comprehension instruction: Examining child × instruction interactions. *Journal of Educational Psychology, 96*(4), 682–698.

Cooper, R. (1967). The ability of deaf and hearing children to apply morphological rules. *Journal of Speech and Hearing Research, 10,* 77–86.

Crandall, K. (1978). Inflectional morphemes in the manual English of young hearing impaired children and their mothers. *Journal of Speech and Hearing Research, 21,* 372–386.

Dail, A. R., & Payne, R. (2010). Recasting the role of family involvement in early literacy development: A response to the NELP report. *Educational Researcher, 39*(4), 330–333.

Davis, J., & Blasdell, R. (1975). Perceptual strategies employed by normal-hearing and hearing-impaired children in the comprehension of sentences containing relative clauses. *Journal of Speech and Hearing Research, 18,* 281–295.

Ehri, L. C., Nunes, S. R., Willows, D. M., Schuster, B. V., Yaghoub-Zadeh, Z., & Shanahan, T. (2001). Phonemic awareness instruction helps children learn to read: Evidence from the National Reading Panel's meta-analysis. *Reading Research Quarterly, 36*(3), 250–287.

Ellis, A. W. (1985). The cognitive neuropsychology of developmental (and acquired) dyslexia: A critical survey. *Cognitive Neuropsychology, 2,* 169–205.

Frankel, K. K., Pearson, P. D., & Nair, M. (2011). Reading comprehension and reading disability. In A. McGill-Franzen & R. Allington (Eds.), *Handbook of reading disability research* (pp. 219–231). New York, NY: Routledge.

Gilman, L., Davis, J., & Raffin, M. (1980). Use of common morphemes by hearing impaired children exposed to a system of manual English. *Journal of Auditory Research, 20,* 57–69.

Gough, P. B., & Tunmer, W. E. (1986). Decoding, reading, and reading disability. *Remedial and Special Education, 7*(1), 6–10.

Gunderson, L., D'Silva, R., & Chen, L. (2011). Second language reading disability. In A. McGill-Franzen & R. Allington (Eds.), *Handbook of reading disability research* (pp. 13–24). New York, NY: Routledge.

Hall, P. K., & Tomblin, J. B. (1978). A follow-up study of children with articulation and language disorders. *Journal of Speech and Hearing Disorders, 43,* 227–241.

Hanson, V. (1989). Phonology and reading: Evidence from profoundly deaf readers. In D. Shankweiler & I. Liberman (Eds.), *Phonology and reading disability: Solving the reading puzzle* (pp. 69–89). Ann Arbor, MI: University of Michigan Press.

Hoover, W. A., & Gough, P. B. (1990). The simple view of reading. *Reading and Writing: An Interdisciplinary Journal, 2,* 127–160.

Izzo, A. (2002). Phonemic awareness and reading ability: An investigation with young readers who are deaf. *American Annals of the Deaf, 147*(4), 18–28.

Jenkins, J. R., Fuchs, L. S., van den Broek, P., Espin, C., & Deno, S. L. (2003). Sources of individual differences in reading comprehension and reading fluency. *Journal of Educational Psychology, 95,* 719–729.

Juel, C. (1988). Learning to read and write: A longitudinal study of 54 children from first to fourth grades. *Journal of Educational Psychology, 80*, 437–447.

Juel, C., & Minden-Cupp, C. (2000). Learning to read words: Linguistic units and instructional strategies. *Reading Research Quarterly, 35*, 458–492.

Kamhi, A. (2009). Prologue: The case for the narrow view of reading. *Language, Speech, and Hearing Services in Schools, 40*, 174–178.

Kamhi, A. G., & Catts, H. W. (2012a). Reading development. In A. G. Kamhi & H. W. Catts (Eds.), *Language and reading disabilities* (3rd ed., pp. 24–44). Upper Saddle River, NJ: Person Education.

Kamhi, A. G., & Catts, H. W. (2012b). Language and reading: Convergences and divergences. In A. G. Kamhi & H. W. Catts (Eds.), *Language and reading disabilities* (3rd ed., pp. 1–23). Upper Saddle River, NJ: Pearson Education.

Kamhi, A. G., & Catts, H. W. (2012c). *Language and reading disabilities* (3rd ed.). Upper Saddle River, NJ: Pearson Education.

Kendeou, P., van den Broek, P., White, M. J., & Lynch, J. S. (2009). Predicting reading comprehension in early elementary school: The independent contributions of oral language and decoding skills. *Journal of Educational Psychology, 101*(4), 765–778.

King, C. (1981). *An investigation of similarities and differences in the syntactic abilities of deaf and hearing children learning English as a first or second language* (Unpublished doctoral dissertation). University of Illinois, Champaign-Urbana.

Laing, E., Hulme, C., Grant, J., & Karmiloff-Smith, A. (2001). Learning to read in Williams syndrome: Looking beneath the surface of atypical reading development. *Journal of Child Psychology and Psychiatry, 42*(6), 729–739.

Lenneberg, E. (1967). *Biological foundations of language.* New York, NY: Wiley.

Luckner, J. L., Sebald, A. N., Cooney, J., Young, J., & Goodwin Muir, S. (2005/2006). An examination of the evidence-based literacy research in deaf education. *American Annals of the Deaf, 150*(5), 443–456.

Mayberry, R. I., del Giudice, A. A., & Lieberman, A. M. (2011). Reading achievement in relation to phonological coding and awareness in deaf readers: A meta-analysis. *Journal of Deaf Studies and Deaf Education, 16*(2), 164–188.

McGill-Franzen, A. (2011). Preface. In A. McGill-Franzen & R. Allington (Eds.), *Handbook of reading disability research* (pp. xi–xii). New York, NY: Routledge.

McGill-Franzen, A., & Allington, R. (Eds.). (2011). *Handbook of reading disability research.* New York, NY: Routledge.

Miller, P., & Clark, M. D. (2011). Phonemic awareness is not necessary to become a skilled deaf reader. *Journal of Developmental and Physical Disabilities, 23*, 459–476.

Mitchell, R. E., & Karchmer, M. A. (2004). Chasing the mythical 10%: Parental hearing status of deaf and hard of hearing students in the United States. *Sign Language Studies, 4*, 138–163.

Nation, K., Clarke, P., Wright, B., & Williams, C. (2006). Patterns of reading ability in children with autism spectrum disorder. *Journal of Autism and Developmental Disorder, 36*, 911–919.

National Reading Panel. (2000). *Report of the National Reading Panel: Teaching children to read— An evidence-based assessment of the scientific research literature on reading and its implications for reading instruction.* Jessup, MD: National Institute for Literacy at EDPubs.

National Early Literacy Panel. (2008). *Developing early literacy: Report of the National Early Literacy Panel.* Washington, DC: National Institute for Literacy. Retrieved from http://www.nifl.gov/earlychildhood/NELP/NELPreport.html

Ormel, E., Hermans, D., Knoors, H., Hendriks, A., & Verhoeven, L. (2010). Phonological activation during visual word recognition in deaf and hearing children. *Journal of Speech, Language, and Hearing Research, 53*(4), 801–280.

Paul, P. (2003). Processes and components of reading. In M. Marschark & P. Spencer (Eds.), *Handbook of deaf studies, language, and education* (pp. 97–109). New York, NY: Oxford University Press.

Paul, P. (2009). *Language and deafness* (4th ed.). Sudbury, MA: Jones & Bartlett.

Paul, P. (2010). Qualitative-similarity hypothesis. In R. Nata (Ed.), *Progress in Education* (Vol. 20, pp. 1–31). New York, NY: Nova Science.

Paul, P. (2012). Qualitative similarity hypothesis. In P. Paul and D. Moores (Eds.), *Deaf epistemologies: Multiple perspectives on the acquisition of knowledge* (pp. 179–198). Washington, DC: Gallaudet University Press.

Paul, P., & Lee, C. (2010). Qualitative-similarity hypothesis. *American Annals of the Deaf, 154*(5), 456–462.

Paul, P., & Wang, Y. (2012). *Literate thought: Understanding comprehension and literacy.* Sudbury, MA: Jason & Bartlett Learning.

Paul, P., Wang, Y., Trezek, B., & Luckner, J. (2009). Phonology is necessary, but not sufficient: A rejoinder. *American Annals of the Deaf, 154*(4), 346–356.

Payne, J. A., & Quigley, S. (1987). Hearing-impaired children's comprehension of verb–particle combinations. *Volta Review, 89*, 133–143.

Perfetti, C. A. (1992). The representation problem in reading acquisition. In P. B. Gough, L. C. Ehri, & R. Treiman (Eds.), *Reading acquisition* (pp. 145–174). Hillsdale, NJ: Erlbaum.

Perfetti, C. A., & Hart, L. (2001). The lexical quality hypothesis. In L. Verhoeven, C. Elbro, & P. Reitsma (Eds.), *Precursors of functional literacy* (pp. 189–214). Amsterdam, the Netherlands: John Benjamins.

Perfetti, C. A., & Sandak, R. (2000). Reading optimally builds on spoken language: Implications for deaf readers. *Journal of Deaf Studies and Deaf Education, 5*(1), 32–50.

Phillips, L. M., Hayward, D. V., & Norris, S. P. (2011). Persistent reading disabilities: Challenging six erroneous beliefs. In A. McGill-Franzen & R. Allington (Eds.), *Handbook of reading disability research* (pp. 110–119). New York, NY: Routledge.

Pressley, M., Allington, R. L., Wharton-McDonald, R., Collins-Block, C., & Morrow, L. (2001). *Learning to read: Lessons from exemplary first-grade classrooms.* New York, NY: Guilford.

Pressley, M., Wharton-McDonald, R., Allington, R. L., Block, C. C., Morrow, L., Tracey, D., et al. (2000). A study of effective first-grade reading instruction. *Scientific Studies of Reading, 5*, 35–58.

Pressnell, L. (1973). Hearing-impaired children's comprehension and production of syntax in oral language. *Journal of Speech and Hearing Research, 16*, 12–21.

Qi, S., & Mitchell, R. E. (2012). Large-scale academic achievement testing of deaf and hard-of-hearing students: Past, present, and future. *Journal of Deaf Studies and Deaf Education, 17*(1), 1–18.

Quigley, S., Wilbur, R., Power, D., Montanelli, D., & Steinkamp, M. (1976). *Syntactic structures in the language of deaf children (final report).* Urbana, IL: University of Illinois, Institute for Child Behavior and Development.

Raffin, M., Davis, J., & Gilman, L. (1978). Comprehension of inflectional morphemes by deaf children exposed to a visual English sign system. *Journal of Speech and Hearing Research, 21*, 387–400.

RAND Reading Study Group (RRSG). (2002). *Reading for understanding: Toward a research and development program in reading comprehension.* Santa Monica, CA; RAND.

Rapp, D. N., van den Broek, P., McMaster, K. L., Kendeou, P., & Espin, C. A. (2007). Higher-order comprehension processes in struggling readers: A perspective for research and intervention. *Scientific Studies of Reading, 11*, 289–312.

Russell, W., Quigley, S., & Power, D. (1976). *Linguistics and deaf children.* Washington, DC: Alexander Graham Bell Association for the Deaf.

Rutter, M., & Yule, W. (1975). The concept of specific reading retardation. *Journal of Child Psychology and Psychiatry, 16*, 181–197.

Scanlon, D. M. (2011). Response to intervention as an assessment approach. In A. McGill-Franzen & R. Allington (Eds.), *Handbook of reading disability research* (pp. 139–148). New York, NY: Routledge.

Schickedanz, J. A., & McGee, L. M. (2010). The NELP report on shared story reading interventions (Chapter 4): Extending the story. *Educational Researcher, 39*(4), 323–329.

Schirmer, B. R., & McGough, S. M. (2005). Teaching reading to children who are deaf: Do the conclusions of the National Reading Panel apply? *Review of Educational Research, 75*(1), 83–117.

Shanahan, T. (2004). Critiques of the National Reading Panel Report: Their implications for research, policy, and practice. In P. McCardle & V. Chhabra (Eds.), *The voice of evidence in reading research* (pp. 235–265). Baltimore, MD: Paul H. Brookes.

Shanahan, T., & Lonigan, C. J. (2010). The National Early Literacy Panel: A summary of the process and the report. *Educational Researcher, 39*(4), 279–285.

Share, D. (1995). Phonological recoding and self-teaching: *Sine qua non* of reading acquisition. *Cognition, 55,* 151–218.

Share, D. (1999). Phonological recoding and orthographic learning: A direct test of the self-teaching hypothesis. *Journal of Experimental Child Psychology, 72,* 95–129.

Share, D., & Stanovich, K. (1995). Cognitive processes in early reading development: Accommodating individual differences into a model of acquisition. *Issues in Education, 1,* 1–57.

Silva, P. A., McGee, R., & Williams, S. M. (1987). Developmental language delay from three to seven years and its significance for low intelligence and reading difficulties at age 7. *Developmental Medicine and Child Neurology, 25,* 783–793.

Snow, C. E. (2010). Reading comprehension: Reading for learning. In P. Peterson, E. Baker, & B. McGraw (Eds.), *International encyclopedia of education* (3rd ed., pp. 413–418). Oxford, UK: Elsevier.

Snow, C. E., Burns, S. M., & Griffin, P. (Eds.). (1998). *Preventing reading difficulties in young children.* Washington, DC: National Academy Press.

Snowling, M., & Hulme, C. (2007). Learning to read with a language impairment. In M. Snowling & C. Hulme (Eds.), *The science of reading: A handbook* (pp. 397–412). Malden, MA: Blackwell.

Stanovich, K. E. (1986). Matthew effects in reading: Some consequences of individual differences in the acquisition of literacy. *Reading Research Quarterly, 21,* 360–407.

Stanovich, K. E. (1988). Explaining the differences between the dyslexic and the garden-variety poor reader: The phonological-core variable-difference model. *Journal of Learning Disabilities, 21*(10), 590–604.

Stanovich, K. E. (1991). Word recognition: Changing perspectives. In R. Barr, M. Kamil, P. Mosenthal, & P. D. Person (Eds.), *Handbook of reading research* (Vol. 2, pp. 418–452). While Plains, NY: Longman.

Stanovich, K. E. (1992). Speculations on the causes and consequences of individual differences in early reading acquisition. In P. Gough, L. Ehri, & R. Treiman (Eds.), *Reading acquisition* (pp. 307–342). Hillsdale, NJ: Lawrence Erlbaum.

Stanovich, K. E. (2000). *Progress in understanding reading: Scientific foundations and new frontiers.* New York, NY: Guilford Press.

Stanovich, K. E., Nathan, R. G., & Zolman, J. E., (1988). The developmental lag hypothesis in reading: Longitudinal and matched reading-level comparisons. *Child Development, 59,* 71–86.

Stanovich, K. E., Nathan, R. G., & Vala-Rossi, M. (1986). Developmental changes in the cognitive correlates of reading ability and the developmental lag hypothesis. *Reading Research Quarterly, 21,* 267–283.

Tomblin, J. B., Records, N., Buckwalter, P., Zhang, X., Smith, E., & O'Brien, M. (1997). Prevalence of specific language impairment in kindergarten children. *Journal of Speech, Language, and Hearing Research, 40,* 1245–1260.

Traxler, C. (2000). The Stanford Achievement Test, 9th edition: National norming and performance standards for deaf and hard-of-hearing students. *Journal of Deaf Studies and Deaf Education, 5*(4), 337–348.

Trezek, B. J., Wang, Y., & Paul, P. V. (2010). *Reading and deafness: Theory, research, and practice.* Clifton Park, NY: Cengage Learning.

Trezek, B. J., Wang, Y., & Paul, P. V. (2011). Processes and components of reading. In M. Marschark & P. Spencer (Eds.), *Handbook of deaf studies, language, and education* (Vol. 1, Part II, pp. 99–114). New York, NY: Oxford University Press.

Tunmer, W., & Hoover, W. (1993). Components of variance models of language-related factors in reading disability: A conceptual overview. In R. J. Joshi & C. K. Leong (Eds.), *Reading disabilities: Diagnosis and component processes* (pp. 135–173). Dordrecht, the Netherlands: Kluwer.

Vauras, M., Kinnunen, R., & Kuusela, L. (1994). Development of learning strategies in high-, average-, and low-achieving primary school children. *Journal of Reading Behavior, 26,* 361–389.

Verhoeven, L. (2011). Language development and reading disabilities. In A. McGill-Franzen & R. Allington (Eds.), *Handbook of reading disability research* (pp. 36–44). New York, NY: Routledge.

Wang, Y., Trezek, B., Luckner, J., & Paul, P. (2008). The role of phonology and phonological-related skills in reading instruction for students who are deaf or hard of hearing. *American Annals of the Deaf, 153*(4), 396–407.

Wang, Y., Kretschmer, R., & Hartman, M. (2008). Reading and students who are d/Deaf or hard of hearing. *Journal of Balanced Reading Instruction, 15*(2), 53–68.

Weber, R. (2006). Function words in the prosody of fluent reading. *Journal of Reading Research, 29*(3), 258–269.

Wharton-McDonald, R. (2011). Expert classroom instruction for students with reading disabilities. In A. McGill-Franzen & R. Allington (Eds.), *Handbook of reading disability research* (pp. 265–272). New York, NY: Routledge.

Wharton-McDonald, R., Pressley, M., & Hampton, J. M. (1998). Literacy instruction in nine first grade classrooms: Teacher characteristics and student achievement. *Elementary School Journal, 99,* 101–128.

Wilcox, J., & Tobin, H. (1974). Linguistic performance of hard-of-hearing and normal hearing children. *Journal of Speech and Hearing Research, 17,* 286–293.

Wolbers, K. A., & Dostal, H. M. (2011). Interventions for the deaf and language delayed. In A. McGill-Franzen & R. Allington (Eds.), *Handbook of reading disability research* (pp. 392–406). New York, NY: Routledge.

Ziegler, J. C., & Goswami, U. C. (2005). Reading acquisition, developmental dyslexia, and skilled reading across languages: A psycholinguistic grain size theory. *Psychological Bulletin, 131*(1), 3–29.

6

Evidence- and Reason-Based Instructional Strategies

Intervention studies are a form of applied research; they examine the effectiveness of a specific instructional approach, method, program, or set of activities on students' learning. Researchers conduct intervention studies to establish direct links between the intervention and anticipated growth in students' knowledge and skills. In this chapter, we review literacy-focused intervention studies that have been conducted recently with d/Deaf and hard of hearing (d/Dhh) students. Each intervention study used either an experimental, quasiexperimental, single-subject, or pretest–posttest design and was conducted between 2000 and 2013. Our goal is to document the effectiveness of specific instructional strategies and approaches that support early English literacy or conventional literacy learning in d/Dhh children and adolescents and to build on the findings from previous reviews (e.g., Luckner, Sebald, Cooney, Young, & Goodwin-Muir, 2005/2006; Schirmer & McGough, 2005; Trezek, Wang, & Paul, 2010).

While intervention research among children and adolescents who have typical hearing is common and has yielded significant findings with respect to evidence-based instructional practices (see, for example, Cain & Oakhill, 2007; Israel & Duffy, 2009), intervention research with d/Dhh students has been rare (see Paul, 2009; Trezek, Wang, & Paul, 2010). Nevertheless, an evidence base is beginning to accrue with respect to instructional interventions designed to promote literacy development in d/Dhh children and adolescents. An integrative review of recent intervention research will provide evidence-based direction for both teachers and researchers whose goal is to promote the literacy development of d/Dhh learners.

Given the major tenet of this book, that d/Dhh learners acquire English language and literacy in ways that are developmentally similar to that of their typically developing peers, that is, the qualitative similarity hypothesis (QSH), we compare the findings of our review to the findings reported by the National Early Literacy Panel (NELP) (2008) and the National Reading Panel (NRP) (2000), comprehensive meta-analyses of literacy interventions conducted with typically developing learners of English literacy. The goal of this comparison is to identify intersections between the bodies of research. Such intersections could provide further support, both evidence and reason based, for the QSH as well as important insights for classroom practice and implications for future research with d/Dhh learners. Major differences between the three reviews would also be informative and would highlight the need for differentiated instruction according to the characteristics of individual profiles (e.g., Valencia, 2011; see also Chapters 1 and 2).

In the following sections, we review early literacy interventions and conventional literacy interventions that have been conducted with d/Dhh learners. Our review is organized to reflect the categories of intervention research identified by the NELP and the NRP. To provide a context for our review and the comparisons we make, we briefly describe both the NELP and the NRP, especially the major findings and recommendations (see also the discussions in Chapters 4 and 5).

EARLY LITERACY INTERVENTIONS

The purpose of the National Early Literacy Panel (2008) was to conduct a synthesis of the experimental and quasiexperimental research on early English literacy development in children from birth through age 5 and on home and family influences on that development. The primary goal of the synthesis was to determine the effectiveness of instructional strategies and practices in supporting both precursor skills (i.e., spoken [through-the-air] language, phonological awareness, and alphabetic knowledge) and conventional literacy skills so that teachers and families could better support young children's English language and literacy development. The panel identified five broad categories of intervention studies in the research literature: code-focused, shared reading, parent and home programs, preschool and kindergarten programs, and language-enhancement interventions.

The code-focused interventions reported statistically significant and moderate to large effects across a wide variety of early literacy outcomes, including spoken language (English), and consistently demonstrated positive effects on children's literacy skills. The shared reading interventions demonstrated statistically significant and moderate effects on children's print knowledge and spoken language skills. Home and parent programs focused on teaching parents instructional techniques to promote their children's linguistic or cognitive development, and these interventions produced statistically significant and moderate to large effects on children's spoken language and general cognitive abilities. Intervention studies that evaluated various aspects (e.g., curricula, policies, extended year) of preschool and kindergarten programs yielded significant and moderate to large effects on children's readiness for reading and spelling instruction. Language-enhancement interventions demonstrated large and statistically significant effects on children's spoken language skills, especially early on. It is important to note that the code-focused, shared reading, home and parent programs, and language-enhancement interventions all improved children's spoken language skills. It is also important to note that the interventions that produced large and positive effects on children's code-related and literacy-related skills were typically delivered through small-group or one-on-one instruction.

In contrast to the wide variety and large number of intervention studies examined by the NELP, we identified only three recent early literacy intervention studies conducted with young d/Dhh children. Two studies investigated code-focused interventions in preschool, kindergarten, and first grade (Beal-Alvarez, Lederberg, & Easterbrooks, 2011; Bergeron, Lederberg, Easterbrooks, Miller, & Connor, 2009). One study examined a shared reading intervention in children's homes (Fung, Chow, & McBride-Chang, 2005). We found no intervention studies that examined the effectiveness of specific parent and home programs for d/Dhh children, although research has documented the home-based literacy experiences of d/Dhh preschoolers (Heineman-Gosschalk & Webster, 2003; Stobbart & Alant, 2008; Swanwick & Watson, 2005) and described resources and support systems for parents (Wood-Jackson, 2011), nor did we identify studies that evaluated preschool or kindergarten interventions or language-enhancement interventions designed specifically for d/Dhh children. In the following sections, we review the code-focused and shared reading interventions we identified.

Code-Focused Interventions

The National Early Literacy Panel (2008) examined intervention studies that were designed to teach young children various aspects of the alphabetic principle (i.e., the knowledge that the sounds in spoken words are represented by letters in written words). This was the largest number of intervention studies that the NELP reviewed, and it included phonological awareness, alphabetic knowledge, and early decoding interventions. Most of the code-focused interventions were conducted in preschool or kindergarten and supplemented regular instructional programming.

We identified only two code-focused intervention studies conducted with young d/Dhh children. Both investigations examined the effectiveness of specific instructional strategies designed to teach phoneme–grapheme correspondences to young children who are d/Dhh, with the goal of supporting the children's acquisition of the alphabetic principle. In the first study, Bergeron et al. (2009) investigated the effectiveness of teaching phoneme–grapheme correspondences using a semantic association strategy. The semantic association strategy was based on an approach from the Children's Early Intervention (CEI) curriculum, which is used to teach phoneme–grapheme correspondences to children with communication disorders (Tade & Vitali, 1994). The semantic association strategy embeds letter–sound instruction within a meaningful story accompanied by a picture that builds a link—a semantic association—between phoneme–grapheme correspondences. For example, the letter *m* is associated with the phoneme /m/ through a story in which a child eats ice cream and says, "Mmm-mmm, that's good." Other curricular programs provide picture cues to help children remember letters, but the semantic association strategy helps children remember phonemes, which are often challenging for d/Dhh children (see Morrison, Trezek, & Paul, 2008).

Bergeron and colleagues modified the CEI approach in two ways. First, after the story was read, the children participated in a multisensory activity in which they acted out the story—in this case, they made ice cream sundaes and practiced saying, "Mmm-mmm, that's good." Second, in subsequent activities in which children were asked to decode words, the researchers used small picture cards to cue the phonemes (e.g., a picture of an ice cream sundae to cue the phoneme /m/). The researchers investigated the effectiveness of the semantic association strategy embedded in two interventions.

In study 1, Bergeron et al. used their enhanced version of the CEI curriculum with five d/Dhh children, ages 3 to 7, who attended preschool, kindergarten, or first grade in oral programs or programs in which Simultaneous Communication and American Sign Language (ASL) were used. Three of the children had cochlear implants; all of the children had some speech perception skills. The intervention was conducted 4 days a week for 35 minutes each day across 8 or 9 weeks in pull-out, small-group instruction.

In study 2, which began in the fall following the first intervention, Bergeron and colleagues implemented and investigated the effectiveness of the semantic association strategy embedded in an early literacy curriculum they had created specifically for d/Dhh preschoolers, called Foundations for Literacy (Lederberg, Miller, Easterbrooks, Bergeron, & Connor, 2009). The foundations curriculum retained the semantic association strategy from the CEI but included new stories and language experiences with modern, culturally inclusive illustrations. The foundations program was designed to provide explicit code-related instruction as well as vocabulary and comprehension instruction to d/Dhh preschoolers who have at least some speech perception skills. The five children who participated in the foundations intervention were 3 to 4 years old and attended an oral preschool program. All of the children had cochlear implants. Although the foundations curriculum was implemented across the academic year, the investigation was conducted 4 days a week for 1 hour through pull-out, small-group instruction for 6 weeks at the beginning of the school year.

Bergeron and colleagues used single-subject design experiments with multiple baselines across content (i.e., phoneme–grapheme correspondences) in both studies to examine the relationship between the interventions and children's acquisition of phoneme–grapheme correspondences. Results of study 1 demonstrated that all of the children learned the phoneme–grapheme correspondences that were taught, and three of the five children maintained knowledge of those correspondences for the remainder of the CEI intervention. Similarly, results of study 2 demonstrated a functional relationship between the foundations intervention and children's acquisition of phoneme–grapheme correspondences. All five children learned the phoneme–grapheme correspondences that were taught during the intervention and maintained these correspondences across the academic year. Moreover, students were able to use learned correspondences in decoding 60% of known words and 30% of novel words. The findings of both intervention studies indicated that the semantic association strategy is an effective method for teaching phoneme–grapheme correspondences to young children who have speech perception abilities. The researchers indicate that the children's learning did not appear to be related to their vocabulary knowledge. They also suggest that the enjoyable nature of the multisensory language experiences were essential to the success of the interventions.

Beal-Alvarez et al. (2011) built on the Bergeron et al. (2009) investigation by examining the effectiveness of the foundations curriculum (Lederberg, Miller, Easterbrooks, & Connor, 2011) to support phoneme–grapheme acquisition in d/Dhh preschoolers with and without speech perception abilities. Children with limited to no speech perception skills were provided additional support through the use of Visual

Phonics, a multimodal system that uses hand cues and written graphemes to teach each of the approximately 46 phonemes of English. In two intervention studies, Beal-Alvarez and colleagues used single-subject design experiments with multiple baselines across content to document student learning.

In the first intervention, 30-minute lessons across a 10-week period in the spring were provided one-on-one to a d/Dhh preschooler who had minimal speech perception skills; the second intervention followed in the fall and was conducted through small-group instruction across the academic year with three d/Dhh preschoolers who had various levels of speech perception skills. The 4-year-old children had unaided hearing losses ranging from 80 to 95 dB and wore hearing aids. Results of both intervention studies demonstrated that all four children mastered the phoneme–grapheme correspondences that were taught and decoded familiar and novel words on posttests; however, some children did not correctly identify novel words after decoding. The researchers suggest that decoding novel words may not be a developmentally appropriate expectation for preschoolers. As in the Bergeron et al. (2009) study, the researchers also indicate that the children's learning did not appear to be related to vocabulary knowledge.

Collectively, the findings of these intervention studies suggest that explicit instruction on phoneme–grapheme correspondences using a multisensory, semantic association strategy, as found in the foundations curriculum, is an effective approach to teaching phoneme–graphemes to d/Dhh children who have speech perception skills and that the instructional approach is also effective for children with limited speech perception if supplemented by Visual Phonics. These findings are noteworthy in light of recent research that suggests that letter–sound knowledge predicts later reading in d/Dhh children (Easterbrooks, Lederberg, Miller, Bergeron, & McDonald-Connor, 2008; Kyle & Harris, 2011). Learning phoneme–grapheme correspondences in the preschool years might support d/Dhh children's acquisition of the alphabetic principle and phonological processing skills early and prevent future delays in learning to read. Longitudinal research is needed to investigate the long-term outcomes of this promising code-focused intervention.

Shared Reading Interventions

Shared reading is considered by many scholars to be the single most important activity adults can do with their children to promote emergent literacy skills (e.g., Anderson, Hiebert, Scott, & Wilkinson, 1985). The NELP examined the effects of interventions that focused on shared reading activities involving parents, teachers, or the combination of parents and teachers reading with children individually or in groups. The studies included in the NELP's review evaluated the effectiveness of the shared reading intervention on precursor (e.g., alphabetic knowledge, phonological awareness, oral [spoken] language) or conventional literacy skills. Results demonstrated moderate effects on measures of oral language, print knowledge, and writing.

Only one shared reading intervention has been conducted with young children who are d/Dhh. In an experimental study, Fung, Chow, and McBride–Chang (2005) examined the effect of dialogic reading (Whitehurst et al., 1988)—a specific approach to shared reading—on the vocabulary development of 28 d/Dhh children who were 5 to 9 years of age and enrolled in oral instructional programs in Hong Kong in kindergarten, first, or second grade. The children's hearing losses ranged from moderate to severe.

In the dialogic approach to shared reading, parents are taught to use the PEER technique—prompt, evaluate, expand, and repeat. First, parents prompt children to say something about the storybook, often using *wh-* and open-ended questions to elicit children's comments. Parents then evaluate the child's response with feedback and expand on the comment by adding new information (e.g., "Yes, that's a pig, and he's making a grunting sound"). Finally, the parent guides the child to repeat what was said or retell the story. The goal of the dialogic approach is to encourage children to take an active role in the shared reading event.

In an 8-week study, Fung and colleagues randomly assigned hearing parents and their d/Dhh children to a dialogic reading group, typical reading group, or control group. Prior to the intervention, the researchers trained parents in the dialogic reading group to use the PEER technique and provided a guidebook that demonstrated standard dialogic reading procedures. These parents were also given a set of eight storybooks with questions attached to each page to help them prompt children's responses. The researchers also provided picture cards for the children to use when responding to questions and for parents to use when prompting story retellings. A calendar checklist reminded parents to read each book with their child twice a week for 15 to 30 minutes each time. Parents in the typical reading group also received the storybooks and calendar but did not participate in the training session or receive other materials. Parents in the control group did not receive materials or training and were only given the storybooks after the intervention was complete. Pretesting demonstrated no statistically significant differences among the children. Posttest results indicated that children in the dialogic reading group scored significantly higher on a receptive vocabulary test than children in the comparison and control group, and the effect size was large. On postintervention questionnaires, parents indicated that the dialogic reading program had been beneficial to their children's learning. Fung and colleagues conclude that high-quality parent–child interactions during the dialogic reading events, and the use of pictorial materials, contributed to the success of the intervention.

A primary challenge in shared reading activities with many d/Dhh children is the children's need to divide their visual attention between the book being shared and the caregiver or teacher's communication (see Spencer, 2000; Swanwick & Watson, 2005). This challenge was not addressed in the Fung et al. (2005) study. If caregivers or teachers are communicating through sign, speech reading, or Cued Speech/Language, the children's visual attention is required and, thus, modifications to the shared reading event must be made. For example, children must be seated in such a way that they can easily look at the parent or teacher as well as the book. The parent or teacher must match her or his communication and book reading to the children's natural attention transfers from the book to the reader.

In the 1990s, researchers sought practical solutions to these challenges by investigating the ways in which d/Deaf parents read to their d/Deaf children (e.g., Akamatsu & Andrews, 1993; Andrews & Taylor, 1987; Lartz & Lestina, 1995). The findings of those studies provided direction for both hearing parents and classroom teachers of d/Dhh children who communicate primarily via sign. The Shared Reading Project (Delk & Weidekamp, 2001) at Gallaudet University was based on the results of those investigations and was specifically designed to demonstrate to parents how to read to their d/Dhh children using strategies that make shared reading most effective. Given that a number of studies in the general research literature suggest that adults' styles of shared reading have differential influences on young children's early understandings of literacy (e.g., Dickinson & Keebler, 1989; Teale & Martinez, 1996), identifying effective strategies for shared storybook reading with d/Dhh children is essential. Future intervention research on shared reading will need to address this challenge.

Although the results of these code-focused and shared reading interventions are promising, the number of studies is extremely small. Considerably more early literacy intervention research is needed in these two areas, as well as in other areas identified by the NELP. If the development of literacy is dependent on the acquisition of major fundamental components, as discussed in Chapters 1 and 2, then investigating these identified NELP areas is a necessary first step in understanding and improving early literacy for d/Dhh children.

Given d/Dhh children's challenges with the acquisition of English, language-enhancement interventions are especially needed. Much of the earlier research on developing the English language has been focused predominantly on the effectiveness of natural, structured, or combined approaches (Paul, 2009). Practical activities for developing receptive and expressive language skills can be found in a few sources (e.g., Easterbrooks & Baker, 2002; Luetke-Stahlman, 1988, 1999; Rose, McAnally, & Quigley, 2004). A synthesis of the available research revealed that there is no superior group of approaches and that many practitioners either use a combined (i.e., some combination of natural and structured methods) approach or reasoned that it is best to use more than one approach (Paul, 2009).

A summary of major points for the early literacy intervention studies discussed here is provided in Table 6.1.

CONVENTIONAL LITERACY INTERVENTIONS

The purpose of the National Reading Panel (2000) was to conduct a synthesis of the experimental, quasiexperimental, and multiple-baseline research on English reading instruction in preschool through grade 12 to identify the skills that are essential to reading development as well as the instructional approaches and methods most effective for teaching reading. No conclusions were drawn from correlational or descriptive studies. The panel investigated several instructional areas, including phonemic awareness, phonics, fluency, vocabulary, and text comprehension, as well as the use of computer technology in reading instruction.

The phonemic awareness interventions yielded large effects for phonemic awareness outcomes and moderate effects for reading and spelling outcomes, suggesting

Table 6.1. Early Literacy Intervention Studies

	Study	Intervention	Population	Methods	Outcomes
Code focused	Bergeron, Lederberg, Easterbrooks, Miller, and Connor (2009).	Study 1: Teaching phoneme–grapheme correspondences using a semantic association strategy. Study 2: Foundations for Literacy curriculum.	Study 1: Five d/Dhh children, 3–7 years; attended preschool, K, or first grade in oral, SimCom, or ASL programs. Three children had cochlear implants; all children had some speech perception skills. Study 2: Five d/Dhh children, 3–4 years; attended oral preschool. All children had cochlear implants.	Single-subject design experiments with multiple baselines across content.	Study 1: All children learned phoneme–grapheme correspondences; three children maintained knowledge throughout the intervention. Study 2: All children learned and maintained phoneme–grapheme correspondences; students used correspondences in decoding 60% of known words and 30% of novel words.
	Beal-Alvarez, Lederberg, and Easterbrooks (2011).	Foundations for Literacy curriculum and Visual Phonics.	Study 1: One d/Dhh preschooler with minimal speech perception skills. Study 2: Three d/Dhh preschoolers (80–95 dB unaided hearing loss); all wore hearing aids and had various levels of speech perception skills.	Single-subject design experiments with multiple baselines across content.	All children mastered phoneme–grapheme correspondences and decoded familiar and novel words on posttests; some children did not correctly identify novel words after decoding.
Shared reading	Fung, Chow, and McBride–Chang (2005).	Dialogic reading.	Twenty-eight d/Dhh children, 5–9 years with moderate to severe hearing losses; attended K, first-, or second-grade oral programs.	Experimental.	Dialogic reading group scored significantly higher on receptive vocabulary test than comparison and control groups.

that teaching children to manipulate phonemes in words can support early English literacy. The phonics interventions demonstrated that systematic phonics instruction was significantly more effective than nonphonics approaches in supporting substantial growth in reading and that early instruction was more effective than phonics instruction introduced after first grade. The fluency interventions examined two primary methods typically used to promote fluency: independent silent reading and guided, repeated oral (spoken) reading. The panel concluded that there was insufficient evidence to draw conclusions about the effectiveness of independent silent reading in promoting reading fluency; however, the available evidence indicated that guided, repeated oral reading had a moderate impact on reading accuracy, fluency, and comprehension.

Studies of vocabulary interventions suggested that direct instruction, repetition, and multiple exposures to target words, learning in rich contexts, and active engagement in learning tasks are essential to vocabulary growth; computer technology also was found to effectively support vocabulary instruction. Interventions on text comprehension instruction demonstrated that six types of instruction, in particular, improve text comprehension: comprehension monitoring, summarization, graphic and semantic organizers, question answering, question generation, and cooperative learning. The use of multiple strategies in combination was found to be the most effective approach. Finally, the computer technology interventions indicated that the addition of speech to computer-presented text, the use of hypertext, and the use of word processing to combine reading with writing instruction appear to have strong potential for supporting reading instruction.

Recent intervention research with d/Dhh students in each of the instructional areas examined by the National Reading Panel (2000) has been rare. In fact, we identified only 18 intervention studies conducted since 2000. Three studies addressed phonemic awareness and phonics instruction (Trezek & Malmgren, 2005; Trezek & Wang, 2006; Trezek, Wang, Woods, Gampp, & Paul, 2007). Similarly, three studies examined the effectiveness of fluency interventions (Enns & Lafond, 2007; Schirmer, Schaffer, Therrien, & Schirmer, 2012; Schirmer, Therrien, Schaffer, & Schirmer, 2009). Vocabulary interventions received the most research attention, with seven recent studies (Barker, 2003; Cannon, Fredrick, & Easterbrooks, 2010; Dimling, 2010; Massaro & Light, 2004; Mollink, Hermans, & Knoors, 2008; Paatsch, Blarney, Sarant, & Bow, 2006; Wauters, Knoors, Vervloed, & Aarnoutse, 2001). Three studies evaluated the effectiveness of text comprehension interventions (Al-Hilawani, 2003; Pakulski & Kaderavek, 2001; Schirmer & Schaffer, 2010). Two intervention studies examined computer technology and reading instruction (Gentry, Chinn, & Moulton, 2004; Wang & Paul, 2011). Each of these intervention studies is reviewed in the sections that follow.

Phonemic Awareness and Phonics Interventions

The National Reading Panel (2000) reviewed phonemic awareness interventions that focused on children's abilities to manipulate phonemes in spoken words, although some of the studies also included phoneme–grapheme instruction. Two types of phonics instruction were also reviewed—systematic phonics, which involves explicit, sequenced instruction on phonics elements, and incidental phonics, which involves teaching phonics elements during teachable moments as they occur in the context of literacy instruction. Although the NRP reviewed phonemic awareness training studies separately from phonics training studies, the panel recognized the potential overlap between phonemic awareness training and phonics instruction. The three intervention studies conducted recently with d/Dhh students examined the effectiveness of phonics treatment packages that included both explicit phonemic awareness training and systematic phonics instruction. The first intervention was conducted with middle school students; the second and third interventions were conducted with kindergarten and first-grade children.

Using a quasiexperimental, pretest–posttest design, Trezek and Malmgren (2005) evaluated the effectiveness of a phonics treatment package with middle school students (i.e., grades 6 through 8). Two teachers and 23 d/Dhh students participated in the study. The students, ages 11 to 15, had hearing losses ranging from slight to profound and attended a self-contained program for d/Dhh students. Students in the treatment group received explicit phonemic awareness and phonics instruction from the first 20 lessons of the Corrective Reading-Decoding A curriculum (Engelmann, Carnine, & Johnson, 1999), a direct instruction approach designed for struggling readers. The researchers augmented these lessons with Visual Phonics as well as computer technology. Specifically, they utilized the animated Baldi technology, in which an avatar of a "talking head" provides d/Dhh students with a visual representation of how mouth shape, lip movement, and tongue placement function in concert to produce specific phonemes and words (see also Barker, 2003; Massaro & Light, 2004, reviewed below). The computer program also included a pictorial glossary to enhance students' acquisition of vocabulary included in the reading curriculum. Students in the comparison group continued to receive the reading instruction that was typical for this d/Dhh program.

After the 8-week intervention, results of the study indicated a highly significant difference between treatment and comparison groups on the posttest. Students in the treatment group significantly outperformed their comparison group counterparts on posttests of the phonemes and words taught as well as a generalization measure. Importantly, performance did not appear to be related to degree of hearing loss, suggesting that d/Dhh students with varying degrees of hearing loss could benefit equally from the phonemic awareness and phonics treatment package.

In a subsequent study, Trezek and Wang (2006) used a pretest–posttest design to evaluate the effectiveness of a phonics intervention supplemented by Visual Phonics on d/Dhh kindergarten and first-grade children's beginning reading skills. The researchers utilized another direct instruction curriculum, Reading Mastery I (Engelmann & Brunner, 1995), a basal reading program for beginning readers that includes explicit phonemic awareness and phonics instruction. The 13 students who participated in the intervention attended a self-contained Total Communication program for students who were d/Dhh. The students, ages 5 to 7 years, had hearing losses ranging from severe to profound; two of the first-grade children had cochlear implants. Students received an average of 48 lessons across the 8-month intervention. The researchers used the Word Reading, Pseudoword Decoding, and Reading Comprehension subtests of the Wechsler Individual Achievement Test II as pretest and posttest measures. Results revealed a statistically significant difference between pretest and posttest scores on

Word Reading, and the effect size was large. Students also outperformed on the Pseudoword Decoding and Reading Comprehension posttests. These findings indicate that given an academic year of instruction from a phonics-based reading curriculum supplemented by Visual Phonics, kindergarten and first-grade children who are d/Dhh can demonstrate progress in beginning reading skills.

In the final intervention, Trezek et al. (2007) built upon the findings of the previous studies by examining the effectiveness of utilizing Visual Phonics to supplement a phonemic awareness and phonics-based reading curriculum that was created by school district personnel where the study was conducted. The year-long intervention was implemented in two kindergarten and two first-grade classrooms in a hearing impaired program that espoused a Total Communication philosophy, although one of the four classrooms utilized an oral/aural approach. The 20 kindergarten and first-grade students who participated in the study were 5 to 8 years old and had hearing losses ranging from mild to profound. Six subtests of the Dominie Reading and Writing Assessment Portfolio (DeFord, 2001) were used as pretest–posttest measures: Sentence Writing Phoneme, Sentence Writing Spelling, Phonemic Awareness Segmentation, Phonemic Awareness Deletion, Phonics Onsets, and Phonics Rimes. Each subtest was administered individually to each student by the classroom teacher. Results of the study revealed a statistically significant difference on all six measures of reading from pretest to posttest and the effect was large, demonstrating the effectiveness of the intervention.

Collectively, the results of these three intervention studies suggest that the use of explicit phonemic awareness and phonics-based reading curriculums, supplemented by Visual Phonics, can support reading achievement in students who are d/Dhh with varying degrees of hearing loss. Given the importance of phonological awareness and phonics knowledge to successful English reading development, these findings make an important contribution to the field, providing direction for classroom teachers about how to teach critical phonological information to students who have limited to no access to the phonology of English. Understanding phonemes as the building blocks of language and developing the ability to use and manipulate those phonemes will provide d/Dhh students the essential foundation for reading instruction (Trezek & Wang, 2006; Trezek, Wang, & Paul, 2010).

Taken together, the results of these three intervention studies establish a line of intervention research that examines how d/Dhh students can be taught to utilize phonological information during beginning English reading instruction. Replication studies with larger numbers of students across grades K to 6 are needed to further substantiate these promising findings.

Fluency Interventions

The National Reading Panel (2000) reviewed two types of fluency intervention studies—interventions that examined the role of independent silent reading in promoting reading fluency and those that examined the effectiveness of guided, repeated oral reading in supporting reading fluency. In independent silent reading approaches (e.g., drop everything and read; sustained silent reading), students read extensively on their own, with minimal guidance or feedback from teachers, to practice using the reading strategies and skills they have learned. In guided, repeated oral reading approaches, students read passages orally and receive explicit guidance and feedback from teachers and/or reading partners. The NRP suggested that independent silent reading may support reading fluency, although no conclusions could be drawn, due to the lack of empirical evidence. However, the panel concluded that repeated oral reading with sufficient guidance and feedback significantly improves reading fluency (see also the discussion in Chapter 5).

We found no recent intervention studies examining independent silent reading with d/Dhh students. The three intervention studies we identified investigated the effectiveness of repeated readings in supporting reading fluency in d/Dhh students. In the first study, Enns and Lafond (2007) developed a fluency intervention that also included a vocabulary component. Using a pretest/posttest design, the researchers documented the progress of two d/Dhh high school students as they participated in the fluency and vocabulary intervention. The 14- and 15-year old students both had dyslexia. They attended a school for d/Dhh students. Every 10 days for 6 months, the students read the same word list or reading passage and received explicit vocabulary instruction on words they had trouble reading. The students read the word lists and passages in ASL; a word-by-word translation was not expected for the passages. Each intervention session focused on building automaticity and vocabulary. Results of the study indicated that both students demonstrated positive results on a reading attitude survey. Students also demonstrated an increase in the number of words read correctly on a sight word reading test and an increase in the raw score of the Test of Early Reading Ability—Deaf/Hard of Hearing version (Reid, Hresko, Hammill, & Wiltshire, 1991). However, these increases were small and would be expected over a 6-month period due to normal development and maturation. Nevertheless, the researchers argue that even a small increase was significant, given that the students' previous progress was limited to one grade level over 9 years of schooling. Enns and Lafond conclude that building fluency through repeated readings and explicit vocabulary instruction may support d/Dhh students' reading development.

Schirmer et al. (2009) combined single-subject and quasiexperimental designs using pre–post measures to examine the effectiveness of a repeated reading intervention on reading fluency in second-grade students who were d/Dhh. Three of the four students had profound hearing losses and one student had a severe hearing loss. All students were reading below grade level. The students attended a state school for d/Dhh students, and ASL was the language of instruction.

The researchers used the reread–adapt and answer–comprehend (RAAC) fluency intervention (Therrien, Gormley, & Kubina, 2006) to supplement students' regular reading instruction, which did not include a reading fluency component. The narrative passages used for the intervention were chosen to match each student's instructional reading level and included themes commonly found in children's literature. The repeated reading portion of the RAAC intervention was used with the students two to three times each week for 5 weeks. Each student received between 8 to 12 individual lessons across the 5-week intervention, depending on student absences. In each lesson, the student read the passages aloud and/or in sign as quickly as possible. The teacher timed the readings and recorded the number of errors. Then the student reread the passage until reaching the criterion of no more than two errors or until reading the passage four times. The teacher then asked four factual and four inferential questions that accompanied each passage and recorded the student's answers.

Results of the study indicated that students significantly improved their reading speed on passages that were reread and on a generalized measure of reading fluency, but overall comprehension did not improve. Moreover, while students correctly answered inferential questions almost as often as they correctly answered factual questions, no pattern of improvement in answering comprehension questions was observed during the intervention. The researchers conclude that pairing fluency and comprehension strategies may be more effective than focusing on fluency alone. They conducted a follow-up intervention study to examine their hypothesis.

In their second study, Schirmer et al. (2012) combined single-subject and quasi-experimental designs to investigate the effect of the RAAC intervention on both fluency and reading comprehension in d/Dhh students. Thirteen students with mild to profound hearing losses participated in the study. The students were in grades 3, 5, and 6 and attended a state school for d/Dhh students that used ASL as the language of instruction. The RAAC intervention was used with the students individually two to three times each week for 8 weeks; each student received between 5 to 19 lessons, depending on student absences and scheduling conflicts. As in the first study, students read passages aloud and/or in sign as quickly as possible, and teachers timed the readings and recorded the number of errors. Then students reread passages until reaching the criterion of no more than two errors or until reading the passage four times. Teachers then asked both factual and inferential questions and recorded students' answers. In subsequent lessons, teachers adjusted the difficulty of the reading material if students could not consistently reach criterion in four readings and/or answered less than half of the comprehension questions correctly.

Again, outcomes of the study indicated that students significantly improved their reading fluency, but overall comprehension did not improve. However, students did demonstrate consistently good comprehension on both literal and inferential questions during the RAAC intervention, which was not the case in the researchers' first intervention study with second-grader students. The researchers suggest that the addition of a comprehension-monitoring component to the intervention had a positive impact on students' comprehension immediately after reading but was not powerful enough to influence more general comprehension.

These intervention studies suggest that guided, repeated readings have the potential to support reading fluency among d/Dhh students; however, some students made limited progress in fluency during the intervention, and comprehension was inadequate. Further research is needed to determine the effectiveness of the repeated readings intervention for supporting reading fluency with comprehension in students who are d/Dhh.

Vocabulary Interventions

Researchers distinguish among several types of vocabularies, including listening vocabulary, speaking vocabulary, reading vocabulary, and writing vocabulary. Based on its comprehensive review, the NRP found that no particular instructional method was most effective for teaching vocabulary; however, it recommended a number of instructional strategies for supporting the development of the various types of vocabularies, including direct instruction, repetition and multiple exposures to target words, learning in meaningful contexts, active engagement in learning tasks, and the use of computer technology to help teach target vocabulary.

Recent vocabulary intervention research among students who are d/Dhh has incorporated a number of these instructional strategies. Moreover, five of the seven intervention studies we identified used what the NRP called a multimedia approach to vocabulary instruction, which involves the use of various forms of media, graphic representations (e.g., semantic mapping), hypertext, and ASL. These seven studies examine interventions designed to promote listening vocabulary, speaking vocabulary, and/or reading vocabulary.

Listening Vocabulary   Barker (2003) and Massaro and Light (2004) examined the effectiveness of a computer-animated tutor for teaching vocabulary to d/Dhh students enrolled in oral elementary day-school programs. The computer-animated tutor displayed line drawings or photographs of target vocabulary words with printed versions of those words while an avatar of a "talking head," nicknamed "Baldi," provided synthesized audiovisual speech that corresponded to the printed words and images. In the Barker (2003) study, all target vocabulary words were nouns that labeled objects the children had seen in their homes, at school, or in the grocery but for which they had no linguistic label. Students photographed many of the items and teachers chose drawings of common objects. There were 27 lessons, most of which contained between 10 and 15 words. Students worked independently to complete each vocabulary lesson, which included a pretest, word presentation, practice, posttest, and word production sequence. The posttest assessed listening vocabulary only. Students identified each target word by clicking on the pictured item as Baldi said each word. Lessons were repeated until students scored 100%. When students received a score of 100% on a lesson's posttest, they advanced to another lesson on the following day. Not all students completed all lessons, but the researchers captured 217 vocabulary-training sessions. Retention was tested 4 weeks after each successfully completed lesson. Results of the single-subject design study indicated that the 16 deaf (profoundly hearing impaired) students, ages 8 to 14 years, memorized a statistically significant number of new words and remembered approximately half of those words 4 weeks later.

The eight students in the Massaro and Light (2004) study were slightly younger, between the ages of 6 and 10 years, and the researchers created individualized vocabulary lessons for each student which included word presentation, perception, reading, spelling, imitation, elicitation, and posttest activities. Students worked through the lessons for approximately 20 to 30 minutes each day, 2 days a week for 10 weeks. Posttests required students to identify each target word by clicking on the pictured item as the avatar Baldi said each word. Using a within-student multiple baseline design, the researchers continuously tested specific vocabulary words while other words were also being tested and trained. Results of the study indicated that students demonstrated significant gains in both listening vocabulary and word production and that students retained almost all of the target vocabulary words 4 weeks after the intervention. The study's findings, as well as those reported by Baker (2003), suggest that a computer-animated tutor may be an effective method of direct vocabulary instruction for students who are d/Dhh. The vocabulary tutor could be tailored to students' individual needs to provide direct and intensive instruction that supplements classroom teaching. The degree to which computer-animated vocabulary tutors are available and utilized in educational settings for d/Dhh students has yet to be fully explored. Further research is needed to document the usefulness of computer technology for supporting d/Dhh students' vocabulary development.

Speaking Vocabulary   Mollink, Hermans, and Knoors (2008) examined the effectiveness of signing in supporting spoken vocabulary development. Fourteen kindergarten and first-grade children, 4 to 8 years of age, participated in the study. All of the children had moderate to severe hearing losses and wore hearing aids. The conversational and instructional language for the children was Signed Supported Dutch, in which spoken Dutch is combined with lexical and syntactic elements from Sign Language of the Netherlands (SLN).

The researchers experimentally examined the vocabulary intervention under four conditions: (1) spoken Dutch only, (2) spoken Dutch and SLN, (3) spoken Dutch and a color, and (4) a control condition that included no training. In the color condition, the examiner named a color in addition to the name of the picture (e.g., "I think about the color purple when I see this picture"). The speech therapist conducted the individual vocabulary training sessions, which were about 10 minutes in length. In each session, 16 pictures of the target vocabulary were shown on a laptop; the therapist named the picture in Dutch and the child repeated the name. Again the therapist named the pictured item, and again the child repeated the name. In the Dutch and SLN condition, the therapist also signed the name of the pictured item. In the Dutch and color condition, the therapist associated the item with a specific color. During the posttests, which were conducted 1 and 5 weeks after the end of the intervention, children were asked to name each picture in spoken Dutch.

Results of the experimental study indicated that the Dutch and SLN condition was most effective for supporting vocabulary learning. Children remembered the target words more accurately when sign and spoken language were used in the vocabulary training. Additional analyses suggested that iconicity (i.e., the extent to which a sign resembles the word it represents) did not have a significant effect overall on learning. Results also demonstrated that the benefits of the vocabulary training endured. Although children could name more pictures correctly at posttest 1 (mean = 39.3%) compared to posttest 2 (mean = 36.5%), the difference was small. Findings of the study corroborated previous research (e.g., Connor, Hieber, Arts, & Zwolan, 2000) in providing support for the use of signing during spoken vocabulary training for d/Dhh children.

Reading Vocabulary   Wauters et al. (2001) examined the effectiveness of signing in supporting English reading vocabulary development. The instructional intervention paired signs and spoken words to written words. Fourteen d/Dhh students, ages 6 to 10, with hearing losses ranging from 75 to 130 dB participated in the study; three of the children had cochlear implants. The children attended a school for d/Dhh students in the Netherlands that used a bilingual approach, that is, spoken Dutch and SLN.

The vocabulary intervention was provided in two conditions: (a) written word and spoken word and (b) written word, spoken word, and sign. All children attended three training periods of approximately 1 hour each and were trained to recognize two word lists of 10 words each. One list was trained in the speech-only condition, and the other list was trained in the speech and sign condition. The target words were presented on a computer screen. First, a picture of the word appeared and the trainer pronounced the word or pronounced and signed the word, depending on the treatment condition. Then the written word appeared on the screen, letter by letter. The children were asked to say or to say and sign the word. The trainer then repeated the word in spoken Dutch or in spoken Dutch and sign. Pretests and posttests of trained words were administered via a computer. A picture appeared on the screen surrounded by four written words, and the child had to choose the target word. The posttest also included 10 untrained words to document generalized training effects. Results of the study demonstrated significant increases in word recognition after the intervention for the speech and sign condition only; however, the intervention did not generalize to untrained words. The researchers suggest that word recognition improves when signs are used in addition to speech during vocabulary training because through the sign a connection is made between the word and its meaning in addition to the phonological information provided by the spoken word.

Paatsch, Blarney, Sarant, and Bow (2006) used pre- and posttest measures to investigate the effectiveness of a 15-week intensive vocabulary intervention on d/Dhh children's reading vocabulary. The 21 children, ages 5 to 12 years, were integrated into a mainstream school with a specialized oral/aural unit for d/Dhh children. Sixteen of the children had hearing losses greater than 90 dB (decibels) HL (hearing level), and 15 children had cochlear implants. Children were trained individually or in small groups by teachers of the d/Deaf and hard of hearing for 20 minutes each day on 70 monosyllabic consonant-vowel-consonant (CVC) words (e.g., *key, fat, doll*). Teachers integrated the target words into themed units being studied in the curriculum. Training activities included oral discussions of word meanings, picture representations of words, putting words into sentences to illustrate semantic and syntactic use of words, and use of dictionaries. School-based activities were also sent home for additional practice. On the posttest measure, students were presented with monosyllabic words one at a time on a computer screen and were asked to give a definition of the word or use the word in a sentence. Results of the study indicated that all students demonstrated statistically significant improvements in word knowledge after the intervention. In addition, the vocabulary training also improved speech perception and reading-aloud scores.

Cannon, Fredrick, and Easterbrooks (2010) investigated the effectiveness of using repeated readings of expository books read in ASL on DVD for supporting reading vocabulary in fifth-grade students who were d/Dhh and also English language learners (ELLs). The four students who participated in the study were reading below kindergarten level. The study employed a multiple-baseline design across three sets of five vocabulary words. Each set of words was introduced during the viewing of one of the three DVDs (five vocabulary words from each DVD). When a student achieved mastery of one set of vocabulary words, the intervention began for the next set of words. The DVDs were designed to support both reading vocabulary and expressive vocabulary by including the illustrations and printed text of the book in the background; thus, students could view the printed vocabulary as the expository text was signed.

In the first phase of the intervention, the researchers pretested students' knowledge of the target words and then students viewed the DVD without teacher intervention. Each DVD was approximately 5 minutes in length and students viewed the DVDs on three consecutive days. Then the researchers assessed students' knowledge of the target vocabulary. Flashcards with pictures of the target words were used for the posttest, which required students to identify each item using ASL. Ongoing data analysis indicated that students were not connecting the target vocabulary words displayed on the DVD to the ASL the interpreter was using to read the book, most likely because ASL does not follow English word order.

So, the researchers initiated a second intervention phase, in which teachers pretested students' knowledge of target vocabulary and then introduced unknown target words. Teachers showed students each word on a flashcard, signed the word, gave students a definition for the word, and pointed to the word as it appeared in various places in the book. Students then viewed the DVDs and took posttests on the target vocabulary. These procedures were used for each set of vocabulary words, with noncurrent baselines collected during the second intervention phase of the previous tier. The study was 6 weeks long, from baseline through final intervention.

Findings of the study indicated that viewing the signed DVDs increased students' recognition of the target words only minimally during the first phase of the intervention. The intervention was more effective when preteaching of the target vocabulary words accompanied the DVDs. The results suggest that direct instruction accompanied by repeated use of the target vocabulary in the DVDs supported the students' word recognition. However, this study did not assess students' comprehension of the meaning of target words. Future investigations of this instructional intervention will need to examine both word recognition and comprehension.

Dimling (2010) examined the effectiveness of a conceptually based vocabulary intervention that included Dolch words and "bridge phrases" (p. 429)—English phrases that require translation into ASL for conceptual understanding (e.g., *clean up, fall down*). All of the Dolch words were content words, and some words had multiple meanings (e.g., *can*). A single-subject multiple baseline design was used to determine the effects of the vocabulary intervention on students' recognition, production, and comprehension of the target words and phrases. Six second-grade students, ages 7 to 9 years, with moderate to profound hearing losses participated in the study. The children used pidgin English signing (i.e., ASL signs in English word order) to communicate.

The classroom teacher taught four, 30-minute conceptually based vocabulary intervention lessons each week. First the word or phrase was introduced in written form, fingerspelling, and sign. Then the teacher engaged students in semantic mapping activities to focus on meaning as well as relationships among words and phrases. Students then practiced creating sentences using the target words or phrases. Teachers taught three Dolch words or three bridge phrases per session for a total of 12 target items per week, and each student had Dolch words and bridge phrases that were selected specifically for that student based on her or his existing knowledge. Teachers assessed students individually twice a week to determine mastery. To assess recognition, the teacher signed each target word or phrase and asked students to label the word or phrase through fingerspelling, voicing, or pointing to the written word or phrase. To assess production, teachers showed students the target words or phrases on flashcards, and students were required to sign or say the word. To assess comprehension, teachers signed, voiced, and showed students the target word or phrases on flashcards and then asked students to provide an example, create a sentence containing the word or phrase, or point to objects in the classroom that represented the word or phrase.

Results of the intervention indicated that all students demonstrated substantial increases in mean number of Dolch words recognized, produced, and comprehended. All students mastered recognition of more than 60% of the Dolch words. Nine students mastered comprehension of more than 75% of the words, and five students mastered production of 90% or more words. The students who mastered 90% are included in the group who mastered at least 75%, just as they are all included in the group that mastered at least 60%. Findings also indicated that all students demonstrated substantial increases in the mean number of bridge phrases recognized and comprehended. Most students also demonstrated substantial increases in bridge phrase productions. Students were more successful at mastering the Dolch sight words than the bridge phrases. On average, students mastered more than 80% of the sight words from the Dolch word vocabulary, compared to 60% of the bridge phrases. The researchers suggest that the bridge phrases were more difficult to comprehend and may have been above the second-grade reading level.

Collectively, the findings of these investigations demonstrate that direct instruction is essential to d/Dhh students' vocabulary development, regardless of the vocabulary intervention employed. The results also indicate that computer-animated vocabulary tutors can successfully support both listening vocabulary and speaking vocabulary in d/Dhh students, although the degree to which this technology is available for instructional use has not been fully determined. The effectiveness of using signs to support the development of spoken vocabulary as well as reading vocabulary also was demonstrated.

Text Comprehension Interventions

The NRP concluded that explicit comprehension instruction can effectively teach students to use comprehension strategies that will increase their understanding of new passages and support general improvements in comprehension. The panel specifically recommended the use of comprehension monitoring, summarization, graphic and semantic organizers, question answering, question generation, cooperative learning, and, in particular, a combination of these instructional strategies to support students' text comprehension. Of these recommended strategies, recent intervention research with d/Dhh students has examined the use of comprehension monitoring, summarization, question answering, and cooperative learning activities in supporting text comprehension. One study examined an intervention designed to support students' listening comprehension (Pakulski & Kaderavek, 2001), and two studies examined instructional interventions designed to support reading comprehension (Al-Hilawani, 2003; Schirmer & Schaffer, 2010).

Listening Comprehension   Pakulski and Kaderavek (2001) used a quasiexperimental design to examine the effectiveness of group role play and oral story retellings on d/Dhh students' metalinguistic awareness of story grammar. Improving students' awareness of story grammar supports their comprehension of narrative text. In the 5-day intervention, trained readers repeatedly read two books (story A and story B) once a day for three days to d/Dhh students who were attending a summer camp for students who communicate orally. The book readings took place in the evenings in students' cabins. On the fourth day, children used props, simple costumes, and puppets to engage in role-play skits for one of the stories that had been repeatedly read across the previous 3 days. The researchers randomly assigned students by cabin to one of the two role-play activities. Children had varying levels of participation in the story role play, but all students watched one of the two story reenactments. Those children who participated used cue cards to prompt their portion of the dialogue. Students who role-played story A then listened to an additional oral reading of story B, and students who role-played story B then listened to an additional oral reading of story A. On the final day of the intervention, the researchers elicited story retellings for both stories from 14 children who completed all aspects of the intervention. These students were between the ages of 7 and 14 and most had moderately severe or greater hearing losses; five of the children had cochlear implants.

The children's oral retellings were transcribed and analyzed using adaptations of the Story Grammar Analysis Protocol (Stein & Glenn, 1982) and the Story Retelling Questionnaire Summary Sheet (Strong, 1998). Each student's story grammar scores were compared across the two conditions: repeated book reading only (condition 1) and repeated book reading plus role play (condition 2). Results of the analysis indicated that the effect of role play (condition 2) was highly significant. Twelve of the students had greater story grammar scores for the role-play condition; scores were tied for the other two students. Students were able to recall more elements of the story for which they had participated in the role-playing skit. The findings suggest that role playing in conjunction with repeated readings can be an effective intervention for supporting students' story grammar macrostructure and ultimately their comprehension of narrative texts.

Reading Comprehension   Al-Hilawani (2003) compared the effectiveness of three methods of reading comprehension instruction on third-grade d/Dhh students' comprehension scores: the key word strategy, modified reciprocal teaching, and a traditional approach to teaching comprehension. The traditional approach to comprehension instruction engaged students in answering questions about passages read. The key word strategy supplemented the traditional approach by selecting key words that would help students retrieve information from memory regarding passages just read. In the modified reciprocal approach, teachers augmented the traditional approach with group discussions that focused on prediction, summarization, and clarification of the passages that were read. Six teachers and 30 third-grade d/Dhh students from three special education centers in United Arab Emirates participated in the 5-day intervention study. The teachers used simultaneous speaking and signing in Arabic for instruction. The children had severe to profound hearing losses and all of them wore hearing aids.

The researcher randomly assigned the teachers to one of the three teaching approaches and trained them in the procedures of that approach. Teachers introduced the reading passage on the first day of the week and met with students for five 45-minute teaching sessions across the week. Then, a reading comprehension test of 12 short-answer recall questions was administered. Results of the analysis showed no significant differences between teaching approaches with regard to detail questions. However, for main idea, word meanings, and inferential questions, the key word and reciprocal teaching approaches were more effective than the traditional approach. The researcher recommended supplementing traditional comprehension instruction with elements of the key word and modified reciprocal teaching approaches. Despite positive results for the key word and reciprocal teaching approaches, however, students' overall comprehension was low, highlighting the difficulties most d/Dhh students experience in text comprehension. Findings of the study demonstrate the need for additional research on comprehension instruction.

More recently, Schirmer and Schaffer (2010) investigated the effects of the guided reading approach on elementary-school d/Dhh students' reading development across 2 years of schooling. The study was conducted at a state school for d/Deaf and hard of hearing students, and ASL was the language of instruction. Guided reading was used with all of the students at the elementary school, but only 19 students for whom the researchers had baseline data were included in the analysis. Fifteen of these students had profound hearing losses, and four students had hearing losses ranging from mild to severe. The students were in grades 1 to 5 at the outset of the intervention, and none were reading at grade level. Guided reading lessons were taught three to four times each week across both academic years of the study. Each lesson included four major components: teacher selection of leveled books, teacher introduction of the book, students' silent reading, and group discussion of the book, including discussion of the problem-solving strategies that students used to construct meaning. The researchers used a single-subject experimental design to investigate the effect of the guided reading protocol. Running records (Clay, 2000) were used to establish baseline and document students' reading progress.

Results indicated that all of the students demonstrated modest progress in reading during the intervention, but progress was far less than the benchmark (i.e., 1 year of progress per year of schooling). All of the students except the oldest group also experienced a regression in scores over the summer months. For most students, it took several months during the school year to regain their previous year's scores. Formal observations of teachers' instruction suggested a lack of fidelity to the guided reading protocol, which might have accounted for the results of the intervention. The researchers argued for the importance of providing teachers with in-class coaching and professional development sessions across the academic year to improve fidelity to the instructional protocol. They also recommended summer reading programs for d/Dhh students and family engagement in shared reading activities to help maintain reading progress.

The findings of these three intervention studies suggest that comprehension instruction and cooperative learning activities can support improvements in d/Dhh students' text comprehension. However, the results also highlight d/Dhh students' slow progress and the difficulties they face in comprehending text. These difficulties are not surprising given the persistent English language deficits of most d/Dhh students (Paul, 2009). To promote growth in text comprehension, readers who are d/Dhh will also need explicit instruction on the nature and structure of the English language and its relationship to ASL and Signed English (see Luckner, et al., 2005/2006; Mayer, 2007; Paul, 2009).

Computer Technology and Reading Instruction

In the NRP's review of studies that examined the use of computer technology to facilitate or enhance reading instruction, the panel concluded that the addition of speech to computer-presented text, the use of hypertext, and the use of word processing to combine reading with writing instruction appear to have strong potential for supporting English reading instruction. The goal of using computer technology as part of a comprehensive reading program is to facilitate instruction in phonemic awareness, phonics, fluency, vocabulary, and/or text comprehension. Two recent intervention studies have explored the effectiveness of using computer technology to support d/Dhh students' text comprehension.

In the first intervention, Gentry et al. (2004) examined the comparative effectiveness of print, sign, and pictures in supporting d/Dhh students' reading comprehension. The researchers embedded children's stories at the third-grade reading level in a multimedia CD-ROM, and each participant in the study received four treatments in random order: (1) printed words only; (2) print and pictures; (3) print and digital video of sign language (ASL, Signed English, or both); and (4) print, pictures, and digital video of sign language (ASL, Signed English, or both). Twenty-eight d/Dhh students, ages 9 to 18 years, from both mainstream and residential school settings participated in the study. All of the children used sign as their primary means of communication, and teachers used a combination of signed English and ASL when communicating with students.

A repeated-measure design was used to analyze the students' English reading comprehension performance. After viewing the selections in each format on a personal computer, students were asked to retell the stories. Results demonstrated significant differences between the treatments. Comprehension was strongest when presented in print-with-pictures format, although only marginally greater than print-with-pictures-and-sign language format, and weakest when stories were presented in print-only format. The use of sign with print but without pictures did not appear to enhance text comprehension. Reading by means of print alone was extremely difficult for the d/Dhh students; the use of pictures significantly aided in the comprehension of written text. The researchers observed that the students typically chose to watch the ASL version of the story first, then switched to the signed English version, and while in that mode compared signs with words. These findings highlighted the need for explicit instruction on the relationships between ASL, signed English, and printed text.

In the second intervention study, Wang and Paul (2011) used a within-subject quasiexperimental design to evaluate the effectiveness of the cornerstones approach, a literature-based approach to reading instruction that integrates computer technology into beginning reading instruction. The researchers compared the effectiveness of cornerstones and teachers' "typical" approaches to reading instruction on d/Dhh students' word identification, word knowledge, and story comprehension. The cornerstones approach to reading instruction uses multimedia technology to present stories in either ASL, Signing Exact English (SEE II), or Cued Speech/Language to accommodate students' communication modalities. The program focuses on building students' word recognition skills, word knowledge (i.e., conceptual knowledge about multiple aspects of words), and background knowledge in order to support text comprehension. The approach includes (1) stories on video with verbatim and edited captions, (2) the use of technology to animate the stories in ASL, SEE II, or Cued Speech/Language and an online hypertext storybook; (3) in-depth word study on specific vocabulary and various levels of comprehension questions, (4) the use of research-based instructional practices, (5) sequenced and consecutive instruction, and (6) the use of technology for interactive games, story maps, graphic organizers, etc. In the "typical" approach, teachers presented stories to their students using methods, materials, and procedures that were typical of their teaching techniques and styles. Five teachers and 22 d/Dhh students, ages 7 to 11 years, participated in the study. The students used a variety of communication methods (i.e., oral, simultaneous speaking and signing, ASL) and their hearing losses ranged from mild to profound.

The researchers utilized an alternating treatment design; each teacher conducted both a cornerstones and a typical lesson in each of three experiments, and each student participated in both the cornerstones and typical interventions. Pretests and posttests for each of the six stories were identical and were administered before and after each intervention. Results of the analysis revealed statistically significant gains from the cornerstones intervention for word identification, but no differences were found for word knowledge and mixed results were reported for story comprehension. These mixed results may have been influenced by carryover effects from the cornerstones approach, which teachers integrated into the typical approach in subsequent experiments, as documented in the researchers' qualitative observation data. The researchers suggest that these carryover effects reflect the feasibility of the cornerstones approach for beginning literacy instruction with d/Dhh students. The study's findings demonstrate the need for further intervention research on the cornerstones approach. In particular, future research will need to examine specific aspects of the technology-infused program to identify the features that are most supportive of specific components of reading instruction.

Together, these two intervention studies suggest that computer technology may be useful for facilitating specific components of reading instruction among d/Dhh students. The studies provide a *first step* in establishing a much-needed line of intervention research that examines the effectiveness of multimedia computer technology in facilitating literacy instruction for students who are d/Dhh.

A summary of major points for the conventional literacy intervention studies discussed here is provided in Table 6.2.

COMPARISON OF FINDINGS WITH RESULTS OF THE NELP AND NRP

The major tenet of this book is that the acquisition of English language and literacy by d/Dhh learners is qualitatively similar to that of native learners of English. We argued throughout this text that certain critical fundamentals facilitate language and literacy learning in both groups. Given our hypothesis—the QSH—we compared the findings of our review of intervention studies with d/Dhh learners to findings reported in the National Early Literacy Panel (2008) and the National Reading Panel (2000), comprehensive meta-analyses that constitute significant and influential bodies of research on literacy interventions among typically hearing learners. We assert that a comparison of our findings to the findings reported in the NELP and the NRP would demonstrate common results and hold important implications for theory, instructional practice, and future research. That is, similar instructional interventions that demonstrated positive results for both groups of learners would suggest qualitative similarities between those learners—providing further evidence for the QSH—and indicate that instructional approaches and methods effective for typically developing learners of English would also be effective with d/Dhh learners. Future research could then build on these similar findings with specific attention to individual profiles based on the fundamentals of literacy development.

To that end, we compared findings in seven broad categories: code-focused, shared reading, phonemic awareness and phonics, fluency, vocabulary, text comprehension, and computer technology interventions. The results of this comparison are detailed in the following paragraphs.

Code-Focused Interventions

The National Early Literacy Panel (2008) found that code-focused interventions implemented via individual or small-group instruction had a significant, substantial, and positive impact on preschool and kindergarten children's phonological awareness, alphabetic knowledge, oral language, and reading and spelling skills, regardless of children's prior literacy skills or their ages. The largest impact was on phonological awareness, defined by the NELP as "the ability to detect, manipulate, or analyze the auditory aspects of spoken language" (p. vii), including the ability to segment words, syllables, or phonemes.

The two code-focused interventions that have been conducted recently with young d/Dhh children focused on phonological awareness and alphabetic knowledge by teaching children specific phoneme–grapheme correspondences, and instruction

Table 6.2. Conventional Literacy Intervention Studies

	Study	Intervention	Population	Methods	Outcomes
Phonemic awareness and phonics interventions	Trezek and Malmgren (2005)	Corrective reading–decoding A curriculum (Engelmann, Carnine, & Johnson, 1999) with Visual Phonics	23 d/Dhh middle school students, 11–15 years; slight to profound hearing losses; self-contained program	Quasiexperimental, pretest–posttest	Treatment group significantly outperformed comparison group on posttests and a generalization measure; performance not related to degree of hearing loss
	Trezek and Wang (2006)	Reading mastery I curriculum (Engelmann & Brunner, 1995) with Visual Phonics	13 d/Dhh K–1 children, 5–7 years; severe to profound hearing losses; two first-grade children had cochlear implants; Total Communication (TC) program	Pretest–posttest	Statistically significant difference between pre- and posttest word reading scores; gains on pseudo-word decoding and reading comprehension posttests
	Trezek, Wang, Woods, Gampp, and Paul (2007)	Phonics-based reading curriculum with Visual Phonics	20 d/Dhh K–1 children, 5–8 years, mild to profound hearing losses; TC and oral/aural programs	Pretest–posttest	Statistically significant difference on six measures of reading from pretest to posttest
Fluency interventions	Enns and Lafond (2007)	Repeated readings with explicit vocabulary instruction	2 d/Dhh high school students; 14 and 15 years; both students had dyslexia; attended school for d/Dhh	Pretest–posttest	Students demonstrated small increase on sight word reading test; small increase in raw score of the Test of Early Reading Ability—Deaf/Hard of Hearing

Study	Intervention	Participants	Design	Results
Schirmer, Therrien, Schaffer, and Schirmer (2009)	Repeated readings portion only of reread–adapt and answer–comprehend (Therrien, Gormley, & Kubina, 2006)	Four second-grade d/Dhh students; severe to profound hearing losses; attended state school for d/Dhh	Single-subject and quasiexperimental designs using pre-and post- measures	Students significantly improved reading speed on passages re-read and on generalized measure of reading fluency; overall comprehension did not improve
Schirmer, Schaffer, Therrien, and Schirmer (2012)	Reread–adapt and answer–comprehend (Therrien, Gormley, & Kubina, 2006)	13 d/Dhh students in grades 3, 5, and 6; mild to profound hearing losses; attended a state school for d/Dhh	Single-subject and quasiexperimental	Students significantly improved reading fluency and demonstrated comprehension of literal and inferential questions; overall comprehension did not improve
Vocabulary interventions				
Barker (2003)	Computer-animated tutor for teaching listening vocabulary	16 profoundly deaf students, 8–14 years; attending an oral program	Single subject	Students memorized a statistically significant number of new words and remembered approximately half of those words on a delayed post test
Massaro and Light (2004)	Computer-animated tutor for teaching listening vocabulary	8 d/Dhh students, ages 6–10 years, attending an oral program	Within-student multiple baseline design	Students demonstrated significant gains in listening vocabulary and word production, and retained most target vocabulary on delayed posttest

(continued)

Table 6.2. Conventional Literacy Intervention Studies (*continued*)

Study	Intervention	Population	Methods	Outcomes
Mollink, Hermans, and Knoors (2008)	Using signs to support spoken vocabulary	14 K–1 d/Dhh children, 4–8 years, with moderate to severe hearing losses; all children wore hearing aids	Experimental	Children in the treatment group (signs and speech) outperformed comparison and control groups on posttest; iconicity did not have a significant effect overall on learning
Wauters, Knoors, Vervloed, and Aarnoutse (2001)	Using signs to support reading vocabulary	14 d/Dhh students, 6–10 years; hearing losses ranging from 75 to 130 dB; three children had cochlear implants; attended a school for d/Dhh	Experimental	Only students in the treatment group (signs and speech) demonstrated significant increases in word recognition; the intervention did not generalize to untrained words
Paatsch, Blarney, Sarant, and Bow (2006)	Explicit instruction on reading vocabulary (monosyllabic CVC words)	21 d/Dhh children, 5–12 years; hearing losses greater than 90 dB HL; 15 children had cochlear implants; specialized oral/aural unit in mainstream school	Pretest–posttest	All students demonstrated statistically significant improvements in word knowledge; intervention also improved speech perception and reading-aloud scores

Cannon, Fredrick, and Easterbrooks (2010)	Repeated readings of expository books read in ASL on DVD to support reading vocabulary	Four fifth-grade d/Dhh students who were also ELLs and reading below kindergarten level	Multiple-baseline design across three sets of vocabulary words	The intervention increased students' recognition of target vocabulary when preteaching of target words accompanied the DVDs
Dimling (2010)	Dolch words and "bridge phrases"—English phrases that require translation into ASL for conceptual understanding (e.g., *clean up; fall down*)	Six second-grade d/Dhh students, 7–9 years; moderate to profound hearing losses	Single-subject with multiple baseline	All students recognized more than 60% of the Dolch words, and four students comprehended more than 75% of the Dolch words; substantial increases in bridge phrases recognized and comprehended
Text comprehension interventions				
Pakulski and Kaderavek (2001)	Repeated book reading plus role play to support listening comprehension	14 d/Dhh students, 7–14 years, moderately severe or greater hearing losses; five children had cochlear implants; oral summer camp	Quasiexperimental	Effect of the intervention was highly significant; students recalled more story elements in the role-play condition.

(continued)

Table 6.2. Conventional Literacy Intervention Studies (*continued*)

Study	Intervention	Population	Methods	Outcomes
Al-Hilawani (2003)	Key word strategy and modified reciprocal teaching	30 third-grade d/Dhh students; severe to profound hearing losses; all children wore hearing aids	Quasiexperimental	No significant differences between interventions on detail questions; for main idea, word meanings, and inferential questions, the key word and reciprocal approaches were more effective than the traditional approach; overall comprehension was low
Schirmer and Schaffer (2010)	Guided reading across 2 years of schooling	19 d/Dhh students in grades 1–5 attending state school for the d/Dhh; 15 students had profound hearing losses; 4 students had mild to severe hearing losses	Single subject	All students demonstrated modest progress in reading but far less than 1 year of progress per year of schooling; all students except the oldest group experienced summer regression

Computer technology interventions				
Gentry, Chinn, and Moulton (2004)	Print, sign, and/or pictures accompanying stories embedded in multimedia CD-ROM	28 d/Dhh students, 9–18 years; attending mainstream and residential schools	Repeated measures	Text comprehension was strongest in the print-with-pictures format, marginally greater than print-with-pictures-and-sign language format, and weakest in print-only format
Wang and Paul (2011)	The cornerstones approach, a technology-infused literature-based reading program	22 d/Dhh students, 7–11 years; hearing losses ranged from mild to profound	Within-subject quasiexperimental	Statistically significant gains for word identification but no differences for word knowledge; mixed results for story comprehension

was provided through one-on-one or small-group instruction (Beal-Alvarez et al., 2011; Bergeron et al. 2009). Findings of both intervention studies demonstrated positive effects on the d/Dhh children's phoneme–grapheme acquisition. These findings reflect those of the NELP and are significant because they demonstrate the feasibility of teaching preschool, kindergarten, and first-grade d/Dhh children fundamental literacy skills that are most predictive of later reading achievement.

Shared Reading Interventions

The shared reading intervention studies reviewed by the NELP demonstrated significant, substantial, and positive impacts on young children's oral language skills and print knowledge. To date, only one intervention study of shared reading has been conducted among young children who are d/Dhh (Fung, Chow, & McBride-Chang, 2005). This study measured the impact of the intervention on children's receptive oral language and demonstrated large and significant positive results, similar to findings reported in the NELP. Future intervention research needs to examine the effectiveness of shared reading for supporting children's print knowledge.

Phonemic Awareness and Phonics Interventions

The National Reading Panel (2000) found that teaching children to manipulate phonemes in words significantly improves their reading. The panel also found that systematic phonics instruction is more effective than incidental approaches or no phonics instruction for children in grades K to 6, with the greatest benefits for earlier instruction. The panel concluded that phonemic awareness training and phonics instruction are essential components of a comprehensive reading program.

Results of recent intervention studies conducted with d/Dhh students corroborate the NRP's findings. These intervention studies demonstrate the effectiveness of phonics treatment packages that include explicit phoneme awareness training and systematic phonics instruction, supplemented by Visual Phonics, on the reading achievement of students in middle school (Trezek & Malmgren, 2005) as well as kindergarten and first grade (Trezek & Wang, 2006; Trezek et al., 2007).

Fluency Interventions

Findings from the NRP's comprehensive review suggested that guided, repeated oral reading had a moderate impact on English reading fluency and comprehension. No evidence was found to support independent silent reading as an instructional method, although it stands to reason that reading practice would improve reading fluency.

Although fluency intervention research with d/Dhh readers has documented improvements in students' fluency through the use of guided, repeated readings of text, in some cases progress was very limited (Enns & Lafond, 2007) and comprehension did not improve (Schirmer et al., 2012; 2009). Fluency is often considered a bridge between word recognition and comprehension (Welsh, 2007), but this did not appear to be the case in the studies reviewed here. Comprehension remained low even when fluency improved.

Since the NRP's report (2000), fluency has taken center stage in classroom reading instruction among children who have typical hearing (Pikulski & Chard, 2005). That is not the case among readers who are d/Dhh. The general research literature continues to suggest that the repeated readings approach is an effective instructional intervention for improving fluency and comprehension (O'Connor, White, & Swanson, 2007; Therrien, 2004). There is a strong need for further research to investigate the effectiveness of this instructional intervention with students who are d/Dhh. Intervention studies also are needed to experimentally test the assertion that fluent reading is developed primarily through extensive independent practice.

Vocabulary Interventions

The largest category of recent intervention studies with d/Dhh students was vocabulary instruction. These interventions incorporated a number of the instructional strategies recommended by the NRP, including the use of computer technology, direct and indirect instruction, repetition and multiple exposures to target words, learning in meaningful contexts, active engagement in learning tasks, and combinations of these strategies. Similarly to the findings of the NRP, the studies documented the effectiveness of the interventions on d/Dhh students' vocabulary growth.

One of the major findings of the NRP was that vocabulary instruction is positively related to English reading comprehension—a finding that is also related to previous research on the relationship between vocabulary knowledge and English reading comprehension for d/Dhh children and adolescents (Paul, 2009). While the current studies we reviewed examined the impact of vocabulary interventions on students' reading vocabularies, no studies examined the impact of a vocabulary intervention on text comprehension. This is an important area for future intervention research to address with d/Dhh children and adolescents.

Text Comprehension Interventions

The NRP concluded that text comprehension instruction can motivate and teach children to use comprehension strategies effectively. Text comprehension interventions among d/Dhh students have examined specific instructional techniques to support both listening comprehension and reading comprehension. The results of one investigation suggest that the use of cooperative group role play enhances students' comprehension of stories that are repeatedly read aloud to them, particularly with respect to understanding story structure (Pakulski & Kaderavek, 2001). Similarly, another study demonstrated that a modified version of reciprocal teaching, in which students worked cooperatively to discuss and summarize passages read and then answered teacher-generated questions, led to gains in reading comprehension (Al-Hilawani, 2003). The third intervention study documented the effectiveness of teaching students to use comprehension monitoring strategies during guided reading lessons (Schirmer & Schaffer, 2010). Cooperative learning, summarization, question answering, comprehension monitoring, and activities that focus students' attention on story structure are all included on the NRP's list of "effective and most promising" (2000, pp. 4–5) comprehension instruction methods. Despite these positive outcomes, however, the d/Dhh students' text comprehension was low overall and they made slower than expected progress, confirming the findings of previous research (see Trezek et al., 2011). This lower performance may reflect a lack of high-quality text comprehension instruction (Schirmer & Schaffer, 2010), including the need for additional attention to the role of metacognition in the comprehension process (e.g., see reviews in Paul, 2009; Trezek et al., 2010).

From another perspective, the reasons for d/Dhh students' lower achievement in text comprehension are most likely due to their struggles with English, particularly English syntax (Wang, Kretschmer, & Hartman, 2008; see also Paul, 2009) and their smaller vocabularies. Text comprehension requires an awareness and understanding of the structure of English, including complex syntactic structures and figurative language; it also requires an extensive knowledge of the words in that text. Given these extenuating factors, we cannot conclude with any degree of certainty whether the text comprehension strategies the NRP has recommended will be effective with readers who are d/Dhh. Nevertheless, we argue that text comprehension interventions must also incorporate explicit instruction on the syntax of English. Considerably more intervention research is needed to identify specific effective instructional techniques and approaches for supporting text comprehension in students who are d/Dhh, and those studies must account for these students' struggles with the vocabulary and syntax of English.

Computer Technology and Reading Instruction

The NRP's major finding with respect to computer technology and reading instruction was that the evidence, albeit limited, suggests the promise of technology for facilitating or enhancing reading instruction. The two recent intervention studies that examined the use of computer technology to facilitate reading instruction with d/Dhh students explored the use of multimedia software packages and hypertext, specific components of computer technology that the NRP found promising for enhancing reading instruction. Both intervention studies demonstrated positive gains for students' word identification and/or text (or story) comprehension.

In the first study, when the printed text of children's stories was presented on multimedia CD-ROM discs, the use of pictures in conjunction with the printed text supported d/Dhh students' text comprehension to a greater degree than did the use of pictures, print, and signs (Gentry, Chinn, & Moulton, 2004). Illustrated reading materials are typically only used through the third grade with hearing students, but this study found that d/Dhh students ranging in age from 9 to 18 years, and from both mainstream and residential school settings, benefitted significantly from the use of pictures to support their reading of printed text.

In the second study, when the printed text of children's stories in the cornerstones approach to reading instruction were presented on multimedia computers and animated in ASL, Signing Exact English, or Cued Speech/Language and students also had access to an online hypertext storybook as well as interactive games, story maps, and graphic organizers on the computer, students' word identification improved significantly. Some students also achieved gains in text (story) comprehension (Wang & Paul, 2011).

Similar to the NRP's findings, these intervention studies suggest that computer technology may be useful for facilitating reading instruction among d/Dhh students, but additional intervention studies with larger populations of students are needed to determine the precise ways in which various forms of technology can most effectively support the teaching of specific components of English reading. Studies also need to investigate the feasibility of integrating technology into classroom literacy instruction. While the use of hypertext to provide signed versions of printed stories appears promising, creating such texts may be cost prohibitive, particularly given the small population of d/Dhh students who would use them. No studies have yet to address the effectiveness of word processing programs that combine reading and writing instruction for d/Dhh students, an area the NRP suggests holds promise for reading instruction.

In sum, the findings of our review on literacy-related interventions with d/Dhh learners demonstrate several similarities with the findings reported by the NELP and the NRP, particularly with respect to code-focused, shared reading, phonemic awareness and phonics, and vocabulary interventions. Differences were also apparent, especially with respect to text comprehension, reflecting—for the most part—the developmental lag in the acquisition of English experienced by most d/Dhh learners. These differences might require further differentiation or enhancement of the recommendations of the reading panels. This does not necessarily mean that the development of text comprehension is qualitatively (developmentally) different. However, similar to other struggling language and literacy learners, it might be that greater attention needs to be paid to specific individual profiles (e.g., Valencia, 2011; see also the discussion in Chapters 1 and 2). In essence, we argue that instructional practices that are effective with typically developing learners of English literacy should be used initially and decisions regarding differentiation and enhancement should be research based.

Intervention research among d/Dhh learners continues to be rare. Since 2000, we identified only 21 studies that investigated literacy-related interventions with d/Dhh children and adolescents. There is still much work to be done if we hope to ameliorate the challenges d/Dhh learners face in the acquisition of English language and literacy.

CONCLUSION

In this chapter, we reviewed recent intervention research that was designed to examine the effectiveness of specific instructional strategies and approaches in supporting early English literacy or conventional literacy learning in children and adolescents who are d/Dhh. The findings of our review highlight particular evidence-based practices that show promise for supporting d/Dhh students' phonemic awareness and phonics knowledge, reading fluency, vocabulary development, and text comprehension. The findings also provide direction for future research on literacy learning and teaching among d/Dhh students. We also compared the findings of our review to findings reported in the National Early Literacy Panel (2008) and the National Reading Panel

(2000) and demonstrated similar results, providing further support based on evidence and reason for the QSH.

REFERENCES

Anderson, R. C., Hiebert, E. H., Scott, J. A., & Wilkinson, I. A. G. (1985). *Becoming a nation of readers: The report of the Commission on Reading.* Washington, DC: National Institute of Education.

Al-Hilawani, Y. A. (2003). Clinical examination of three methods of teaching reading comprehension to deaf and hard-of-hearing students: From research to classroom applications. *Journal of Deaf Studies and Deaf Education, 8*(2), 146–156.

Akamatsu, C. T., & Andrews, J. F. (1993). It takes two to be literate: Literacy interactions between parent and child. *Sign Language Studies, 81,* 333–360.

Andrews, J. F., & Taylor, N. (1987). From sign to print: A case study of picture book "reading" between mother and child. *Sign Language Studies, 56,* 261–274.

Barker, L. (2003). Computer-assisted vocabulary acquisition: The CSLU vocabulary tutor in oral-deaf education. *Journal of Deaf Studies and Deaf Education, 8*(2), 187–198.

Beal-Alvarez, J. S., Lederberg, A. R., & Easterbrooks, S. R. (2011). Grapheme–phoneme acquisition of deaf preschoolers. *Journal of Deaf Studies and Deaf Education, 17*(1), 39–60.

Bergeron, J. P., Lederberg, A. R., Easterbrooks, S. R., Miller, E. M., & Connor, C. M. (2009). Building the alphabetic principle in young children who are deaf or hard of hearing. *Volta Review, 109*(2–3), 87–119.

Cain, K., & Oakhill, J. (Eds.). (2007). *Children's comprehension problems in oral and written language.* New York, NY: Guilford Press.

Cannon, J., E., Fredrick, L. D., Easterbrooks, S. R. (2010). Vocabulary instruction through books read in American Sign Language for English-language learners with hearing loss. *Communication Disorders Quarterly, 31*(2), 98–112.

Clay, M. M. (2000). *Running records for classroom teachers.* Portsmouth, NH: Heinemann.

Connor, C., Hieber, S., Arts, H., & Zwolan, T. (2000). Speech, vocabulary, and the education of children using cochlear implants: Oral or Total Communication? *Journal of Speech, Language, and Hearing Research, 43*(5), 1185–1204.

DeFord, D. (2001). *Dominie Reading and Writing Assessment Portfolio* (3rd ed.). Carlsbad, CA: Dominie.

Delk, L., & Weidekamp, L. (2001). *Shared Reading Project: Evaluating implementation processes and family outcomes: Sharing results.* Washington, DC: Laurent Clerc National Deaf Education Center, Gallaudet University.

Dickinson, D., & Keebler, R. (1989). Variation in preschool teachers' styles of reading books. *Discourse Processes, 12,* 353–375.

Dimling, L. M. (2010). Conceptually-based vocabulary intervention: second graders' development of vocabulary words. *American Annals of the Deaf, 155*(4), 425–448.

Easterbrooks, S., & Baker, S. (2002). *Language learning in children who are deaf and hard of hearing: Multiple pathways.* Boston, MA: Allyn & Bacon.

Easterbrooks, S. R., Lederberg, A., Miller, E., Bergeron, J., & McDonald-Connor, C. (2008). Emergent literacy skills during early childhood in children with hearing loss: Strengths and weaknesses. *Volta Review, 108*(2), 91–114.

Engelmann, S., & Brunner, E. C. (1995). *Reading mastery I.* Columbus, OH: Science Research Associates.

Engelmann, S., Carnine, L., & Johnson, G. (1999). *Corrective reading decoding level A: Word-attack basics.* Columbus, OH: Science Research Associates.

Fung, P., Chow, B. W., & McBride-Chang, C. (2005). The impact of a dialogic reading program on deaf and hard-of-hearing and early primary school-aged students in Hong Kong. *Journal of Deaf Studies and Deaf Education, 10*(1), 82–95.

Gentry, M. M., Chinn, K. M., & Moulton, R. D. (2004). Effectiveness of multimedia reading materials when used with children who are deaf. *American Annals of the Deaf, 149*(5), 394–403.

Heineman-Gosschalk, R., & Webster, A. (2003). Literacy and the role of parents of deaf children. *Deafness and Education International, 5*(1), 20–38.

Israel, S., & Duffy, G. (Eds.). (2009). *Handbook of research on reading comprehension.* New York, NY: Routledge.

Lartz, M., & Lestina, L. (1995). Strategies deaf mothers use when reading to their young deaf or hard of hearing children. *American Annals of the Deaf, 140*, 358–362.

Lederberg, A. L., Miller, E. M., Easterbrooks, S. R., Bergeron, J. P., & Connor, C. M. (2009). *Foundations for literacy.* Unpublished curriculum, Georgia State University, Atlanta, GA.

Lederberg, A. R., Miller, E. M., Easterbrooks, S. R., & Connor, C. M. (2011). *Foundations for literacy.* Unpublished curriculum, Georgia State University, Atlanta, GA.

Lederberg, A. R., & Spencer, P. E. (2009). Word-learning abilities in deaf and hard-of-hearing preschoolers: Effect of lexicon size and language modality. *Journal of Deaf Studies and Deaf Education, 14*(1), 44–62.

Luckner, J., Sebald, A., Cooney, J., Young, J., & Goodwin-Muir, S. (2005/2006). An examination of the evidence-based literacy research in deaf education. *American Annals of the Deaf, 150*(5), 443–456.

Luetke-Stahlman, B. (1998). *Language issues in deaf education.* Hillsboro, OR: Butte Publications.

Luetke-Stahlman, B. (1999). *Language across the curriculum: When students are deaf or hard of hearing.* Hillsboro, OR: Butte Publications.

Massaro, D. W., & Light, J. L. (2004). Improving the vocabulary of children with hearing loss. *Volta Review, 104*(3), 141–174.

Mollink, H., Hermans, D., & Knoors, H. (2008). Vocabulary training of spoken words in hard-of-hearing children. *Deafness and Education International, 10*(2), 80–92.

Morrison, D., Trezek, B., & Paul, P. (2008). Can you see that sound? A rationale for a multisensory intervention tool for struggling readers. *Balanced Reading Instruction, 15*(1), 11–26.

National Early Literacy Panel. (2008). *Developing early literacy: Report of the National Early Literacy Panel.* Washington, DC: National Institute for Literacy. Retrieved from http://www.nifl.gov/earlychildhood/NELP/NELPreport.html.

National Reading Panel. (2000). *Report of the National Reading Panel: Teaching children to read—An evidence-based assessment of the scientific research literature on reading and its implications for reading instruction.* Jessup, MD: National Institute for Literacy at EDPubs.

O'Connor, R. E., White, A., & Swanson, H. L. (2007). Repeated reading versus continuous reading: Influences on reading fluency and comprehension. *Exceptional Children, 74*(1), 31–46.

Paatsch, L. E., Blamey, P.J., Sarant, J. Z., & Bow, C. P. (2006). The effects of speech production and vocabulary training on different components of spoken language performance. *Journal of Deaf Studies and Deaf Education, 11*(1), 39–55.

Pakulski, L. A., & Kaderavek, J. N. (2001). Narrative production by children who are deaf or hard of hearing: The effect of role play. *Volta Review, 103*(3), 127–139.

Paul, P. (2009). *Language and deafness* (4th ed.). Sudbury, MA: Jason & Bartlett.

Pikulski, J. J., & Chard, D. J. (2005). Fluency: Bridge between decoding and reading comprehension. *Reading Teacher, 58*(6), 510–519.

Reid, D. K., Hresko, W. P., Hammill, D. D., & Wiltshire, S. (1991). *Test of early reading ability—Deaf or hard of hearing.* Austin, TX: Pro-Ed.

Rose, S., McAnally, P., & Quigley, S. (2004). *Language learning practices with deaf children* (3rd ed.). Austin, TX: Pro-Ed.

Schirmer, B. R., & McGough, S. M. (2005). Teaching reading to children who are deaf: Do the conclusions of the National Reading Panel apply? *Review of Educational Research, 75*(1), 83–117.

Schirmer, B. R., & Schaffer, L. (2010). Implementation of the guided reading approach with elementary school deaf students. *American Annals of the Deaf, 155*(3), 377–385.

Schirmer, B. R., Schaffer, L., Therrien, W. J., & Schirmer, T. N. (2012). Reread–adapt and answer–comprehend intervention with deaf and hard of hearing readers: Effect on fluency and reading achievement. *American Annals of the Deaf, 156*(5), 469–475.

Schirmer, B. R., Therrien, W. J., Schaffer, L., & Schirmer, T. N. (2009). Repeated reading as an instructional intervention with deaf readers: Effect on fluency and reading achievement. *Reading Improvement, 46,* 168–177.

Spencer, P. (2000). Looking without listening: Is audition a prerequisite for normal development of visual attention during infancy? *Journal of Deaf Studies and Deaf Education, 5*(4), 291–302.

Stein, N., & Glenn, C. (1982). Children's concept of time: The development of a story schema. In W. J. Friedman (Ed.), *The developmental psychology of time* (pp. 255–282). New York, NY: Academic Press.

Stobbart, C., & Alant, E. (2008). Home-based literacy experiences of severely to profoundly deaf preschoolers and their hearing parents. *Journal of Developmental and Physical Disabilities, 20*(2), 139–153.

Strong, C. (1998). *The Strong narrative assessment procedure.* Eau Claire, WI: Thinking Publications.

Swanwick, R., & Watson, L. (2005). Literacy in the homes of young deaf children: Common and distinct features of spoken language and sign bilingual environments. *Journal of Early Childhood Literacy, 5*(1), 53–78.

Tade, W. J., & Vitali, G. J. (1994). *Children's early intervention for speech-language reading (CEI).* East Aurora, NY: Slosson Education.

Teale, W. H., & Martinez, M. (1996). Reading aloud to young children: Teachers' reading styles and kindergarteners' text comprehension. In C. Pontecorvo, M. Orsolini, B. Burge, & L. Resnick (Eds.), *Children's early text construction* (pp. 321–344). Mahwah, NJ: Lawrence Erlbaum.

Therrien, W. J. (2004). Fluency and comprehension gains as a result of repeated reading: A meta-analysis. *Remedial and Special Education, 25,* 252–261.

Therrien, W. J., Gormley, S., & Kubina, R. M. (2006). Boosting fluency and comprehension to improve reading achievement. *Teaching Exceptional Children, 38*(3), 22–26.

Trezek, B., & Malmgren, K. (2005). The efficacy of utilizing a phonics treatment package with middle school deaf and hard-of-hearing students. *Journal of Deaf Studies and Deaf Education, 10*(3), 256–271.

Trezek, B., & Wang, Y. (2006). Implications of utilizing a phonics-based reading curriculum with children who are deaf or hard of hearing. *Journal of Deaf Studies and Deaf Education, 11*(2), 202–213.

Trezek, B., Wang, Y., & Paul, P. (2010). *Reading and deafness: theory, research, and practice.* Clifton Park, NY: Delmar/Cengage Learning.

Trezek, B., Wang, Y., & Paul, P. (2011). Processes and components of reading. In M. Marschark & P. Spencer (Eds.), *The Oxford handbook of deaf studies, language, and education* (2nd ed., Vol. 1, pp. 99–114). New York, NY: Oxford University Press.

Trezek, B., Wang, Y., Woods, D., Gampp, T., & Paul, P. (2007). Using visual phonics to supplement beginning reading instruction for students who are deaf or hard of hearing. *Journal of Deaf Studies and Deaf Education, 12* (3), 373–384.

Valencia, S. (2011). Reader profiles and reading disabilities. In A. McGill-Franzen & R. Allington (Eds.), *Handbook of reading disability research* (pp. 25–35). New York, NY: Routledge.

Wang, Y., Kretschmer, R., & Hartman, M. (2008). Reading and students who are d/Deaf or hard of hearing. *Journal of Balanced Reading Instruction, 15*(2), 53–68.

Wang, Y., & Paul, P. (2011). Integrating technology and reading instruction with children who are deaf or hard of hearing: The effectiveness of the Cornerstones Project. *American Annals of the Deaf, 156*(1), 56–68.

Wauters, L., Knoors, H., Vervloed, M., & Aarnoutse, C. (2001). Sign facilitation in word recognition. *Journal of Special Education, 35*(1), 31–41.

Welsch, R. G. (2007). Using experimental analysis to determine interventions for reading fluency and recalls of students with learning disabilities. *Learning Disability Quarterly, 20,* 115–129.

Whitehurst, G. J., Falco, F. L., Lonigan, C. J., Fischel, J. E., BeBaryshe, B. D., Valdez-Menchaca, M. C., & Caulfield, M. (1988). Accelerating language development through picture book reading. *Developmental Psychology, 24*(4), 552–559.

Wood-Jackson, C. (2011). Family supports and resources for parents of children who are deaf or hard of hearing. *American Annals of the Deaf, 156*(4), 343–362.

7

Understanding and Conducting Research on Language and Literacy

Understanding how to teach or develop English language or literacy in children and adolescents who are d/Deaf and hard of hearing (d/Dhh) has been challenging, and frustrating, for scholars, researchers, and educators. From one perspective, we know more about the natures of English language and literacy than we do about the manner in which to facilitate their growth in individuals (see discussion in Paul, 2009). There seems to be a knowledge–practice gap that defies the construct of the range of *evidence-based* or *best practices* as advocated by the National Reading Panel (2000) and the National Early Literacy Panel (2008) and has educational implications, as discussed in Chapter 6 of this book.

From another perspective, this knowledge–practice gap may be an illusion or, more likely, a situation that exists because of the limited, narrow, and problematic types of research that have been conducted, thus far, on English language and literacy development of d/Dhh children and adolescents. In our view, such research may predominantly rely on simple (or no) theoretical models or may employ designs that do not respect the complex nonunitary natures of English language and English literacy. Perhaps, for example, there is no way to know everything completely and empirically about language acquisition, especially for the purpose of teaching it to individuals (e.g., Chomsky, 2006; see also, varying perspectives in Crystal, 1995, 1997, 2006). The same assertion has been proffered for English literacy development, especially with respect to the teaching of *comprehension* (Paul, 1998; cf. Pearson & Johnson, 1978; Raphael, George, Weber, & Nies, 2009).

Nevertheless, given our integrative analyses of existing research presented previously in this book, we assert that certain aspects of language and much of literacy can be taught or facilitated in a classroom (or elsewhere) (e.g., see Chapter 6; see also Raphael et al., 2009; Stahl & Nagy, 2006). If it has been difficult to develop language and literacy skills in d/Dhh children, then—similar to the case for other children who are struggling readers and writers—it might be that little is known about the manner in which these children acquire English language and literacy, including the learning of English as a second language. Thus, we need to improve our theorizing and research designs to obtain a better understanding of the individual profiles of these children and adolescents (McGill-Franzen & Allington, 2011; Valencia, 2011; Vellutino, 2003). The development of individual profiles requires not only a deeper understanding of the constructs of English language and English literacy and their relationships but also adequate descriptions of the demographics (e.g., hearing, cognition, etc.) and sociocultural variables of the d/Dhh population under study. Consequently, we can proceed—albeit cautiously—from theory to research, including instructional/intervention research, to effective (e.g., *evidence-based*) practices or *best practices.*

In this chapter, we begin with a brief discussion of the epistemological underpinnings of research (and theory and practice). Then, we analyze a selection of research designs, relate this analysis to the understanding of English language and literacy, and proffer suggestions for utilizing additional perspectives because of the complexity of these constructs. Next, the chapter provides a discussion of selective investigations, specifically targeting d/Dhh children and adolescents. We delineate a few problems associated with the research studies and their respective findings, including the challenges of conducting particular types of research on d/Dhh individuals. Finally, we provide directions for further research within a metaparadigmatic framework in which synergy across research designs is powerful for eventual implementation of comprehensive language and literacy instruction.

EPISTEMOLOGICAL UNDERPINNINGS

Paul and Moores (2010) have argued that discussions of epistemological underpinnings should be the purview not only of theorists and researchers but of all educators, because conducting research is or should be a collaborative process involving major stakeholders such as teachers and researchers. The complexity of these epistemological underpinnings notwithstanding (Paul & Moores, 2012a, 2012b), one of the real dangers is misinterpretation, either of extant theory or specific research investigations.

In reflecting and conducting research on English language and English literacy, there are a number of critical questions to explore, several of which have been addressed previously in this book:

> What is language, particularly the English language?
> What does it mean to possess proficiency in the English language?
> What is English literacy?
> What does it mean to be literate in written English?
> What is the relationship between English language and English literacy?
> How do the perspectives on these questions relate to the acquisition of English as
> a second language or in a bilingual situation?

The manner in which we should examine these questions, even the nature and wording of the questions themselves, are pervasively influenced by an individual's epistemological framework (Lehrer, 2000; Noddings, 1995, 2007; Paul & Moores, 2012a; Pring, 2004; Ritzer, 2001). This might result in dissensions involving the use of scientific research paradigms (often called the standard epistemology or a variant of the main theme) versus the use of nonscientific paradigms (e.g., multiple epistemologies not involving the scientific method). Even more interesting is the fact that the nature and wording of questions are also influenced by professionals' perceptions of the meaning of *deafness* reflected, perhaps, in the employment of terms such as *Deaf, hearing loss, Deaf identity, hearing impairment, deafness,* and so on. Thus, tensions might emerge between theorists and researchers who utilize mainstream or clinical/medical/cognitive-individual paradigms versus those who favor social, cultural, or sociocultural paradigms for theorizing, conducting research, and implementing practice (Paul & Moores, 2012b; Ritzer, 2001).

A number of researchers, particularly those who espouse social and/or cultural paradigms, are reluctant or simply refuse to provide an adequate amount of demographic information on d/Dhh individuals, especially information related to speech and hearing acuities or proficiencies of the samples under investigation (Paul, 2011a). In these scholarly works, the presence of all-encompassing *learning* assumptions is evident such as the following, not exhaustive, list (Paul & Moore, 2010, p. 418):

- Individuals who are d/Deaf learn differently from hearing individuals.
- Anything based on sound/speech is not appropriate for d/Deaf learners.
- Most of deaf education is focused on deficits, not cultural or individual proclivities.
- Models for teaching should be based solely or predominantly on patterns of interactions involving sign language using dyads such as Deaf mothers/teachers and d/Deaf children.
- American Sign Language (or any sign language) is the natural language of d/Deaf individuals.
- The Deaf brain or the Deaf mind is different from the hearing brain or the hearing mind.
- Mainstream theories and research are inappropriate or not sufficient for understanding d/Deaf individuals.

Even more striking in investigations is the application of incomplete or truncated models of the English language (e.g., not considering all components or perspectives as delineated by the American Speech-Language-Hearing Association [ASHA] (1983) and those associated with English literacy (e.g., downplaying or misinterpreting the contributions of phonology or phonemic awareness; see National Early Literacy Panel, 2008; National Reading Panel, 2000; see also the discussions in Chapters 1 & 2). These issues become compounded in light of the misinterpretations of research findings, especially the findings on second-language acquisition (Mayer 2009; Mayer & Leigh, 2010; Mayer & Trezek, 2011; Mayer & Wells, 1996; Paul, 1998; Trezek, Wang, & Paul, 2010).

We recognize that there are limits to the use of the scientific approach (e.g., objective methodology) for an ultimate or complete understanding of the development of English language and English literacy. In fact, we contend that this is the case for any other psychological or physiological endeavor. The use of the scientific approach via either quantitative or qualitative explorations is still necessary, and this can be accomplished even within the framework of multiple epistemologies (Paul & Moores, 2010, 2012a, 2012b; Moores & Paul, 2012), especially within what has been labeled a metapardigmatic framework (e.g., Wang, 2010, 2012). Nevertheless, such endeavors are flawed if there is not an adequate understanding of the uses, interpretations, and limits of research designs, as discussed in the next section.

RESEARCH DESIGNS

Possessing the knowledge, skills, and dispositions for conducting effective research is the *sine qua non* of doctoral education programs in universities (e.g., Hancock & Paul, 2005; see also Boote & Beile, 2005; Freeman, deMarrais, Preissle, Roulston, & St. Pierre, 2007; Koro-Ljungberg, Yendol-Hoppey, Smith, & Hayes, 2009). Despite the risks of oversimplification or overgeneralization, Paul (2005) has argued for an improvement in the research preparation of doctoral students in education programs, particularly those who will work with future doctoral education students and who will be responsible for teacher preparation. There might be a shortage, currently and in the future, of qualified and knowledgeable university professors for teacher preparation of children and adolescents who are d/Dhh (Benedict, Johnson, & Antia, 2011; Johnson, 2013). However, if these professors are not employed in comprehensive research institutions (also known as Research 1 institutions) or in institutions that value research, then effective educational research on d/Dhh children might be in jeopardy.

We the authors recognize that the meaning of effective educational research, and the construct of *research* itself, is shrouded in controversies (Noddings, 2007; Pring, 2004). We assume that ultimately educational research is concerned with addressing and improving issues in schools, particularly learning and achievement. If educational researchers and their research endeavors are not considered to be worthy or effective, it is not unheard of that a college or school of education may be deemed also to be unimportant or unnecessary—consider, for example, the closing of the School of Education at the University of Chicago and others elsewhere (e.g., Pring, 2004).

If the focus of research is on academic learning, then the educational researcher needs to possess a deep knowledge of the content areas under investigation—in our case, English language and English literacy—as well as being adept in research methodology. However, as noted by Loadman (2005), "Blind adherence to a methodology is worse than weak methodology intelligently applied" (p. 281). We suggest that "blind adherence" to a school of thought, a specific view on *deafness*, or a specific theory or practice is the worst of all. Future researchers need to possess a frame of mind that embraces different perspectives, research paradigms, and epistemologies, given that the problems of learning and achievement are complex and involve collaboration (Berlinger, 2005; Loadman, 2005; Noddings, 2007; Pring, 2004). With respect to general research on language and literacy, we begin with an analysis of a selection of research designs.

Analysis of Research Designs on English Development

Research designs do not always fall neatly into exclusive categories. In an attempt to minimize redundancy, we categorize research designs on English development into two broad areas: primary/empirical research (i.e., quantitative, qualitative, and mixed) and secondary research (i.e., quantitative meta-analysis, narrative review, research integration or synthesis, and reason-based research). In general, research on English language or literacy development has migrated from concentrating predominantly on development as an internal/individual psychological process to a more comprehensive understanding that incorporates the linguistic structures and contributions of language and social and/or cultural factors along with the psychological or cognitive domains (Israel & Duffy, 2009; McGill-Franzen & Allington, 2011; Ruddell & Unrau, 2004; Stubbs, 1980). Accordingly, research designs used to examine English development are becoming increasingly intricate, mainly because theorists and researchers have argued that such development is not unitary in nature.

The classification scheme used here is a convenient way of simplifying the complex research designs that are currently employed. We discuss the natures, including limitations, of these types of research. As mentioned previously, part of the misunderstanding and misinterpretation in research on language or literacy and d/Dhh children and adolescents is due to a neglect to consider the technical merits of conducting specific types of research investigations.

Primary or Empirical Research: Quantitative, Qualitative, and Mixed   *Experimental and quasiexperimental.*   With a focus on the collection, analysis, and interpretation of numeric (i.e., quantifiable) data, *quantitative researchers* attempt to describe, explain, and predict language or literacy behaviors (Gall, Gall, & Borg, 2003; Gay & Airasian, 2000; Loadman, 2005). Based primarily on a positivist epistemology framework (Noddings, 2007; Paul & Moore, 2012b; Ritzer, 2001), quantitative researchers often examine language or literacy behaviors under controlled conditions via experiments to identify cause-and-effect relationships. The ultimate theoretical goal of this research thrust is explanatory adequacy (Chomsky, 2006; Lund, 2003; Paul, 2009)—that is, the establishment of generalizations, laws, theories, and so on.

A true experimental study has three essential elements: comparison, control, and manipulation (Cunningham, Stanovich, & Maul, 2011; Gall et al., 2003; Gay & Airasian, 2000). An experimental design employs random assignment of units to conditions to control the experimental treatments. Random assignments ensure that each unit has the same probability of being assigned to given conditions because assignment to each condition is based solely on chance. However, controlled experimentation is more easily conducted in laboratory sciences such as physics and chemistry than in field-based sciences such as sociology and education, particularly investigations of language or literacy. The close cousin of experimental design is quasiexperimental design, which compares existing groups (e.g., children in one classroom with those in another) using various types of design and/or statistical control to ensure that the groups are as comparable as possible in every condition except for receiving the experimental treatment(s).

The primary goal of experimental and quasiexperimental research is to create hypothetical *counterfactuals*, which means to infer treatment effects by comparing them with what would have happened if the treatment had not been administered (e.g., Dawes, 1994). From one perspective, experimental and quasiexperimental methods are considered the *gold standard* for implementing scientifically based (i.e., objective methodology) reading instruction (National Early Literacy Panel, 2008; National Reading Panel, 2000), and funding agencies in the United States (e.g., Institute of Education Sciences) give preference to educational research that uses experimental and quasiexperimental designs. The best practices or evidence-based practices in language or literacy instruction are typically defined narrowly as instruction that results in statistically greater student achievement or performance based on quantifiable measures derived from carefully controlled experiments (e.g., Bradley & Reinking, 2011).

Nevertheless, it is not easy to employ true experimental or quasiexperimental designs in language or literacy research because of the wide variation inherent in classrooms or schools, which often can have significant influences on the effectiveness of an intervention and which simply cannot be investigated in one experiment. Instructional interventions are never implemented in a vacuum, and complex interactions among variables with multiple effects operate in any instructional context. That is, artificial conditions created in experimental and quasiexperimental explorations are often impossible to create in actual classrooms and schools (e.g., Bradley & Reinking, 2011). In addition, the requirement that interventions be implemented with fidelity (i.e., treatment fidelity) denies the possibilities and realities of adapting instruction to continually fluctuating variables in classrooms, which is the essence of effective teaching.

Correlational research.   Within the umbrella of quantitative research, an alternative to true experimental and quasiexperimental designs is correlational investigations. In correlational studies, a researcher's ability to examine the nature of the relationship between certain variables is significantly limited when the elements of control and manipulation are removed (Gall et al., 2003; Gay & Airasian, 2000). Analytic techniques paired with correlational data represent a middle ground between unqualified inference and simple association. One of the most important limitations of correlational analyses is that the mere presence of a relationship between two variables cannot guarantee that changes in one variable cause changes in another. Cunningham and colleagues (2011) use a widely cited example to illustrate: "Here we might consider the well-worn example of the correlation between an increase in ice cream consumption and a rise in drowning deaths during the summer months. The presence of this correlation does not justify a conclusion that eating ice cream causes people to drown" (p. 51).

Cunningham and colleagues (2011) identify two salient potential problems of correlational evidence: (1) *third-variable problem*, where both variables are related to a third variable that affects both variables to some degree (e.g., in the case of eating ice cream and drowning, the confounding variable is heat), and (2) *directional problem*, where the mere existence of a correlation cannot ascertain which of the two variables may be influencing the other (e.g., Does a student become a better reader because s/he reads more or does a student read more because s/he is a better reader?).

With respect to inherent (e.g., sex or age), ethical (e.g., human malnutrition or socioeconomic status), or logistical (e.g., random assignment of students into different classrooms) conditions, correlational studies are left as a viable alternative to experimental and quasiexperimental studies. Furthermore, although potential confounding variables cannot be *experimentally* controlled, some specific variables might be *statistically* controlled through the use of regression-based statistical modeling techniques, such as multiple regression, path analysis, and structural equation modeling (SEM) (Hancock & Mueller, 2006; Schumacker & Lomax, 2010).

From another perspective, statistical modeling in literacy research should be used with caution, as Schatschneider and Petscher (2011) conclude:

> All models are wrong. . . . It means that all models are imperfect representations of what is occurring in nature. Models by their very nature are reductionistic and will not be able to fully explain the complex relationship we are attempting to understand. Statistical models will never tell us with certainty whether something is an exact cause of something else. Probability is inherent in every statistical model, and probabilities imply the possibility that a model is incorrect. But simply because this is true, it does not imply that models are not useful. Statistical models provide us with an incrementally better understanding of reading ability and development. They aid us in advancing our understanding of the components and correlates of reading, they give us ideas about which correlates may be fruitful to intervene with in order to enable more students to read, and they provide us with the ability to predict if our interventions will work on future students. (p. 64)

In essence, certain statistical techniques can be extremely useful, particularly when the potential third variables are known and thus can be accounted for (Cunningham, Stanovich, & Maul, 2011).

Qualitative research.   With respect to theory and research motivated by a constructivist epistemology (Paul & Moores, 2012b; Wang, 2010, 2012), some researchers have inquired whether a reduction of complex constructs such as English language or literacy to a few quantifiable variables could lead to an oversimplification of the nature of these constructs. That is, the research outcomes might be incomplete and/or provide an unjustifiably superficial understanding of the constructs (e.g., Sailors & Flores, 2011).

By collecting, analyzing, and interpreting nonnumeric data such as words, drawings, pictures, images, and observations, *qualitative researchers* explore, uncover, describe, and construct an understanding of language or literacy behaviors. Although experimental or quasiexperimental researchers seek to isolate factors for causal implications, the goal of qualitative studies is to explain, describe, and provide insights into human behaviors in context by addressing research questions such as *why, how does it work, why is it happening*, and *what does it look like* (e.g., Purcell-Gates, 2011).

One procedure to ensure validity in qualitative research is *triangulation*, that is, the gathering of data from different sources to confirm the validity of data. Qualitative procedures for studying English language or literacy include interviews, observations, think alouds, focus groups, and document analyses. Arising from the qualitative research tradition, recent qualitative studies within online contexts also include some unique qualitative and quantitative procedures such as recording of Internet usage statistics, online interviews, online focus groups, archived transcripts of online speech, social network analyses, screenshot captures, monitoring of screen moves, and eye trackings (e.g., Greenhow, 2011).

Although not designed to provide statistical generalizability of results, qualitative research findings typically provide insights into issues of concern that others can consider and reflect upon. Educators and researchers consider whether the context of a given study is similar enough to their own context to warrant application of the research findings (e.g., Purcell-Gates, 2011).

Mixed methods. As noted by Duffy in his 1981 research address to the National Reading Conference (Duffy, 1991; also see Loadman, 2005), there seem to be parallel universes of quantitative and qualitative researchers with no contact or interaction; however, this situation is changing with the recent emergence of mixed research methodology. *Mixed research* is a research paradigm that involves much more than the mixing or combination of quantitative and qualitative methods (e.g., Onwuegbuzie & Mallette, 2011). Focusing on useful outcomes, the mixed-methods approach to research allows more epistemological flexibility in methodology and encourages a democratic application of multiple perspectives (Tashakkori & Teddlie, 1998, 2003). Proponents assert that this approach minimizes the limitations associated with attempts to provide a complete view of a complex construct such as English language or English literacy in a single isolated paradigm. It should be noted, however, that mixed methods, or the use of any type of methodology, is not a panacea either.

Intervention studies in English language or English literacy research using mixed methods possess some unique characteristics that are different from those that employ pure quantitative or qualitative methods. For example, the intervention can be studied in an authentic instructional environment where variations or conditions are allowed to occur naturally and where instructional responses to these variations or conditions can be adaptive and iterative without the constriction of implementation fidelity in quantitative methods. Furthermore, intervention studies using mixed methods often promote democratic ideas and invite more authentic collaborative relationships between researchers and teachers (and sometimes students) in setting research agendas and modifying the selected interventions to reduce the infamous research (knowledge)–practice gap. As discussed previously, the knowledge–practice divide is one of the major factors that contributes to the denigration of the value or worth of educational research (Paul, 2005; Pring, 2004).

It needs to be reiterated that the application of mixed-research methods is not simply mixing or combining different methods together. The research questions, sources of data, and types of analyses and interpretations should support each other and rest on clear and carefully examined epistemological assumptions. Dressman and McCarthey (2011) suggest:

> The ways in which researchers consider the nature of knowledge may conflict with one another; therefore, simply combining methods together may not produce the types of useful data we need to make classrooms better places for our students but may result in a hodgepodge of information without theoretical grounding. (p. 461)

In essence, the range of epistemological strengths and weaknesses associated with different designs reminds us that all primary research designs have some significant contributions and important limitations.

Secondary Research   Secondary research is the secondary analysis of empirical studies, which include quantitative metadata analyses of a set of empirical studies within a well-defined domain or qualitative, narrative integrative reviews of the research literature in a specific area or construct. Based on multimethod combinations, secondary researchers attempt to systematically collect and analyze the various aspects of relevant published and unpublished (e.g., dissertations) research. The range of methods include computer searches of subject indexes (e.g., ERIC, PsycInfo, Proquest UMI Dissertations, Medline, and Google Scholar) or citation indexes (e.g., SSCI and SCI), and a *snowball* method, which entails the use of reference lists from key or prominent publications in the field. Thus, progress in research on English language or English literacy can occur by the accumulation of evidence from different interlocking studies, each of which might be of a fairly low contribution, but taken together can present a coherent picture and warrant firmer conclusions (e.g., Stanovich, 2000).

Quantitative metadata analyses involve the use of rigid, replicable statistical approaches to test hypotheses and uncover trends and gaps in a field or area of inquiry, in a way that is similar to the methodological approaches used in primary research (e.g., Bus, van IJzendoorn, & Mol, 2011). Although the unit of analysis in primary research is the individual participants (or classes or other groups), the unit of quantitative metadata analysis is the study's results. Via a specifically designed coding system, quantitative metadata analysis reanalyzes the data collected in the primary study (or studies), employing different statistical methods to reassess the original outcome(s). Generally speaking, the statistic used to assess the effectiveness of a treatment or any other variable is the effect size (ES), for example, Cohen's *d*, which measures the differences between the mean of the treatment group and the mean of the control group in standard deviation units.

One of the primary concerns of quantitative metadata analysis is the "file drawer" problem (Begg, 1994; Cohen, 1990; Rosenthal, 1991), that is, research papers reporting significant results are much easier to publish than those with null (i.e., nonsignificant) results regardless of the quality of the study. Thus, the majority of research papers remain in the file drawers of disappointed researchers, and the minority of papers with significant results, which are published, might inflate the real or actual picture of the phenomena under exploration. To address this publication bias, it is better to collect and analyze studies, regardless of publication status, and to ascertain post hoc whether publication status leads to differences in combining effect size (e.g., Bus et al., 2011).

Another potential problem of quantitative metadata analysis is the possibility of averaging out the most promising effects of the best classrooms, teachers, and programs. Still another concern is the exclusion of successful interventions that have not been evaluated in the required manner because of selection constraints in identifying studies for inclusion (Bus et al., 2011; Dickinson, Freiberg, & Barnes, 2011).

Taken together, the conduct of secondary research does enable researchers to construct models of associations between theoretically important variables that have not yet been combined in separate empirical (primary) studies. As such, researchers might be able to demonstrate where the model still is incomplete (e.g., Bus et al., 2011). The findings of secondary research, however, should not be applied in lieu of primary research findings to obtain an understanding of the English language and English literacy development of children and adolescents who were not part of the original empirical studies under exploration. Even in light of this situation and due to limited primary research data, secondary research designs can still play a major role in understanding constructs or phenomena, especially if one ascribes to a developmental similarity model of English language and literacy acquisition—as is the case with this book (e.g., Stanovich, 2000).

A summary of major points on research designs is provided in Table 7.1.

Table 7.1. Analysis of Research Designs on English Development

Primary or empirical research

Quantitative research

- Based primarily on a positivist epistemology framework
- Focus on the collection, analysis, and interpretation of numeric (i.e., quantifiable) data
- Attempt to describe, explain, and predict language or literacy behaviors
  - *Experimental and quasiexperimental*
    - A true experimental study has three essential elements: comparison, control, and manipulation
    - A quasiexperimental study compares existing groups using various types of design and/or statistical control to ensure that the groups are as comparable as possible in every condition except for receiving the experimental treatment(s)
    - The primary goal of both is to create hypothetical *counterfactuals*, inferred treatment effects generated by comparing them with what would have happened if the treatment had not been administered
    - Limitations:
      - There is wide variation inherent in classrooms or schools, and artificial conditions created in experimental and quasiexperimental explorations are often impossible to create in actual classrooms and schools
      - The requirement that interventions be implemented with fidelity denies the possibilities and realities of adapting instruction to continually fluctuating variables in classrooms
  - *Correlational research*
    - Can be used in situations where variables cannot be experimentally controlled and/or manipulated due to inherent (e.g., sex or age), ethical (e.g., human malnutrition or socioeconomic status), or logistical (e.g., random assignment of students into different classrooms) reasons
    - Can statistically control potential confounding variables through the use of regression-based statistical modeling techniques

(*continued*)

Table 7.1. Analysis of Research Designs on English Development (*continued*)

- Limitations:
  - The mere presence of a relationship between two variables cannot guarantee that changes in one variable cause changes in another
    - *Third-variable problem,* where both variables are related to a third variable which affects both variables to some degree
    - *Directional problem,* where the mere existence of a correlation cannot ascertain which of the two variables may be influencing the other
  - Statistical models by their very nature are reductionistic and will not be able to fully explain the complex relationships in language and literacy research

Qualitative research

- Based primarily on a constructivist epistemology framework
- Focus on the collection, analysis, and interpretation of nonnumeric data such as words, drawings, pictures, images, and observations
- Attempts to explore, uncover, describe, and construct an understanding of language or literacy behaviors in context
- Uses triangulation to ensure validity
- Common procedures: interviews, observations, thinking aloud, focus groups, and document analyses; within online contexts, procedures include recording of Internet usage statistics, online interviews, online focus groups, archived transcripts of online speech, social network analyses, screenshot captures, monitoring of screen moves, and eye tracking

Mixed methods

- Allow more epistemological flexibility in methodology and encourage a democratic application of multiple perspectives
- Unique characteristics for intervention studies:
  - Can study the intervention in an authentic instructional environment where variations or conditions are allowed to occur naturally and where instructional responses to these variations or conditions can be adaptive and iterative without the constriction of implementation fidelity in quantitative methods
  - Often promote democratic ideas and invite more authentic collaborative relationship between researchers and teachers (and sometimes students) in setting research agendas and modifying the selected intervention
- The research questions, sources of data, and types of analyses and interpretations should support each other and rest on clear and carefully examined epistemological assumptions

Secondary Research

Quantitative metadata analyses

- Use rigid, replicable statistical approaches to test hypotheses and uncover trends and gaps in a field or area of inquiry
- Unit of analysis is the reviewed study's results
- Reanalyze the data collected in the primary study (or studies), employ different statistical methods to reassess the original outcome(s) via a specifically designed coding system

- Limitations:
  - *File drawer problem*: the majority of research papers remain in the file drawers of disappointed researchers because of null results regardless of the quality of the study, and the minority of published papers with significant results might inflate the real or actual picture of the phenomena under exploration
  - The possibilities of averaging out the most promising effects of the best classrooms, teachers, and programs
  - The exclusion of successful interventions that have not been evaluated in the required manner because of selection constraints in identifying studies for inclusion

Qualitative review

- Qualitative, narrative integrative reviews of the empirical studies in a specific area or construct

The Notion of Best Practices

Researchers have used an array of options of primary and secondary research designs to examine the English language and English literacy development of children and adolescents. Nevertheless, it seems that the term *best practices* in language or literacy instruction is still narrowly defined as instruction that results in statistically greater student achievement based on quantifiable measures derived from carefully controlled experiments. The artificially created best practices that have resulted from this type of research have encountered various practical problems via attempts at implementation in the classroom. The two most obvious problems, mentioned previously, are the incapability to reflect the complex interactions among variables and the adaptation of instruction to continually fluctuating variables operating in a classroom instructional context.

From another perspective, the construct of best practices, based predominantly or only on the outcomes of experimental research, has been challenged (Paul, 2009; Pearson, 2004; Tierney, 2008). As indicated previously, it can be argued that these best practices have not taken into account the intricate sociocultural worlds of students, including the nature and influence of parents and caregivers or teacher–student interactions (e.g., Tierney, 2008). This is a criticism often levied against the findings and recommendations of both the National Early Literacy Panel (2008) and the National Reading Panel (2000). It might also be that the construct of best practice is best applied at the micro level—that is, the individual student level—rather than the macro or group level. This is especially true for individuals with disabilities or in special education programs, who have a complex set of needs that proceed beyond those of individuals without disabilities (see the various articles in Paul, 2008; for deafness, see also Easterbrooks & Baker, 2002; Rose, McAnally, & Quigley, 2004).

In essence, it is possible that the complex intertwined web of interactions within the classroom and other social milieus of students render it nearly impossible or extremely challenging to come to a complete understanding of the effectiveness of instructional approaches on a group level only. As suggested by Paul (2009, p. 427), based on the works of Kumaravadivelu (2006) and Prabhu (1990):

1. Different methods are best or useful with respect to the different teaching contexts, involving the interactions of teachers and students.
2. All methods are partially true or valid, depending on how a method is defined and how the results are actually measured.
3. The notion of good and bad methods is itself misguided; in fact, the notion of a method is most likely misguided in that it does not capture the entirety of the teaching and learning process. Furthermore, a method described in theory and taught and implemented in isolated, contrived situations lacks ecological validity.

Perhaps, it is best to proffer a range of effective practices as guidelines, rather than a narrow, limited "cookbook" approach. Clearly the constructs of either best or evidence-based practices imply that there are certain fundamentals that need to be addressed for all children to acquire and make progress in English language and literacy—which is also one of the basic premises of this book. With the proliferation of research design tools, the research community has made some progress in understanding the development of English. However, the gap between research and practice might never be closed if the best practices (or evidence-based practices) suggested by research do not attend to meticulous details and reflect the complex dynamics of the classroom. Different research designs have influenced our understanding of English development in distinctive ways, and no single research design has or should have a monopoly in the field. In fact, no specific research design or paradigm is a panacea. Synergy across research designs or paradigms is not only possible but also powerful, productive, and advisable (e.g., Duke & Mallette, 2011).

Previously, we have discussed the dangers of adherence to a specific methodology or research paradigm. Pearson (2004) has argued that one should not be confined by scientific research only—there is value in "just plain messing around" (p. 235). Pearson implies that it is critical to mess around to discover or uncover a range of factors in the teaching–learning context. Of course, after a certain amount of messing around, it is important to formulate a conceptual framework, which can lead to the development of a model or theory that can eventually guide research and apply findings to instruction.

Multiple Perspectives

Constructs as complex as language and literacy have to be investigated through multiple theoretical and research perspectives. It is counterproductive to argue whether, for example, English reading is primarily or predominantly a cognitive process or a social process or an environmental/behavioral process. Even if one favors a sociocultural or an environmental/behavioral framework, this does not mean that cognitive strategies/processes/skills are not applicable, especially for struggling readers or writers. In fact, as argued by McIntyre (2011): "A sociocultural perspective on children with reading disabilities does not discount other explanations for reading failure or other recommendations for instruction" (p. 54). Another researcher, Hayes (2004), has remarked that it is doubtful that all or even most of the English reading difficulties of children can be explained or accounted for via the lens of social factors such as ethnicity, race, and gender. In a similar vein, all or most English literacy challenges cannot be explained predominantly via a cognitive or an environmental/behavioral framework.

Perhaps a good starting point is to formulate a working model of English language or literacy acquisition, even if models are imperfect, and to recognize the contributions of various epistemological or theoretical frameworks, either separately or combined in some fashion (Paul & Moores, 2012a, 2012b; Wang, 2012). It is no surprise that several literacy models exist, ranging from the simple view of reading (Gough & Tunmer, 1986; Hoover & Gough, 1990) to the comprehensive componential model of reading (Joshi & Aaron, 2012) to an array of approaches that incorporate cognitive, affective, and social factors and their combinations (Ruddell & Unrau, 2004) to those that highlight the strong role of language (Dickinson, Golinkoff, & Hirsch-Pasek, 2010; Shanahan, 2006) or the connections between reading and writing (Shanahan, 1984; Shanahan & Lomax, 1986, 1988; Tierney & Pearson, 1983). Without oversimplifying, it is possible to synthesize the common elements across models and proffer the following (Paul, 2012, p. 4):

> *English reading = English language comprehension/competency (through-the-air) + access skills (primarily decoding skills) + cognitive skills (e.g., comprehension, metacognition, working memory, etc.) + sociocultural factors (e.g., home environment, teacher– student relations, etc.) + affective factors (e.g., motivation, interest, etc.) + whatever* (e.g., see various chapters in Cain & Oakhill, 2007; Israel & Duffy, 2009; McGill-Franzen & Allington, 2011).

Whichever model is accepted or developed needs to consider that the various components (or subconstructs) of English reading require differentiated instruction or research because of the varying needs of children at different age levels and with different backgrounds, the demands of the reading tasks, the requirements of schools, and so on (Kamhi & Catts, 2012; McGill-Franzen & Allington, 2011; National Early Literacy Panel, 2008; National Reading Panel, 2000). As noted in Chapters 1 and 2, the need for differentiation is due to the intricate nature of developing, in this case, a reader or individual profile, which can guide the contents of an effective instructional approach (e.g., Valencia, 2011) and which is still contingent on the notion of fundamentals. In essence, the constructs of differentiation and reader profile seem to argue against blind adherence to one all-encompassing research framework or model or to the generalization of findings of a particular type of study to all members of the subgroups of a specific population.

We do not intend to offer a complete list, but we do discuss the common application of a few specific perspectives in research on English language and literacy, particularly English reading, in the ensuing paragraphs. We consider, briefly, three commonly used models: the simple view of reading (SVR; Gough & Tunmer, 1986; Hoover & Gough, 1990), a popular model used in research on struggling readers and writers (Kamhi & Catts, 2012); the convergent skills model of reading (CSMR) (Vellutino, Tunmer, Jaccard, & Chen, 2007), and the componential model of reading (CMR), which seems to be gaining adherents (Joshi & Aaron, 2012). We also discuss reading– writing connections (Shanahan, 2006; Tierney & Pearson, 1984).

We contend that these perspectives, synthesized briefly here, are applicable to children and adolescents who are d/Dhh as well to other populations of children. Even more important is the need to delineate common elements across these perspectives, rather than to focus on only one. This might be one productive way to interpret the need for multiple perspectives or a multiparadigmatic approach to the challenges of developing English language and literacy skills in d/Dhh individuals (Paul & Moores, 2012b; Wang, 2012).

Simple View of Reading (SVR)   The SVR asserts that English reading comprehension is composed of two basic, independent components: word decoding and language (i.e., linguistic or through-the-air/oral) comprehension (Gough & Tunmer, 1986; Hoover & Gough, 1990). In this model for understanding reading disability (or delay or difference), the following equation is often proffered: R (reading comprehension) = D (decoding) × L (linguistic or language comprehension). If D = 0 or if L = 0, then R is problematic—and obviously 0. In reality, perhaps assigning a value of 0 is somewhat unrealistic; nevertheless, the intricate relationship among these three broad constructs is the essence of the SVR.

Despite the criticisms of this model (e.g., Hoffman, 2009), it does have empirical support (see reviews in Joshi & Aaron, 2012; Kamhi & Catts, 2012). The decoding construct seems to stress the importance of phonemic awareness and other phonological processes. The discussion of linguistic or language comprehension is similar to the main points presented in Chapter 2 of this book—namely, proficiency in the separate components of the English language and in the integrated use of these components. What is meant by language comprehension in SVR might be limited, given that prior knowledge and metacognitive skills are not explicitly considered but might be implied (Kamhi & Catts, 2012; Trezek et al., 2010). Language comprehension is not the same as story comprehension (i.e., listening to a story and answering questions or retelling major points)—albeit it is a critical component of story comprehension. The constructs of the SVR can be related to several of the major findings and recommendations of both the National Early Literacy Panel (2008) and the National Reading Panel (2000).

Convergent Skills Model of Reading (CSMR)   The CSMR has elements that are similar to the SVR, albeit there seems to be a predominant focus on the hierarchy of skills in a progressive manner (Vellutino, Tunmer, Jaccard, & Chen, 2007). In the CSMR, it is argued that the predicted relationship between English language and English reading progresses from the primacy of code-based decoding skills toward English semantic and syntactic abilities. In other words, code-based decoding skills are most critical for early reading development or the learning-to-read period, whereas English language skills, particularly the use of receptive and expressive language, become critical for the reading-to-learn period (see also, the discussion in Chapters 2, 3, and 4 of this book).

As aptly stated by Vellutino et al. (2007),

> Phonological skills such as phoneme segmentation and phonological (letter–sound) decoding would carry greater weight as determinants of success in beginning

reading than would visual skills, but as children acquire a high degree of proficiency in word identification and other word-level skills, language comprehension and the underlying oral language processes would likely become the primary sources of variability in reading because individual differences in word identification and phonological decoding diminish as a source of such variability. In addition, the more diverse and more advanced reading materials to which developing readers are increasingly exposed tend to make greater demands on higher level language skills (e.g., vocabulary and syntactic knowledge). (p. 4)

Vellutino et al. (2007) also assert that not only are English language comprehension processes critical for advanced reading but also that these processes do not become fully operative until the reader has acquired a sufficient proficiency level in word identification, which facilitates the understanding of written text that would typically be comprehended in spoken language (i.e., through-the-air discourse). Similar to those of the SVR, the basic tenets of the CSMR can be related to the major findings of the National Early Literacy Panel (2008) and the National Reading Panel (2000).

Componential Model of Reading (CMR)   Two of the major criticisms of earlier English reading models, including the SVR and the CSMR, are their lack of comprehensiveness and the linearity of the processes (Hoffman, 2009; Joshi & Aaron, 2012; Paul, 1998, 2009; Pearson, 2004). As discussed previously, the predominant focus has been on cognitive factors (e.g., cognitive strategies, memory, decoding, comprehension, etc.); thus, there is a need to incorporate factors associated with other domains (see also, Chapter 4), as in the CMR. In fact, the CMR is similar to the English reading equation posed previously in this chapter (Paul, 2012).

The CMR categorized factors into three major domains: cognitive, psychological, and ecological (Joshi & Aaron, 2012). Cognitive factors include the traditional focus on word identification and comprehension. Psychological factors belong to what can be labeled as the affective domain (see the attitude-influence model in Mathewson, 2004; see also, Miller & Faircloth, 2009) and include motivation, interest, and teacher beliefs and expectations—and, according to Joshi and Aaron (2012), gender issues. The ecological domain seems to contain variables that are synonymous with sociocultural factors such as the home (including language) environment, teacher–student interactions, classroom environment, and so on. All three domains need to be considered in a cohesive fashion because each domain seems to account for a certain percentage of the variance in the development of English reading comprehension in research studies (Joshi & Aaron, 2012; Paris & Hamilton, 2009).

Reading–Writing Connections   In attempting to understand the development of English written language, we can pose a line of questions that focuses on the relationships between reading and writing:

> Does reading come before or after writing or are both of these domains developed simultaneously?
> What is the role of language, particularly the English language, in the development of English reading and writing?

Does reading contribute to the development of writing or does writing contribute to the development of reading?

Are there specific skills attributed to the process of writing?

As argued elsewhere, the perspectives on these questions remind us that neither reading nor writing is a unitary process (Mayer, 2010; Mayer & Trezek, 2011; Paul, 2009, 2011, 2011a).

Theory and research on English reading have pervasively influenced perspectives on the development of English writing (see also, the discussion of research in Chapter 4; Hayes, 2004; Paul, 2009; Williams, 2004, 2011). For example, as an amalgam of the information-processing and social views, cognitive–interactive proponents assert that developments in reading and writing are interrelated at both the word level and the discourse level (Bear & Templeton, 1998; Lipson & Wixson, 2013; Tierney, 1992). Readers construct meaning when they comprehend in much the same way as writers construct meaning when they compose. Meaning is constructed as a function of the dynamic interplay between the information-processing abilities of readers/writers and the contexts of reading/writing events. The reading and writing performance of a learner is influenced not only by reader/writer (or internal) factors such as comprehension, composition, vocabulary development, word identification and spelling, fluency, grammar, usage and the mechanics of writing, prior knowledge, knowledge about reading and writing, attitude, and motivation but also by contextual (or external to the individual) factors such as settings, instructional practices, and instructional resources.

The sophistication of the reading and writing process clearly suggests how difficult, and probably fruitless, it is to search for a single causative, all-encompassing factor for less-skilled performance of a learner (be it phonology or comprehension or the use of American Sign Language) because research has adequately demonstrated that variability in performance is normal in the reading and writing process and is influenced by several variables (e.g., Lipson & Wixson, 2013). In addition, the literacy education/research field is still driven by the search for pathology to use one set of materials and tasks to predict performance because of the erroneous belief that the reading and writing processes are static and unitary and can be precisely measured at some point in time. Moving discussions of reading and writing disabilities/difficulties away from simply specifying deficits, the interactive view of reading and writing (e.g., Lipton & Wixson, 2013), for example, focuses on the specification of the conditions under which a student can and will learn, that is, how each student performs under different conditions and which set of considerations is most probable to facilitate learning.

In brief, English reading and writing are interactive and consist of various similar subprocesses, and both are based on or strongly related to English language development. The reading–writing connection is complex and dynamic, which should be taken into consideration in language or literacy research and practice. Tierney and Pearson (1983) have aptly summarized the reading–writing connection:

> What drives reading and writing is this desire to make sense of what is happening—
> to make things cohere. A writer achieves that fit by deciding what information to

include and what to withhold. The reader accomplishes that fit by filling in gaps . . . or making un-cued connections. All readers, like all writers, ought to strive for this fit between the whole and the parts and among the parts. (p. 572)

A summary of major points on three of the most commonly used English reading models, discussed in this section, is presented in Table 7.2.

Table 7.2. Three Commonly Used Models in Research on English Language and Literacy

Simple view of reading (SVR)

- English reading comprehension is composed of two basic, independent components: word decoding and language comprehension
- R (reading comprehension) = D (decoding) × L (linguistic or language comprehension)
- Decoding construct stresses the importance of phonemic awareness and other phonological processes
- Linguistic or language comprehension stresses proficiency in the separate components of the English language and in the integrated use of these components
- Limitation:
  - What is meant by language comprehension might be limited, given that prior knowledge and metacognitive skills are not explicitly considered, but might be implied

Convergent skills model of reading (CSMR)

- The predicted relationship between English language and English reading progresses from the primacy of code-based decoding skills toward English semantic and syntactic abilities
- Code-based decoding skills are most critical for early reading development of the learning-to-read period whereas English language skills, particularly the use of receptive and expressive language, become critical for the reading-to-learn period

Componential model of reading (CMR)

- Factors for English reading are categorized into three major domains:
  - Cognitive factors:
    - Word identification
    - Comprehension
  - Psychological (i.e., affective) factors:
    - Motivation
    - Interest
    - Teacher beliefs and expectations
    - Gender issues
  - Ecological (i.e., sociocultural) factors:
    - Home (including language) environment
    - Teacher–student interactions
    - Classroom environment
- All three domains need to be considered in a cohesive fashion because each domain accounts for a certain percentage of the variance in the development of English reading comprehension in research studies

Common Elements Across Perspectives   Based on the integration of research concerning the perspectives discussed previously, the accumulated evidence has confirmed strong reciprocal continuous relations between early through-the-air (receptive and expressive) English language learning and later English literacy development (e.g., Dickinson et al., 2010; Shanahan, 2006). For example, the Center for the Improvement of Early Reading Achievement affirms that "oral language is the foundation on which reading is built, and it continues to serve this role as children develop as readers" (Hiebert, Pearson, Taylor, Richardson, & Paris, 1998, Topic 1, p. 1). By the late elementary school years, children's English reading comprehension is highly correlated with language abilities nourished from earlier years (e.g., Dickinson et al., 2011). Proponents of models of reading, such as SVR, CSMR, and CMR, assert that once English decoding skills are established, English language comprehension, which is supported by English semantic and syntactic abilities, plays the primary role in predicting English reading comprehension.

As discussed in Chapters 2, 3, and 4, language is an evolving, self-reinforcing, interdependent system in which one component (e.g., phonology) relates to and supports the emergence of others (see also Crystal, 1995, 1997, 2006; Dickinson et al., 2011). For example, phonemic awareness is partially a by-product of early vocabulary development because the size of a preschooler's vocabulary is associated with the ability to attend to the sounds of the language (McGinness, 2005; Munson, Kurtz, & Windsor, 2005; Storkel, 2001, 2003). Within the language system, the rate at which children acquire vocabulary is associated with their syntactic knowledge because syntactic cues are used to assist in determining the meanings of new words (e.g., Harris, Golinkoff, & Hirsh-Pasek, 2011). Developmentally, early English language acquisition can self-reinforce into long-term effects. Consider this: children's language processing speed and receptive vocabulary size at 25 months predicts their vocabulary at 8 years of age (e.g., Marchman & Fernald, 2008; Stahl & Nagy, 2006).

The role of language in literacy development seems to be indisputable (e.g., Shanahan, 2006); however, there are few English language interventions that have been shown to be effective in the research literature (e.g., National Early Literacy Panel, 2008). The overall results of large multistate and national studies, such as Early Reading First (ERF; Early Reading First Evaluation, 2007), Head Start (Administration for Children and Families, 2010), Early Head Start (Love et al., 2005), and public prekindergarten (Howes et al., 2008), suggest that programmatic early childhood initiatives have minimum to null effects on different aspects of children's English language development. In a national randomized controlled trial, the Head Start Impact Study (Administration for Children & Families, 2010) revealed that, compared to a control group, 4-year-old children who spent one year in Head Start benefitted little on vocabulary learning with no significant effects on phonological processing or oral comprehension whereas the 3-year-olds benefitted slightly more in vocabulary and phonological processing. In one of the most comprehensive meta-analyses of early literacy, the National Early Literacy Panel (2008) found no significant difference in children's oral language outcomes between programs that used a literacy-focused curriculum and those that did not.

The dearth of effective English language interventions might be due to the fact that the multifaceted nature of language (see Chapter 2) requires broad-based and comprehensive interventions, which are more difficult to design and to demonstrate effectiveness than the ones that are narrowly targeted. In addition to the design problem, implementation difficulty cannot be ignored either. Low-quality implementations, which might be a result of poor professional preparation and support of teaching or to lack of resources or capacity in classroom settings, were common in several language intervention programs. In addition, the fidelity of the intervention was problematic because implementation was either not evaluated or not reported. Finally, English language skill itself was much more difficult to improve than other skills such as letter knowledge and letter–sound relationships. Dickinson and colleagues (2011) conclude:

> First, language studies may provide insufficiently detailed information to shed much light on what is and what is not working in interventions, due to averaging out of effects across many classrooms, lack of attention to fidelity of implementation, and lack of detailed examination of those programs and methods that are effective in improving children's language. Also, language abilities are particularly difficult skills to change, in terms of both teaching practices and children's learning. Doing so requires intensive, sustained intervention, which likely requires high researcher involvement and professional development for teachers. (p. 343).

In essence, to design interventions that have substantial and sustained impact on children's English language learning in ways that can be translated into recommendations for improving English reading comprehension, it is critical to understand how to measure language skill as a construct. For example, the Peabody Picture Vocabulary Test, 4th ed. (PPVT-4; Dunn & Dunn, 2007), a measure of receptive language, is commonly used as a measure of language skills. However, vocabulary is only one element of the language system, and broader measures of semantic knowledge and syntactic knowledge are stronger long-term predictors than receptive vocabulary alone (McGuinness, 2005; National Early Literacy Panel, 2008).

At the beginning of this section, we advocated a multiperspective approach with a focus on integrating research findings across research-based comprehensive English language and literacy models. With respect to the basic tenets of the qualitative similarity hypothesis (QSH), the fundamentals apply to all individuals attempting to learn English as a first or second language. In developing English language or literacy models or designing English language or literacy interventions, researchers and educators should keep in mind the indispensable intertwined role of English language (through-the-air) proficiency and the challenges associated with English language interventions.

RESEARCH ON d/Dhh CHILDREN AND ADOLESCENTS

Language and literacy research on children and adolescents who are d/Dhh inherits the complexity and dynamics of general language and literacy research and possesses additional characteristics unique to these individuals. That is, language and literacy research on d/Dhh children and adolescents entails not only the issues discussed previously in this chapter but also specific matters that require consideration, for example, the need for adequate descriptions of demographics as well as challenges for conducting comprehensive experimental research on this low-incidence population.

Need for Adequate Descriptions of Demographics

As discussed in Chapter 1, the term *d/Deaf and hard of hearing* refers to individuals with a wide range of hearing loss; thus, there is a need to delineate causes, types, degrees, and age at onset of the hearing loss. The line of demarcation between *hard of hearing* and *deaf* is not clear in the research literature (see Chapter 1); however, the use of these terms, without accompanying information, is ambiguous and not helpful for facilitating communication among theorists, researchers, and educators. Inadequate or lack of demographic information can lead also to misinterpretations of research findings along with overgeneralizations and oversimplifications of the constructs under study (see Allman, 2002; Paul, 2009; Paul, 2011a; Paul & Moore, 2012b).

There is also a distinction between being *deaf*, which relates to the audiometric description of hearing loss, and being *Deaf*, which refers to identification with Deaf culture, which has its own set of values, social structure, mores, forms of artistic expression, and language, American Sign Language (ASL) (Paul & Wang, 2012; see also Chapter 1). Nevertheless, the distinction between deaf and Deaf still might not be clear due to the idiosyncratic formation of Deaf identity (Leigh, 2009). Most d/Deaf individuals are born into a non-Deaf world where the language of family/community might not be fully accessible, which can preclude the complete development of their sense of who they are. The gray area between the Deaf world and the hearing world—despite the ambiguity and overgeneralizations of these constructs—leads to their struggles in figuring out who they are and how they can fit in (Wang, 2012; see also McKee & Hauser, 2012, for another perspective).

It should be emphasized that the language experiences of students who are d/Dhh vary significantly as well. American Sign Language (ASL) is widely misunderstood as the primary or first language for most students who are d/Dhh (see discussion in Chapter 2). In fact, based on the 2009–2010 survey of about 38,000 students who are d/Dhh in the United States (Gallaudet Research Institute, 2011), only about 5.8% of these children regularly use ASL at home and about 23% of the children have family members who regularly use some form of signing (see also, Johnson, 2013; Paul, Wang, Trezek, & Luckner, 2009). The majority of d/Dhh students are now educated in general education classrooms, and most of these students rely upon speech alone, followed by speech and sign. Only a minority of students uses sign alone, let alone ASL, for receptive and expressive language. It should also be remembered that up to 50% (and probably more) of the d/Dhh students have an additional disability (Guardino, 2008).

The use of *sign* might entail a visual–manual language such as ASL alone or in some combination with several of the artificially developed Manually Coded English (MCE) systems that use ASL-based signs and English grammar sign makers to represent the structure of English. Examples of these communication systems include signed English, Seeing Essential English (SEE I), Signing Exact English (SEE II), Conceptually Accurate Sign English (CASE), pidgin sign English, and contact signing (Paul, 2009). There is even variation in the predominant use of speech—that is, in conjunction with communication or instructional modes such as Cued Speech/ Language (e.g., LaSasso, Crain, & Leybaert, 2010) or Visual Phonics (e.g., Trezek et al., 2010) and within specific oral methods/programs (e.g., Beattie, 2006).

The need for adequate demographics is essential in describing the achievement level of students who are d/Dhh. In the past research literature, it has been commonly reported that the vast majority of students with severe to profound hearing loss and some with moderate hearing loss might not read much better than a fourth-grade level when compared to individuals who are typical English language readers or writers (e.g., Paul, 2009). With the advent of early intervention, including early amplification—contributing to a changing landscape (e.g., Mayer & Leigh, 2010; Johnson, 2013)—this has become an overcharacterization of the performance of these individuals (e.g., Anita, Kreimeyer, & Reed, 2010; Easterbrooks & Beal-Alvarez, 2012).

Thus, to minimize misinterpretations and overgeneralizations, adequate demographic and achievement data should include but not be limited to

1. degree of hearing loss,
2. age at onset of hearing loss,
3. gender,
4. ethnicity,
5. presence of additional identified disabilities,
6. mode of communication (speech, sign, ASL, etc.),
7. years in educational program and type of program (e.g., oral, Total Communication, bilingual),
8. years using amplification such as cochlear implants or hearing aids,
9. speech and audiologic data,
10. available achievement data (e.g., language and literacy), and
11. hearing and socioeconomic status (SES) of parents/caregivers.

All of these variables have an intricate nature and should be documented in detail in research investigations. Consider, for example, degree of hearing loss. The estimated breakdown is depicted in Table 7.3. In the past, there has been much discussion in the research literature on learners with severe to profound hearing loss (Moores, 2001; Paul, 2009; see also Chapter 2). It is critical to include investigations of the English language and English literacy development of children in the slight to moderately severe range because this group represents the vast majority of children with hearing loss in educational programs (e.g., American Speech-Language-Hearing Association, 2011; Gallaudet Research Institute, 2011).

In essence, the heterogeneous nature of d/Dhh children and adolescents requires theorists and researchers to provide adequate descriptions of demographics and other achievement information. In addition, it might be beneficial to explore the effectiveness of multiple pathways in developing English language and literacy.

Table 7.3. Degree of Hearing Loss, Hearing Loss Range, and Percentage of Students

Degree of hearing loss	Hearing loss (dB HL)	Percentage
Slight	16–25	18.9
Mild	26–40	13.3
Moderate	41–55	14.2
Moderately severe	56–70	12.3
Severe	71–90	13.8
Profound	90+	27.5

Note: Based on information in American Speech-Language-Hearing Association (2011) and the Gallaudet Research Institute (2011).

Challenges and Issues

Global Linear Relationships   It is an oversimplification to consider a one-size-fits-all or all-encompassing factor to solve all of the language and literacy difficulties of these children and adolescents. A few examples of the misinterpretations, overgeneralizations, and the challenges in conducting comprehensive investigations are discussed in this section.

Previously, we argued that English language and English literacy are not unitary constructs in which it is possible to discover one predominant factor for understanding their development. The search for the one factor (i.e., all-encompassing variable) undermines the complexity of these constructs. Research that attempts to establish a global linear relationship (often a correlation) between, for example, a specific broad factor (e.g., ASL, CSL, SEE) and the acquisition of English is limited, incomplete, and misleading.

The most common examples in previous years have been research documenting the effects of the use of a particular English sign system such as Signed English or SEE—again, within a global linear manner (e.g., Paul, 2009, 2011). All English sign systems provide only limited access to the acquisition of the English language—and this access is not adequate either for through-the-air English proficiency or for the early and advanced development of English literacy skills (Paul, 2009, 2011; Paul & Wang, 2012).

LaSasso and Crain (2010) have proffered the *degraded input* or *structural limitation hypotheses* as an explanation for this relative lack of success with the use of English sign systems. These scholars asserted that, in spite of their effectiveness in introducing vocabulary and syntax of English, the sign systems represent English at the morphological level—albeit incompletely—rather than at the phonological or phonemic level (see also Paul, 2001, 2009, and the discussion in Chapter 2). Therefore, these systems might not be effective in assisting children in acquiring the beginning and in-depth awareness of the sound structures of words (Trezek et al., 2010), which seems to be critical for learning the alphabetic system or the relationship between letters and sounds (e.g., Cain & Oakhill, 2007; McGuinness, 2004, 2005). In discussing structural limitation or degraded input hypotheses, Lassaso and Crain (2010) remarked that the signed portion of MCE [i.e., English sign] systems may not provide enough structured input for learners to use their innate biological language-learning capabilities to learn English. The task of learning English via MCE sign systems has been described as being similar to that of a hearing child trying to learn English in a (hypothetical) system that presents French or Japanese vocabulary in English word order with English prefixes and suffixes added to the French or Japanese word. (p. 306; words in brackets added)

Other examples of global linear (and correlational) relationships can be found in the research literature involving English language or literacy development and cochlear implants (e.g., Spencer, Marschark, & Spencer, 2011) or CSL (e.g., Paul, 2009), often with d/Dhh children and adolescents in *oral* programs. This is not to deny that there are some positive research findings (e.g., Antia et al., 2010; Johnson, 2013; LaSasso et al., 2010; Wang, Trezek, Luckner, & Paul, 2008). Nevertheless, these findings have not established a global linear relationship, and the specific reasons for any documented success are not always clear (e.g., Paul, 2009; Spencer et al., 2011)—most likely due to inadequate reporting of demographics or misinterpretations of findings, based on the utilized research designs.

There has been an increasing emphasis on understanding the effects of the use of ASL as a first language or in an ASL–English bilingual program on learning English as a second language. As mentioned previously, ASL is used with a small percentage of d/Dhh children in the schools or as a first language in the home. Despite attention to this emotionally laden research focus, it has been argued that there has not been a substantial amount of empirical research addressing this relationship, particularly using complex research models (Moores, 2008; Paul, 2009, 2011). Even more problematic is the interpretation of prominent second-language theories and of specific correlational investigations as evidence for such a relationship, as discussed in the ensuing paragraphs (see also, the discussion in Chapter 3).

Much of the controversy surrounding ASL and English has entailed the construct of *transfer* in second-language learning. Although transfer can be positive or negative (that is, either enhancing or interfering with second-language acquisition), it is not yet well understood. With children whose first language is a spoken one (e.g., Spanish, French, etc.), the bulk of the evidence indicates that transfer principles, particularly the production of errors, are predominantly developmental in nature in learning a second language, in this case, English (McLaughlin, 1984, 1985, 1987; Paul, 2001, 2009). The application of transfer principles for individuals whose first language is based on nonspoken language structures (e.g., sign languages) or does not possess a written representation or language (e.g., sign languages and many spoken languages in nonliterate societies) to the acquisition of a second language, particularly the written language (reading and writing), is also not clear.

Proponents of ASL–English programs or, more specifically, those who favor the predominant use of ASL as the main method of communication and instruction, have misinterpreted the theoretical models of Cummins and Vygotsky (see discussions in Mayer & Akamatsu, 2011; Mayer & Wells, 1996; Paul, 1998, 2001, 2009). Based on their interpretations of, for example, Cummins's (1989) developmental/linguistic interdependence model, they have asserted that through-the-air skills obtained from the use of ASL (full-blown receptive and expressive language skills) not only transfer wholesale but also can assist predominantly in the development of English, including English reading/writing skills. Along with their interpretations of Vygotsky's inner speech construct (e.g., Vygotsky, 1962, 1978), these proponents argued that English phonology is not critical in the development of English literacy (i.e., English reading). Furthermore, they argued that it is possible to bypass the spoken (through-the-air) form of a language (e.g., English) and still learn to read and write in that language. In many ASL–English programs, this leads to the use of English written language only (i.e., English print), and the development of English literacy seems to entail mostly comparisons of the two languages and the use of ASL to describe the grammar and so on of English (for a description/survey of bilingual programs, see LaSasso & Lollis, 2003; Rose et al., 2004).

We have already addressed the issue of phonology, particularly with respect to the learning of through-the-air English, which has been argued to be critical for learning to read and write English (e.g., Chapters 1 to 5). We also acknowledged that there is much more to English reading (and writing) than the use of phonology. Our focus here is on the misinterpretations of Cummins's interdependence model, which applies particularly to two spoken languages, both of which have a written language component. In essence, it is not clear if Cummins's model can be applied if the orthographies of the two languages are vastly dissimilar or if one of the languages does not possess a written language system.

Given the differences between ASL (sign only) and English (spoken and written), the transfer from the through-the-air form of ASL to the written form of English is neither automatic nor clear-cut. It has been argued that second-language learners can use their knowledge of their first language in acquiring information (e.g., about topics or grammar, etc.) about the second language. However, acquiring adequate, independent print literacy skills in a second language such as English requires an understanding of the alphabetic principle, which is in turn dependent upon access to phonology and morphology of English (Mayer & Trezek 2011; Paul, 2009, 2011; Paul & Wang, 2012). Finally, the models of Cummins and Vygotsky do not support or even suggest the notion that learning to read and write English is possible by only utilizing its secondary written language system (i.e., print) with explanations of this system in the first or home language (Mayer & Wells, 1996; Paul, 1998, 2009). There is simply no strong evidence of an established correlation between proficiency in the through-the-air form (i.e., oral or sign) of one language and proficiency in reading/writing of a second language, at least in research motivated by the work of Cummins and others in second-language reading and writing.

Let us be clear here: We are not arguing against the need or benefits of an ASL–English bilingual–bicultural program for some children and adolescents. Rather, we (and others) have asserted that the use of or proficiency in ASL, by itself, cannot account for the development of complex English literacy skills. In essence, any first language, by itself, is not sufficient for the development of reading and writing skills in a second language.

This leads to another major—and misleading—interpretation: the results of studies establishing a correlation between ASL and English proficiency. As discussed previously, the results of correlations should be interpreted cautiously because of the third-variable and directional problems. Novice researchers in the social sciences quickly learn that correlation does not imply causation, and ironically, the next lesson they frequently learn is that correlational data are often all we have in many areas of the social sciences including education (Cunningham et al., 2011).

The findings of correlational studies are used as the primary evidence or the predominant variable to support the use of ASL to teach English as a second language or for the establishment of ASL–English bilingual–bicultural programs. For example, Strong and Prinz (1997; see also, DeLana, Gentry, & Andrews, 2007; Prinz, 1998) conducted one of the seminal studies on the correlations between linguistic proficiency in a sign language and performance level in a written language. They assessed proficiency in ASL and written English of 160 d/Deaf children, aged 8 to 15 years, and found that d/Deaf children with the higher two levels of ASL significantly outperformed children in the lowest ASL ability level in written English after controlling for age and nonverbal intelligence. Interestingly, the relationship between ASL level and English literacy was not significant for the subgroup of older children (aged 12–15) with deaf mothers; thus, that subgroup was excluded from a subsequent analysis.

Strong and Prinz concluded that bilingual d/Deaf children could benefit from having even a moderate fluency in ASL. One obvious limitation of the study was the need to investigate the reason(s) for the insignificant correlation between ASL level and English literacy for older children: A third variable is a possibility. Another limitation was that it was unclear if the higher levels of literacy compared favorably with age peers who are typically developing literacy learners (Mayer & Akamatsu 2011; Mayer & Leigh, 2010). This limitation is also apparent in several other similar studies (e.g., Chamberlain & Mayberry, 2000; Hoffmeister, 2000; Padden & Ramsey, 2000; see the review in Wang, 2012). As discussed repeatedly, the role of the English language on English literacy development of children, including children who are d/Dhh, is indisputable. However, these correlational studies do not answer the question of whether language proficiency itself is sufficient for literacy development, let alone the role of language proficiency of ASL in developing English literacy development as a second language.

In fact, Moores and Sweet (1990) found no correlation between English reading or writing and ASL proficiency for two groups of congenitally deaf students, 16 to 18 years of age, 65 of whom had hearing parents and 65 of whom had deaf parents. High correlations were identified between English reading and two measures of English grammar/structure (i.e., the Test of Syntactic Abilities and the Signed English Morphology Test). Nevertheless, the English reading/ASL correlation was only .06 for d/Deaf children of d/Deaf parents and .04 for deaf children of hearing parents (see further discussion in Moores & Meadow-Orlans, 1990).

Aside from the third-variable problem, the directional problem of correlational studies in language/literacy research on individuals who are d/Dhh is also pronounced. For example, Chamberlain and Mayberry (2008) assessed the linguistic comprehension skills of 31 skilled and less skilled d/Deaf adult readers in ASL, MCE (Manually Coded English), and written English and their syntactic skills in ASL; they then collected questionnaire data on the readers' print exposure as well as speech use and comprehension. The results reported that skilled d/Deaf readers demonstrated greater levels of ASL syntactic ability and narrative comprehension. Chamberlain and Mayberry concluded that ASL syntactic proficiency contributed significantly to the development of skilled English reading of d/Deaf bilinguals. However, as the authors discussed, because ASL signers are immersed in an English milieu and their reading language is English, it is technically impossible to draw any strong conclusion about whether ASL syntactic proficiency contributed to the development of written English.

In sum, using correlational studies on ASL proficiency and written English proficiency to support the use of ASL to directly teach written English without the spoken/signed (through-the-air) form is problematic because of the limitations of correlational designs. Mere correlations between sign language proficiency and English written language proficiency or evidence of sign language influence in English written language development do not necessarily mean that there is linguistic transfer from sign language to English, much less a positive transfer (Wang, 2012). From another perspective, the findings of these correlational studies underestimate the complexity and nonunitary nature of the construct of English literacy. It is important to examine the reasons behind the correlations and to move into, for example, experimental or more complex research paradigms.

Construct Validation   Related to the issue of global linearity and the complexity of constructs such as English language and literacy, discussed previously, is the notion of construct validation. As in other areas of science, theorists and researchers are concerned with establishing the viability of potentially important variables and constructs. This is especially true for subconstructs associated with a complex overall construct such as proficiency in English language or English literacy. Construct validity involves the generalizations of observations to higher-order constructs that the observations are purported to represent (Schatschneider & Petscher, 2011).

Constructs such as *decoding ability* and *vocabulary knowledge* are unobservable constructs, and researchers must infer the existence of these constructs through samples of behaviors via the use of specific assessments. The threat to construct validation seems to be prominent in research on some d/Dhh children and adolescents, for example, when measuring the phonological knowledge of these individuals. More often than not, the results of specific tasks associated with determining phonological knowledge or other aspects of phonological processing might be unreliable because of individuals' ability to access information presented via the use of speech.

This does not mean that phonological knowledge or the use of phonological processing is not important for developing English literacy—that is, as part of the overall equation of English literacy. It might mean there is a need to develop certain tasks that have potential for assessing the same types of information in a relatively unconfounded manner. However, there might be challenges in assessing phonological knowledge via the use of alternative means such as the use of English signs, Visual Phonics, or CSL if such means are leading children toward the desired responses (i.e., give away the right answers). More important, it might require researchers and educators to understand the potential limits or benefits of certain subtests on a particular assessment such as the DIBELS, that is, for whom and under what conditions can such an assessment be administered (Luckner, 2013).

Single-Subject and Qualitative Research: Cautionary Use of Metaparadigmatic Approaches   Recent applications of single-subject experimental designs and qualitative case studies in language and literacy research for d/Dhh children have provided an integrated, detailed, and powerful analysis of the impact of interventions (e.g., Bergeron, Lederberg, Easterbrooks, Miller & Connor, 2009; Syverud, Guardino, & Selznick, 2009). There are important concerns and issues, however, that need to be kept in mind for these two research paradigms.

Single-subject experimental design allows an examination of the effects of an experimental treatment or treatments when obtaining groups of subjects or establishing comparability among and between groups is difficult (Neuman, 2011). With replication, single-subject experimental design can build important theoretical links in establishing generalizability by determining if the intervention is effective for other individuals and in other settings (some researchers might argue for *transferability* instead of *generalizability*; see Cooper, Heron, & Heward, 2007). The prerequisite for replication is, of course, a description of participants, settings, and intervention with sufficient details allowing for other researchers to duplicate the experiment. In contrast to waiting for extended posttest evaluations, single-subject experimental studies examine ongoing practice to measure changes in behavior for a particular individual.

One of the greatest limitations of using single-subject experimental design is the issue of *carryover effects*, especially in an A-B-A design where treatments will be returned to baseline because, once a skill is learned, it generally cannot be unlearned easily. Carryover effects are also an issue in other designs (e.g., multiple-baseline or alternating treatment) where one treatment might influence or blend with another, and it might be impossible to attribute the effects of a target behavior to a particular treatment. Another confounding factor that might be present in some single-subject experimental studies is *order effect*, that is, the ordering of the treatment instead of the treatment alone accounts for the effect.

Qualitative case study has long been stereotyped as "a weak sibling among social science methods" (Ying, 1994, p. xiii), partially because its focus is not on establishing generalizability. Although it does not offer information on causality regarding teaching practice and learning, it provides information on the "dimensions and dynamics of classroom living and learning" (Dyson, 1995, p. 51). Qualitative case study is nonexperimental and descriptive, but observing behavior is not the only way of conducting a case study. Although a case study is most often used when the researcher has no control over the behaviors being studied, it can also be used in situations where the researcher changes the environment that is being investigated. In addition, case study is a study of a bounded system, which could be a child, a teacher, or a classroom. Finally, as in other qualitative studies, case study uses multiple sources of evidence that must be analyzed into themes or patterns—for example, sources such as observations, interviews, and collection of artifacts and documents (Barone, 2011). One of the primary limitations of qualitative case studies is the unintended consequence of encouraging unwarranted generalizations, although they are intended to be particularistic and descriptive using narrative as the communication vehicle (Dressman & McCarthey, 2011).

Sharing a common emphasis on individuals instead of larger populations, single-subject experimental and case study approaches are derived from different assumptions, research designs, and data collection methods. However, their differences do not prevent researchers from combining the two approaches by broadening their definitions of what is acceptable as data and how data can be represented (Cihak, 2011). Qualitative data commonly used in case studies such as interview responses and narrative descriptions can be used to support quantitative definitions of *baseline* or *effect* and triangulated with quantitative data to strengthen the results or help explain unanticipated outcomes within the context of single-subject designs.

These two broad types of research designs, single-subject and qualitative, are used often in investigations involving d/Dhh children and adolescents. Combining them in some fashion is a good example of conducting multiparadigmatic scientific investigations. This might be more necessary than not because deafness is a low-incidence disability with a number of variables that need to be considered. Thus, true large-scale experimental intervention studies in language and literacy research within the field are and might continue to be rare.

A summary of the challenges and issues in research on d/Dhh children and adolescents is presented in Table 7.4.

Table 7.4. **Challenges and Issues in Research on d/Dhh Children and Adolescents**

Global Linear Relationships

- Research that attempts to establish a global linear relationship (often a correlation) between a specific broad factor and the acquisition of English is limited, incomplete, and misleading

- Examples:

  - Research documenting the effects of the use of a particular English sign system such as Signed English or Signing Exact English on the acquisition of English:

    - These sign systems, indeed all English sign systems, provide only limited access to the acquisition of the English language, and this access is not adequate either for through-the-air English proficiency or for the early and advanced development of English literacy skills

    - *Structural limitation* or *degraded input hypotheses*

  - Research documenting the effects of cochlear implants, often with d/Dhh children and adolescents in *oral* programs, on the acquisition of English:

    - In spite of some positive outcomes, the findings have not established a global linear relationship, and the specific reasons for any documented success are not always clear, most likely due to inadequate reporting of demographics or misinterpretations of findings based on the utilized research designs

- Research documenting the effects of the use of American Sign Language as a first language or being in an ASL–English bilingual program on the acquisition of English:
  - There has not been a substantial amount of empirical research addressing this relationship, particularly using complex research models
  - The interpretation of prominent second-language theories as evidence for such a relationship is problematic
  - The interpretation of specific correlational investigations as evidence for such a relationship is problematic

Construct Validation

- Constructs such as *decoding ability* and *vocabulary knowledge* are unobservable constructs, and researchers must infer the existence of these constructs through samples of behaviors via the use of specific assessments
- The threat to construct validation seems to be prominent in research on some d/Dhh children and adolescents, for example, when measuring the phonological knowledge of these individuals:
  - The results might be unreliable due to individuals' ability to access information presented via the use of speech
  - There might be challenges in the use of alternative means such as English signs, Visual Phonics, or CSL if such means are leading children toward the desired responses (i.e., give away the right answers)
  - Researchers and educators need to understand the potential limits or benefits of certain subtests on a particular assessment, that is, for whom and under what conditions can such an assessment be administered

Single-Subject and Qualitative Research: Cautionary Use of Metaparadigmatic Approaches

- Limitations of single-subject experimental design:
  - Carryover effects
  - Order effects
- Limitations of qualitative case study design:
  - The unintended consequence of encouraging unwarranted generalizations
- The two research designs can be combined by broadening the definitions of what is acceptable as data and how data can be represented
- Combining both research designs in some fashion is used often in investigations on d/Dhh children and adolescents because deafness is a low-incidence disability with a number of variables that need to be considered

CONCLUSION

Dewey (1946, 1998) claimed that those who teach without understanding the underlying theoretical frameworks might be following a road that leads to nowhere. In fact, all teachers operate within a certain framework, whether they are cognizant of this framework or not. Teachers often hold problem-solving-based theoretical models; that is, they generally ignore some sources of data (e.g., findings from certain types of research designs) if the data do not occur in the settings in which they work or address the problems they encounter (e.g., Lipson & Wixson, 2013). For a process as complex as

English language or English literacy development, synergy across epistemologies and research designs has almost become a necessity.

In primary research, based mainly on a positivist epistemology, quantitative researchers often examine language and literacy behaviors under controlled conditions via experimental or quasiexperimental studies to identify cause-and-effect relationships. However, for inherent, ethical, or logistical reasons, correlational studies actually dominate the field, particularly when specific variables can be statistically controlled via the use of regression-based statistical modeling techniques. Meanwhile, correlational designs should always be used with caution because of third-variable and directional problems.

Alternatively, based primarily on constructivist epistemology, qualitative researchers explore, discover, describe, and construct an understanding of language and literacy behaviors in the field or ecologically valid environments. Mixed-methods research, involving much more than the combination of quantitative and qualitative methods, is a growing trend in the field of language and literacy research. Focusing on useful outcomes, mixed-methods research allows more epistemological flexibility in method and analysis and encourages a democratic involvement of multiple perspectives.

A careful investigation of the underpinnings of research for children and adolescents who are d/Dhh reveals that there are no substantial categorical differences between conducting research on this population and on other populations in general language and literacy research. This is in tandem with the basic principles of the qualitative similarity hypothesis (QSH), the major focus of this book. Of course, as mentioned in this chapter, there are a few additional challenges and considerations for conducting research on children and adolescents who are d/Dhh such as awareness of the need for complete descriptions of demographics and the limitations, uses, and interpretations of specific research designs. Equally as important is the understanding of the nonunitary complex constructs of English language and English literacy, especially those debated within the larger fields of developing English as a first or second language.

There have been a number of correlational studies, especially involving a specific English sign system (e.g., SEE), CSL, or ASL. However, as is the case in general language and literacy research, there exists the danger of using correlations to establish cause-and-effect relationships without attention to its innate third-variable and directional limitations. In addition, the findings of correlational studies might be interpreted in such a manner that undermines the complexity of constructs or the threats to construct validity.

Because deafness is a low-incidence disability, there are relatively few large-scale experimental or quasiexperimental research investigations related to it. Instead, single-subject experimental designs and qualitative case studies in language and literacy research have provided a growing understanding of the impact of instructional interventions. Combining these research paradigms might be a fruitful approach for future investigations, and this provides an example of what is meant by the use of metaparadigmatic frameworks in which varying epistemological beliefs are valued and epistemological limitations are considered.

REFERENCES

Administration for Children and Families. (2010). *Head Start impact study: Final report*. Washington, DC: U.S. Department of Health and Human Service.

Allman, T. M. (2002). Patterns of spelling in young deaf and hard of hearing students. *American Annals of the Deaf, 147*, 46–64 .

American Speech-Language-Hearing Association (ASHA) Committee on Language (1983, June). Definition of language. *ASHA, 25*, 44.

Antia, S., Kreimeyer, K., & Reed, S. (2010). Supporting students in general education classrooms. In M. Marschark & P. Spencer (Eds.), *The Oxford handbook of deaf studies, language, and education* (Vol. 2, pp. 72–92). New York, NY: Oxford University Press.

Barone, D. M. (2011). Case study research. In N. K. Duke & M. H. Mallete (Eds.), *Literacy research methodologies* (2nd ed., pp. 7–27). New York, NY: Guilford Press.

Bear, D. R., & Templeton, S. (1998). Explorations in developmental spelling: Foundations for learning and teaching phonics, spelling, and vocabulary. *Reading Teacher, 52*, 222–242.

Beattie, R. G. (2006). The oral methods and spoken language acquisition. In P. E. Spencer & M. Marschark (Eds.), *Advances in the spoken language development of deaf and hard-of-hearing children* (pp. 103–135). New York, NY: Oxford University Press.

Begg, C. B. (1994). Publication bias. In H. Cooper & L. V. Hedges (Eds.), *The handbook of research synthesis* (pp. 399–409). New York, NY: Russell Sage Foundation.

Benedict, K., Johnson, H., & Antia, S. (2011). Faculty needs and doctoral preparation in education of deaf and hard of hearing students. *American Annals of the Deaf, 156*(1), 35–46.

Bergeron, J. P., Lederberg, A. R., Easterbrooks, S. R., Miller, E. M., & Connor, C. M. (2009). Building the alphabetic principle in young children who are deaf or hard of hearing. *Volta Review, 109*(2–3), 87–119.

Berlinger, D. (2005). Toward a future as rich as our past. In C. Hancock & P. Paul (Eds.), *Essays on the role and nature of research within the PhD program in education* (pp. 53–91). Columbus, OH: Ohio State University, College of Education.

Boote, D. N., & Beile, P. (2005). Scholars before researchers: On the centrality of the dissertation literature review in research preparation. *Educational Researcher, 34*(6), 3–15.

Bradley, B. A., & Reinking, D. (2011). Revisiting the connection between research and practice using formative and design experiments. In N. K. Duke & M. H. Mallete (Eds.), *Literacy research methodologies* (2nd ed., pp. 188–212). New York, NY: Guilford Press.

Bus, A. G., van IJzendoorn, M. H., & Mol, S. E. (2011). Meta-analysis. In N. K. Duke & M. H. Mallete (Eds.), *Literacy research methodologies* (2nd ed., pp. 270–300). New York, NY: Guilford Press.

Cain, K., & Oakhill, J. (Eds.). (2007). *Children's comprehension problems in oral and written language*. New York, NY: Guilford Press.

Chall, J. S. (2000). *The academic achievement challenge: What really works in the classroom?* New York, NY: Guilford Press.

Chamberlain, C., & Mayberry, R. I. (2000). Theorizing about the relationship between ASL and reading. In C. Chamberlain, J. Morford, & R. I. Mayberry (Eds.), *Language acquisition by eye* (pp. 221–260). Mahwah, NJ: Erlbaum.

Chamberlain, C., & Mayberry, R. I. (2008). American Sign Language syntactic and narrative comprehension in skilled and less skilled readers: Bilingual and bimodal evidence for the linguistic basis of reading. *Applied Psycholinguistics, 29*, 367–88.

Chomsky, N. (2006). *Language and mind* (3rd ed.). New York, NY: Cambridge University Press.

Cihak, D. (2011). Single-subject and case-study designs. In A. McGill-Franzen & R. L. Allington (Eds.), *Handbook of reading disability research* (pp. 419–433). New York, NY: Routledge.

Cohen, J. (1990). Things I have learned (so far). *American Psychologist, 45*, 1304–1312.

Cooper, J., Heron, T., & Heward, W. (2007). *Applied behavior analysis* (2nd ed.). Upper Saddle River, NJ: Prentice Hall.

Cummins, J. (1989). A theoretical framework for bilingual special education. *Exceptional Children, 56*, 111–119.

Cunningham, A. E., Stanovich, K. E., & Maul, A. (2011). Of correlations and causes: The use of multiple regression modeling in literacy research. In N. K. Duke & M. H. Mallete (Eds.), *Literacy research methodologies* (2nd ed., pp. 50–69). New York, NY: Guilford Press.

Crystal, D. (1995). *The Cambridge encyclopedia of the English language.* New York, NY: Cambridge University Press.

Crystal, D. (1997). *The Cambridge encyclopedia of language* (2nd ed). New York, NY: Cambridge University Press.

Crystal, D. (2006). *How language works.* London, England: Penguin.

Dawes, R. M. (1994). *House of cards: Psychology and psychotherapy built on myth.* New York, NY: Free Press.

DeLana, M., Gentry, M. A., & Andrews, J. (2007). The efficacy of ASL/English bilingual education: Considering public schools. *American Annals of the Deaf, 152*(1), 73–87.

Dewey, J. (1946). *The public and its problems.* Chicago, IL: Gateway.

Dewey, J. (1998). *How we think.* Boston, MA: Houghton Mifflin.

Dickinson, D. K., Freiberg, J. B., & Barnes, E. M. (2011). Why are so few interventions really effective? A call for fine-grained research methodology. In S. B. Neuman & D. K. Dickinson (Eds.), *Handbook of early literacy research* (Vol. 3, pp. 337–357). New York, NY: Guilford Press.

Dickinson, D. K., Golinkoff, R. M., & Hirsch-Pasek, K. (2010). Speaking out for language: Why language is central to reading development. *Educational Researcher, 10*(4), 305–310.

Dressman, M., & McCarthey, S. J. (2011). Toward a pragmatics of epistemology, methodology, and social theory. In N. K. Duke & M. H. Mallete (Eds.), *Literacy research methodologies* (2nd ed., pp. 441–463). New York, NY: Guilford Press.

Duffy, G. (1991). What counts in teacher education? Dilemmas in educating empowered teachers. In J. Zutell & S. McCormick (Eds.), *Learner factors/teacher factors: Issues in literacy research and instruction* (pp. 1–18). Chicago, IL: National Reading Conference.

Duke, N. K., & Mallette, M. H. (2011). Conclusion. In N. K. Duke & M. H. Mallete (Eds.), *Literacy research methodologies* (2nd ed., pp. 464–471). New York, NY: Guilford Press.

Dunn, L. M., & Dunn, D. M. (2007). *Peabody Picture Vocabulary Test (PPVT-4)* (4th ed.). San Antonio, TX: Pearson.

Dyson, A. (1995). Children out of bounds: The power of case studies in expanding visions of literacy development. In K. Hinchman, D. Leu, & C. Kinzer (Eds.), *Perspectives on literacy research and practice* (pp. 39–53). Chicago, IL: National Reading Conference.

Early Reading First Evaluation. (2007). *National evaluation of Early Reading First.* Washington, DC: U.S. Department of Education.

Easterbrooks, S., & Baker, S. (2002). *Language learning in children who are deaf and hard of hearing: Multiple pathways.* Boston, MA: Allyn & Bacon.

Easterbrooks, S., & Beal-Alvarez, J. (2012). States' reading outcomes of students who are d/Deaf and hard of hearing. *American Annals of the Deaf, 157*(1), 27–40.

Freeman, M., deMarrais, K., Preissle, J., Roulston, K., & St. Pierre, E. A. (2007). Standards of evidence in qualitative research: An incitement to discourse. *Educational Researcher, 36*(1), 25–32.

Gall, M., Gall, J., & Borg, W. (2003). *Educational research: An introduction* (7th ed.). Boston, MA: Allyn & Bacon.

Gallaudet Research Institute. (2011, April). *Regional and national summary report of data from the 2009–2010 annual survey of deaf and hard of hearing children and youth.* Washington, DC: Gallaudet University.

Gay, L., & Airasian, P. (2000). *Educational research: Competencies for analysis and application* (6th ed.). Upper Saddle River, NJ: Merrill/Prentice-Hall.

Gough, P. B., & Tunmer, W. E. (1986). Decoding, reading, and reading disability. *Remedial and Special Education, 7*(1), 6–10.

Greenhow, C. M. (2011). Research methods unique to digital contexts. In N. K. Duke & M. H. Mallete (Eds.), *Literacy research methodologies* (2nd ed., pp. 70–86). New York, NY: Guilford Press.

Guardino, C. (2008). Identification and placement for deaf students with multiple disabilities: Choosing the paths less followed. *American Annals of the Deaf, 153*(1), 55–64.

Hancock, C., & Paul, P. (Eds.). (2005). *Essays on the role and nature of research within the PhD program in education.* Columbus, OH: Ohio State University, College of Education.

Hancock, G. R., & Mueller, R. O. (Eds.). (2006). *Structural equation modeling: A second course.* Greenwich, CT: Information Age.

Harris, J., Golinkoff, R. M., & Hirsh-Pasek, K. (2011). Lessons from the crib to the classroom: How children really learn vocabulary. In S. B. Neuman & D. K. Dickinson (Eds.), *Handbook of early literacy research* (Vol. 3, pp. 49–65). New York, NY: Guilford Press.

Hayes, J. (2004). A new framework for understanding cognition and affect in writing. In R. Ruddell & N. Unrau (Eds.), *Theoretical models and processes of reading* (5th ed., pp. 1399–1430). Newark, DE: International Reading Association.

Hiebert, E. H., Pearson, P. D., Taylor, B. M., Richardson, V., & Paris, S. G. (Eds.). (1998). *Every child a reader: Applying reading research in the classroom.* Ann Arbor, MI: Center for the Improvement of Early Reading Achievement.

Hoffman, J. (2009). In search of the "simple view" of reading comprehension. In S. Israel & G. Duffy (Eds.), *Handbook of research on reading comprehension* (pp. 54–66). New York, NY: Routledge.

Hoffmeister, R. (2000). A piece of the puzzle: ASL and reading comprehension in deaf children. In C. Chamberlain, J. Monford, & R. Mayberry (Eds.), *Language acquisition by eye* (pp. 143–64). Mahwah, NJ: Lawrence Erlbaum.

Hoover, W. A., & Gough, P. B. (1990). The simple view of reading. *Reading and Writing, 28,* 127–160.

Howes, C., Burchinal, M., Pianta, R., Bryant, D., Early, D., Clifford, R., et al. (2008). Ready to learn? Children's pre-academic achievement in pre-kindergarten programs. *Early Childhood Research Quarterly, 23,* 27–50.

Israel, S., & Duffy, G. (Eds.). (2009). *Handbook of research on reading comprehension.* New York, NY: Routledge.

Johnson, H. (2013). Initial and ongoing teacher preparation and support: Current problems and possible solutions. *American Annals of the Deaf, 157*(5), 439–449.

Joshi, R. M., & Aaron, P.G. (2012). Componential model of reading (CMR): Validation studies. *Journal of Learning Disabilities, 45*(5), 387–390.

Kamhi, A., & Catts, H. (2012). *Language and reading disabilities* (3rd ed.). Boston, MA: Pearson Education.

Koro-Ljungberg, M., Yendol-Hoppey, D., Smith, J. J., & Hayes, S. B. (2009). Epistemological awareness, instantiation of methods, and uninformed methodological ambiguity in qualitative research projects. *Educational Researcher, 38,* 687–699.

Kumaravadivelu, B. (2006). *Understanding language teaching: From method to postmethod.* Mahwah, NJ: Erlbaum.

LaSasso, C. J., & Crain, K. L. (2010). Cued language for the development of deaf students' reading comprehension and measured reading comprehension. In C. J. LaSasso, K. L. Crain & J. Leybaert (Eds.), *Cued Speech and Cued Language for deaf and hard of hearing children* (pp. 285–321). San Diego, CA: Plural Publishing.

LaSasso, C. J., Crain, K. L., & Leybaert, J. (Eds.). (2010). *Cued Speech and Cued Language for deaf and hard of hearing children.* San Diego, CA: Plural Publishing.

LaSasso, C., & Lollis, J. (2003). Survey of residential and day schools for deaf students in the United States that identify themselves as bilingual–bicultural programs. *Journal of Deaf Studies and Deaf Education, 8,* 79–90.

Lehrer, K. (2000). *Theory of knowledge* (2nd ed.). Boulder, CO: Westview Press.

Leigh, I. W. (2009). *A lens on deaf identities*. New York, NY: Oxford University Press.

Lipson, M. Y., & Wixson, K. K. (2013). *Assessment of reading and writing difficulties: An interactive approach*. Upper Saddle River, NJ: Pearson.

Loadman, W. (2005). A brief history and view of the preparation of educational researchers: Or rescind the law of the hammer. In C. Hancock & P. Paul (Eds.), *Essays on the role and nature of research within the PhD program in education* (pp. 266–299). Columbus, OH: Ohio State University, College of Education.

Love, J. M., Kisker, E. E., Ross, C., Raikes, H., Constantine, J., Boller, K., et al. (2005). The effectiveness of Early Head Start for 3-year-old children and their parents: Lessons for policy and programs. *Developmental Psychology, 41*, 885–901.

Luckner, J. (2013). Using the dynamic indicators of basic early literacy skills with students who are deaf or hard of hearing: Perspectives of a panel of experts. *American Annals of the Deaf, 158* (1), 7–19.

Lund, N. (2003). *Language and thought*. New York, NY: Routledge.

Mallete, M. H., & Duke, N. K. (2011). Introduction. In N. K. Duke & M. H. Mallete (Eds.), *Literacy research methodologies* (2nd ed., pp. 1–6). New York, NY: Guilford Press.

Marchman, V. A., & Fernald, A. (2008). Speed of word recognition and vocabulary knowledge in infancy predict cognitive and language outcomes in later childhood. *Developmental Science, 11*, F9–F16.

Mathewson, G. (2004). Model of attitude influence upon reading and learning to read. In R. Ruddell & N. Unrau (Eds.), *Theoretical models and processes of reading* (5th ed., pp. 1431–1461). Newark, DE: International Reading Association.

Mayer, C. (2009). Issues in second language literacy education for learners who are deaf. *International Journal of Bilingual Education and Bilingualism, 12*(3), 325–334.

Mayer, C. (2010). The demands of writing and the deaf writer. In M. Marschark & P. Spencer (Eds.), *Oxford handbook of deaf studies, language, and education* (Vol. 2, pp. 144–155). New York, NY: Oxford University Press.

Mayer, C., & Akamatsu, C. T. (2011). Bilingualism and literacy. In M. Marschark & P. Spencer (Eds.), *Oxford handbook of deaf studies, language, and education* (2nd ed., Vol. 1, pp. 144–155). New York, NY: Oxford University Press.

Mayer, C., & Leigh, G. (2010). The changing context for sign bilingual education programs: Issues in language and the development of literacy. *International Journal of Bilingual Education and Bilingualism, 13*(2), 175–186.

Mayer, C., & Trezek, B. J. (2011). New (?) answers to old questions: Literacy development in D/HH learners. In D. Moores (Ed.), *Partners in education: Issues and trends from the 21st International Congress on Education of the Deaf Conference Proceedings* (62–74). Washington, DC: Gallaudet University Press.

Mayer, C., & Wells, G. (1996). Can the linguistic interdependence theory support a bilingual–bicultural model of literacy education for deaf students? *Journal of Deaf Studies and Deaf Education, 1*(2), 93–107.

McGill-Franzen, A., & Allington, R. (Eds.). (2011). *Handbook of reading disability research*. New York, NY: Routledge.

McGuinness, D. (2004). *Early reading instruction: What science really tells us about how to teach reading*. Cambridge, MA: MIT Press.

McGuinness, D. (2005). *Language development and learning to read: The scientific study of how language development affects reading skill*. Cambridge, MA: MIT Press.

McIntyre, E. (2011). Sociocultural perspectives on children with reading difficulties. In A. McGill-Franzen & R. Allington (Eds.), *Handbook of reading disability research* (pp. 45–56). New York, NY: Routledge.

McKee, M., & Hauser, P. (2012). Juggling two worlds. In P. Paul & D. Moores (Eds.), *Deaf epistemologies: Multiple perspectives on the acquisition of knowledge* (pp. 45–62). Washington, DC: Gallaudet University Press.

McLaughlin, B. (1984). *Second-language acquisition in childhood: Vol. 1. Preschool children* (2nd ed.). Hillsdale, NJ: Erlbaum.

McLaughlin, B. (1985). *Second-language acquisition in childhood: Vol. 2. School-age children* (2nd ed.). Hillsdale, NJ: Erlbaum.

McLaughlin, B. (1987). *Theories of second-language learning.* Baltimore, MD: Edward Arnold.

Miller, S., & Faircloth, B. (2009). Motivation and reading comprehension. In S. Israel & G. Duffy (Eds.), *Handbook of research on reading comprehension* (pp. 307–322). New York, NY: Routledge.

Moores, D. (2001). *Educating the deaf: Psychology, principles, and practices* (5th ed.). Boston, MA: Houghton-Mifflin.

Moores, D. (2008). Research on Bi-Bi instruction. *American Annals of the Deaf, 153*(1), 3–4.

Moores, D., & Meadow-Orlans, K. (Eds.). (1990). *Educational and developmental aspects of deafness.* Washington, DC: Gallaudet University Press.

Moores, D., & Paul, P. (2012). Retrospectus and prospectus. In P. Paul & D. Moores (Eds.), *Deaf epistemologies: Multiple perspectives on the acquisition of knowledge* (pp. 255–258). Washington, DC: Gallaudet University Press.

Moores, D., & Sweet, C. (1990). Relationships of English grammar and communicative fluency in reading in deaf adolescents. *Exceptionality, 1,* 97–106.

Munson, B., Kurtz, B. A., & Windsor, J. (2005). The influence of vocabulary size, phonotactic probability, and wordlinkeness on nonword repetitions of children with and without specific language impairment. *Journal of Speech, Language, and Hearing Research, 48,* 1033–1047.

National Early Literacy Panel. (2008). *Developing early literacy: Report of the National Early Literacy Panel.* Jessup, MD: National Institute for Literacy.

National Reading Panel. (2000). *Report of the National Reading Panel: Teaching children to read—An evidence-based assessment of the scientific research literature on reading and its implications for reading instruction.* Jessup, MD: National Institute for Literacy at EDPubs.

Neuman, S. B. (2011). Single-subject experimental design. In N. K. Duke & M. H. Mallete (Eds.), *Literacy research methodologies* (2nd ed., pp. 383–403). New York, NY: Guilford Press.

Noddings, N. (1995). *Philosophy of education.* Boulder, CO: Westview Press.

Noddings, N. (2007). *Philosophy of education* (2nd ed.). Boulder, CO: Westview Press.

Onwuegbuzie, A. J., & Mallette, M. H. (2011). Mixed research techniques in literacy research. In N. K. Duke & M. H. Mallete (Eds.), *Literacy research methodologies* (2nd ed., pp. 301–330). New York, NY: Guilford Press.

Padden, C., & Ramsey, C. (2000). American Sign Language and reading ability in deaf children. In C. Chamberlain, J. Morford, & R. Mayberry (Eds.), *Language acquisition by eye* (pp. 165–189). Mahwah, NJ: Erlbaum.

Paris, S., & Hamilton, E. (2009). The development of children's reading comprehension. In S. Israel & G. Duffy (Eds.), *Handbook of research on reading comprehension* (pp. 32–53). New York, NY: Routledge.

Paul, P. (1998). *Literacy and deafness: The development of reading, writing, and literate thought.* Needham Heights, MA: Allyn & Bacon.

Paul, P. (2001). *Language and deafness* (3rd ed.). San Diego, CA: Singular.

Paul, P. (2005). Epilogue. In C. Hancock & P. Paul (Eds.), *Essays on the role and nature of research within the PhD program in education* (pp. 311–319). Columbus, OH: Ohio State University, College of Education.

Paul, P. (2009). *Language and deafness* (4th ed.). Sudbury, MA: Jones & Bartlett.

Paul, P. (2011). A perspective on language and literacy issues. In D. Moores (Ed.), *Partners in education: Issues and trends from the 21st International Congress on the Education of the Deaf* (pp. 51–61). Washington, DC: Gallaudet University Press.

Paul, P. (2011a). What's in a word (label, phrase, term, etc.)? *American Annals of the Deaf, 156*(3), 235–238.

Paul, P. (2012). What is a theory good for? *American Annals of the Deaf, 157*(1), 3–6.

Paul, P., & Moores, D. (2010). Toward an understanding of epistemology and deafness. *American Annals of the Deaf, 154*(5), 417–420.

Paul, P., & Moores, D. (Eds.). (2012a). *Deaf epistemologies: Multiple perspectives on the acquisition of knowledge.* Washington, DC: Gallaudet University Press.

Paul, P., & Moores, D. (2012b). Toward an understanding of epistemology and deafness. In P. Paul & D. Moores (Eds.), *Deaf epistemologies: Multiple perspectives on the acquisition of knowledge* (pp. 3–15). Washington, DC: Gallaudet University Press.

Paul, P., & Wang, Y. (2012). *Literate thought: Understanding comprehension and literacy.* Sudbury, MA: Jones & Bartlett.

Paul, P., Wang, Y., Trezek, B., & Luckner, J. (2009). Phonology is necessary, but not sufficient: A rejoinder. *American Annals of the Deaf, 154*(4), 346–356.

Pearson, P. D. (2004). The reading wars. *Educational Policy, 18*(1), 216–252.

Pearson, P. D., & Johnson, D. (1978). *Teaching reading comprehension.* New York, NY: Holt, Rinehart, & Winston.

Prabhu, N. (1990). There is no best method—Why? *TESOL Quarterly, 24,* 161–176.

Pring, R. (2004). *Philosophy of educational research* (2nd ed.). New York, NY: Continuum.

Prinz, P. (Ed.). (1998). ASL proficiency and English literacy acquisition: New perspectives [Special issue]. *Topics in Language Disorders, 18*(4).

Purcell-Gates, V. (2011). Ethnographic research. In N. K. Duke & M. H. Mallete (Eds.), *Literacy research methodologies* (2nd ed., pp. 135–154). New York, NY: Guilford Press.

Raphael, T., George, M., Weber, C., & Nies, A. (2009). Approaches to teaching reading comprehension. In S. Israel & G. Duffy (Eds.), *Handbook of research on reading comprehension* (pp. 449–469). New York, NY: Routledge.

Ritzer, G. (2001). *Explorations in social theory: From metatheorizing to rationalization.* Thousand Oaks, CA: Sage.

Rose, S., McAnally, P., & Quigley, S. (2004). *Language learning practices with deaf children* (3rd ed.). Austin, TX: Pro-ed.

Ruddell, R., & Unrau, N. (Eds.). (2004). *Theoretical models and processes of reading* (5th ed.). Newark, DE: International Reading Association.

Rosenthal, R. (1991). *Meta-analytic procedures for social research* (rev. ed.). Newbury Park, CA: Sage.

Sailors, M., & Flores, M. (2011). Observational research. In A. McGill-Franzen & R. L. Allington (eds.), *Handbook of reading disability research* (pp. 444–455). New York, NY: Routledge.

Schatschneider, C., & Petscher, Y. (2011). Statistical modeling in literacy research. In M. L. Kamil, P. D. Pearson, E. B. Moje, & P. P. Afflerbach (Eds.), *Handbook of reading research* (Vol. 4, pp. 54–65). New York, NY: Routledge.

Schumacker, R.E., & Lomax, R. G. (2010). *A beginner's guide to structural equation modeling* (3rd ed.). New York, NY: Routledge.

Shanahan, T. (1984). The reading–writing relation: An exploratory multi-variate analysis. *Journal of Educational Psychology, 76*(3), 466–477.

Shanahan, T. (2006). Relations among oral language, reading, and writing development. In C. MacArthur, S. Graham, & J. Fitzgerald (Eds.), *Handbook of writing research* (pp. 171–183). New York, NY: Guilford Press.

Shanahan, T., & Lomax, R. (1986). An analysis and comparison of theoretical models of the reading–writing relationship. *Journal of Educational Psychology, 78*(2), 116–123.

Shanahan, T., & Lomax, R. (1988). A developmental comparison of three theoretical models of the reading–writing relationship. *Research in the Teaching of English, 22*(2), 196–212.

Spencer, P., Marschark, M., & Spencer, L. (2011). Cochlear implants: Advances, issues, and implications. In M. Marschark & P. Spencer (Eds.). *The Oxford handbook of deaf studies, language, and education* (2nd ed., Vol. 1, pp. 452–470). New York, NY: Oxford University Press

Stahl, S., & Nagy, W. (2006). *Teaching word meanings.* Mahwah, NJ: Erlbaum.

Stanovich, K. E. (2000). *Progress in understanding reading: Scientific foundations and new frontiers.* New York, NY: Guilford Press.

Storkel, H. L. (2001). Learning new words: Phonotactic probability in language development. *Journal of Speech, Language, and Hearing Research, 44,* 1321–1337.

Storkel, H. L. (2003). Learning new words II: Phonotactic probability in verbal learning. *Journal of Speech, Language and Hearing Research, 46,* 1312–1323.

Strong, M., & Prinz, P. M. (1997). A study of the relationship between ASL and English literacy. *Journal of Deaf Studies and Deaf Education, 2*(1), 37–46.

Stubbs, M. (1980). *Language and literacy: The sociolinguistics of reading and writing.* Boston, MA: Routledge & Kegan Paul.

Syverud, S. M., Guardino, C., & Selznick, D. N. (2009). Teaching phonological skills to a deaf first grader: A promising strategy. *American Annals of the Deaf, 154,* 382–388.

Tashakkori, A., & Teddlie, C. (1998). *Mixed methodology: Combining qualitative and quantitative approaches.* Thousand Oaks, CA: Sage.

Tashakkori, A., & Teddlie, C. (Eds.). (2003). *Handbook of mixed methods in social and behavioral research.* Thousand Oaks, CA: Sage.

Tierney, R. J. (1992). Ongoing research and new directions. In J. W. Irwin & M. A. Doyle (Eds.), *Reading/writing connections: Learning from research* (pp. 247–259). Newark, DE: International Reading Association.

Tierney, R. (2008). Reading and children with disabilities: Searching for better guidance. *Balanced Reading Instruction, 15*(2), 89–98.

Tierney, R. J., & Pearson, P. D. (1983). Toward a composing model of reading. *Language Arts, 60,* 568–580.

Trezek, B., Wang, Y., & Paul, P. (2010). *Reading and deafness: Theory, research and practice.* Clifton Park, NY: Cengage Learning.

Valencia, S. (2011). Reader profiles and reading disabilities. In A. McGill-Franzen & R. Allington (Eds.), *Handbook of reading disability research* (pp. 25–35). New York, NY: Routledge.

Vellutino, F. (2003). Individual differences as sources of variability in reading comprehension in elementary school children. In A. P. Sweet & C. E. Snow (Eds.), *Rethinking reading comprehension* (pp. 51–81). New York, NY: Guilford Press.

Vellutino, F. R., Tunmer, W. E., Jaccard, J. J., & Chen, R. (2007). Components of reading ability: Multivariate evidence for a convergent skills model of reading development. *Scientific Studies of Reading, 11,* 3–32.

Vygotsky, L. (1962). *Thought and language.* Cambridge, MA: MIT Press.

Vygotsky, L. (1978). *Mind in society: The development of higher psychological processes.* Cambridge, MA: Harvard University Press.

Wang, Y. (2010). Without boundaries: An inquiry of Deaf epistemologies through a metaparadigm. *American Annals of the Deaf, 154*(5), 428–434.

Wang. Y. (2012). Educators without borders: A metaparadigm for literacy instruction in bilingual bicultural education. In P. Paul & D. Moores (Eds.), *Deaf epistemologies: Multiple perspectives on the acquisition of knowledge* (pp. 199–217). Washington, DC: Gallaudet University Press.

Wang, Y., Trezek, B., Luckner, J., & Paul, P. (2008). The role of phonology and phonological-related skills in reading instruction for students who are deaf or hard of hearing. *American Annals of the Deaf, 153*(4), 396–407.

Williams, C. (2004). Emergent literacy of deaf children. *Journal of Deaf Studies and Deaf Education, 9*(4), 352–365.

Williams, C. (2011). Adapted interactive writing instruction with kindergarten children who are deaf or hard of hearing. *American Annals of the Deaf, 156*(1), 23–34.

Yin, R. K. (1994). *Case-study research: Design and methods* (2nd ed.). Thousand Oaks, CA: Sage.

8

From the Past to the Future: Reflections on the QSH

In this chapter are two essays in which David Bloome, Kouider Mokhtari, and Carla Reichard reflect on the merits of the qualitative similarity hypothesis (QSH). The contributors are well known in their respective fields and evaluate the QSH with respect to their own epistemological and research paradigms. We respond to selective remarks in these essays in Chapter 9.

ESSAY I

The Social Turn in Language and Literacy Research and the Qualitative Similarity Hypothesis: Particularity, Practice, Time, and Part–Whole Relations

David Bloome
Ohio State University

Peter Paul, Ye Wang, and Cheri Williams have composed an impressive book and review of research articulating what they call the "qualitative similarity hypothesis." They are especially concerned with the development of reading and writing skills in children and students who are d/Deaf and hard of hearing. From my perspective, a major accomplishment of their essay is the assertion that children and students who are d/Deaf and hard of hearing should be treated on an equal basis with other children and students. One need not be an expert in educational research to recognize their marginalization and deficit framing by dominant educational institutions. Some may argue that Paul, Wang, and Williams have not gone far enough in articulating or warranting their thesis of personhood, but within the paradigm of experimental, quasiexperimental, and clinical research (what they call "scientific" research), their argument is eloquent, persuasive, and needed.

There are multiple frames, perspectives, and paradigms in research and scholarship on language and literacy. While there are some places where these different

approaches might converge, there are unbridgeable differences in foundational definitions of the phenomena under consideration, in what counts as knowledge and knowing, in units of analysis, in the goals of research and scholarship, in the relationship of
researchers to the researched, in the rhetorical presentation, in the warranting of the-
ses, and more. Yet, despite recognizing these differences, many language and literacy
scholars appreciate perspectives beyond their own while also recognizing the inherent
incompleteness of the scholarly endeavor to understand and articulate the human condition. This is the position in which I find myself. My research, which I also claim as
"scientific" (although employing a different definition of "scientific" than Paul, Wang,
and Williams), has been grounded in the social turn in linguistic and educational research and has been associated with interactional sociolinguistics, microethnographic
discourse analysis, and cultural anthropology. None of this is to be found in the argument made in Paul, Wang, and Williams's essay, although there is a history of research
that could have been called on to support their thesis regarding the personhood of
children and students who are d/Deaf and hard of hearing with regard to language and
literacy (e.g., Kim, 2012; Marshall, 1996; Maxwell, 1985; Miller, 2001; Poveda, Pulido,
Morgade, Messina, & Hédlová, 2008; Ramsey & Padden, 1998; Senghas & Monaghan,
2002; Wilcox, 1994; among many others).

Here, I frame a relationship between the argument Paul, Wang, and Williams
have made regarding personhood, language, literacy, and education—what they call the
"qualitative similarity hypothesis"—and the conduct of research on personhood, language, literacy, and education grounded in the social turn in language and educational
research. To do so, I focus on particularity, practice, time, and part–whole relations.

PARTICULARITY

The qualitative similarity hypothesis (QSH) asserts that "the acquisition of English by
any individual is developmentally similar to that of native learners and to that of typical literacy learners of English. This developmental similarity suggests that there are
certain critical fundamentals that facilitate and enhance the acquisition process. These
fundamentals . . . apply to the learning of English as either a first or second language"
(Chapter 1, p. 1). The QSH applies both to oral and through-the-air language as well
as written language. In general and in principle, as the evidence marshaled by Paul,
Wang and Williams suggests, this is perhaps so, but language and literacy learning
does not happen "in general" or "in principle" but in the messy and complex particularities in which specific people find themselves (Bloome, 2005); these particularities
matter at least as much as the general principles.

The particularities of a language and literacy learning event include the specific
people there, what they are specifically doing, their histories with each other and the
place in which they find themselves, what they have been talking about, what they are
now talking about, their specific bodies, the furniture in the place, the specific texts they
have in front of them, the physical condition of those texts, the specific emotional and
affective tenor they have brought with them and constructed, and so much more. All
of this is implicated in the meaningfulness of the social event they are constructing, of

the particular cognitive–linguistic–cultural literacy practices that are being made public and available for taking up, of the particular ways in which the students/children adapt, modify, and transform those cognitive–linguistic–cultural practices within and for the particular situations in which they find themselves (see Banquedano-Lopez, Solis, & Kattan, 2005; Becker, 2000; Pahl & Rowsell, 2005; Street, 1993; van Leeuwen, 2008).

As I read Chapter 1, it seemed to me that Paul, Wang, and Williams were continuously undermining dichotomies and supplanting them by a call to consider the particular child and the particular situation. For example, in discussing whether children who are d/Deaf and hard of hearing might have a reading disability or a reading difficulty, they dismiss such a dichotomy and instead argue that "this either–or syndrome or dichotomy is not only unproductive but also masks the complexity of developing proficiency in both English language and English literacy" and they call for "deciding the specific issues that need to be addressed for each child. These issues may indeed be both inside and outside the child" (p. 17). I wish that they had problematized the dichotomy of the "inside" versus the "outside." If they had done so, they would have had plenty of company (e.g., Bateson & Bateson, 2000; Bruner, 2008; Gee, 1992; Lave, 1996; Vygotsky, 1978; Wertsch, Del Río, & Alvarez, 1995). It will no longer do to view the mind as integral in and of itself, as somehow existing separate from the "outside," nor will it do to conceptualize the "outside" as if it is not the product and process of the human mind and human minds (both historically and in the present) in constant, reciprocal interaction with each and every human mind.

This discussion of "inside versus outside" leads me to one area of difference I have with Paul, Wang, and Williams. When they discuss "context" they refer to a series of categorical mediating variables (e.g., poverty, socioeconomic status, learning environment, gender, health, etc.) as if language and literacy learning occur in general and in principle "inside" and are mediated by contextual factors. Recent discussions of context (e.g., Duranti & Goodwin, 1992; Erickson & Shultz, 1977) have defined context otherwise. The boundaries between people and their activities and the contexts in which they act have been erased; what counts as central are the particularities of what specific people do in particular situations with each other, with all the complexities of those situations, social relationships, and connections to other events, situations, settings, and institutions. There is no "out there" out there; it is "here," "now," "in your head," "in your face," in the event, in the interaction; and it is here in particular and specific. Researchers and educators do not get to marginalize the particular situations in which people live nor the people with whom they live as if the real was "in general" and "in principle." The "in general" and "in principle" are the by-products of an ontological perspective, not an emic understanding of how particular people live their lives in particular spaces and times—and such an understanding is a critical foundation for any theorizing of language and literacy learning.

What Paul, Wang, and Williams insert into the particular events that specific people construct as they teach and learn language and literacy is a warranted argument about the equality of personhood for children and students who are d/Deaf and hard of hearing. The question to ask is not whether such an assertion is true; rather, what does it mean to insert such a claim with all its warrants into particular events with particular people? What, within particular situations for particular, specific people, does "similar" mean? If taken as a description of the given and extant realities of the particular lives, events, and histories of specific people it could be an absurdity, a non sequitor, an insult, and a platitude, or it could be a call to action. I take it as a call to action, a particular, warranted rhetoric that Paul, Wang, and Williams insert into the particularities of people's lives and events. What is at issue is how such a call to action, warranted "in general" and "in principle," can be taken up by whom, when, where, and how.

PRACTICE

Paul, Wang, and Williams write that "decoding without comprehension (i.e., constructing and extracting meaning) is not reading" (p. 135). This bold statement is key to their argument for equality in personhood. As they point out, early reading instruction has primarily focused on the decoding of written language into oral language and not on comprehension. Such a focus has been supported by national policy reports. There have been at least three unfortunate consequences to the focus of early reading instruction on decoding print into oral language. The first is the marginalization of reading for meaning for young children (they learn that reading in school is for the purpose of "accurate" oral performance instead of a search for meaning). Second, and key to the argument I make here, it establishes a hegemonic view of reading development (it happens this way, only this way, and it is natural, obvious, and inherent in the nature of being human). Third, it frames any deviation from this route to reading development as deficient and deficit. In the face of such deficit framing, Paul, Wang, and Williams assert that "the inability to hear does not, by itself, predict a child's cognitive ability or potential for learning" (p. 141).

There is a slippage from the way learning to read is organized in American schools (and schooling based on American models) to assumptions about reading development itself. Most reading instruction programs for young children begin with decoding written to oral language and only emphasize comprehension in later grades. This becomes the assumed inherent nature of reading development, supported by national policy documents that fail to recognize the slippage despite serious criticisms (see Camilli, Kim, & Vargas, 2008; Camilli, Vargas, & Yurecko, 2003; Garan, 2002).

Rather than view reading development as something inherently "inside," reading development can alternatively be framed as the ongoing learning (or acquisition) of a series of practices, ways of using language (spoken, written, through-the-air, signed, etc.) that involve both the "inside" and the "outside." (Indeed, having problematized the dichotomy between the "inside" and "outside" it is important to view the "inside" and "outside" as mutually defining each other.) Briefly, a practice can be defined as a cultural way of doing something. It is shared, public, and learned; it is a social construction held not by an individual per se but by a collective—a family, a classroom, a school, a community, a society, etc. As such, the practices of reading may be multiple (a collective may have a series of different ways of reading depending on the types of situation; the practice of reading in church differs from the practice of reading at bedtime with children, reading a legal brief, reading a love letter, etc.; see Baynham, 1995; Besnier,

1995; Pahl & Rowsell, 2005; Street, 1995 for discussion of reading practices). From this point of view, there is no such thing as "reading" outside of a practice. Reading at school is better characterized as school instruction reading practices (cf., Street & Street, 1991). There is not one school reading practice but multiple, differing school reading practices. Indeed, reading practices even within a classroom can vary, with different achievement-oriented reading groups acquiring different practices (see Borko & Eisenhart, 1987). What one learns in school are school reading practices; their applicability outside of school depends on the acquired communicative competence of people to recontextualize (cf. van Leeuwen, 2008) and adapt (cf. Banquedano-Lopez et al., 2005; Becker, 2000) school reading practices to other situations. Viewing reading development as the learning and acquisition of a set of practices involving written language defenestrates reading development as monolithic and the inherent marginalization of those who are not of the corpus on whom the dominant model of reading development was based.

For some reading and literacy scholars, a practice view of reading and a developmental view of reading are mutually exclusive perspectives. Not so: if the dichotomy of the "inside" and "outside" is problematized and if the centrality of a singular, "generalized" model of reading development is defenestrated, then theories of reading development can focus on multiple, diverse pathways centered on the acquisition of diverse repertoires of written language practices. Understanding that the foundations of reading development are themselves culturally, linguistically, and cognitively diverse and multiple is key to recognition of diverse pathways. One of the underlying concepts that require analysis and problematizing is time.

TIME

One of the subthemes in the book by Paul, Wang, and Williams is time. They employ terms such as *delay, timeline, mature, beginning school years, grades, development, timeframe, early literacy,* and *critical period,* among others. More subtle references to time can be found in their references to the Matthew effect, instructional programs, and the term *child* itself. Beyond their references to time, reading education in the United States and many other places around the world are framed and defined in terms of time (see Adam, 1990; Anderson-Levitt, 1996; Ben-Peretz & Bromme, 1990; Bloome, Beierle, Grigorenko, & Goldman, 2009; Lemke, 2000; Mercer, 2008). Consider the U.S. Department of Education's "Race to the Top" program, whose title embraces time as a competitive concept.

From my perspective, the narrative that Paul, Wang, and Williams promote with regard to the reading education of children and students who are d/Deaf and hard of hearing involves a different chronotope.

Chronotope is a term borrowed from the literary scholarship of Bakhtin (1981):

> We will give the name *chronotope* (literally, "time space") to the intrinsic connectedness of temporal and spatial relationships that are artistically expressed in literature . . . spatial and temporal indicators are fused into one carefully thought-out, concrete whole. [Time] thickens, takes on flesh, becomes artistically visible; likewise,

space becomes charged and responsive to the movements of time, plot, and history. . . . [I]t is precisely the chronotope that defines genre and generic distinctions. . . . The chronotope as a formally constitutive category determines to a significant degree the image of man [*sic*] in literature as well. The image of man [*sic*] is always intrinsically chronotopic. (pp. 84–85)

Chronotopes vary. In some literary works, the protagonist goes on a journey but neither the protagonist nor the world ages or changes. The sequencing of adventures the protagonist has does not matter. In other literary works, the sequence of events matters, the hero ages and changes, and so does the world. The movement through time and space can be linear, layered, inverted, and otherwise creatively constructed. Units of time can be consistent and uniform or varied, with particular moments of time greatly expanded juxtaposed with units of time that are fleeting. Chronotopes vary widely and it is part of the literary craft in the manufacture of a chronotope.

All narratives have an implied chronotope, including the narratives created by educational and reading researchers in their descriptions of (and prescriptions for) children's reading development. The thing to ask about a theory of reading development is not whether there is an implied chronotope but rather what the chronotope is and what its consequences are for defining what it means to be human and how reading development is defined within that framework of what it means to be human.

In an article examining the classroom experiences of children with special needs, Bloome and Katz (1997) note that classrooms and instructional programs are organized around differing chronotopes. They write (pp. 220–221)

Every literacy practice, including those at school, is grounded in a cultural conception of time and space. It is not just how students use time and space to read and write or how time and space constrain their reading and writing, but rather how conceptions of time and space define reading and writing practices, define readers and writers, and define reading and writing difficulties. For example, if the classroom chronotope is similar to "adventure-time," classroom literacy practices become adventures and obstacles to overcome, i.e., things that happen to the student without changing him or her (in the sense of character development or personal evolution). Reading and writing difficulties are obstacles the student was not able to overcome; time stops, and the student is stuck in that space. If time and space in the classroom are defined as goods to be accumulated and exchanged, then classroom literacy practices become consumer items to be acquired through barter. Reading and writing difficulties, within such a chronotope, are the lack of sufficient goods (time and space) to make the exchange, and the remediation of reading and writing difficulties becomes the provision of additional goods (time and space) or the bartering for social practices other than literacy practices. If the classroom chronotope is defined by community time and space (in terms of social action on the world outside the classroom), classroom literacy practices become tools for manipulating time and space, and reading and writing difficulties are defined by the inability of students to take action on the world and to make changes.

What if time is taken out of learning to read or reconceptualized as contingent on the task? For example, consider those reading practices in which readers are engaged, alone or with others, in reading a religious text in which what matters is the engagement itself and not how quickly one read it or how many comprehension questions one answered correctly at the end of the passage. Time in such situations is not something to be conquered but a condition to be savored. Similarly so, bedtime story reading can be a time for parents and children to savor loving relationships in which books are the props for being so; unless bedtime story reading is recontextualized within a school chronotope in which it becomes merely a part of a "race to the top" and the loving relationships get demoted to facilitative, mediating factors.

In part, it is holding the unreflected chronotope that allows the reading development of children who d/Deaf and hard of hearing, among others, to be viewed as inherently having reading difficulties and reading disabilities, as being cognitively less than their peers. However, it will not do to merely wish away dominant educational chronotopes. They must be supplanted by other chronotopes, and both educators and students must be helped to understand how to move through time and space in ways with new chronotopes based on the recognition of equality of personhood.

PART–WHOLE RELATIONSHIPS

Fundamental to any ethnographic study is inquiry about the relationships of parts and wholes. For example, it is not sufficient to study instruction on vocabulary in particular without exploring what larger "wholes" of which such instruction is a part. It may be part of a broader scheme for the teaching of reading and/or part of an institutional response to high-stakes testing; the social organization of the particular way in which vocabulary instruction is done in that particular school may be part of a sorting process in that school and community that will provide academic advantages to some students based on a cultural ideology of differential and hierarchical intellectual ability. It may be part of an effort to be "scientific" and "research based" and thus support the identity of the educators as "professional," distinguishing them from other people who cannot claim such an identity. It may be part of a broader definition of reading held locally and nationally; it may be part of a response to a federally sponsored funding program and thereby diminish a sense of local community with a sense of national community. Or, it may be none of these. Whatever the relationship of the part to the whole (and the whole to the parts), no part is sufficiently defined (nor methodologically adequate) without documenting the relationship of part and whole.

It is not easy to document or describe the relationship of parts and wholes as such relationships are often dynamic and frequently contested. Consider the issues of language raised by Paul, Wang, and Williams as they might get played out in a particular classroom for children and students who are d/Deaf and hard of hearing. Some people may be constructing a relationship between the instruction of those students and a broader ideology contesting a deficit framing of those students; others might be constructing a relationship emphasizing integration, assimilation, and finding their place within the broader society; others might be constructing a relationship of self-sufficiency, pride, and community with others who are d/Deaf and hard of hearing; and still others may be viewing the instruction within a whole primarily concerned with efficient resource distribution.

The relationships between part and wholes are not given, but are constructed by people as they act and interact with each other within the various positions they hold. The particular way a teacher organizes her instruction, the texts she chooses for her students to read, and the particular way she communicates with parents may all be part—knowingly or otherwise—of how the teacher is attempting to construct a relationship between what happens in her classroom with larger wholes. Her efforts only matter if others take them up, and as they take them up they will reshape the teacher's efforts of constructing a relationship of parts to whole. Similarly so, a school board president may promulgate particular policies attempting to construct a relationship between a broader economic whole for the community or municipality and the particular classrooms within the school district. Perhaps the school board president attempts to create and implement policies that will educate the particular students in her school district for the needs of businesses in that community. However, the particular whole–part construction promulgated by the school board president only matters if and how those proposals are taken up by others.

In brief, it is not so much a description of part–whole relationships as it is a description of how part–whole relationships are being constructed, by whom, when, where, how, and with what consequences. It is this recognition that part–whole relationships are constructed by people within the particular situations in which they locate themselves that makes it difficult to be optimistic about Paul, Wang, and Williams's argument about literacy learning and the equality of personhood of children and students who are d/Deaf and hard of hearing. How their construction of the part (the QSH) is taken up by others in construction of the whole (the relationship of reading and literacy to personhood within our society) will be key in who benefits, when, and where. More simply stated, what happens in a particular classroom is important and cannot be discounted, but it is not enough. What happens in particular classrooms needs to also incorporate construction of a relationship between the part (the local) and the whole (the macro), and it is in those constructions that equality of personhood will be taken up (or not) and defined, and the economic, cultural, social, intellectual, and linguistic benefits a society has to offer be distributed. More succinctly stated, equality "in general" and "in principle" may be a beginning, but it is not a lived equality and in abstraction it is not an equality on which children or students can rely.

Final Comments

There have been many discussions in educational research about how diverse perspectives might be brought together. In some discussions of how ethnographic and qualitative research might be brought together with research oriented to generalizations and decontextualized principles, one approach has been to conceptualize ethnographic and qualitative research as providing grounded questions and hypotheses that might be tested through generalizing research and clinical studies. Such a scheme has the inherent problem of translating constructs generated through different epistemological frames (and chronotopes) into those of generalizing research and clinical studies. In brief, it is liable to be merely an exercise in interpellation (cf. Althusser, 1971; see Bloome, Katz, Solsken, Willett, & Wilson-Keenan, 2000).

Bloome, Carter, Christian, Otto, and Shuart-Faris (2005) write that there are four ways in which relationships among different traditions and perspectives can be constructed. The first is that one perspective subsumes the other, redefining the other so that the substance of meaning of the other is lost and only the accouterments remain (an example of which is briefly discussed in the preceding paragraph). The second is parallel play. The perspectives exist side by side, with researchers holding all of them in mind although there is no substantive integration. The third is the null set; the different perspectives exist and are recognized, but no meaningful relationship is created among them. The fourth is the creation of a new perspective generated by the synergy of juxtaposing the different perspectives.

In my view, educational change is not so much a rules and principles process (as in, follow these rules and principles) as a learning from cases process. To make an analogy with playing chess, a novice can learn how to play chess by following the rules for how the pieces move and some general principles of play, but that novice will never become a good chess player until she studies actual games played by masters and others. It is in the studying of actual games, in exploring the particular moves made in particular games, that one begins to recognize patterns and schemes that can be applied to the analysis of one's own games. Of course, one's own games are never going to be exactly like those one has studied. The point is not reproduction. One needs to become adept at applying to one's own games the sequences and patterns one has extracted from the study of others' games. In my view, this is similarly so in educational change whether at the classroom, school, district, state, or national levels. As Robinson wrote more than 25 years ago,

> It will no longer do, I think, to consider literacy as some abstract, absolute quality attainable through tutelage and the accumulation of knowledge and experience. It will no longer do to think of reading as a solitary act in which a mainly passive reader responds to cues in a text to find meaning. It will no longer do to think of writing as a mechanical manipulation of grammatical codes and formal structures leading to the production of perfect or perfectible texts. Reading and writing are not unitary skills nor are the reducible to sets of component skills falling neatly under discrete categories (linguistic, cognitive); rather, they are complex human activities taking place in complex human relationships. (1987, p. 329)

Note: David Bloome is EHE Distinguished Professor of Teaching and Learning in the Department of Teaching and Learning of the Ohio State University College of Education and Human Ecology. Bloome's research focuses on how people use spoken and written language for learning in classroom and nonclassroom settings and how people use language to create and maintain social relationships, to construct knowledge, and to create communities, social institutions, and shared histories and futures. Building on sociolinguistic, anthropological, and cognitive perspectives of language and literacy learning, Bloome's research focuses on children in preschool, early elementary, middle childhood, and early adolescence. He is a former president of the National Council of Teachers of English and of the National Conference on Research in Language and Literacy. He is a former middle school and high school teacher. He is the director of the Center for Video Ethnography and Discourse Analysis, director of the Columbus

Area Writing Project, former coeditor of *Reading Research Quarterly*, and founding editor of *Linguistics and Education: An International Research Journal*. In 2008, Bloome was inducted into the Reading Hall of Fame. He is the coauthor of six books, editor or coeditor of five books on language and literacy in education, and author or coauthor of numerous journal articles and book chapters. Bloome's current scholarship focuses on four areas related to writing and reading education: (1) the social construction of intertextuality as part of the reading, writing, and learning processes, (2) discourse analysis as a means for understanding reading, writing, and literacy events in and outside of classrooms, (3) narrative development among young children as a foundation for learning and literacy development in schools, and (4) students as researchers and ethnographers of their own communities.

REFERENCES

Adam, B. (1990). *Time and social theory*. Philadelphia, PA: Temple University Press.

Althusser, L. (1971). *Lenin and philosophy and other essays*. London, England: Unwin.

Anderson-Levitt, K. (1996). Behind schedule: Batch-produced children in French and U.S. classrooms. In B. A. Levinson, D. E. Foley, & D. C. Holland (Eds.), *The cultural production of the educated person: Critical ethnographies of schooling and local practice* (pp. 57–78). Albany, NY: State University of New York Press.

Bakhtin, M. (1981). *The dialogic imagination*. Trans. C. Emerson & M. Holquist. Austin, TX: University of Texas Press.

Banquedano-Lopez, P., Solis, J., & Kattan, S. (2005). Adaptation: The language of classroom learning. *Linguistics and Education, 16*, 1–26.

Bateson, G., & Bateson, M. C. (2000). *Steps to an ecology of mind*. Chicago, IL: University of Chicago Press.

Baynham, M. (1995). *Literacy practices*. London, England: Longman.

Becker, A. (1988). Language in particular: A lecture. In D. Tannen (Ed.), *Linguistics in context* (pp. 17–35). Norwood, NJ: Ablex.

Becker, H. (2000). The etiquette of improvisation. *Mind, Culture and Activity, 7*(3), 171–176.

Ben-Peretz, M., & Bromme, R. (Eds.). (1990). *The nature of time in schools: Theoretical concepts, practitioner perceptions*. New York, NY: Teachers College Press.

Besnier, N. (1995). *Literacy, emotion, and authority*. Cambridge, England: Cambridge University Press.

Bloome, D. (2005). Introductions to the study of classroom language and literacy, in particular. In R. Beach et al. (Eds.), *Multidisciplinary perspectives on literacy research* (pp. 275–292). Cresskill, NJ: Hampton Press.

Bloome, D., Beierle, M., Grigorenko, M., & Goldman, S. (2009). Learning over time: Uses of intercontextuality, collective memories, and classroom chronotopes in the construction of learning opportunities in a ninth grade language arts classroom. *Language and Education, 23*(4), 313–334.

Bloome, D., Carter, S., Christian, B., Otto, S., & Shuart-Faris, N. (2005). *Discourse analysis and the study of classroom language and literacy events: A microethnographic approach*. Mahwah, NJ: Erlbaum.

Bloome, D., & Katz, L. (1997). Literacy as social practice and classroom chronotopes. *Reading and Writing Quarterly, 13*(3), 205–225.

Bloome, D., Katz, L., Solsken, J., Willett, J., & Wilson-Keenan, J. (2000). Interpellations of family/community and classroom literacy practices. *Journal of Educational Research, 93*(3), 155–164.

Borko, H., & Eisenhart, M. (1987). Reading ability groups as literacy communities. In D. Bloome (Ed.), *Classrooms and literacy* (pp. 107–134). Norwood, NJ: Ablex.

Bruner, J. (2008). Culture and mind: Their fruitful incommensurability. *Ethos, 36*(1), 29–45.

Camilli, G., Kim, S. H., & Vargas, S. (2008). A response to Steubing et al. "Effects of systematic phonics instruction are practically significant": The origin of the National Reading Panel. *Educational Policy Analysis Archives. 16*(16). Retrieved March 13, 2013, from http://www.eric. ed.gov/PDFS/EJ809416.pdf

Camilli, G., Vargas, S., & Yurecko, M. (2003). Teaching children to read: The fragile link between science and federal education policy. *Education Policy Analysis Archives, 11*(15). Retrieved from http://epaa.asu.edu/ojs/article/view/243.

Duranti, A., & Goodwin, C. (Eds.). (1992). *Rethinking context: Language as an interactive phenomenon.* Cambridge, England: Cambridge University Press.

Erickson, F., & Shultz, J. (1977). When is a context? *Newsletter of the Laboratory for Comparative Human Cognition, 1*(2), 5–12.

Garan, E. (2002). *Resisting reading mandates: How to triumph with the truth.* Portsmouth, NH: Heinemann.

Gee, J. P. (1992). *The social mind: Language, ideology, and social practice.* New York, NY: Bergin & Garvey.

Kim, M. (2012). Intertextuality and narrative practices of young deaf students in classroom contexts: A microethnographic study. *Reading Research Quarterly, 47*(4), 404–426.

Lave, J. (1996). Teaching, as learning, in practice. *Mind, Culture, and Activity, 3*(3), 149–164.

Lemke, J. (2000). Across the scales of time: Artifacts, activities, and meanings in ecosocial systems. *Mind, Culture, and Activity, 7*(4), 273–290.

Marshall, M. (1996). Problematizing impairment: Cultural competence in the Carolines. *Ethnology, 35*(4) 249–263.

Maxwell, M. (1985). Some functions and uses of literacy in the deaf community. *Language in Society, 14*(2), 205–221.

Mercer, N. (2008). The seeds of time: Why classroom dialogue needs a temporal analysis. *Journal of the Learning Sciences, 17,* 33–59.

Miller, P. J. (2001). Enacting stories, seeing worlds: Similarities and differences in the cross-cultural narrative development of linguistically isolated deaf children. *Human Development, 44,* 311–336.

Pahl, K., & Rowsell, J. (2005). *Literacy and education: Understanding the new literacy studies in the classroom.* London, England: Paul Chapman.

Poveda, D., Pulido, L., Morgade, M., Messina, C., & Hédlová, Z. (2008). Storytelling with sign language interpretation as a multimodal literacy event: Implications for deaf and hearing children. *Language and Education, 22*(4), 320–342.

Ramsey, C., & Padden, C. (1998). Natives and newcomers: Gaining access to literacy in a classroom for deaf children. *Anthropology and Education Quarterly, 29*(1), 5–24.

Robinson, J. L. (1987). Literacy in society: Readers and writers in the worlds of discourse. In D. Bloome (Ed.), *Literacy and schooling* (pp. 327–353). Norwood, NJ: Ablex.

Senghas, R. J., & Monaghan, L. (2002). Signs of their times: Deaf communities and the culture of language. *Annual Review of Anthropology,* 69–97.

Street, B. (Ed.). (1993). *Cross-cultural approaches to literacy.* Cambridge, UK: Cambridge University Press.

Street, B. (1995). *Social literacies.* London, UK: Longman.

Street, B., & Street, J. (1991). The schooling of literacy. In D. Barton & R. Ivanic (Eds.), *Writing in the community* (pp. 143–166). London, England: Sage.

Van Leeuwen, T. (2008). *Discourse and practice: New tools for critical discourse analysis.* Oxford, England: Oxford University Press.

Vygotsky, L. S. (1978). *Mind in society.* Cambridge, MA: Harvard University Press.

Wertsch, J. V., Del Río, P., & Alvarez, A. (Eds.). (1995). *Sociocultural studies of mind.* Cambridge, England: Cambridge University Press.

Wilcox, S. (1994). Struggling for a voice: An interactionist view of language and literacy in Deaf education. In V. John-Steiner, C. P. Panofsky, & L. W. Smith (Eds.), *Sociocultural approaches to language and literacy: An interactionist perspective* (pp. 109–138). Cambridge, England: Cambridge University Press.

ESSAY 2

The Promises and Potential Vulnerabilities of the Qualitative Similarity Hypothesis
Kouider Mokhtari and Carla A. Reichard

In this essay, we examine the promises and vulnerabilities of the qualitative similarity hypothesis (QSH) construct as delineated by Paul, Wang, and Williams. Even though the book focuses primarily on the validity of the QSH construct for developing English language and literacy by children and adolescents who are d/Deaf and Hard of Hearing (d/Dhh), our response takes into account the construct's potential for all students, including English learners. In our review, which focuses primarily on content presented in Chapters 1, 3, 4, and 7, we note that the QSH construct has substantial merit and that it has practical implications for effectively addressing the language and literacy needs of all students, including those who have identified language and learning needs. In light of the challenges and complexities involved in studying children and adolescents who are d/Dhh, we further argue that even though QSH has ample extant theoretical and research support, further validation of the construct should be subjected to more rigorous empirical testing. Finally, we conclude by recognizing the complexities involved in becoming literate in any language and recommend that the field of literacy is a critical area of research and scholarship that needs to be investigated by scholars beyond the boundaries of the traditional reading and writing education fields.

Book Content Overview

Paul, Wang, and Williams examine the validity of the QSH and its potential for helping d/Dhh individuals develop their English language and literacy skills. The essence of the QSH, according to the authors is that (a) the acquisition of English language and literacy by any individual, including d/Dhh individuals, is developmentally similar to that of typical native English speakers/learners, (b) there is a set of fundamental skills that help develop or enhance the English language and literacy learning processes, and (c) these fundamental skills apply to learning to read and write in English as a first and a second language. These essential concepts have important implications for effectively addressing the English language and literacy needs and challenges of all children, including d/Dhh individuals.

THE DIFFERENCE THIS BOOK MAKES

This book is unique. To our knowledge, there are no books that address the construct of a qualitative similarity hypothesis. Designed for researchers, teacher educators, and language and literacy professionals who work with d/Dhh students, this book presents essentials for teachers of d/Dhh students to support their English language and literacy development. Each chapter clearly lays out answers to pressing questions about the validity of QSH and its implications for addressing the language and literacy challenges of all students, pointing out that teachers should be more focused on how best to address student needs and less worried about determining whether these students have "reading disabilities" or "reading difficulties" (see Chapter 1). As well, the authors maintain that despite the various controversies that exist in the field with respect to what contributes most to successful language and literacy acquisition among English learners, there are striking similarities when it comes to developing reading comprehension skills. Comparable to monolingual peers, academic vocabulary skills appear to be a significant challenge for these students regardless of whether they are hearing or d/Dhh English learners (see Chapter 3). In Chapter 4, the authors examined research on emergent and conventional literacy for children and adolescents with and without hearing challenges. They provide evidence showing that barring differences in developmental progress growth patterns, children and adolescents with hearing challenges develop emergent as well as conventional literacy skills in much the same way as their hearing peers. Finally, in Chapter 7, the authors offer constructive insights with respect to understanding and conducting research in language and literacy with children and adolescents who are d/Dhh. They point out that while standard research methods and paradigms can be used equally well with children and adolescents with or without hearing loss, conducting research with students who are d/Dhh poses unique challenges that require greater synergies across epistemologies and research designs.

Its broad yet thorough view of theory, process, and research that support the notion of QSH among students with and without hearing loss distinguishes this book. The authors do an outstanding job in taking the discussions of issues pertaining to QSH across the disciplines of first-language acquisition, second-language learning, first- and second-language literacy development, speech and hearing sciences, and other human learning sciences. The fact that the book is based on theory and research informing QSH allows researchers and practitioners to understand how QSH is grounded and how theory can be actualized in the classroom. Thus, the book fills an important gap for a coherent, theoretically consistent, and research-based portrait of how d/Dhh children acquire literacy knowledge and skills.

THE PROMISE OF THE QUALITATIVE SIMILARITY HYPOTHESIS

The QSH construct has great intellectual merit from both theoretical and research standpoints. The construct also has practical implications for effectively addressing the language and literacy needs of all students, including those with documented language and learning needs. The authors make a very strong case for the notion that the acquisition of English language and literacy by any individual is developmentally similar to that of typical native English speakers, that a set of critical fundamental skills exists that helps develop or enhance the English language and literacy learning processes, and that these fundamental skills apply to learning to read and write in English as a first and a second language. Support for these arguments comes from various fields of inquiry, including linguistics and literacy. For illustration, we offer three examples from linguistics and literacy, respectively, in support for the QSH construct.

The first example pertains to the notion of "language universals." Linguistics scholars (e.g., Chomsky, 1965; Chomsky & Halle, 1991; Halle, 1962) identify various types of language universals. Some of the most relevant language universals are the so-called absolute universals, which comprise certain aspects of language (e.g., vowels, verbs, pronouns) generally found in all known human languages. When considering absolute universals, Chomsky maintains that the organization of human communication would be impossible unless every language manifested these particular linguistic structures. In his theory of universal grammar, he offers an explanation based on the innate predispositions of human beings, arguing that language constitutes an independent faculty of the mind that embodies certain highly specific structural properties. The fact that certain aspects of language appear to be manifested universally is thus explained in the context of biological development. In line with this approach, it is often argued that every child manages to acquire a highly complex linguistic system within a relatively short space of time and comes to demonstrate linguistic knowledge, which could not possibly have been acquired on the basis of experience alone.

The second example comes from the field of literacy and pertains specifically to the issue of transfer of language and literacy skills and strategies across languages when learning to read and write. Researchers agree that reading comprehension skills and strategies have a long and important history in first- and second-language learning thanks to the work of August and Shanahan (2006), Pressley and Afflerback (1995), Jimenez, Garcia, and Pearson (1996), and many others. It is generally agreed that possessing literacy skills in a first language aids the development of second-language literacy skills, and indeed, there are many studies that support this argument. For instance, Jimenez et al. (1996) found that good readers effectively transferred knowledge back and forth between Spanish and English, using cognates as well as translation strategies. Taileffer and Pugh (1998) examined the reading strategies of students reading in English as a second language. They found that students transferred first-language reading comprehension strategies into second-language reading. They further found that good first-language reading strategies could compensate for weak second-language learning proficiency, a finding consistent with the compensatory models of reading and language learning. In a design similar to that of Taileffer and Pugh, Mokhtari and Reichard (2004) showed that similar reading comprehension strategies were used by first- and second-language college readers most specifically at higher levels of proficiency, suggesting that first- and second-language reading tends to become more qualitatively similar at greater levels of language proficiency.

Finally, whether one is thinking about the processes involved in learning to read in a first or a second language, or considering the needs of typically developing readers or readers with special language or hearing needs, it is important to keep in mind that one of the most compelling findings in reading research is that children who get off to a slow start in reading rarely catch up with their peers. As several studies have shown, poor first-grade readers almost invariably continue to be poor readers (e.g., Francis, Shaywitz, Stuebing, Shaywitz, & Fletcher, 1996; Torgesen, 1998). This pattern of behavior is, to a great extent, true for first-language readers, second-language readers, and students who are d/Dhh—and this is quite consistent with the major tenets of the QSH.

Potential Vulnerabilities of the Qualitative Similarity Hypothesis

As we noted previously, the QSH has its well-deserved intellectual merits. On the other hand, it has had its share of vulnerabilities. In recent years, the construct has been subjected to some criticism by a group of scholars representing cross-disciplinary fields at the University of Toronto and Gallaudet University. Some of these scholars recently examined some of the major tenets of the QSH, especially as they pertain to addressing the needs of d/Dhh students. The main criticism appears to be focused on the role of phonology during the early reading development stages for students with hearing challenges. The main thrust of these criticisms, which are described in a series of published articles (e.g., Allen et al., 2009; Hall, Ferreira, & Mayberry, 2012; Kargin et al., 2012; Mayberry, del Giudice, & Lieberman, 2010; Miller & Clark, 2011), are focused on the relations of phonemic awareness and phonological decoding to reading development in students who are d/Dhh. The gist of most of the criticism leveled at the QSH construct is rooted in the finding that many highly skilled readers who are d/Dhh do not show evidence of using phonemic awareness and phonological coding when recognizing written words (e.g., Mayberry et al., 2010; Miller & Clark, 2011). Research conducted by these scholars indicates that while the ability to identify speech sounds and associate them with spelling patterns can be helpful in learning to read, this skill has been found to play a minor role. As well, these researchers argue that students who are d/Dhh, much like their hearing peers, need other basic skills such as language comprehension and memory for language, as well as a lot of time reading. These variables have been found to play larger roles in reading development.

We find these criticisms perplexing when considering the key tenets of the QSH, which take into account layers of language beyond the sound system of language, namely word-level skills (e.g., morphological awareness) and sentence-level skills (e.g., syntactic or grammatical awareness). In fact, research indicates that both morphological awareness and syntactic awareness contribute significantly to the process of learning to read and comprehend what one reads for students varying in language and literacy proficiencies. In other words, morphological processing contributes directly to language comprehension. Readers who "know" the internal structure of words have a distinct advantage not only in word decoding but also in vocabulary and comprehension. Snow, Burns, and Griffin (1998) maintain that knowledge of morphology is important because it helps readers connect word forms and meanings within the structure of sentences. For example, "children learn that events having already occurred are marked by morphological inflections such as 'ed'. For children, sensitivity to morphology may be an important support skill in reading and spelling" (p. 74).

Similarly, recent advances in language and literacy research suggest that while vocabulary knowledge deficits are at the core of reading problems among upper-grade students, deficits in metalinguistic awareness skills such as syntactic or grammatical awareness, here defined as children's understanding of the syntactic structure of sentences and their ability to deliberately reflect on and manipulate that structure, are likely to play a larger role in explaining reading comprehension variance than originally assumed (e.g., Cain, 2010; Scott, 2004; Tunmer & Bowey, 1984). In fact, syntactic awareness has been shown to aid reading comprehension in direct ways such as when attempting to comprehend words within individual sentences and integrating the meaning of multiple sentences in larger units of texts, as well as in indirect ways such as when making grammaticality judgments or correcting grammatical errors in sentences (e.g., Tunmer & Bowey, 1984). Poor readers have been shown to differ on a number of syntactic processing tasks (e.g., sentence correction, grammaticality judgments) and these differences, according to some researchers (e.g., Tunmer & Bowey, 1984) suggest the existence of a syntactic processing deficit among some struggling readers. These findings provide support for the notion that all students, including those with hearing impediments, go through similar processes when learning to read, and those processes include developing an awareness of aspects of language that go beyond the phonemic or sound layers of language. We concur with the authors of the QSH that phonological awareness is a necessary but not sufficient condition for learning to read by typically developing readers as well as by readers who find learning to read difficult.

SUMMARY AND IMPLICATIONS

In summary, we have argued that the QSH makes a significant contribution to the field of first- and second-language and literacy. Although not entirely new (see Stanovich's Matthew effect and developmental lag hypothesis constructs [Stanovich, 1986]), the notions that the acquisition of English language and literacy by any individual is qualitatively similar to that of typical native English speakers and that a set of essential fundamental skills underlie the development of English language and literacy learning processes hold great promise for explaining the processes involved in learning to read among various types of learners. The key tenets of the QSH construct also have important implications for effectively addressing the English language and literacy needs and challenges of all children, including d/Dhh individuals.

    One of the most obvious implications of the QSH is that schools and families should focus on early identification and prevention of language and reading difficulties in young children, including d/Dhh children, experiencing literacy problems. The best solution to the problem of reading failure, according to literacy researcher Joe Torgeson, is for schools to allocate resources for early identification and prevention (Torgeson, 1998, 2004). Indeed, as we indicated earlier, early identification of children at risk of having reading difficulty is critical, as research has shown that it is unlikely they will ever fully catch up.

A related implication of the QSH construct pertains to addressing critical layers of language beyond phonology. These layers of language include developing students' awareness of how words are formed (i.e., morphological awareness) as well as how sentences are structured (i.e., syntactic awareness). Learning to read does not stop at third grade. Once students develop basic word decoding skills, they need to learn aspects of language that will enable them not only to read words accurately and fluently but also to understand what they read. Results of research completed during the past two decades or so have provided evidence that some developing readers (estimates vary from 10 to 15%) turn out to be poor comprehenders despite their performance on phonemic awareness tasks and their ability to read words rapidly and accurately (Nation & Snowling, 1999). Snow, Burns, and Griffin (1998) stated that "the picture that is emerging is of a group of children who have difficulties with language comprehension but unlike many children with severe language impairment, poor comprehenders read accurately and have good phonemic (speech) processing skills" (p. 549). This research has shown that phonemic awareness is a necessary but not sufficient condition for proficient reading. Indeed, recent advances in reading research suggest that while phonemic deficits are at the core of some specific reading problems, deficits in morphological and syntactic skills are likely to play a larger role than originally assumed (e.g., Carlisle, 2010; Scott, 2004).

Finally, we conclude by pointing to an important implication for further research that might help enhance our understanding of the processes involved in becoming literate by all students, including those with hearing loss. It is evident that literacy development is a critical area for research and scholarship that draws from various fields of inquiry that are beyond the traditional borders of the literacy education field. These fields include but are not limited to languages and linguistics, speech and hearing sciences, educational and cognitive psychology, and other human learning sciences. The field of literacy has progressed at a remarkable speed during the past few decades. However, it would benefit a great deal from models and theories of literacy development that draw from these cross-disciplinary fields.

Note: Kouider Mokhtari serves as the Anderson-Vukelja-Wright Endowed Professor of Education within the School of Education at The University of Texas at Tyler, where he engages in research, teaching, and service initiatives aimed at enhancing teacher practice and increasing student literacy achievement outcomes. His research focuses on the acquisition of language and literacy by first- and second-language learners, with particular emphasis on children, adolescents, and adults who can read but have difficulties understanding what they read. His research has been published in books (e.g., *Reading Strategies of First and Second Language Learners: See How They Read*, with Ravi Sheory, 2008; and *Preparing Every Teacher to Reach English Learners*, with Joyce Nutta and Carine Strebel, 2012), as well as journals such as *The Reading Teacher, Journal of Adolescent and Adult Literacy, Journal of Educational Psychology, Canadian Modern Language Review, Journal of Research in Reading,* and *System: An International Journal of Educational Technology and Applied Linguistics.* His coauthored book *Preparing Every Teacher to Reach English Learners* has been selected for the 2013 AACTE Outstanding Book Award. The award recognizes exemplary books that make a significant contribution to the knowledge base of educator preparation or of teaching and learning with implications for educator preparation. He currently serves as co-chair of the Literacy and English Learners Committee of the International Reading Association, whose work is focused on enhancing the education of English learners. He also serves as coeditor of *Tapestry: An International Cross-disciplinary Journal,* which is dedicated to the advancement of research and instruction for English language learners.

Carla Reichard is assistant director of Sponsored Research at The University of Texas at Tyler. Her research interests include metacognition, measurement, and student retention.

REFERENCES

Allen, T., Clark, M. D., del Giudice, A., Koo, D., Lieberman, A., Mayberry, R., & Miller, P. (2009). Phonology and reading: A response to Wang, Trezek, Luckner, and Paul. *American Annals of the Deaf, 154*(4), 338–345.

August, D., & Shanahan, T. (Eds.). (2006). *Developing literacy in second-language learners: A report of the National Literacy Panel on Language-Minority Children and Youth.* Mahwah, NJ: Lawrence Erlbaum.

Cain, K. (2010). *Reading development and difficulties.* West Sussex, England: British Psychological Society.

Carlisle, J. F. (2010). An integrative review of the effects of instruction in morphological awareness on literacy achievement. *Reading Research Quarterly, 45*(4), 464–487.

Chomsky, N., & Halle, M. (1991). *The sound pattern of English.* New York, NY: Harper & Row.

Chomsky, N. (1965). *Aspects of the theory of syntax.* Cambridge, Massachusetts: MIT Press.

Francis, D. J., Shaywitz, S. E., Stuebing, K. K., Shaywitz, B. A., & Fletcher, J. M. (1996). Developmental lag versus deficit models of reading disability: A longitudinal, individual growth curves analysis. *Journal of Educational Psychology, 88,* 3–17.

Hall, M., Ferreira, V., & Mayberry, R. (2012). Phonological similarity judgments in ASL: Evidence for maturational constraints on phonetic perception in sign. *Sign Language & Linguistics, 15*(1), 104–127.

Halle, M. (1962). Phonology and generative grammar. *Word, 18,* 54–72.

Jiménez, R. T., Garcia, G. E., & Pearson, P. D. (1996). The reading strategies of bilingual Latina/o students who are successful English readers: Opportunities and obstacles. *Reading Research Quarterly, 57*(6), 576–578.

Kargin, T., Guldenoglu, B., Miller, P., Hauser, P., Rathman, C., Kubus, O., & Spurgeon, E. (2012). Differences in word processing skills of deaf and hearing individuals reading in different orthographies. *Journal of Developmental Physical Disabilities, 24,* 65–83.

Mayberry, R., del Guidice, A., & Lieberman, A. (2010). Reading achievement in relation to phonological coding and awareness in deaf readers: A meta-analysis. *Journal of Deaf Studies and Deaf Education, 16*(2), 164–188.

Miller, P., & Clark, D. (2011). Phonemic awareness is not necessary to become a skilled deaf reader. *Journal of Developmental Physical Disabilities, 23,* 459–476.

Mokhtari, K., & Reichard, C. (2004). Investigating the strategic reading processes of first and second language readers in two different cultural contexts. *System: An International Journal of Educational Technology and Applied Linguistics, 32*(3), 379–394.

Nation, K., & Snowling, M. J. (1999). Developmental differences in sensitivity to semantic relations among good and poor comprehenders: Evidence from semantic priming. *Cognition, 70,* B1–13.

Pressley, M., & Afflerbach, P. (1995). *Verbal protocols of reading: The nature of constructively responsive reading.* Hillsdale, NJ: Lawrence Erlbaum.

Scott, C. (2004). Syntactic contributions to literacy learning. In C. A. Stone, E. R. Silliman, B. J. Ehren, & K. Apel (Eds.), *Handbook of language and literacy: Development and disorders* (pp. 340–362). New York, NY: Gilford Press.

Snow, C. E., Burns, M. S., & Griffin, P. (1998). *Preventing reading difficulties in young children.* Washington, DC: National Academy Press.

Stanovich, K. E. (1986). Matthew effects in reading: Some consequences of individual differences in the acquisition of literacy. *Reading Research Quarterly, 21,* 360–407.

Taillefer, G., & Pugh, T. (1998). Strategies for professional learning in L1 and L2. *Journal of Research in Reading, 21*(2), 96–108.

Torgesen, J. K. (2004). Avoiding the devastating downward spiral: The evidence that early intervention prevents reading failure. *American Educator, 28*(3), 6–19.

Torgeson, J. K. (1998). Catch them before they fall: Identification and assessment to prevent reading failure. *American Educator, 22*(1-2), 32–39.

Tunmer, W. E., & Bowey, J. A. (1984). Metalinguistic awareness and reading acquisition. In W. E. Tunmer, C. Pratt, & M. L. Herriman (Eds.), *Metalinguistic awareness in children* (pp. 144–168). New York, NY: Springer-Verlag.

9

Conclusion: Reflections and Directions

All intelligent thoughts have already been thought; what is necessary is only to try to think them again.

—Johann Wolfgang Von Goethe

The qualitative similarity hypothesis (QSH) is not a novel construct—whether it (as well as other developmental similarity models) qualifies as one of the "intelligent thoughts" that should be reexamined is left to the judgment of our readers and the community of researchers and theorists invested in exploring the development of English language and English literacy. To minimize misinterpretations and to obtain an adequate understanding of the QSH, we emphasize that there are macro and micro subconstructs, which should be discussed and investigated separately as well as in unison.

In this chapter, we summarize the salient tenets of the QSH with respect to the development of English language and literacy, particularly in d/Deaf and hard of hearing (d/Dhh) children and adolescents and in other children who are labeled as struggling readers and writers. We highlight the theoretical background of the QSH and relate this to the constructs of disciplinary structure (or knowledge) and critical period. Then, we proceed with the research and educational implications for developing English language and literacy skills. Much of this synthesis is based on the information that has been presented in Chapters 1 to 7.

With this springboard, we respond to the gist of several selective remarks in the essays of the reactants in Chapter 8. Areas of agreement are reflective of the complexity and viability of the QSH and the need for further research within the micro and macro components. We argue that the points of disagreement or dissensions are mostly due to a lingering misunderstanding of some of our assertions, as noted also in one of the reactants' essays (Mokhtari & Reichard, Chapter 8). However, a few of the dissensions are also due to differences emerging from epistemological and metaphysical underpinnings, as per our interpretations of selected statements from the other reactant's essay (Bloome, Chapter 8). These different world views or mental frameworks—if not addressed carefully—can lead to unproductive debates and limited progress in the understanding, development, and improvement of English for all children (e.g., Noddings, 2007; Pring, 2004; Ritzer, 2001).

In the last section of this chapter, we proffer directions for further research on the merits of the QSH in light of research on other similar constructs (e.g., Stanovich's developmental lag hypothesis [e.g., 1988]). Despite the caveats inherent in the degraded input hypotheses associated with the use of English signing and cochlear implants (e.g., LaSasso, Crain, & Leybaert, 2010; Leybaert & LaSasso, 2010), we agree with Mayer and Leigh (2010) that future researchers and scholars need to work with an evolving cohort of d/Dhh children and adolescents who possess demographics that are quite different from those of the previous cohorts due to advancements in technology (i.e., early detection and amplification) and early intervention programs.

With respect to further research, this range of demographics in the new cohort of d/Dhh students will influence the contents of debates on the meanings of the word *d/Deaf* (e.g., Paul & Moores, 2010, 2012a) and cause the line of demarcation between *deaf* and *hard of hearing* to become blurry and, possibly, indistinguishable. In addition, there will be controversial and varying interpretations of the question "Can it be a good thing to be deaf?" (e.g., Cooper, 2012), especially when comparing the achievement levels associated with English language and literacy of d/Dhh students to those of peers who are typical learners. Of course, as we argued in Chapter 7, these assertions will become clear only if investigators employ sophisticated operational sample descriptions (within reason!) and research designs that take into account the multifaceted components of English language and English literacy. In essence, it should be possible to develop effective or evidence-based practices, most likely on the individual level, with guidance from research findings on the group level. In our view, effective practices are dependent on the viability of the development of individual profiles.

REFLECTIONS ON THE QUALITATIVE SIMILARITY HYPOTHESIS

It is no simple feat to evaluate the merits of the QSH—which is no different from the controversies associated with the assessments of other complex constructs, some of which might have a slippery or ill-structured nature (e.g., Flavell, 1985; Paul, & Moores, 2010, 2012a; see also the discussions for reading constructs in Cartwright, 2009; Paris & Hamilton, 2009). In fact, complex constructs are always difficult to define operationally and completely and might not have an established agreed-upon conceptual structure (either loosely or well defined), especially for understanding teaching and learning. This point can certainly be gleaned from the essay of Bloome (in Chapter 8).

What might be overlooked in the criticisms from some researchers (e.g., Allen et al., 2009; Miller & Clark, 2011) is that the intricate nature of the QSH is contingent, in part, on understanding the complexity of the constructs under study, such as

English language and English literacy. This has led to a rendition of fundamentals as evident in the responses to the following questions:

What is the nature of the English language?
What is the nature of English literacy?
What are the relationships between these two entities for both first- and second-language learners?

We have attempted to demonstrate that these questions and others reflect the nonunitary natures of English language and literacy and render it extremely challenging to conduct research and develop skills in these constructs, including their subconstructs (e.g., Kamhi & Catts, 2012).

To address viability and applicability, it needs to be underscored that the QSH is a descriptive (narrative), testable construct comprised of micro and macro subconstructs. Each construct should be investigated separately as well as in unison with others. For example, consider English reading as the overall construct that has been addressed by the QSH. The English reading subconstructs (which can function also as broad constructs) might be the alphabetic system and print comprehension. Within the alphabetic system and print comprehension are additional subconstructs such as letter knowledge and letter–sound relationships (alphabetic system) and making inferences and answering questions on varying difficulty levels (print comprehension).

To express the interrelations among constructs, it is possible to use a descriptive narrative approach or develop a mathematical equation with weights assigned based on the variances in research investigations (e.g., the simple view of reading in Gough & Tunmer, 1986; Joshi & Aaron, 2012; cf. Hoffman, 2009). Whether one employs a narrative or mathematical model, it is incumbent on the researcher or scholar to explain and justify (either empirically or in a secondary research manner) the viability and contribution of each construct/subconstruct as well as the manner in which the constructs/subconstructs work together.

The QSH concerns the acquisition of through-the-air English (i.e., speaking and/or signing) and English literacy (i.e., reading and writing). It is asserted that the acquisition of English as a first or second language by any individual is *developmentally similar* to that of native learners/users and to that of typical literacy learners of English. The acquisition process is contextualized with respect to the importance of certain critical fundamentals, which are reflective of the structure of the particular discipline under study (i.e., English language or English literacy). In addition, this acquisition process is affected by a critical or optimal timeframe of development for both language (e.g., Lenneberg, 1967) and literacy (e.g., Stanovich, 1986, 1988). The research on cerebral plasticity does not undermine the critical timeframe but it does proffer qualifications.

We acknowledge that, in the past, the QSH has been grounded predominantly in cognitive–linguistic theories for both English language and English literacy. There has been some support for the QSH via interpretations of research findings within a sociocultural framework or a sociocognitive framework that rely heavily on variables, artifacts, and practices associated with the social context (Paul, 2012; Paul & Wang,

2012; Williams, 2004, 2011, 2012). If this *support* is contentious, we have argued that the contention is due mostly to the condition of a paradigm shift rather than a paradigm elaboration of cognitivism (e.g., Gaffney & Anderson, 2000). As discussed later, the shift is due to different epistemological underpinnings and the resultant implications for research and practice.

The assertion that the overall and within-construct acquisition and development (i.e., manner) of English is qualitatively similar can result in controversial discussions about the content of the curriculum for a particular discipline or content area and the manner in which instruction should be differentiated. This assertion is not related to the rate of acquisition—which might differentiate the QSH somewhat from other developmental models (e.g., Stanovich's developmental lag hypothesis [e.g., 1988]). That is, it does not matter whether a child's acquisition of English is slower or faster or on par with typical learners or users. The crux is that such acquisition is developmentally similar for both first- and second-language learners. It is this assumption that has caused the most dissension, especially for proponents of strong social or cultural models (e.g., Allen et al., 2009; Miller & Clark, 2011; Tierney, 2008; see also Bloome's essay in Chapter 8).

We emphasize here that the argument for developmental similarity is based on fundamentals and is contingent on research documenting the constructs of disciplinary structure and critical or optimal period. The structure of the discipline refers to certain discipline components of varying difficulty levels. Certain components seem to be precursors for the acquisition of more difficult components. The critical or optimal period involves a timeline for maximizing the acquisition and beneficial effects of a bona fide through-the-air language as well as for print literacy.

Some evidence for the QSH for d/Dhh children and others who are struggling readers and writers has been presented in this book. Specific literacy instructional techniques (i.e., effective or evidence-based practices) have been proffered in Chapter 6. With respect to the notion of individual profiles, we have discussed the limitations of both instruction and research in Chapter 7. Considering the dissensions, we maintain that some of these are misinterpretations; however, it is also the case of different worldviews involving the convoluted constructs of fundamentals, disciplinary structures, and critical or optimal time periods as discussed in the next section.

THE REACTANTS' ESSAYS

Both essays in Chapter 8 focus on a few of the strengths and weaknesses of the QSH. Mokhtari and Reichard frame their essay on "promises" and "vulnerabilities," citing research support and instructional implications—but also the need for stronger and additional empirical research investigations. Bloome also remarks on the merits, but his essay highlights the differences of the QSH with respect to his epistemological stance—the social framework (e.g., the social turn; sociocultural).

It should be remembered that there are dangers of oversimplification and misrepresentations when presenting ideas out of context for discussion purposes. We should know this well, mainly because it is the same argument that can be applied to a number of critics of the QSH (e.g., Allen et al., 2009; Miller & Clark, 2011). Nevertheless, it is important to attempt such a discussion, and it is better if the dialogue from different perspectives continues rather than be terminated or, to use Bloome's word, become "unbridgeable."

Bloome's Essay

To understand and appreciate several of Bloome's points, it is important to proffer our interpretations of his epistemological stance and its implications for research, assessment, and instruction. Bloome remarks that his research "has been grounded in the social turn in linguistic and educational research and has been associated with interactional sociolinguistics, microethnographic discourse analysis, and cultural anthropology" (p. 227). He further states that his view of *scientific* research is different from—perhaps broader than—ours, and he suggests that this might be one reason for the exclusion of this research thrust in our synthesis of investigations on "personhood," language, and literacy with respect to d/Dhh children and adolescents.

The exclusion of specific research investigations is, most likely, because it is not clear to us that such research has or will lead to an improvement in the development of English language and literacy in struggling readers and writers. Rather, we intentionally chose to examine mostly experimental/quasi-experimental research because we were making comparisons to the findings of the National Reading Panel (NRP) and the National Early Literacy Panel (NELP). The NRP and NELP have had widespread influences on classroom practices, so it made sense to frame our argument around this comparison.

We appreciate varying perspectives, including Bloome's, and indeed we have endorsed the use of multiple epistemologies or paradigms (see Chapter 7). We certainly hope that our approach is not reflective of the remarks by Blackburn (2005, words and italics added): "Attempts to understand others . . . are exercises of power: We [*i.e., those who conduct what might be called scientific research*] impose them, trample on their difference, and force them into our own mould" (p. 199). This is certainly not our interpretation of our research or our attempts to understand the English language and literacy development of d/Dhh children and adolescents.

From another perspective, as remarked by Paul and Moores (2012b): "It is unlikely that scientific researchers . . . would promote hypotheses that are ad hoc—that is, tailor-made principles that are not generalizable and are confined to a specific situation or context" (p. 8). This seems to be the case for some, but not all, of the research that has been motivated by multiple epistemologies, although this does not mean that the findings are not important or do not have value (Paul & Moores, 2012, 2012a, 2012b; Pring, 2004; Ritzer, 2001).

We suspect that Bloome does not subscribe to any strong version of a standard epistemology, but we are not certain if he is predominantly or solely a proponent of only multiple epistemologies (see discussions of these constructs in Paul & Moore, 2012a; Ritzer, 2001). Our definition of *science* does include qualitative or ethnographic research—especially sociocultural research in educational settings—and we assume that such research, along with the quantitative versions, leads or can lead to an improvement of English language and literacy skills. In fact, a number of our citations and suggested practices in Chapter 6 have been influenced by the results of qualitative/sociocultural investigations (as well as by those influenced by behavioral and cognitive paradigms). Nevertheless, the reference point for improvement (e.g., individual or group comparisons) and the manner in which this is to be accomplished (type of instruction, assessment, etc.) are contentious or might be viewed predominantly as *power issues* with respect to the varying epistemologies of researchers and theorists (e.g., Noddings, 2007; Pring, 2004; Ritzer, 2001). We have discussed power issues with respect to the debate on reading disabilities versus reading differences in Chapter 1 and on language disabilities and language differences in Chapter 2.

There is little question that Bloome's epistemology pervasively influences his perspectives on what counts as data, interpretations of personhood, views on language and literacy development, and his remarks on our "inside the head/outside the head" phrase. For example, Bloome mentions that we neglected to incorporate "a history of research that could have been called on to support [our] thesis regarding the personhood of children and students who are d/Deaf and hard of hearing with regard to language and literacy" (p. 227). Setting aside the ambiguous notion of personhood—a controversial social justice label—much of the research that Bloome cites (e.g., the works of Maxwell, Miller, Ramsey & Padden, and Wilcox) seems to impose a particular view of personhood, language, and literacy—mostly under the umbrella of American Sign Language (ASL) and the Deaf identity.

As discussed previously in this book, ASL is used by a small minority of d/Dhh children and adolescents in U.S. schools. Including ASL as the predominant variable in any definition of personhood with reference to language and literacy development does not, in our view, represent the situation for the overwhelming majority of d/Dhh students in P–12 educational settings. ASL is the first language of some Deaf children and should be considered for that group in educational contexts—not, as discussed in Chapter 2, for all or even most d/Dhh children and adolescents. In addition, the research on ASL and the subsequent or concomitant development of English has resulted in overgeneralizations and misinterpretations (see Chapter 7; see also, Paul, 2009, 2012; Wang, 2012). In any case, the intertwinement of personhood, language, and literacy needs to take into account the evolving landscape of education, particularly the changing demographics of d/Dhh students, as emphasized strongly in Chapter 7 (see also Mayer & Leigh, 2010).

Next we turn to Bloome's comments on the QSH with respect to his discussion of the constructs of particularity, practice, time, and part–whole relations. Only a few of our reactions, mostly general, are proffered respectfully here. Taken together, Bloome's constructs seem to question a strong focus on the development of English language and literacy in general or in principle. Indulging in a rich interpretation, we might surmise that Bloome's constructs call into question the current practices of standardized assessments, content standards, and instruction of literacy in the schools. Arguably, this could mean that more attention should be expended on understanding the specific and broad social situations and contexts of learners' lives as they acquire or engage in language and literacy practices and events (in our case, English).

We suspect that Bloome's criticisms of current literacy/reading school practices, based on a "deficit" model (see comments in his *Practice* section), also are related to several of his points in the *Particularity* section. Running the risk of oversimplification on our part, we notice that Bloome avers that "viewing reading development as the learning and acquisition of as a set of practices involving written language defenestrates reading development as monolithic and the inherent marginalization of those who are not of the corpus on whom the dominant model of reading development was based" (p. 230). Whether a particular model of reading development, based on written language, adopted by American schools marginalizes (or excludes) certain subgroups of the school population requires more space than can be devoted here.

Clearly, this marginalization can be extended to the use of content standards, curricula, standardized assessments, instructional practices, and research motivated by specific models of reading/literacy. In light of Bloome's complex remarks regarding the construct of "time," this marginalization can be extended further to the discussion of the Matthew effects (Stanovich, 1986)—which, for better or worse, has caused some school districts to use reading on a third grade level as the litmus test for promotion to the fourth grade (e.g., the State of Ohio). Nevertheless, "time" as expressed and discussed within the construct of the QSH is related to optimal timeframes of learning English language and literacy for maximum benefits within the framework of academic achievement. The QSH does not intend for "time" to become a punitive variable. It states that as the time it takes to adequately learn a language and to read and write with proficiency in that language lengthens, the more difficult the task becomes and the more problematic subsequent development and understanding of other content areas becomes.

We are sensitive and respectful, and even agree with several of Bloome's assertions, especially if his "particularity" construct is somewhat similar to our call for individual profiles (see Chapter 1). However, we frame our situation differently—and we have no doubt that our interpretations are motivated by our epistemologies. First, we do not believe that any focus on improvement invokes a deficit model per se or results necessarily in a marginalization of any subgroup (albeit it might result in marginalization if the social worlds of individuals are denigrated or ignored). The use of the word *deficit* in reading/literacy practices is influenced by an interpretation of a model of education or of teaching and learning based on an epistemology such as behaviorism, cognitivism, social constructivism, or any number of permutations and combinations (e.g., Fenstermacher & Soltis, 2004). The teacher might be viewed as a manager, facilitator, or a liberator—or permutations or combinations of all three broad models.

Whether the role of the teacher is situated within a "deficit" framework is an interpretation of instructional style, not necessarily a reflection of the actual tenets or aspects of the teaching–learning model. We believe that such a separation of interpretation and basic principles of a model (or theory) is desirable and possible. In fact, this issue is similar to debates involving the products of writing and the interpretations associated with such products (e.g., see Paul & Wang, 2012).

We leave to others the further discussion of the relevancy of educational or school practices to the broader social world, including whether these practices are limited and unproductive. Rather, we have argued that it is not possible to understand and address individual profiles or the "particularity" of language and literacy development without an appeal to general principles or fundamentals. This requires an understanding of disciplinary structures as discussed previously in this book and summarized in the earlier part of this chapter.

We think that Bloome would agree with our assumption that there is a mismatch among the artifacts, language usage, and social practices of the home and surrounding cultural worlds of children and the classroom usage, artifacts, and practices relating to the social and academic language and requirements of schools. In our view, this mismatch requires culturally relevant instructional techniques to deliver the critical fundamentals of developing language and literacy as required by schools. In short, we reassert that understanding the structure of a discipline such as English language and literacy is critical to minimizing the mismatch between the cognitive capability of the individual and her or his learning via the instruction of the discipline.

We might not have clearly articulated our view on the "inside-the-head/outside-the-head" phenomenon, especially the relationships between these two broad constructs. This is not an either/or dichotomy; however, ultimately reading and acquiring knowledge is predominantly an inside-the-head phenomenon facilitated by outside-the-head factors. In our discussions of the dichotomies between language or reading *difficulties* and language or reading *disabilities* (Chapters 1 and 2), we argue that attention must be paid to both groups of factors for the development or improvement of English language and literacy. We extend Bloome's chess analogy to make our points.

Chess is a game that entails command of inside-the-head (e.g., cognitive, socioemotional) and outside-the-head (e.g., cultural) variables (for popular and informative accounts, see Schiller, 2003; Shahade, 2005). Excellent chess players are cognizant of the opening moves and variations, the need to plan and strategize, advantageous board positions—especially those in previously played games—the other players' strengths and weaknesses, and so on. They also need to exhibit patience and perseverance and, occasionally, be willing to take risks (the surprise element!), considering the fact that there are hundreds of possible moves and positions in the game. It might be oversimplifying to argue that the social and cultural factors play supporting roles in the development of masters and grandmasters (and this does depend on one's definition of social variables). Good role models, teachers, consulting teams for analyzing positions during a game, and initiatives to build motivation and confidence are important. Nevertheless, the inside-the-head aptitude wins tournament games. In fact, it is possible that most excellent chess players spend a substantial amount of time practicing and studying alone.

To use a controversial exemplar, one of the world's greatest women chess players, Judith Polgar, use to refuse to play in or even endorse women's only tournaments in the early period of her career—a view heavily influenced by her father (for a popular account, see Shahade, 2005). Polgar rarely plays women chess players unless they compete in general (open to all) matches. She has implied that the social and cultural worlds of women's tournaments prevent female players from reaching the highest echelons of the game, or, to put it in our framework, to exhibit the necessary cognitive and socioemotional skills to withstand the pressures of tournaments, which can persist for a couple of months or more. (Note: Of course, the counterargument is that the general tournaments are not women-friendly, similar to the environments of some workplaces). As it is, there are few women in the top 10 rankings of the chess world, considering both men and women, and Polgar has been there—she achieved the title of grandmaster at the age of 15 years, 4 months, and was the youngest person ever to reach this milestone at that time. We are not suggesting that playing chess is exactly similar in nature to learning to read and write English; however, the analogy does exemplify our inside-the-head/outside-the-head view on the development of English language and English literacy skills.

Perhaps we have misunderstood some of Bloome's main points or, more likely, we have reinterpreted his points within our mental framework to justify our position. We contend that fundamentals, critical or optimal periods, and discipline structures are important for developing English language and literacy skills in an educational sociocultural environment. We appreciate Bloome's comment that this situation might not be completely "unbridgeable", especially if scholars and researchers are willing to cross the "divide" to dialogue and learn from each other.

Essay by Mokhtari and Reichard

Much of the essay by Mokhtari and Reichard seems to be congruent with our major assertions regarding the QSH—even though their epistemological framework is not explicitly stated in their essay. They presented a balanced treatment of the QSH with their rendition of major points within two main categories: *promises* and *vulnerabilities*. Mokhtari and Reichard examine the validity of the QSH with respect to individuals attempting to acquire English literacy skills, whether as a first or second language. These scholars, along with Bloome, also aver that the complexity of constructs such as language and literacy requires theorists and researchers to examine research and resultant findings from scholars outside of the traditional fields associated with reading research. This point also has been made strongly by McGuinness (2004, 2005), who proposes that research on English language acquisition needs to be taken more seriously in understanding the acquisition of English literacy skills.

In their *Promise* section, Mokhtari and Reichard espouse the theoretical, research, and implication merits of the QSH. They agree that the construct of developmental similarity (in the QSH) has strong theoretical and research support and does apply to all individuals attempting to learn English. With reference to the interdisciplinary approach, Mokhtari and Reichard proffer additional examples that can be applied to buttress the major assumptions of the QSH. These examples include the work of Chomsky's "language universals"; one of the major constructs in second language research: the transfer principle; and a construct associated with the Matthew effects (Stanovich, 1986). With respect to the last example, Mokhtari and Reichard imply that it is critical to address the language and literacy needs of students, particularly those who are struggling readers and writers, during the early literacy period. They also recognize that many of these struggling literacy learners might never catch up with their peers who are typically developing literacy learners despite the allocation of resources and attention.

It is instructive to comment further on one of Mokhtari and Reichard's examples, which might be most applicable for addressing a few of the dissensions involving the QSH (e.g., Allen et al., 2009; Miller & Clark, 2011). Mokhtari and Reichard state that "it is generally agreed that possessing literacy skills in a first language aids the development of second language literacy skills, and indeed, there are many studies that support this argument" (p. 239). We have attempted to elaborate on this point in this book (see especially Chapter 3). We emphasize that literacy in one's first or home language is not a guarantee that one will develop an equally commensurate level of literacy in the second language, particularly in English. Individuals still need to learn and to manipulate the second language in nonliterate situations (e.g., through the air), and this will facilitate the acquisition of second-language literacy. As we have stressed repeatedly, it is extremely difficult to proceed from a first language with no written form (such as ASL and a number of spoken languages) to the acquisition of the written form of the second language—that is, English. There is more to second language acquisition of English literacy than (1) knowing English through the air, (2) knowing any first language—spoken or signed, (3) being able to read/write in the first language, and so on. English language and English literacy are not unitary constructs that are influenced by one all-encompassing variable.

Mokhtari and Reichard also agree with us about some of the criticisms of the QSH. They notice that several of these criticisms are focused narrowly on the roles of phonology and phonemic awareness, which are only part of the construct of the QSH. We have acknowledged the varying roles of phonology in the development of English literacy and have also attempted to clarify the reasons for this phenomenon (e.g., in Chapters 1, 3, and 4). Similar to the remarks of Mokhtari and Reichard and others (e.g., McGuinness, 2004, 2005), knowledge of the language—*particularly the language of print*—plays a major role in the acquisition of literacy skills. It seems to us that phonology plays a major role in the acquisition of through-the-air English proficiency (see Chapter 2) and is necessary but not sufficient for the development of English literacy skills.

Mokhtari and Reichard remark that "recent advances in reading research suggest that while phonemic deficits are at the core of some specific reading problems, deficits in morphological and syntactic skills are likely to play a larger role than originally assumed" (p. 242). In essence, Mokhtari and Reichard conclude, "we concur with the authors of the QSH that phonological awareness is a necessary but not sufficient condition for learning to read by typically developing readers as well as by readers who find learning to read difficult" (p. 241). We have argued that, in order for individuals to use through-the-air English as part of the English literacy acquisition process, they need to have proficiency in all components of English (e.g., phonology, morphology, syntax, etc.) separately as well as in unison.

In discussing the merits (promises) of the QSH, Mokhtari and Reichard seem to accept the constructs of fundamentals, critical periods, and disciplinary structures as important for understanding the QSH and its implications. In their *Summary and*

Implications section, they reiterate the need for literacy researchers and scholars to consider a cross-disciplinary approach for understanding literacy acquisition. Finally, Mokhtari and Reichard reiterate their previous argument that even though QSH has ample extant theoretical and research support, further validation of the construct should be subjected to more rigorous empirical testing.

FINAL REMARKS

As noted by both reactants' essays in Chapter 8, there is a need for additional empirical (i.e., primary) research on the merits of the QSH. We agree strongly that more rigorous empirical investigations are needed to validate or qualify the major tenets of the QSH—albeit such research is often difficult to conduct and multiparadigmatic approaches and designs need to be considered (see Chapter 7). Future research also needs to address issues such as the nonunitary aspects of both English language and English literacy, the diversity of demographics in d/Dhh children and adolescents, and the strengths and limitations of assessments, research designs, and instructional practices.

Nonunitary aspects remind us that there is no all-encompassing factor to account for all or even most of the variance in investigations on the development of English language and English literacy. This precludes factors, sometimes touted as panaceas, such as the use of ASL, Cued Speech/Language (CSL), semantics, phonology, and so on. Rather, future research explorations should examine the contributions of a specific English sign system or ASL or CSL or specific aspects of these language/communication systems to the specific development of or aspects of English and not be focused on the global correlational effects of these factors. There seems to be some promise in this suggested line of research as exemplified by the recent work of Colin, Leybaert, Ecalle, and Magnan (2013) on the use of CSL.

Another implication of the nonunitary notion is that investigations should be based on comprehensive models of English language and literacy, which have been influenced by prevailing descriptions of the major constructs or subconstructs. In our view, it is best that investigations be modeled after those utilized in the larger fields of developing English as a first or second language. For example, as discussed in Chapter 3, the results of research on English Language Learners (i.e., ELLs) have provided evidence that the development and implementation of effective instructional practices should, at the least, start from those practices that have been supported by research for language and literacy instruction for typically developing monolingual English-speaking children (albeit with a few accommodations and adaptations) (see also the essay by Mokhtari and Reichard in Chapter 8).

From another perspective, we can obtain a better understanding of the developmental trajectories of d/Dhh children and adolescents. Consider the discussion in Chapter 4 on research in the final phase of emergent literacy for d/Dhh children and those who are typical English literacy learners. It has been demonstrated that the alphabetic principle (e.g., letter–sound relationships) is essential for movement into early conventional literacy, and the inadequate acquisition of this principle might explain, in part, the reason that the literacy learning trajectories of a number of d/Dhh children diverge from those of their peers who are typical literacy learners. Whereas most typical literacy learners acquire these fundamental constructs and transition from emergent literacy into early conventional literacy, a number of d/Dhh children, particularly those with severe to profound hearing loss, experience much difficulty and do not proceed adequately into conventional literacy.

Considering theory and research from the larger fields, including children who are struggling readers/writers and those who are ELLs, should also minimize misunderstandings regarding the nonunitary natures of English language and literacy. For example, based on Cummins's linguistic interdependence theory, the components of a language such as English—phonology, morphology, and syntax—are language specific. It is not possible to develop a deep adequate knowledge of these *forms* of English via the use of or explanation from a different language such as ASL or French or some other language (e.g., Paul & Wang, 2012; Wang, 2012).

We have reiterated in this chapter and elsewhere (see Chapter 7) that future researchers need to be cognizant of the emerging demographics of a new cohort of d/Dhh children and adolescents. Providing adequate descriptions of the demographics of samples is not only an important technical merit of investigations but also is critical for the development of individual profiles. These profiles should consider both inside-the-head and outside-the-head factors such as the wide array of linguistic (e.g., language parameters/components), cognitive (e.g., working memory), social (e.g., home environment), and affective (e.g., motivation) variables. The varying effects of instructional strategies and practices as well as the application of research findings can be effectively contextualized with respect to the demographic and achievement data on the participants.

Throughout this book, we have emphasized strongly and repeatedly that the reference standard for the QSH is the *typical* development of English language and literacy. Thus, typically developing individuals may be hearing, Deaf, deaf, or hard of hearing and may even have a disability (e.g., language/learning disability; dyslexia). However, progress on understanding the QSH and other developmental similarity models is contingent on the construction of adequate language and literacy assessments and being cautious about the constraints and interpretations of these assessments with respect to, for example, the speech, hearing, language, and cognitive demands for perception and production aspects of the tests.

We certainly endorse more research on the social and cognitive worlds of children and adolescents as well as a better understanding of the relationships between the practices and artifacts of schools and those of institutions outside of schools. As mentioned previously, we have endorsed a multiparadigmatic approach (e.g., see Chapter 7; Wang, 2010, 2012), which encourages scientific and multiple epistemological research endeavors. One of the major challenges, as noted by Paul and Moores (2012b), is to arrive at an agreement on the descriptions of the ends (outcomes such as achievement scores, etc.) while permitting varying perspectives and approaches on the means (formal and informal measures, diversity in instruction and instructional styles, etc.) for accomplishing the ends.

From another perspective, it might be important to encourage and permit these worldview differences to persist for theorizing, research, and practice for the sake of understanding rather than resolution (e.g., Pring, 2004; Ritzer, 2001). In our view, this is bound to slow down progress—assuming that we can agree on a description/definition of that construct (e.g., Noddings, 2007; Pring, 2004, Ritzer, 2001). Nevertheless, it is our position that adhering strongly to a specific ideology, philosophy, epistemology, definition/view of "deafness" or "social justice," and so on is—as discussed in Chapter 7—unproductive for solving complex educational problems and for preparing individuals to live and prosper in a diverse world.

In sum, we have asserted that the construct of the QSH is applicable to d/Dhh individuals, indeed to all individuals attempting to learn English. As discussed throughout this book, meta-analyses have uncovered a few insubstantial differences in research and instructional effectiveness due to factors such as race/ethnicity, age, family income, or disability status. Thus, what is effective for typical learners of English in a first or second language should also be effective (with some accommodations) for *all* children regardless of their status and background. This is not intended as a *one-size-fits-all* approach; rather, we believe that this is a good place to start in any attempt to understand and remedy the English language and literacy challenges of d/Dhh children and adolescents.

REFERENCES

Allen, T., Clark, M. D., del Giudice, A., Koo, D., Lieberman, A., Mayberry, R., & Miller, P. (2009). Phonology and reading: A response to Wang, Trezek, Luckner, and Paul. *American Annals of the Deaf, 154*(4), 338–345.

Blackburn, S. (2005). *Truth: A guide*. New York, NY: Oxford University Press.

Cartwright, K. (2009). The role of cognitive flexibility in reading comprehension: Past, present, and future. In S. Israel & G. Duffy (Eds.), *Handbook of research on reading comprehension* (pp. 115–139). New York, NY: Routledge.

Colin, S., Leybaert, J., Ecalle, J., & Magnan, A. (2013). The development of word recognition, sentence comprehension, word spelling, and vocabulary in children with deafness: A longitudinal study. *Research in Developmental Disabilities, 34*, 1781–1793.

Cooper, R. (2012). Can it be a good thing to be deaf? In P. Paul & D. Moores (Eds.), *Deaf epistemologies: Multiple perspectives on the acquisition of knowledge* (pp. 236–251). Washington, DC: Gallaudet University Press.

Fenstermacher, G., & Soltis, J. (2004). *Approaches to teaching*. New York, NY: Teachers College, Columbia University.

Flavell, D. (1985). *Cognitive development* (2nd ed.). Englewood Cliffs, NJ: Prentice-Hall.

Gaffney, J., & Anderson, R. (2000). Trends in reading research in the United States: Changing intellectual currents over three decades. In M. Kamil, P. Mosenthal, P.D. Pearson, & R. Barr (Eds.), *Handbook of reading research* (Vol. III, pp. 53–74). Mahwah, NJ: Lawrence Erlbaum.

Gough, P. B., & Tunmer, W. E. (1986). Decoding, reading, and reading disability. *Remedial and Special Education, 7*(1), 6–10.

Hoffman, J. (2009). In search of the "simple view" of reading comprehension. In S. Israel & G. Duffy (Eds.), *Handbook of research on reading comprehension* (pp. 54–66). New York, NY: Routledge.

Joshi, R. M., & Aaron, P.G. (2012). Componential model of reading (CMR): Validation studies. *Journal of Learning Disabilities, 45*(5), 387–390.

Kamhi, A., & Catts, H. (2012). *Language and reading disabilities* (3rd ed.). Boston, MA: Pearson Education.

LaSasso, C. J., Crain, K. L., & Leybaert, J. (Eds.). (2010). *Cued Speech and Cued Language for deaf and hard of hearing children.* San Diego, CA: Plural.

Lenneberg, E. (1967). *Biological foundations of language.* New York, NY: Wiley.

Leybaert, J., & LaSasso, C. (2010). Cued Speech for enhancing speech perception and first language development of children with cochlear implants. *Trends in Amplification, 14*(2), 96–112.

Mayer, C., & Leigh, G. (2010). The changing context for sign bilingual education programs: Issues in language and the development of literacy. *International Journal of Bilingual Education and Bilingualism, 13*(2), 175–186.

McGuinness, D. (2004). *Early reading instruction: What science really tells us about how to teach reading.* Cambridge, MA: MIT Press.

McGuinness, D. (2005). *Language development and learning to read: The scientific study of how language development affects reading skill.* Cambridge, MA: MIT Press.

Miller, P., & Clark, D. (2011). Phonemic awareness is not necessary to become a skilled deaf reader. *Journal of Developmental Physical Disabilities, 23,* 459–476.

Noddings, N. (2007). *Philosophy of education* (2nd ed.). Boulder, CO: Westview.

Paris, S., & Hamilton, E. (2009). The development of children's reading comprehension. In S. Israel & G. Duffy (Eds.), *Handbook of research on reading comprehension* (pp. 32–53). New York, NY: Routledge.

Paul, P. (2009). *Language and deafness* (4th ed.). Sudbury, MA: Jones & Bartlett.

Paul, P. (2012). Qualitative similarity hypothesis. In P. Paul and D. Moores (Eds.), *Deaf epistemologies: Multiple perspectives on the acquisition of knowledge* (pp. 179–198). Washington, DC: Gallaudet University Press.

Paul, P., & Moores, D. (2010). Toward an understanding of epistemology and deafness. *American Annals of the Deaf, 154*(5), 417–420.

Paul, P., & Moores, D. (Eds.). (2012a). *Deaf epistemologies: Multiple perspectives on the acquisition of knowledge.* Washington, DC: Gallaudet University Press.

Paul, P., & Moores, D. (2012b). Toward an understanding of epistemology and deafness. In P. Paul & D. Moores (Eds.), *Deaf epistemologies: Multiple perspectives on the acquisition of knowledge* (pp. 3–15). Washington, DC: Gallaudet University Press.

Paul, P., & Wang, Y. (2012). *Literate thought: Understanding comprehension and literacy.* Sudbury, MA: Jones & Bartlett.

Pring, R. (2004). *Philosophy of educational research* (2nd ed.). New York, NY: Continuum.

Ritzer, G. (2001). *Explorations in social theory: From metatheorizing to rationalization.* Thousand Oaks, CA: Sage.

Schiller, E. (2003). *Encyclopedia of chess wisdom: The gold nuggets of chess knowledge: Opening, middle game, endgame, strategies, tactics, psychology, more.* New York, NY: Cardoza.

Shahade, J. (2005). *Chess bitch: Women in the ultimate intellectual sport.* Los Angeles, CA: Siles.

Stanovich, K. (1986). Matthew effects in reading: Some consequences of individual differences in the acquisition of literacy. *Reading Research Quarterly, 21,* 360–407.

Stanovich, K. (1988). *Children's reading and the development of phonological awareness.* Detroit, MI: Wayne State University Press.

Tierney, R. (2008). Reading and children with disabilities: Searching for better guidance. *Balanced Reading Instruction, 15*(2), 89–98.

Wang, Y. (2010). Without boundaries: An inquiry of Deaf epistemologies through a metaparadigm. *American Annals of the Deaf, 154*(5), 428–434.

Wang. Y. (2012). Educators without borders: A metaparadigm for literacy instruction in bilingual bicultural education. In P. Paul & D. Moores (Eds.), *Deaf epistemologies: Multiple perspectives on the acquisition of knowledge* (pp. 199–217). Washington, DC: Gallaudet University Press.

Williams, C. (2004). Emergent literacy of deaf children. *Journal of Deaf Studies and Deaf Education, 9*(4), 352–365.

Williams, C. (2011). Adapted interactive writing instruction with kindergarten children who are deaf or hard of hearing. *American Annals of the Deaf, 156*(1), 23–34.

Williams, C. (2012). Promoting vocabulary learning in young children who are d/Deaf and hard of hearing: Translating research into practice. *American Annals of the Deaf, 156*(5), 501–508.

About the Authors

Peter V. Paul is a professor in the Department of Teaching and Learning in the College of Education and Human Ecology at The Ohio State University. One of his major responsibilities is teacher education for individuals interested in the education of d/Deaf and hard of hearing (d/Dhh) students. Dr. Paul has published extensively on the language and literacy development of d/Dhh children and adolescents and has several international and national presentations. He received the OSU's College of Education 2000 Senior Research Award and the Richard and Laura Kretschmer National Leadership Award (Ohio School Speech Pathology Educational Audiology Coalition, October 2010). Dr. Paul has served on several editorial boards, including those in the general area of reading (*Reading Research Quarterly*; *Balanced Reading Instruction*), and is the current editor of the *American Annals of the Deaf* (since January 2011). He has a bilateral, profound hearing loss (and now has cochlear implants in both ears) and is the father of a son, Peter Benedict, who has Down syndrome and autism.

Ye Wang is an associate professor and the program coordinator for the Education of the d/Deaf and Hard of Hearing (EDHH) Program in the Department of Communication Sciences and Disorders, Missouri State University. As a Coda (i.e., child of Deaf adults), Dr. Wang is a teacher educator preparing teachers of the d/Deaf and hard of hearing students as well as a researcher. After 3 years of assistant professorship at Teachers College, Columbia University, Dr. Wang was invited by Missouri State University to lead the EDHH program in the fall of 2008. She has authored/co-authored numerous books, book chapters, and peer-reviewed academic journal articles. Her primary research interest is the language and literacy development of students who are d/Deaf and hard of hearing. Her other research and scholarly interests include multiple literacies, technology and literacy instruction, inclusive education, research methodology and early intervention. Currently, Dr. Wang is serving as the senior associate editor for *American Annals of the Deaf.*

Cheri Williams is a professor in the Literacy and Second Language Studies program in the School of Education at the University of Cincinnati. She teaches graduate courses in emergent and early literacy as well as advanced seminars on theoretical and methodological frameworks for literacy research. Dr. Williams has published extensively on emergent and early literacy learning and instruction among children who are typically developing and those who are d/Deaf and hard of hearing. Her research appears in the leading journals in the fields of literacy and deaf education; she also has numerous national presentations. In 2010, Dr. Williams was inducted into the University of Cincinnati's Academy of Fellows for Teaching and Learning, and she recently received the American Educational Research Association (AERA) Special Interest Group (SIG) for Research on the Education of Deaf Person's 2013 Best Paper Award for research on early writing among children who are d/Deaf and hard of hearing. Dr. Williams has served on a number of editorial boards, including the *American Annals of the Deaf*, *The Volta Review*, and *Language and Education*.

Index

affective aspects. *See* affective domain

affective domain, 2–3, 7, 10–12, 18, 34, 37, 203

alphabetic knowledge, 57, 80, 82–83, 92, 132, 138, 152–153, 155, 173

alphabetic principle, 12, 82, 85, 88, 90–91, 100, 108, 153, 155, 212

American Sign Language (ASL), 1–2, 10, 26, 28, 32, 41, 102–103, 140, 142, 154, 162–167, 170–172, 182, 190, 204, 208–214, 218, 250, 254–256. *See also* ASL/English bilingualism-biculturalism

articulatory-auditory loop, 31, 37, 44

ASD. *See* autism spectrum disorders (ASD)

ASL. *See* American Sign Language (ASL)

ASL/English bilingualism–biculturalism (BiBi), 65–68, 70–71

autism. *See* autism spectrum disorders (ASD)

autism spectrum disorders (ASD), 34, 132–133

automaticity, 90, 92, 94, 103, 132–133, 162. *See also* prosodic reading

Baldi, 160, 164

basic interpersonal communication skills (BICS), 60

Bell, Alexander Graham, 28

BiBi. *See* ASL/English bilingualism–biculturalism (BiBi)

BICS. *See* basic interpersonal communication skills (BICS)

bottleneck hypothesis, 133. *See also* lexical quality hypothesis (LQH); verbal efficiency model

brain plasticity, 12

CALP. *See* cognitive academic language proficiency (CALP)

carryover effects, 172, 215. *See also* order effects

CASE. *See* Conceptually Accurate Sign English (CASE)

catch–up trajectories, 61–62

CEI. *See* Children's Early Intervention (CEI)

Children's Early Intervention (CEI), 153–154

Chomsky's view of explanatory adequacy, 3

CI. *See* cochlear implants (CI)

clinical versus cultural views of deafness, 16

CMR. *See* componential model of reading (CMR)

cochlear implantation. *See* cochlear implants (CI)

cochlear implants (CI), 37, 40, 43–44, 85–88, 99, 101–102, 109, 154, 160, 166, 169, 209, 211, 246

code-focused intervention, 82, 138, 152–153, 155, 157, 173, 183

cognitive academic language proficiency (CALP), 60

cognitive-processing, 90

cognitivism, 2–3, 8, 17–18, 90, 248, 251

collaborative strategic reading, 94

componential model of reading (CMR), 201, 203

comprehension monitoring, 58, 90, 96, 106, 133, 140, 159, 163, 168–169, 181

concept-oriented reading instruction (CORI), 97

Conceptually Accurate Sign English (CASE), 209

Condition of Education 2011, 54

constructivism, 90, 251

contact signing, 209

content words, 103, 105, 111, 142–143, 167. *See also* function words

conventional literacy, 11, 79, 83, 85, 90, 98, 107–109, 111, 138, 151–152, 155, 157, 173–179, 183, 238, 255–256

convergent skills model of reading (CSMR), 201–203

core deficit models of reading, 91

CORI. *See* concept–oriented reading instruction (CORI)

critical or optimal period, 3–4, 12–13, 248, 253

CSL. *See* Cued Speech/Language (CSL)

CSMR. *See* convergent skills model of reading (CSMR)

Cued Speech/Language (CSL), 28, 37, 43–45, 68, 70, 100, 109, 156, 172, 182, 209–211, 214, 218, 255

Cummins's linguistic interdependence theory, 57, 65, 70, 256

DEAF–WORLD, 1

decoding, 10–15, 55, 57–63, 91–94, 106, 129–135, 139, 143, 153–155, 160–161, 201–203, 206, 214, 229, 240–242

degraded input hypotheses, 210

developmental lag hypothesis (DLH), 4, 13–14, 34, 127–129, 241, 246, 248

developmental similarity, 1–4, 19, 197, 227, 245, 248, 256

disciplinary structure, 4–6, 12, 245–248, 252–254

DLH. *See* developmental lag hypothesis (DLH)

dyslexia, 2, 14–17, 47, 126, 130, 162, 256. *See also* reading difficulty; reading disability

early hearing detection and intervention (EHDI), 67, 85

EHDI. *See* early hearing detection and intervention (EHDI)

ELLs. *See* English Language Learners (ELLs)

embodied cognition, 18. *See also* situated cognition

emergent literacy, 12, 35–36, 57, 79–80, 82–90, 108–109, 111, 155, 238, 255–256

English Language Learners (ELLs) d/Deaf and hard of hearing students who are, 64–69: ASL/English bilingualism–biculturalism, 65–66;

263